D1263823

THE BEAT GENERATION

PETER LANG
New York • Washington, D.C./Baltimore • Bern
Frankfurt am Main • Berlin • Brussels • Vienna • Oxford

THE BEAT GENERATION

CRITICAL ESSAYS

EDITED BY
Kostas Myrsiades

PETER LANG
New York • Washington, D.C./Baltimore • Bern
Frankfurt am Main • Berlin • Brussels • Vienna • Oxford

Library of Congress Cataloging-in-Publication Data

The Beat Generation: critical essays / edited by Kostas Myrsiades.
p. cm.
Includes bibliographical references and index.
1. American literature—20th century—History and criticism.
2. Beat generation. 3. Kerouac, Jack, 1922–1969—Criticism
and interpretation. I. Myrsiades, Kostas.
PS228.B6 B4244   810.9'0054—dc21   2001038848
ISBN 0-8204-5778-7

Die Deutsche Bibliothek-CIP-Einheitsaufnahme

The beat generation: critical essays / ed. by: Kostas Myrsiades.
–New York; Washington, D.C./Baltimore; Bern;
Frankfurt am Main; Berlin; Brussels; Vienna; Oxford: Lang.
ISBN 0-8204-5778-7

Cover design by Dutton & Sherman Design

The paper in this book meets the guidelines for permanence and durability
of the Committee on Production Guidelines for Book Longevity
of the Council of Library Resources.

Printed in the United States of America

CONTENTS

PREFACE

We have now passed the fifty-year mark since the Beats first came upon the literary scene, and although the academy's hostility towards the Beats has not completely abated, it has certainly diminished. Today mainstream publishers are adding many Beat titles to their lists, and students of Beat literature can draw upon a wealth of critical resources that have been published in the last twenty years.

As the essays gathered in this collection indicate, Kerouac is still the undisputed king of the Beats followed by Burroughs and Ginsberg. At the same time however, the Beat movement is shown to be broader and more far reaching than previously thought, encompassing names like Oscar Zeta Acosta and William Kotzwinkle and suggesting influences on contemporary German and Dutch literature on authors like Wolf Wondratschek, Rolf Dieter Brinkmann, Jorg Fauser and Simon Vinkenoog.

The majority of the essays included in this anthology, however, are on four of the most established figures of the Beat Generation—Jack Kerouac, William S. Burroughs, Allen Ginsberg, and Gary Snyder. The essays on the whole, on the other hand, provide a more encompassing view of the Beat Generation and attempt to show not only the Beats' relevancy to us today, but also their significance and influence as a major literary movement of the late twentieth century.

The sixteen essays selected here open with an overview by Robert Bennett who assesses the Beats for the present generation and speculates how they should be taught in the universities of the twenty-first century concluding,

> If Beat literature is to continue to have relevance in contemporary American universities, which are shaped by both feminist and minority discourses, then the Beat canon must be expanded to include a wider range of Beat voices in order to develop a more self-critical understanding of the Beat Generation's multiple voices, internal contradictions, and political limitations. (17)

Of these sixteen essays seven are on Jack Kerouac. The first two by Ann Douglas and Ronna C. Johnson survey the entire Kerouac oevre and place it in its historical setting emphasizing this avant-garde author's innovative prose and categorizing his works in relation to postmodernism. The remaining four Kerouac essays by Erik R. Mortenson, Steve Wilson, Nancy McCampbell Grace, and Fiona Patton deal with five Kerouac novels: *On the Road*, *Maggie Cassidy*, *The Subterraneans*, *Tristessa*, and *Doctor Sax*.

William Burroughs is represented in two essays by Douglas G. Baldwin and Timothy S. Murphy, which first give an overview of Burrough's work and then focus on his best known work, *Naked Lunch*. In the next three essays, Terence Diggory, Jaap van der Bent, and Robert Kern deal respectively with the two Beat poets that have received the most recognition and can be found represented in most standard poetry anthologies: Allen Ginsberg and Gary Snyder. The remaining three essays by A. Robert Lee, Robert E. Kohn, and Anthony Waine and Jonathan Wooley look beyond the established Beats to argue for a more international Beat canon that includes Chicano writer Oscar Zeta Acosta, the neglected author William Kotzwinkle, and the influence the Beats have had on a generation of West German poets since 1960.

Half of the essays included in this anthology first appeared in a special issue of *College Literature* dedicated to teaching Beat literature (27.1 Winter 2000) guest edited by my colleague Jenny Skerl to whom the present editor is indebted not only for her help in the production of an excellent issue but also for introducing me to a body of literature that made me aware of the great recent interest in the Beats and the plethora of Beat criticism waiting to be printed.

INTRODUCTION

Teaching the Beat Generation to Generation X
Robert Bennett

In a 1959 article titled "Squaresville U.S.A. vs. Beatsville," *Life* magazine contrasted Hutchinson, Kansas and Venice, California as representative examples of the "two extremes of present-day U.S. life and attitudes": the "homey pleasures of Squaresville" and the "far-out freedom of Beatsville" (31). Beginning with pictures of three conservatively dressed "square" girls from Hutchinson juxtaposed against a picture of Lawrence Lipton performing jazz poetry for a coterie of Venice Beats, this article describes how Hutchinson personifies "traditionally accepted American virtues—a stable, prosperous community, given to conservatism but full of get-up-and-go"—while Venice "throbs with the rebellion of the beatnik, who ridicules U.S. society as 'square,' talks a strange language and loves to chant his poetry while jazz bands or bongo drums play accompaniments" (31). While this contrast between the Beats and the Squares tends to reduce 1950s America to oversimplified stereotypes, it also exemplifies a widely shared consensus that the Beats and the Squares defined two opposing poles of post-WWII American culture. As David Halberstam explains in *The Fifties* (1993), the Beats are frequently regarded as having been the "first to protest what they considered to be the blandness, conformity, and lack of serious social and cultural pur-

pose in middle-class life in America" (295). Similarly, John Clellon
Holmes's Beat manifesto, "The Philosophy of the Beat Generation,"
defines the Beat Generation as a "kind of passive resistance to the
Square society in which [it] lives" (1958, 38), and Allen Ginsberg's
"America" more colorfully tells "square" America to "Go fuck yourself
with your atom bomb" (1959, 39). Even though "square" publications
like *Life* and Beat poets like Ginsberg chose opposing sides in this
intra-cultural conflict, they shared a similar sense that the Beat
Generation's opposition to "square" America marked a new and
definitive rupture within post-WWII American culture.

   Given how pervasively this Beat-vs.-Square dichotomy has influenced traditional accounts of both the 1950s in general and the Beat
Generation in particular, it seems almost impossible to teach a
course on Beat culture without invoking some variation on this Beat-
vs.-Square opposition. In fact, this dichotomy generally provides not
only the theoretical foundation, but also what I will call the pedagogical unconscious that organizes how Beat literature is both concep-
tualized and taught. Consequently, numerous resources exist to help
teachers develop courses that explore how and why the Beat
Generation emerged in opposition to its historical adversary: the
dominant, white, middle-class, suburban, "square" culture of 1950s
America. One can read almost any major Beat work—such as
Ginsberg's *Howl and Other Poems*, Jack Kerouac's *On the Road*, or
William Burroughs's *Naked Lunch*—more or less at face value and
easily identify its numerous "hipper-than-thou" attacks on "square"
values such as an all-consuming work ethic, sexual repression, cultur-
al xenophobia, militaristic patriotism, and suburban materialism.
Moreover, these primary texts can be augmented with both works of
secondary criticism—such as John Tytell's *Naked Angels* and the
Whiney Museum of American Art's anthology, *Beat Culture and the
New America, 1950-1965*—and various multimedia texts, ranging
from Lawrence Ferlinghetti's jazz poetry performances to Dennis
Hopper's video documentary, *The Source*. Collectively, these pri-
mary, secondary, and auxiliary texts abundantly document the Beat
Generation's critique of the mainstream culture of 1950s America.

What is more difficult, however, is to create a course that critically analyzes and conceptually complicates oversimplified notions of this Beat-vs.-Square dichotomy. Nevertheless, educators must directly confront this task of deconstructing the binary opposition between the Beats and the Squares if they want to develop a more comprehensive understanding of the Beat Generation which goes beyond superficial stereotypes and partisan sloganeering. Before I analyze in greater detail both how and why oversimplified contrasts between the Beats and the Squares limit how educators teach Beat culture, let me begin with a single example taken from William Lawlor's *The Beat Generation: A Bibliographical Teaching Guide* (1998). Even though Lawlor's teaching guide ranks among the most comprehensive resources for Beat scholars, it more or less projects the traditional opposition between the Beats and the Squares onto the pedagogical context of teaching Beat culture. Defining the Beats as "representatives of the counterculture" whose "validity and worth" is often marginalized in certain "academic and professional circles," Lawlor argues that educators who teach Beat culture bear "a special responsibility to justify Beat studies" because a "body of academicians judicious about maintaining rigor and discipline" is "sometimes skeptical about the Beats" (14, 1–2). Consequently, Lawlor concludes:

> The responsibility to justify Beat literature is different from the responsibility to justify the study of other works. When one teaches Edmund Spencer's The Faerie Queene, John Milton's Paradise Lost, or John Bunyan's The Pilgrim's Progress, one is confident of the academy's approval, but feels a responsibility to justify the study of this literature to students. . . . In contrast, when one teaches the literature of the Beat Generation, one must justify the material not to students, who often are ready to celebrate Jack Kerouac, Allen Ginsberg, and William Burroughs, but to colleagues, academicians, and professionals, who in some cases doubt the validity and literary worth of On the Road, Howl and Other Poems, and Naked Lunch. (Lawlor 1998, 1–2)

In short, Lawlor argues that teaching Beat culture inverts the traditional pedagogical scene of instruction, so that instead of educating students to accept canonical standards Beat educators must expand the literary canon itself to include students' alternative Beat aesthetic sensibilities. Thus Lawlor more or less invokes the same Beat-vs.-Square dichotomy, which also structures many theoretical conceptualizations of Beat culture, in order to describe the pedagogical scene of instruction in Beat classrooms. Only now the "far-out freedom" of contemporary students and unorthodox Beat educators is contrasted against the "homey pleasures" of "square" academicians and canonical orthodoxy. In effect, Lawlor defines Beat classrooms as academic Beatsvilles opposed to the larger "Squaresville" of the university that surrounds them. Ultimately, Lawlor's parallel construction of Beat culture and the pedagogical context in which it is taught clearly demonstrates how academic conceptualizations of the Beat Generation shape the pedagogical strategies used to teach Beat literature.

While I agree both with Lawlor's attempt to expand the canon to include the Beats and with his interest in students' innate aesthetic responses, both projects include serious complications that Lawlor does not fully address. To begin with, I believe that Lawlor has mislocated, and consequently misconstrued, the real source of contemporary academic resistance to Beat culture. It is true that some vestiges of New Criticism still influence contemporary literary studies, and these residual theoretical assumptions obviously discredit the "validity and worth" of Beat literature. However, Lawlor's argument ignores how New Critical assumptions have already been seriously eroded by multiple waves of poststructuralism, deconstructionism, New Historicism, feminism, multiculturalism, and other forms of critical theory and cultural studies. Consequently, Lawlor fails to explain why resistance to Beat literature continues in contemporary academic contexts where canons are repeatedly reconfigured, boundaries between high and low culture are easily transgressed, and counterhegemonic cultural practices are taught on a daily basis. One cannot fully account for contemporary academic resistance to Beat literature, therefore, without recognizing how it also derives from a critical disapproval of the Beat Generation's sexism, racism, and apoliticism as much as it emerges from a vestigial New Critical veneration of canonical orthodoxy. While I still accept Lawlor's challenge of justifying Beat literature to "colleagues, academicians, and professionals," recognizing these additional sources of resistance to Beat culture significantly alters what it means to justify Beat literature because there is a world of difference between how one would justify Beat literature to colleagues trained in New Criticism and how one would justify it to colleagues trained in feminism or African American studies. Consequently, taking into account this wider range of contemporary resistances to the Beats requires submitting Beat culture itself to a more careful critical scrutiny that goes beyond simply replacing a "square" literary tradition with the "Beat" sensibilities of students who are "ready to celebrate Jack Kerouac, Allen Ginsberg, and William Burroughs" (Lawlor 1998, 2). Instead, Beat educators must explore more critical and multidimensional dialogues not only between Beat literature and a "square" New Critical literary tradition but also between Beat literature and various forms of contemporary criticism. Within such a pedagogical context, one cannot assume in advance, as Lawlor does, that academic "rejection contributes to the attractiveness of the Beats as representatives of the counterculture" (14). While much academic criticism of the Beats is reactionary and ill-conceived, other critiques of the Beats are relevant and insightful. Moreover, confronting these critiques forces scholars and educators to develop a more complex understanding of both the Beat Generation itself and its relationship to 1950s America.

In addition to complicating Lawlor's explanation of why Beat culture is marginalized, I also want to reevaluate why contemporary students are so "ready to celebrate" it. While Lawlor implies that contemporary students celebrate Beat culture because their aesthetic sensibilities somehow understand and resemble it, I am not fully convinced that contemporary students' interest in Beat culture can always be equated with their espousal of Beat countercultural sensibilities. My experience teaching Beat texts has confirmed Lawlor's claim that many contemporary students are indeed "ready to celebrate" the Beats, but I am concerned that many of these students want to celebrate the Beats precisely because it is much easier to *celebrate* them today than it was to *be* them in the 1950s. To begin with, there is a qualitative difference between actively producing a contemporary cultural revolution and belatedly consuming that revolution fifty years after the fact. After all, many contemporary students have been introduced to Beat culture not at bohemian poetry readings or in seedy jazz clubs but rather by advertisements for Gap khakis or by Rhino Record's three-volume *Beat Generation* CD. After recognizing how many contemporary references to Beat culture invoke the Beats for nostalgic or commercial purposes, one cannot effectively teach Beat culture to contemporary students without critically analyzing how the Beat Generation's cultural project has already been either largely accomplished or seriously co-opted for other purposes, and consequently it no longer functions as an active or progressive countercultural movement. Unless students can critically distinguish between authentic countercultural movements and the various ways in which those movements are neutralized, co-opted, and commodified, they might celebrate a contemporary image of the Beat Generation which significantly differs from the Beat Generation's historical reality. Moreover, it is much easier for contemporary students to reject the values of 1950s America today than it was for the Beats to reject those values in the 1950s. Consequently, one cannot unproblematically promote the Beat Generation as countercultural icons for a contemporary generation of students whose cultural milieu is itself more Beat than "square." Finally, looking back with the benefit of hindsight, it has become increasingly evident that the Beats themselves remained trapped within many of the patriarchal, racist, and homophobic assumptions of "square" America, and consequently the Beat revolution only partially realized the kind of radical cultural critique it hoped to achieve. Having taught Beat texts to contemporary California students—at a time when California has simultaneously legalized marijuana for medical purposes and criminalized Affirmative Action—I am convinced that what needs to be emphasized in Beat courses is precisely the incompleteness of the Beat revolution. In the same way that the Beats only critiqued certain dimensions of "square" America, contemporary America often remembers and celebrates only certain dimensions of the Beat Generation. To celebrate the Beat Generation's passionate advocacy of casual drug use and sexual experimentation, without critiquing its sexist construction of masculine identity and its often meager contribution to the Civil Rights Movement, is to promote an uncritical and politically reactionary interpretation of the Beats' legacy to contemporary America. Consequently, teaching Beat Generation texts to Generation X students requires much more than simply encouraging students to "celebrate" the Beat Generation as "representatives of the counterculture" (Lawlor 1998, 14). Instead, a critical Beat pedagogy should analyze both the successes and the failures of the Beat counterculture, and it should simultaneously challenge students to be self-critical about their own investments in that counterculture.

While I am by no means suggesting that we entirely discard all descriptions of 1950s America as a conflict between the Beats and the Squares, I do believe that an oversimplified and uncritical understanding of the Beats' opposition to "square" America severely limits both scholars' analyses of Beat culture and educators' pedagogical strategies for teaching it. By exploring how theoretical and pedagogical issues mutually influence each other, the rest of my paper will describe how educators can construct more complex pedagogical strategies for teaching Beat literature by developing a more complex understanding of the binary opposition between the Beats and the Squares.

Looking back from a contemporary perspective, it is easier to recognize that the cultural complexities of 1950s America cannot be reduced to a simplistic confrontation between the Beats and the Squares. It no longer requires a radical feminist perspective to problematize *Life* magazine's description of the "homey pleasures of Squaresville." After all, not everyone was allowed either to participate in or to share equally in the "homey pleasures" of "square" America's patriarchal families, suburban homes, and racially segregated institutions. As works such as Ralph Ellison's *Invisible Man*, John Okada's *No-No Boy*, and N. Scott Momaday's *House Made of Dawn* demonstrate, "square" America marginalized, excluded, alienated, and even interred many racial minorities. Similarly, works such as Sylvia Plath's *The Bell Jar*, Tennessee Williams's *The Glass Menagerie*, and J. D. Salinger's *The Catcher in the Rye* describe how even people included in "square" America often experienced it as a site of anxiety, entrapment, hypocrisy, and injustice rather than as a sanctuary of "homey pleasures." Moreover, one doesn't have to belong to the Moral Majority to question whether the Beat Generation was really as "far-out" and "free" as it presented itself. In Kerouac's *On the Road*, for example, Sal Paradise claims that he wants to explore cultural alterity:

> At lilac evening I walked with every muscle aching among the lights of 27th and Welton in the Denver colored section, wishing I were a Negro, feeling that the best the white world had to offer was not enough ecstasy

for me, not enough life, joy, kicks, darkness, music, not enough night, [and he desires to be a] Denver Mexican, or even a poor overworked Jap, anything but what I was so drearily, a 'white man' disillusioned. . . . I was only myself, Sal Paradise, sad, strolling, in this violet dark, this unbearably sweet night, wishing I could exchange worlds with the happy, true-hearted, ecstatic Negroes of America." (Kerouac 1957, 180)

How seriously can we take Paradise's soliloquy, however, when the next page describes him going to see a "rich girl I knew" who "pulled a hundred-dollar bill out of her silk stocking and said, 'You've been talking of a trip to Frisco; that being the case, take this and go and have your fun'" (181)? As Halberstam points out, it was "no small irony that the magic ingredient that allowed them [the Beats] to forgo regular jobs and still manage reasonably comfortable lives was the sheer affluence of the mainstream culture that they so disdained; the country was so rich that even those who chose not to play by its rules were protected" (1993, 301). A critical analysis of the Beat Generation, therefore, must explore how these kinds of ironies and contradictions complicate simplistic oppositions between the Beats and the Squares.

To develop such a critical pedagogy, instructors need to restructure Beat courses in such a way that these ironies and contradictions become an integral part of rather than an anomalous afterthought to a critical analysis of post-WWII American culture. At the very least, instructors can draw attention to how these ironies and contradictions complicate traditional accounts of the opposition between the Beats and the Squares. For example, why did Hutchinson's "square" teenagers invite Lawrence Lipton to "cool" them in to Beat culture if "square" America was really so horrified by the Beats, and why did the nomadic Kerouac keep returning home to his "square" mother's home and rich girlfriends for more cash if the Beats were so committed to "protesting the narcotic tobacco haze of Capitalism" (Ginsberg 1959, 13)? As these examples demonstrate, "square" and Beat worlds not only crossed and interpenetrated, but also enabled and sustained, each other in ways that are much more interesting and complex than either the Beats or *Life* magazine readily admit.[1] Consequently, instructors can further emphasize these contradictions by self-consciously assigning Beat texts that discuss them more openly. While *On the Road* and "Howl" attempt to represent the Beats and the Squares as diametrically opposed antagonists, a work like Ginsberg's "America" more candidly confesses how even Ginsberg struggled to free himself from the "insane demands" of "square" America's cultural hegemony, which caused him to be "obsessed by Time magazine" and "read it every week" (1959, 41). A wider exposure to Beat interviews, diaries, letters, and other candid autobiographical materials can also reveal more of the complexity of the Beat Generation's struggle to free itself from its powerful cultural adversary. Moreover, reinterpreting Beat texts as sites of overlapping, conflicting, and contradictory cultural exchanges—instead of as declarations of a cultural war between the Beats and the Squares—not only produces a more complex understanding of these texts themselves, but it fundamentally alters the theoretical and pedagogical foundation of Beat studies. Instead of simply portraying the Beat Revolution either as an unproblematic antidote to post-WWII America's culture of complacence and conformity, or as a radical, progressive countercultural movement which simply needs to be valorized, replicated, and defended against a "square" New Critical academy, both the Beats and the Squares should be understood as complex and interrelated cultural movements, which need to be carefully analyzed, evaluated, and contextualized without reducing them to oversimplified polar opposites.

Another way to draw attention to the contradictions and ironies of Beat culture is to study Beat texts in comparative contexts that highlight these contradictions. For example, I have attempted to expose some of the contradictions in Kerouac's *On the Road* by teaching it together with works such as Carolyn Cassady's *Off the Road*, Ted Joans's "Travelin'," and Ana Castillo's *The Mixquiahuala Letters*. When contrasted with Cassady's *Off the Road* and Joans's "Travelin'," Kerouac's free-spirited nomads often seem more timid and conservative, more burdened by guilt and culturallylimited aspirations, and more aided by self-serving narcissism and socioeconomic and patriarchal privileges than Kerouac presents them. While Kerouac hyperbolizes Sal and Dean's trip across the U.S.-Mexican border as a journey into a "magic land" where they can "leave everything behind" and enter a "new and unknown phase of things" as "other Americans haven't done before us," Joans's travels range more widely from "Elkhart Indiana" to "Ibadan Nigeria," "Oaxaca Mexico," "Nova Scotia," "Ireland," "London England," "Belgium," and "Venice"

(Kerouac 1957, 276; Joans 1961a). Moreover, Joans describes his travels with both more cosmopolitan awareness of each location's cultural specificity and less touristic hysteria about its exotic differences. Similarly, when contrasted with Castillo's novel, it becomes more clear that Kerouac's *On the Road* celebrates Sal and Dean's objectification of their cultural others while Castillo self-consciously represents the limitations of her characters' cultural stereotypes and celebrates their attempts to overcome those stereotypes instead of the stereotypes themselves.

Another way to help students deconstruct the binary opposition between the Beats and the Squares is to develop a more complex understanding of "square" America by assigning revisionist histories of the 1950s, such as Stephanie Coontz's *The Way We Never Were: American Families and the Nostalgia Trap* (1992) or Joel Foreman's anthology, *The Other Fifties: Interrogating Midcentury American Icons* (1997). As Foreman explains, we must complicate our conception of the "1950s as either simple, innocent, happy, unanimously supportive of a broad spectrum of beliefs, or radically separated from the 1960s by a culture of complacence" (1997, 1). Similarly, Coontz argues that the stereotypical 1950s American family "evaporates on closer examination" because underneath "the polished facades of many 'ideal' families, suburban as well as urban, was violence, terror, or simply grinding misery that only occasionally came to light" (1992, 9, 35). Instead of uncritically accepting sanitized images of "square" America "that are still delivered to our homes in countless reruns of 1950s television sit-coms," we should critically analyze how the "reality of these families was far more painful and complex than the situation-comedy reruns or the expurgated memories of the nostalgic would suggest" (23, 29). Given that the Beat Generation emerged in opposition to square America, courses on Beat culture need to develop a more complex understanding of "square" America both to understand better how and why the Beats rejected it and to contextualize that rejection comparatively with respect to other contemporaneous social and cultural movements. This can be done not only by reading revisionist histories like Coontz's and Foreman's, but also by analyzing more complex literary representations of "square" America. Writers such as Ellison, Salinger, Plath, Okada, Momaday, Williams, Gwendolyn Brooks, James Baldwin, and Gilbert Sorrentino also explored the numerous dysfunctions, hypocrisies, and contradictions that lurked beneath 1950s America's "square" façade, but their works often develop both a more complex view of "square" America's internal contradictions and a broader understanding of the multiple social and political groups that co-existed on the margins of "square" America. For example, Williams's *The Glass Menagerie* explores many of the same themes as Kerouac's *On the Road*, but it explores the complexities of "square" America instead of casually dismissing it. Similarly, Plath's *The Bell Jar* compliments Ginsberg's "Howl" by providing an alternative description of how and why "square" America caused the "best minds" of its generation to be "destroyed by madness" (Ginsberg 1959, 9). As Plath's novel demonstrates, Ginsberg's "angelheaded hipsters" who "went out whoring through Colorado in myriad stolen night-cars" and "threw potato salad at CCNY lecturers on Dadaism" were not the only ones driven to madness and suicidal despair by the social constraints of 1950s America (Ginsberg 1959, 9, 14, 18). Pairing Beat texts with other representations of "square" America not only helps correct media stereotypes of the 1950s, but it also helps students better appreciate that the Beat Generation rejected post-WWII American culture not only because of its privileged, "square," middle-class, suburban affluence but also because many Beats experienced the "violence, terror, or simply grinding misery that only occasionally came to light" in representations of post-WWII America (Coontz 1992, 9).

In addition to deconstructing simplistic stereotypes of "square" America, a critical analysis of Beat literature must also complicate idealized and nostalgic representations of the Beat Generation itself by critically analyzing how many Beat writers remained at least partially trapped within the "square" culture they attempted to critique. In this respect, Jack Kerouac's *On the Road* not only provides what the *New York Times* critic, Gilbert Millstein, described as "the testament . . . of the Beat Generation," but it also exemplifies how the Beats' countercultural revolution replicated many of post-WWII America's "square" cultural assumptions (1957, 27). It is true that *On the Road* articulates an alternative vision of America from the perspective of the "mad ones, the ones who are mad to live, mad to talk, mad to be saved, desirous of everything at the same time, the ones

who never yawn or say a commonplace thing, but burn, burn, burn
like fabulous yellow roman candles exploding like spiders across the
stars and in the middle you see the blue centerlight pop and everybody goes 'Awww!'" (Kerouac 1957, 8). Nevertheless, even Kerouac's
"mad ones" still espoused many of the narrow-minded conventions
of "square" America. An obvious example of this can be found in
their reinterpretation of sexuality. At the same time that Kerouac
and his characters rejected "square" America's repressed sexuality by
exalting sex as "the one and only holy and important thing in life,"
they retained "square" America's sexism both by describing women
as "awfully dumb and capable of doing horrible things" and by
expecting women to "make breakfast and sweep the floor" while the
men "sat around dumbly smoking butts from ashtrays" (4–5).
Similarly, Kerouac travels into African American, Chicano, and
Mexican cultures, but his sense of cultural diversity replicates many
of "square" America's cultural stereotypes. Not only does he reduce
African Americans to blackface stereotypes of the "happy, true-hearted, ecstatic Negroes of America" (180) and exoticize Mexico as a
"pornographic hasheesh daydream" (291), but he also conflates these
cultural stereotypes into an undifferentiated multicultural mélange:
"The mambo beat is the conga beat from Congo, the river of Africa
and the world; it's really the world beat" (287). Moreover, it is this
same procrustean disregard for cultural particularities that allows
Kerouac to want to become a "Negro," "Denver Mexican," and "poor
overworked Jap" all at the same time (180). Consequently, even
though Kerouac reverses "square" America's xenophobic fear of cultural difference, he retains many of its reductive racist and sexist
stereotypes.

   In particular, an excellent way to introduce students to the more
problematic aspects of Beat culture is to expand the Beat canon to
include works by both minority and female Beat writers. In many
instances, these less canonical Beat texts directly challenge the Beat
Generation's idealized representations of itself by pointing out how
the Beat Generation promotes many of the dominant culture's racist
and sexist conventions. For example, Ted Joans's *The Hipsters*
(1961b) satirizes the Beats by describing them as Jivey Leaguers,
Creepniks, Folkniks, and Hipper-Than-Thouniks to point out various
contradictions and self-deceptions in the Beat Generation's idealized

representations of itself. According to Joans's parodic definitions, a "Jivey Leaguer" is a "half-way cat whose sole concern is to be a part of everything which he puts down or cashes-in-on as it suits his eternal search for girls in his well-dressed-to-bore tight faggotaire clothes"; a "Creepnik" is someone "always on the scene digging lonely young chicks, pets that are left alone, and other valuables that he can steal"; and a "Hipper-Than-Thounik" is an "overread writer or painter of sorts who speaks as an astute authority on every subject, even sex, which she knows only from books" (1961b, 16, 17, 21). With each parody, Joans challenges the Beat Generation's false pretentions of being deeper, hipper, or more artistic than it really is. Similarly, Joans's "Rent-A-Beatnik" ad in the *Village Voice*, in which he offered to rent himself out as an authentic Beatnik companion who could help Squares appear more hip at parties, parodied the Beat counterculture as a trendy, superficial revolution focused more on fashion than substance. In *All of Ted Joans And No More* (1961a), poems such as "We Split the Beat Scene," "Shoe Fits?," and "Jivey Leaguer" also criticize the Beats for being racist. For example, "Jivey Leaguer" criticizes Beat Jivey Leaguers who are "afraid of undiluted democracy" because they claim to be "superior" but refuse to let African Americans "have Civil Rights" (90–91). Similarly, Joans criticizes these sexual rebels who eagerly "invade the Village searching for a Free-Lay" but would "die if I banged your sister someday" because their liberated libidos remain trapped by racist prejudices (92). Other critical parodies of the Beat Generation can also be found in works such as Bob Kaufman's "Bagel Shop Jazz," Amiri Baraka's "Poem for Halfwhite College Students," and La Loca's "Why I Choose Black Men for My Lovers."

In addition, several minority and female Beat writers have either rewritten canonical Beat texts or reinterpreted Beat history from alternative perspectives. For example, Carolyn Cassady's *Off the Road: My Years with Cassady, Kerouac, and Ginsberg* redescribes many of the characters and events in Kerouac's *On the Road* from a female perspective that exposes and reverses many of Kerouac's sexist assumptions and self-serving descriptions. In particular, Cassady's account problematizes Kerouac's representations of his sexual virility by describing him as a "somewhat inhibited" lover and explaining how Cassady "manipulated circumstances" to seduce Kerouac, rather than the other way around (1992, 455, 453). Similarly, Diane di Prima's *Memoirs of a Beatnik* reinterprets the Beat counterculture described in works such as Kerouac's *The Subterraneans* by focusing on how women actively participated in and helped create the Beat revolution instead of just passively standing around and washing the dishes as Kerouac often implies. For example, instead of continuing sexist stereotypes that reduce females to passive sexual objects or prostitutes, di Prima describes how Beat women also "initiate[d] the dance that would satisfy my own desire and bring delight to the creature beside me" (1998, 5). Another critical revision of Beat literary conventions can be found in Amiri Baraka's *Dutchman and the Slave* (1964), which signifies on Kerouac's representations of Charlie Parker in *The Subterraneans* (1958) and *Mexico City Blues* (1959). Even though jazz significantly influenced both Kerouac and Baraka, these two writers often interpreted jazz in radically different ways. For example, Kerouac describes Parker as "the kindest jazz musician there could be" and wonders if Parker is "looking to search if really I was that great writer I thought myself," while Baraka interprets Parker's music as telling the "hip white boys [who] scream for Bird": "Up your ass, feeble-minded ofay! Up your ass" (Kerouac 1958, 14; Baraka 1964, 35). While neither representation can be taken as a definitive authentic interpretation of Parker's music, the contrast between the two representations exemplifies some of the tensions and contradictions within the Beat Generation itself. Because works by African American and female Beat writers often explicitly represent these tensions, including these works as essential contributions to the Beat canon makes it much more difficult to celebrate Beat writers such as Kerouac, Ginsberg, and Burroughs as unproblematic representatives of the cultural conflicts of post-WWII America. It is true that the central core of Beat writers did develop a significant critique of "square" America, but their cultural critique only represented one way, and not necessarily the most radical or most progressive way, of questioning and redefining 1950s American culture. If Beat literature is to continue to have relevance in contemporary American universities, which are shaped by both feminist and minority discourses, then the Beat canon must be expanded to include a wider range of Beat voices in order to develop a more self-critical understanding of the Beat Generation's multiple voices, internal contradictions, and political limitations.

Another way to complicate simplistic notions of the Beat counterculture's revolution against "square" America is to analyze more critically the nature and function of countercultural movements themselves. While Halberstam is correct that the Beats were "pioneers of what would eventually become the counterculture" (1993, 295), many contemporary students lack a critical understanding of how countercultural traditions have functioned in post-WWII America. In the same sense that many contemporary students' understanding of "square" America derives largely from reruns of 1950s sitcoms, much of their understanding of the Beat counterculture derives from media images of the Beat culture as it is represented in commercial advertisements and movies. Consequently, they develop a naïve and romanticized view of countercultural movements, which often prevents them from either understanding or participating in significant acts of cultural critique. To help students begin to recognize some of the limitations of and contradictions within countercultural movements, it is useful to assign a work like Thomas Frank's *The Conquest of Cool: Business Culture, Counterculture, and the Rise of Hip Consumerism* (1997), which analyzes how the media and capitalist economy misrepresent and co-opt countercultural movements. As Frank explains, not only has "business dogged the counterculture with a fake counterculture, a commercial replica that seemed to ape its every move for the titillation of the TV-watching millions and the nation's corporate sponsors," but corporate culture has made "rebel youth culture" itself "the cultural mode of the corporate moment, used to promote not only specific products but the general idea of life in the cyber-revolution. Commercial fantasies of rebellion, liberation, and outright 'revolution' against the stultifying demands of mass society are commonplace almost to the point of invisibility in advertising, movies, and television programming" (1997, 7, 4). For example, Coca-Cola sends replicas of Ken Kesey's bus, *Further*, "around the country to generate interest in the counterculturally themed beverage" Fruitopia, while "Nike shoes are sold to the accompaniment of words delivered by William S. Burroughs and songs by The Beatles, Iggy Pop, and Gil Scott Heron ('the revolution will not be televised')" (4). In addition to studying a work like

Frank's *The Conquest of Cool*, it can also be instructive to have students locate and analyze their own examples of how Beat culture has been commodified and repackaged for Generation X consumers. Examples of such commodification can be found not only in contemporary advertisements, but also in new multimedia Beat tributes such as Dennis Hopper's documentary *The Source* and the rapidly proliferating Jack Kerouac CD collections. Further evidence of this commodification can also be seen in the historical evolution of Beat book covers, which have increasingly moved away from City Lights' somber black-and-white cover for the original edition of Ginsberg's *Howl and Other Poems* (1959) to the seductive, picture-packed retro-nostalgia of Penguin's recent edition of Kerouac's *Book of Blues* (1995). Consequently, it can be useful to ask students to compare accounts of the famous Six Gallery poetry reading with Dennis Hopper's recreation of Beat poetry performances in *The Source* or to analyze how the work of a particular Beat writer has been repackaged and reinterpreted in different contexts. By contrasting contemporary examples of repackaged Beat culture with Beat texts, students can develop a more critical understanding of how the Beat Generation's current appeal might differ from its historical reception in the 1950s.

After reading a work like Frank's history of the collusion between countercultural movements and the business culture of corporate capitalism, students are also better prepared to critically analyze their own investments in Beat culture. For example, they can be challenged to explain why the Beat Generation has become so popular with their own generation if it was really such a countercultural threat to 1950s America. Confronting critical questions like this not only helps students complicate their view of the Beat Generation as a countercultural movement, but it helps them develop a more self-critical understanding of their own eagerness to celebrate it. After all, would they be so ready to celebrate Kerouac, Ginsberg, and Burroughs if these writers really opposed the cultural and corporate logic of their own historical moment? It can prove instructive, therefore, to require students to analyze the contemporary relevance of the Beat counterculture for a contemporary audience, instead of simply celebrating their critique of 1950s "square" America, because this forces students to directly address their own investments—both in the Beats and in their own cultural moment. Another way to help students explore the contemporary relevance of Beat culture is to assign texts such as Maxine Hong Kingston's *Tripmaster Monkey: His Fake Book* or Jessica Hagedorn's *Gangster of Love*, which rewrite Beat themes in contemporary contexts. Moreover, Generation X students need to confront why they are so ready to celebrate the writing of Kerouac, Ginsberg, and Burroughs, but are less comfortable about works by more marginal Beat writers such as di Prima, Baraka, and Kaufman. Consequently, assigning students to write papers that compare and contrast canonical white, male Beat writers with more marginalized female and minority Beats can help students more directly confront how their own investments in the Beat counterculture both derive from a particular, narrow construction of the Beat canon and reflect their own particular cultural and class sensibilities. Ultimately, educators who teach the Beat Generation to Generation X must develop more critical pedagogical strategies, which force students to analyze whether or not they celebrate Beat literature because its countercultural revolution allows them to rebel against authority without ever really doing what Gayatri Spivak refers to as the "careful project of un-learning our privilege as our loss" (1990, 9).

In conclusion, I believe that a central pedagogical objective of teaching Beat literature is to complicate a commonly held oversimplified understanding of the 1950s as a cultural war between the Beats and the Squares, and I have attempted to explain several reasons why these two movements cannot be taken as *the* extremes of post-WWII American culture. To begin with, overemphasizing the Beats and the Squares obscures other historical and cultural forces, ranging from the expanding media culture to the escalating Civil Rights movement, which provide equally valid reference points not only for plotting 1950s history in general but also for understanding the historical evolution of the Beats and the Squares themselves. For example, the Beat Generation appears far less radical or progressive when it is contrasted against the Civil Rights Movement than when it is contrasted against "square" America. The Beat Generation did critique 1950s America, but it was neither the only nor the most radical movement of its day. Moreover, in addition to contextualizing the Beat Generation within a broader spectrum of 1950s cultural movements, teachers should expose students to a more expansive sense of the Beat canon itself. The canonical white, male core of Kerouac, Ginsberg, and Burroughs should be studied alongside the alternative perspectives of both African American Beats such as Baraka, Joans, and Kaufman and female Beats such as Diane di Prima, Carolyn Cassady, and Hettie Jones. This comparative approach will help students develop a more critical understanding not only of the Beat counterculture's limitations but also of alternative ways to construct countercultural practices. Finally, despite the Beat Generation's rejection of certain "square" values, it never entirely dismantled the cultural logic of post-WWII America. Instead, its particular countercultural vision deconstructed certain cultural taboos at the same time that it retained both other forms of sexual and racial privilege and covert economic ties to the same postwar affluence that it despised. In short, the Beat Generation was not a radical repudiation of "square" America but rather a strong, but partial, cultural critique, which ultimately branched out to form a complex network of alliances with other countercultural movements, ranging from the aesthetic experimentation of abstract expressionist painters and the Black Mountain poets to the political activism of the Civil Rights and feminist movements. In certain ways, the Beat Generation's complex network of alliances even extended back into the dominant "square" culture itself either to preserve certain forms of privilege or to get some extra cash when the money ran out on the road.

I have emphasized these limitations of Beat culture, however, not simply to point out the inevitable fact that nobody can completely escape the logic and practices of their own culture, but rather because I believe that our theoretical conceptions of Beat culture significantly influence both how and why we teach Beat literature. In particular, assuming that the Beat Generation was an unproblematic countercultural movement has direct pedagogical consequences because it leads educators both to represent Beat literature as a counterhegemonic assault on the literary canon and to ally themselves with the cultural sensibilities of their Generation X students who are "ready to celebrate" Beat icons. I believe, however, that educators need to develop more critical pedagogical strategies for teaching Beat culture, which will problematize, rather than simply deny or defend, the validity and worth of Beat texts. More importantly, I

believe that this kind of critical analysis will encourage Generation X
students to develop a more self-critical understanding of how their
personal investments in Beat culture often derive not from authenti-
cally countercultural practices but rather from a complex amalgamation of conflicting desires, ranging from a healthy disrespect for
authority and a genuine interest in other cultures to an attempt to
bulwark what remains of their cultural and social privileges and a
profound misunderstanding of their own entrapment within the
postmodern logic of late capitalism. In short, Generation X's relationship to the Beat Generation resembles the Beat Generation's relationship to the dominant "square" culture of 1950s America because
both relationships emerge out of a complex network of both progressive and reactionary desires. As educators who want to teach
the Beat Generation to Generation X students, our task is to develop
new critical pedagogical strategies that will enable our students to
recognize, analyze, and explore—rather than oversimplify and fore-
close—what Beat literature has to teach us about the full range of
these conflicting desires.

Notes

1 While the Life article, "Squaresville U.S.A. vs. Beatsville" (1959), attempts tomain-
tain a simple opposition between the Beats and the Squares by pointing out that
the girls from Hutchinson rescinded their "prankish invitation" after Lipton
accepted it, this explanation doesn't fully square with the article's other claims
about the girls being "whisked away to seclusion by their distressed parents" and
about the Beatniks being "reinvited by other teen-agers" until the local police
and town fathers intervened (31, 36).

WORKS CITED

Baraka, Amiri. 1964. *Dutchman and The Slave*. New York: William Morrow.
Cassady, Carolyn. 1992. "From Off the Road." In *The Portable Beat Reader*, ed.
Ann Charters. New York: Penguin.
Castillo, Ana. 1986. *The Mixquiahuala Letters*. New York: Doubleday.
Coontz, Stephanie. 1992. *The Way We Never Were: American Families and the
Nostalgia Trap*. New York: Basic Books.
di Prima, Diane. 1998. *Memoirs of a Beatnik*. 1969. Reprint. New York: Penguin.
Foreman, Joel, ed. 1997. *The Other Fifties: Interrogating Midcentury American
Icons*. Chicago: University of Illinois Press.
Frank, Thomas. 1997. *The Conquest of Cool: Business Culture, Counterculture,
and the Rise of Hip Consumerism*. Chicago: University of Chicago Press.
Ginsberg, Allen. 1959. *Howl and Other Poems*. San Francisco: City Lights Books.
Halberstam, David. 1993. *The Fifties*. New York: Fawcett Columbine.

Holmes, John Clellon. 1958. "The Philosophy of the Beat Generation." *Esquire*, February, 35–38.

Joans, Ted. 1961a. *All of Ted Joans and No More*. New York: Excelsior.

———. 1961b. *The Hipsters*. New York: Corinth.

Kerouac, Jack. 1957. *On the Road*. New York: Penguin.

———. 1958. *The Subterraneans*. New York: Grove.

———. 1959. *Mexico City Blues*. New York: Grove.

Lawlor, William. 1998. *The Beat Generation: A Bibliographical Teaching Guide*. Englewood Cliffs, NJ: Salem Press.

Millstein, Gilbert. 1957. "Books of the Times." *New York Times*, 5 September, 27.

Spivak, Gayatri. 1990. *The Post-Colonial Critic: Interviews, Strategies, Dialogues*, ed. Sarah Harasym. New York: Routledge.

"Squaresville U.S.A. vs. Beatsville." 1959. *Life*, 21 September, 31–37.

CHAPTER ONE

Telepathic Shock and Meaning Excitement:
Kerouac's Poetics of Intimacy
Ann Douglas

Explaining the special nature of his friendship with Jack Kerouac, Allen Ginsberg said that early in their relationship he realized that, "If I actually confessed the secret tendencies of my soul, he would understand nakedly who I was" (Watson 1995, 37). I think a number of Kerouac's readers even today feel the same way. I, for one, seem to know Kerouac better, he's *dearer* to me, than all but a few people in my actual life, and the extended confessions he called his "true-story novels" tell me that I am somehow just as important to him.

Every writer enters into a relationship with his reader, offering at the outset a kind of contract that lets the reader know what she must give to live inside this book, and what she will get in return. But few writers try to tell their readers everything that ever happened to them as Kerouac does over the many volumes of the "Duluoz legend"; few writers deliver the magical intensity of intimacy that *Dr. Sax, On the Road, Visions of Cody, Visions of Gerard, Maggie Cassady*, and *Big Sur* bring. Kerouac's ambition was as modest as it was grandiose, as slight as it was large. For every long shot in his "bookmovies," those moments when people "recede in the plain

til you see their specks dispersing" (1991, 156), there's a closeup.
"See close, my face now," Kerouac writes in *Dr. Sax*, "in the window
of the Sarah Avenue house," "a little kid with blue eyes," munching on
a Macintosh apple (1977, 82). Kerouac never wants to move out of
our sight or reach. "He flew low," Victor-Lévy Beaulieu has written,
and near, very near (1975, 165).

Kerouac said he wrote for "companionship," recounting what he
read on "the face of the person who opened the door," out of compassion for "someone going beyond the streetlamp into the dark"
(quoted in Nicosia 1983, 231, 345). Pledging himself to "100% personal honesty" (Charters 1995a, 356), Kerouac makes the reader his
confidant, taking her into his most private thoughts and experiences, into areas which the world sometimes seems to prohibit us
from sharing with anyone—our feelings about our bodies, our self-
imagings, the moods that inspire and afflict our need to believe. He
meant the reading of his books to break a taboo, for himself and his
readers. The things a man wishes to unsay, he remarked, are precisely
what American literature is "awaiting and bleeding for." "I have
renounced fiction and fear," he wrote Neal Cassady on December 28,
1950 (Charters 1995a, 248).

After telling us the story of his relationship with the Mexican
drug addict, Tristessa, Kerouac closes his narrative by saying, "I'll
write long sad tales about people in the legend of my life—this part
is my part of the movie, let's hear yours" (1992, 96). There's no period in the text, no punctuation at all, after "yours." The story is left
unfinished, open, like the last bar of Charlie Parker's version of
"Embraceable You," encouraging the reader to come into the same
bar of music, to put her image into the same frame with his, her
breath taking up where his left off. At this moment, you're all he has,
and maybe at this moment he's all you have, or need.

So, Kerouac, for some of us, becomes almost synonymous with
our private lives, the secret culture of our inmost thoughts and affec-
tions, the legend as well as the history of our existence. I know that
for me he's inextricably bound up with the circumstances of my life
at the time I first read *On the Road* in 1958 when I was sixteen.
Howl, too, circulated at the boarding school I attended, part of an
underground of forbidden literature that included *Forever Amber*
and Pierre Louÿs's *Aphrodite*. Though we barely understood

Ginsberg's homosexual allusions, we could aspire to being "the best minds" of our generation, and I thought I knew what it might mean to be "destroyed by madness."

On the Road was different. Unlike *Howl*, or *The Subterraneans* and *Visions of Cody*, later books by Kerouac published without editorial revision, there was little in it that my mother would have censored. In fact, when I persuaded her to read *On the Road* decades later, what bothered her was not so much the sexual promiscuity or the drug-taking of its characters—although, of course, she noted them—but its heartwrenching sadness. To her surprise, she'd fallen in love with Kerouac's sweetness and wit, and the fact that, as she told me, "It's the saddest book I ever read," affected her like a misfortune befalling a brilliant but improvident friend. She sensed that what was unusual and perhaps forbidden here was Kerouac's emotional expressiveness, his willingness to travel so far with so little luggage, so few judgments as ballast or currency, making himself helpless before the transience of experience, helpless as an agent and individual, though not as an artist. "Don't you know what's so utterly sad about the past?" Kenny Wood asks Peter Martin in *The Town and the City*. "It has no future. The things that come afterward have all been discredited" (Kerouac 1978, 110).

Back in 1959, *On the Road* told me and my friends, all young women from the uppermiddle classes reared in privileged, densely settled, even stratified regions of the United States, that we were part of a continent rather than a country, a kind of fabulous *terra incognita* not fully detailed on any map, shading on one side into a colder, mysterious northern land and on the other into a more tropical and seductive climate. In Kerouac's novel, the continent had been strangely emptied out of the people usually caught on camera, yet it was filled with other people, people in motion, of various races and ethnicities, speaking many tongues, migrating from one place to another as seasonal laborers, wandering around as hobos and hitchhikers, meeting each other in brief but somehow lasting encounters. *On the Road* told me that being an American meant being "somebody else, some stranger . . . [whose] whole life was a haunted life, the life of a ghost" (1991, 17).

Decades later, in the mid-1970s, I began teaching Kerouac in courses at Columbia University. Around the same time, I met and fell in love with Jay Fellows, a man for whom *On the Road* had also been a revelation, who saw himself as Kerouac's twin. He wasn't altogether mistaken. Like Jack, he was dazzlingly good-looking, intelligent, and athletic, and he, too, had played (in the same position) on the Horace Mann football team; he, too, made up in speed and tenacity what he lacked in sheer size. He, too, was written up in the city papers; he, too, went on to Columbia, only to leave the glories of football for the ecstatic struggles of authorship. Though he was never as famous as Jack was, he, too, became a cult figure to a small circle of friends and acquaintances before he published his first book; his books, too, were language experiments drenched in pastness, and they, too, met with little comprehension. His relationship with his mother, like Jack's with Memere, was all-absorbing in ways that precluded certain kinds of adult experience. He, too, drank himself to death in a fury of helpless disappointment when he was only a few years older than Jack had been at the time of his death.

At Jay's memorial service at St. Mark's Church in the Village, where the fortieth anniversary reading of *On the Road* took place this past September, I read Lucien Carr's words about Jack's end. Jack was "a man on the run," "ruining [his] soul," Carr says. Then he asks, "What can a man do for his brother? *What can a man do for love?*" "*Nothing,*" he answers. "*Nothing*" (Gifford and Lee 1978, 319). I don't believe this story of Kerouac's influence is entirely exceptional, and I can't think of another writer whose books get so intensely entangled with the lives and psyches of his readers.

In *Life on the Screen*, a study of virtual reality and on-line culture, the critic Sherry Turkle makes the point that even very young computer users can distinguish the hyperreality of on-line life from the reality of the off-screen world. To them, the on-line world feels "conscious," that is, capable of multiple activities, but not "alive"; it doesn't provide bodies with real skin (1996, 84). It's an important distinction, one that serves to delimit what is represented from what is experienced, but Kerouac's effort as an author was, I think, precisely to erase it, to use the "spontaneous prose" of "personal secret idea words" (Charters 1995b, 484) to make the world his pages chronicle as real as bodies with real skin, creating what he called "real unreality" (Charters 1992, 221), a world rapturous and magical, as obstreperous, funny, hopeful, and infinitely forlorn as our own bodies—those unmalleable masses of matter that are, willy-nilly, our only representatives in the world. Train, dress, and carry it as you may, your body tells anyone who cares to read more about yourself than you would willingly tell anyone, including yourself.

It is the body's open secrets, its status as obstacle and door to salvation, that Kerouac fashioned a new prose style to tell—what it felt like to be "Home at Christmas" as a small boy going to sleep on a winter night in Lowell, seeing a "great bulging star white as ice beating in the dark field of heaven, "hearing the apple tree outside his window "cracking black limbs in frost," smelling the "softcoal heat of the furnace in the cellar ,"knowing the bird outside was sleeping "with his muffly feathers inward" (Charters 1995b, 49). Later, in *Big Sur*, we learn what it was to be a grown, though not grown-up, man struggling with the devils of alcoholism, flagging creativity, and spiritual despair, "a bentback mudman monster groaning underground in hot steaming mud pulling a long hot burden nowhere," slipping back into formlessness as another death approaches, "nature giving us birth and eating us back" (Kerouac 1981a, 8).

In a bad moment recounted in *Big Sur*, Kerouac opens Boswell's *Life of Samuel Johnson* and instantly finds himself "in an entirely perfect world again" (1981a, 86). For inveterate readers like Kerouac, like myself, reading can be an experience of total self-sufficiency; he called it "absorbing" rather than reading a book. We have what we always wanted—ourselves, accompanied by no rivals, no parents or peers, bothered, in fact, by no people at all except those our imaginations choose to invest with reality. It's just us, at last, and a complete world, one mysteriously landscaped, as the world outside seldom is, to our deepest needs.

Yet, there's another, very different experience found in reading Kerouac. Despite the culture of intimacy he creates, Kerouac tells us again and again that his writing reflects, as "literature should," "real life in this real world" (1981b, 10). In *Vanity of Duluoz*, he explains that his novels form a "contemporary history record [of] what really happened and what people really thought" (1994, 190). Kerouac's editor and biographer Ann Charters has reminded us of what meticulous and extensive records Kerouac kept of his career and his times; he meant his work to be in some sense verifiable. Seymour Krim, still among Kerouac's most insightful critics, thought he had left "the

most authentic prose record" available of the "screwy, neo-adoles-
cent" post-WWII era (1965, xxv). Kerouac is an historian as well as a
novelist and an autobiographer; that's what the phrase "true story
novel" is meant to tell us. I like the phrase "auto-history"[1] for
Kerouac's project as well; it swerves away from the objective/subjec-
tive, world/self dyad, suggesting an investigation of the private self
through its historical era and viceversa. Kerouac's style, that explo-
sive, tender, confessional vehicle of what he called "telepathic shock
and meaning excitement" (Charters 1995b, 484), was devised, in
other words, as part of his effort to read, not just himself or Neal
Cassady or Memere, but the larger life of his times.

Like F. Scott Fitzgerald, Kerouac had an infallible eye for the cultural detail that served as a harbinger of important social change. He
noted the white T-shirt Marlon Brando wore in *A Streetcar Named
Desire* and the new masculine image it represented (Charters
1995b, 560). Perhaps more surprisingly, in *Vanity of Duluoz*, published in the late 1960s just before the first personal computers
were being marketed, he anticipated the deconstructionist doubts
such technology would cast on the traditional understanding of
authorship. People might think, as one recent letter writer had, that
he didn't write his own books, that there was no "Jack Kerouac" at
all, that his words "just suddenly appeared on a computer" somewhere. To Kerouac this sophistry was of a piece with a new popular
phrase, one he detested, "you're putting me on," which seemed to rest
on the assumption that everyone was more or less lying more or less
all the time, that there were no such things as truth and falsehood or
an authentic self (1994, 13, 14). Kerouac doesn't use the term, of
course, but, in fact, he's describing the "postmodern" perspective and
era, whose beginnings historians and theoreticians today date to the
same years, the early 1960s, that Kerouac was alluding to.[2]

It's not that Kerouac was sure that there was an authentic self.
Indeed, his work is a sometimes agonized exploration of precisely
this question: what, if anything, keeps the self consistent from
moment to moment? Who provides the continuity for his "book-
movie?" He openly wonders if the man writing *Big Sur* can be the
same person who wrote *On the Road* a decade earlier. The Beat
movement took place on the cusp of postmodernity; it's the negoti-
ating ground, the borderland between modernity and postmoderni-

ty, and Kerouac knew it. But he couldn't start a book from the assumption that there was no self, answerable in some way to the God in whom he never stopped believing. For Kerouac, the fact that God is outnumbered or forgotten doesn't mean that God isn't still present; a belief betrayed is not the same thing as a belief abandoned. Kerouac's refusal of editing or revision, his injunction to "make the mind the slave of the tongue" (Charters 1995b, 11), presupposes at the very least that there is a story to be told, a story that insists on being told, even if there is no truth to find.

I believe that Kerouac's style is the most important innovation in American prose since Hemingway's very different stylistic breakthrough twenty-five years earlier. As Hemingway's prose was a response to the new technological and metaphysical realities ushered in by World War I, so Kerouac's "spontaneous prose" reflected the realities of a very different but equally influential wartime period, that of WWII and the Cold War that quickly succeeded it. Such a response, whether one is speaking of Hemingway or Kerouac is, of course, not an altogether conscious process. It's rather a matter of the pressures at work on the writer at a given time, and the acuity, originality, and depth of the resources he brings to meet them. It has more to do with alchemy than politics.

Kerouac's ethos of openness, his insistence that he comes before us totally unarmed, unprepared, and unguarded, ready to keep absolutely nothing back, makes the most sense when we realize that he was writing at a time when national preparedness, particularly military preparedness, took on proportions unprecedented in Western history. In the wake of Hiroshima, as hostilities between the United States and the Soviet Union, its recent ally, intensified into a staged battle between the putative forces of good and evil, the bomb was defined as "the property of the American people" (Isaacson and Thomas 1986, 321)[3]; extraordinary measures were taken to see that the "secret" of its composition was kept. Knowledge was tightly compartmentalized; each person working on the bomb was to know only what he needed to know for his particular job. The prerogative of the big picture, the overview, belonged to a tiny elite, increasingly immune from scrutiny or interference.[4]

Various top-secret state documents of the day promulgated the doctrine of "plausible deniability"; the covert actions of the CIA, itself

new in 1947, its assassination plots and "roll back" strategies, were to
be conducted in such a way that no one in the top echelons of the
U.S. government could be held accountable if they were exposed.[5]
Knowledge was viewed for the first time, not as the result of discovery and collaboration, of tapping into a free-flowing source that pre-
dated and exceeded the individual mind, but as a commodity owned
by a particular set of minds in a particular nation. Knowledge could-
n't travel; it could only be stolen and smuggled across enemy lines.[6]
The category of "classified information" covered ever-greater portions
of the national experience; borders were appearing in new places,
policed as never before.

Everyone was under surveillance by someone, it seemed, by
neighbors and fellow citizens, if not the FBI. Under President
Truman's Loyalty Program, thousands of people were compelled to
tell their stories to their employers or even the House Committee on
Un-American Activities, to confess and renounce their leftist pasts
and "choose the West," in Dwight Macdonald's phrase, or suffer the
consequences (1958, 197–201).[7] The writer Mary McCarthy referred
to such well-rehearsed confessions, Cold War melodramas prepack-
aged to yield a predictable denouement, as "sensational fact-fictions,"
a genre in which lies and truth could no longer be distinguished
from one another (1961, 75–76).

It was in this atmosphere that Kerouac wrote his "true-story novels," a term that could serve as a critical revision of McCarthy's "sensational fact-fictions." In the age that invented the idea of classified
information, Kerouac's effort was to *de*classify the secrets of the
human body and soul; "100% personal honesty" countered "plausible
deniability," improvisation replaced planning, fluidity defied compart-
mentalization, and magic supplanted mystification. In Kerouac's
work, choices arise only *not* to be made.

The apparent formlessness that attends Kerouac's narratives, the
absence of conventional plotting that made the critic Norman
Podhoretz fume in 1958 that there was "no dramatic reason" for anything that happened in Kerouac's fiction (1958, 315), was in part a
response to a world in which there seemed to be too many reasons
for things to happen as they did, in which events felt predetermined
and overdetermined, in which cues to the unexpected were no
longer heard. Drama means that something doesn't happen because

something else does. In its crudest form, the girl tied to the railroad tracks isn't run over by the train *because* her lover arrives just in time to cut her free; drama presupposes alternatives and a choice between them. Whether the agent is represented as God or human resourcefulness or happenstance, one side wins and the other loses. Drama is about control threatened and regained; it's part of the special effects of power. Kerouac, however, meant to slip the leash of the preconditioned and overcontrolled. As Mardou Fox asks in *The Subterraneans*, "what's in store for me in the direction I *don't* take?" (Kerouac 1981c, 30)—a question that refuses the distinction between offstage and onstage on which drama depends.

The America Kerouac describes in *The Subterraneans* is full of the ghosts of prior, displaced inhabitants; they signal the directions the nation itself did not take that nonetheless still lie open, waiting to be reimagined. As Mardou tells Leo about her life, he sees her Native American ancestors, "wraiths of humanity treading lightly the surface of the ground so deeply suppurated with the stock of their suffering you have only to dig a foot down to find a baby's hand" (1981c, 28–29). Mardou's ancestors, of whom she is not at this moment talking or thinking, bleed into her narrative, recoloring its figures, shifting its key; to Leo, she is not one person but many. The unknown is as real as the known; what has not happened, what has not been told, isn't obliterated by what has. In a similar fashion, the "clash of the streets beyond the window's bare soft sill" (1981c, 28) provides the soundtrack to Mardou's narrative; the presumably unrelated activities and noises of outside filter inside, into the room in which the lovers are sitting—words themselves exist in close proximity to the sounds that predate, accompany, and succeed their formulations.

From the opening page of *The Subterraneans*, Kerouac has been pulling the reader inside the story as well. "I must explain," he says to the reader, how he was feeling when he was introduced to Mardou; further "confessions must be made" about his "lecherous propensities" (1981c, 3, 5). On yet another track of the multiple mix that is his narrative, Kerouac is hypothesizing our responses as extensions and alternatives to his own; he feels us out there transforming and modifying what he's telling us. We are the future of the text, a future just becoming visible in its present, as surely as Mardou's ancestors are the past into which its present disappears. Kerouac's presentation of his sexuality follows the same logic; the love story of Leo and Mardou is interrupted, overlaid with a secondary tale about Leo's confused overtures to the successful, homosexual author Arial Lavalina. Yet neither the biographical Kerouac or his fictive stand-in here are homosexual or even bisexual in any conventional sense. It's rather that Kerouac won't ever shut off an alternative script— inevitably the contours of his homosexual impulses surface through the heterosexual patterns that in actual fact dominate them.

Nor will Kerouac choose between apparently conflicting temporal modes or points of view. Telling us about the day, a few months prior to the writing of the story, on which he first met Mardou as he was walking down the street with Larry O'Hara, he places us at the same time at the moment of writing, as he sits in the "sadglint of my wallroom," listening to Sarah Vaughan on the radio (1981c, 3). Destabilizing the self, unmooring the story, as Kerouac does here, is to maximize his own vulnerability, but as Charlie Parker liked to tell other musicians, if you "act just a little bit foolish and let yourself go, better ideas will come [to you]" (Reisner 1991, 187). Embarrassment and failure may attend a readiness to loose the self from its conventional frame, yet to entertain alternative selves, to go out of character, letting accident usurp the role of decision, putting the guest in the chair of the host, the child in the place usually reserved for the adult, is the key to the kind of art that both Kerouac and Parker sought to create; an art in which anarchic simultaneity rather than sequence is the principle of order, a narrative leaching over borders, dissolving compartmental walls, reversing outsides and insides, and returning us to a state of mental and physical flux. Differentiation here is but one of the forms that undifferentiation takes.[8]

It is important in this context that Kerouac was not a native English speaker. He was raised speaking the local French-Canadian dialect joual, the largely working class and oral idiom he continued to use with his mother throughout his life. In a 1950 letter, he explained to a French-Canadian reviewer that "All my knowledge rests in my 'French-Canadianness' and nowhere else . . . . I never spoke English before I was six or seven . . . . The reason I handle English words so easily is because it is not my own language. I refashion it to fit French images. Do you see that?" (Charters 1995a, 229). Linguistically, Kerouac always led a double life; the idiom of his novels was American English but his imagination was joual. His writing is less a translation of his native tongue into English than a relexification of English; he deanglicizes it, undoing the routinization process that created Standard English and condemned all its variants as the idiom of the illiterate.[9]

Kerouac's dual language track, the balance he struck between the written text and an earlier oral performance, also had echoes in the wider life of his times. The Cold War era was the period that saw the liberation of the nations of Africa and Asia from colonial rule; it marked the start of the so-called postcolonial era in which we live today, and which the new academic field of Postcolonial Studies is designed to elucidate. Postcolonial theory tells us that one people has been subjugated but not entirely erased by another, that one language has been empowered over another without being able to eradicate it. The critic Chantal Zabus, writing about the imposition of English as the official language for the parts of West Africa formerly under British rule, says that the native's original, unwritten "source" language presses as a palimpsest behind the "target" or official, acquired, imperial language in which he writes, reshaping and reinterpreting it for its own ends (1995, 314–18). The English spoken in West Africa, in other words, refuses to exorcize its ghostly African predecessor; in our postcolonial era, Anglo-English proper has been transformed by its own alternative lives, whether it be the English spoken in Africa or India or Ireland.

Like the native West African dialects, like the Celtic and Breton tongues of his distant forefathers, the joual that haunts and reshapes Kerouac's American English is also in some sense a "colonial" language; it, too, is the idiom of a people defeated in war, left behind by modernization, a people who claim their identity not on the strength of the battles they have won or the land they rule but solely on the strength of the language they speak. The battle was lost, the land is gone, only the language remains, a language now carrying more history than conventional meaning knows how to accommodate.[10] Kerouac's fabled memory was essentially a genealogical one; it was his task, as Victor-Lévy Beaulieu puts it, "to keep the minutes for collectivities in the process of disappearing" (1975, 167–68). Kerouac's readers fall in love with him in part because he positions himself so openly and nakedly as a lover, the acolyte, and historiographer of the otherwise forgotten. To leave this life without recording the things only he remembered would have been for Kerouac the unpardonable sin.

The lover's stance, however, is always a complex one. As Roland Barthes describes it in *A Lover's Discourse*, love is about giving up control, being compelled or seduced to trust something or someone not ourselves because we believe, if only for a moment, that the rewards of such exposure justify the risk. But once we tell a third party about our experience of love, Barthes says, as sooner or later we inevitably do, we begin to betray it, because in any narrative we fashion, we ourselves, not the beloved, emerge in some guise as the hero; it is well-nigh impossible to tell a story without putting oneself in charge. Kerouac, too, knew that narratives are always involved with authority, with self-promotion. "It's difficult to make a real confession," he tells the reader early in *The Subterraneans*, "when you're such an egomaniac all you can do is take off on long paragraphs about minor details about yourself" (1981c, 5). He can't narrate the story of this love affair without getting involved in big "word constructions" that "betray" it (1981c, 13). Kerouac can't escape his own narrative authority, but he can attempt to diminish it more radically than any writer had yet been able to do. "I always wanted to write a book to defend someone [else]," he says in *Desolation Angels*, "because to defend myself [is] an indefensible trip" (1980, 364). In all his books, he keeps handing narrative authority over to someone or something else, even as he explores his own reactions to the process.

Kerouac's most charmed, most perfect narratives are, I think, the Lowell novels about his pre-English, joual-speaking childhood, stories in which his brother Gerard and his parents are at least as important as he is. As Joan Acucello has noted, the memoir of childhood gains its enchantment, its special poetry of disinterestedness, from the fact that its premises were set by others (1997, 6). The kingdom of childhood is a magical one precisely because little anxiety need be expended on borders and boundaries—they are not choices, but givens, even absolutes, to be reinvented and transformed by the imagination, not challenged by the mind. "Isn't it true," Kerouac asks in *On the Road*, "that you start your life a sweet child believing in everything under your father's roof?" "The day comes, however, when that certainty no longer holds, when you know that you are running the show, if only because it is painfully clear that no one else is. Then, Kerouac says, "you go shuddering through nightmare life" (1991, 105).

Kerouac put off this nightmare as long as he possibly could. The first books that cover his postchildhood years, novels largely written in the early to mid-1950s, are complex acts of homage focused on someone not himself—on Dean/Cody or Japhy Ryder or Mardou or Tristessa. "I was a lout compared, I couldn't keep up with them," Sal remarks in *On the Road*, contrasting himself with Dean Moriarity and Carlo Marx; they "danced down the street like dingledodies, and I shambled after, as I've been doing all my life after people who interest me" (1991, 7, 8). *They* set the terms of the story, he doesn't. But in the books that Kerouac wrote in the late 1950s and 1960s, *Desolation Angels, Big Sur, Vanity of Duluoz,* and *Satori in Paris,* the authority of others has failed. The only person's wake in which he now finds himself is his own, and the rage and pain of these books reveal the depths of the disorientation this entailed. "No characters," is the way he describes his time alone on Desolation Peak in *Desolation Angels,* just "myself . . . face to face with . . . Hateful . . . me" (1980, 4). Kerouac unable to relocate himself in the multiple orbits of others, in an expanding universe of untried alternatives, is a writer almost unable to write. "I'm sick of words," he tells us in *Desolation Angels* (1980, 5); "I hate to write," he bursts out in *Big Sur* (1981a, 41).

Kerouac has grown angry with his readers; they, too, have come to represent the forces of constraint rather than the possibilities of expansion. The reader no longer echoes and varies the author's existence, but checks and misunderstands it. He's writing in the flatter, deader style of *Vanity of Duluoz,* he tells us, because he's learned that no one understood the enchanted bravura style of the books he valued most. There's just Stella left to listen, the "dear wifey" to whom he addresses *Vanity of Duluoz.* He ends by telling her to forget the story he's just told: "Go to sleep. Tomorrow's another day." Nothing really matters, he says, but his need for the next drink of wine (1994, 268).

While I would never claim that *Vanity of Duluoz,* much less *Satori in Paris,* are comparable as artistic achievements to *Dr. Sax* or *Visions of Cody,* for me, they complete rather than betray the Duluoz legend, and I think it's in part because, though Kerouac claims to place no hopes in me, his reader, I as his reader am still part of the story. If the reader is now one of the bad guys, so to speak, so is he, and he is telling her why she, and he, have failed, detailing and exposing the paucity of his invention as fully as he once displayed its plenitude. F. Scott Fitzgerald remarked that while his friend and rival Ernest Hemingway stood for "the authority of success," he represented "the authority of failure," and this authority, the authority, one might say, of non-authority, seems the logical goal of Kerouac's project, a project in which every presence was always shaded by a host of absences. Besides, what other writer has told his reader what it feels like to fail without trying to convert artistic bankruptcy into narcissistic gold, without using his failure as a fresh opportunity to showcase the resources he can still bring to bear on its explication? No, Kerouac is writing here because he has to, because the only promise he has found he can honor is his pledge to keep his files, and his reader, up to date, to tell the true story of what he saw and how he saw it to the bitter end. This was all, he said, he'd ever had to offer, and if impoverishment was where he was, impoverishment laid bare would be what the reader got.

In a late, enraged essay titled "After Me the Deluge," published posthumously in 1969 in *The Los Angeles Times*, after ranting against his putative heirs, the hippies, beatniks, and anti-war protesters of the day, Kerouac suddenly realizes that they, too, are "inconsolable orphans," "all so *lonered*." Then he turns to the reader and asks, "Ever look closely at *anybody* and see that particularized patience all their own, eyes hid, waiting with lips sewn down for time to pass, for something to succeed, for the long night of life to take them in its arms and say, 'Ah, Cherubim, this silly, stupid business . . . What *is* it, existence?'" (Charters 1995b, 578). Don't look around to see who he's talking to—it's you. It's your turn, to take up the tale, to put your image in the same frame with his, your breath picking up where his left off.

Notes

1 John Lucaks used the term to define Dwight Macdonald's projected, never completed autobiography (see Wreszin 1994, 473).
2 The most influential attempts to date to define the postmodern era have been Harvey (1990), Huyssen (1986), and Jameson (1991).

3 The words are those of Truman's Secretary of the Navy James Forrestal quoted in Isaacson and Thomas (1986, 321).
4 For the history of nuclear secrecy, see Boyer (1994). On the elite's monopoly of knowledge in the Cold War era, see Mills (1956).
5 For the CIA and the doctrine of plausible deniability, see Grose (1994) and Thomas (1995).
6 On the new status of knowledge in the post-WWII era see Lyotard (1984, xxiii–6).
7 For domestic surveillance, see Whitfield (1991).
8 I am indebted, in my analysis of Kerouac's style to Tallman (1960, 153–69), still the best single essay on the subject.
9 See Williams (1966, 214–19) for an influential discussion of the imposition of Standard English.
10 See During (1987, 32–47).

Works Cited

Acucello, Joan. 1997. "Leaps and Bounds." *New York Times Book Review*, 19 January, 6.

Beaulieu, Victor-Lévy. 1975. *Jack Kerouac: A Chicken Essay*. Trans. Sheila Fischman. Toronto: Coach House Press.

Boyer, Paul M. 1994. *By the Bomb's Early Light: American Thought and Culture at the Dawn of the Atomic Age*. 1985. Reprint. Chapel Hill: University of North Carolina Press.

Charters, Ann, ed. 1992. *The Beat Reader*. New York: Penguin Books.

———, ed. 1995a. *The Letters of Jack Kerouac 1940-1956*. New York: Viking.

———, ed. 1995b. *The Portable Jack Kerouac*. New York: Viking.

During, Simon. 1987. "Postmodernism or Postcolonialism Today." *Textual Practice* 1: 32–47.

Gifford, Barry, and Lawrence Lee. 1978. *Jack's Book*. New York: St. Martin's Press.

Grose, Peter. 1994. *Gentlemen Spy: The Life of Allen Dulles*. Boston: Houghton Mifflin.

Harvey, David. 1990. *The Condition of Postmodernity: An Inquiry Into the Origins of Cultural Change*. Cambridge, MA: Blackwell.

Huyssen, Andreas. 1986. *After the Great Divide: Modernism, Mass Culture, Postmodernism*. Bloomington: Indiana University Press.

Isaacson, Walter, and Evan Thomas. 1986. *The Wise Men: Six Friends and the World They Made: Acheson, Bohler, Harriman, Kennan, Lovett, McCloy*. New York: Simon and Schuster.

Jameson, Frederic. 1991. *Postmodernism, or The Cultural Logic of Late Capitalism*. Durham: Duke University Press.

Kerouac, Jack. 1977. *Dr. Sax: Faust Part Three*. 1959. Reprint. New York: Grove Press.

———. 1978. *The Town and the City*. 1950. Reprint. New York: Harcourt Brace Jovanovich.

———. 1980. *Desolation Angels*. 1965. Reprint. New York: Perigee Books.

————. 1981a. *Big Sur*. 1962. Reprint. New York: McGraw Hill.

————. 1981b. *Satori in Paris*. 1966. Reprint. New York: Grove Press.

————. 1981c. *The Subterraneans*. 1958 Reprint. New York: Grove Press.

————. 1991. *On the Road*. 1957. Reprint. New York: Penguin Books.

————. 1992. *Tristessa*. 1960. Reprint. New York: Penguin.

————. 1994. *Vanity of Duluoz: An Adventurous Education 1935-1946*. 1968. Reprint. New York: Penguin Books.

Krim, Seymour. 1965. Introduction to *Desolation Angels*, by Jack Kerouac. New York: Coward-McCann.

Lyotard, Jean-François. 1984. *The Postmodern Condition: A Report on Knowledge*. Trans. Geoff Bennington and Brian Massumi. Minneapolis: University of Minnesota Press.

Macdonald, Dwight. 1958. "I Choose the West." In *Memoirs of a Revolutionist*. 1957. Reprint. New York: Meridian Books.

McCarthy, Mary. 1961. *On the Contrary*. New York: Farrar, Straus.

Mills, C. Wright. 1956. *The Power Elite*. New York: Oxford University Press.

Nicosia, Gerald. 1983. *Memory Babe: A Critical Biography of Jack Kerouac*. New York: Grove Press.

Podhoretz, Norman. 1958. "The Know-Nothing Bohemians." *Partisan Review* (Spring): 315.

Reisner, Robert, ed. 1991. *Bird: The Legend of Charlie Parker*. 1962. Reprint. New York: DaCapo Press.

Tallman, Warren. 1960. "Kerouac's Sound." *Evergreen Review* 4: 153–69.

Thomas, Evan. 1995. *The Very Best Men: Four Who Dared: The Early Years of the CIA*. New York: Simon and Schuster.

Turkle, Sherry. 1996. *Life on the Screen: Identity in the Age of the Internet*. New York: Simon and Schuster.

Watson, Steven. 1995. *The Birth of the Beat Generation: Visionaries, Rebels and Hipsters*. New York: Pantheon.

Whitfield, Stephen. 1991. *The Culture of the Cold War*. Baltimore: Johns Hopkins University Press.

Williams, Raymond. 1966. *The Long Revolution*. Rev. ed. New York: Harper.

Wreszin, Michael. 1994. *A Rebel in Defense of Tradition: The Life and Politics of Dwight Macdonald*. New York: Basic Books.

Zabus, Chantal. 1995. "Relexification." In *The Post-colonial Studies Reader*, ed. Bill Ashcroft, Gareth Griffiths, and Helen Tiffin. New York: Routledge.

CHAPTER TWO

"You're putting me on":
Jack Kerouac and the Postmodern Emergence
Ronna C. Johnson

Of the triumvirate of principal male Beat writers—Allen
Ginsberg, William S. Burroughs, and Jack Kerouac—Kerouac's
literary historical significance and artistic achievement remain
underestimated. This is so in part because his writing has been over-
shadowed by his mass culture image—his media-driven fame for
Beat nonconformity, artistic purity, freewheeling living. The journalist
David Halberstam recycles the standard dismissal of Beat literature
in his 1993 tome, *The Fifties*: "Writers they might have been, but in
the end their lives tended to be more important than their books"
(112). Eclipsed by such reductive views, Kerouac's literature has
eluded critical understanding also because it is liminal; it demarcates
a widely unremarked transitional moment in U.S. arts and culture. I
see Kerouac as a seminal figure in postwar literary advances, a *pre*-
postmodernist whose work evinces the turn from modes and ideolo-
gies of late high modernism to those of the nascent postmodern.
Kerouac's hybrid literary forms and composition techniques—amal-
gamations of African-American cultural and musical styles with
canonical European-derived literary ones—manifest his pivotal sta-

tus. Preceding the postmodern literary and cultural advent it delineates, Kerouac's work clarifies the postmodern cusp.

Both his literature and the trajectory of his career as a public figure attest that as he produced his innovative texts, Kerouac confronted a postwar era neither fitted to modernism nor yet committed to the postmodern. In its technical innovation and deconstructions of the postwar social his work anticipated formal, artistic, and cultural phenomena that would be theorized later in poststructuralist thought.[1] While his liminality—his position between modernism and the postmodern, partaking of both—can be seen as an adaptation to his fluctuating post-Bomb moment, it is also arguable that his idiosyncratic literature helped to define and clarify a transitional moment there for him to fill. His work and life demonstrate that postmodernism did not emerge full-blown in the late 1960s as an artistic and cultural *fait accompli*, but rather, was produced in an era of transition and experimentation that Kerouac marked and embodied. For not only did his work evince as yet unrecognized postmodern effects, but in an ironic, surreal reversal, Kerouac himself became a commodified object of nascent postmodern tendencies: a mass media icon. The collapse of distinctions between his media image and fiction produced Kerouac as an icon, but also marks the postmodern condition his literature intimated. Thus, his status as a cult hero expresses even as it obscures his focal position in the postmodern emergence, the way his literature registers the postmodern advent his iconic image embodies.

This essay examines the postmodernity of Kerouac's mass media fame, arguing that his dismissal as a writer and the ironic eclipse of his pre-postmodernism by his mass culture image are not unmediated postmodern effects. First, a textual analysis of Kerouac's 1959 television appearance on *The Steve Allen Show* documents operations of his mass media fame *in vivo*, exploring Kerouac's efforts to subvert its misrepresentations and reconstructions. Then, a discussion of Kerouac's narrativization of his celebrity in *Desolation Angels* (1965) and *Vanity of Duluoz* (1967) shows the way these late novels comment on distortions of media scrutiny, as, with his signature reflexiveness, Kerouac critiqued the hyperreal effects of his iconic fame in his books. The two parts of *Desolation Angels*, which Kerouac wrote in two periods straddling his celebrity advent, compare the writer-protagonist's condition before and after becoming famous. The bitter meditations of *Vanity of Duluoz* revisit hopes made vain by success. In both texts fame is depicted as a notoriety caused by intrusive, sensationalizing media attention, as represented by Kerouac's experience on *The Steve Allen Show*. Performing a precociously postmodern self-cannibalization by making his appropriation and transformation into a mass media object a subject of his work, Kerouac's late novels deconstruct and critique his fame, feasting on the media forces that feasted on Jack Kerouac.

Kerouac's position on a postwar artistic, literary, and cultural divide is manifested in his concern to participate in modernist tradition and his analogous drive to invent a new expression to challenge and reconfigure that same tradition. Ellen G. Friedman has written "the master narratives strangely seem more alive in the beats' work than they do in the works of modernity. They are the context of the beats' rebellion" (1993, 250). But in Kerouac the master or canonical narratives are modified by a competing impulse to reconfigure, to out-invent tradition. Kerouac is neither modernist ephebe nor postmodern innovator but liminal and transitional. His "beat rebellion"— his departure into the new—does "legitimate master narratives" as Friedman claims, but it also exposes their disintegration, delineating Jean-François Lyotard's defining idea of the postmodern condition as the obsolescence of master narratives. Kerouac's location in and clarification of a pre-postmodern interval went unrecognized in his time because he preceded such theories naming and defining the postmodern; of necessity, then, this discussion utilizes later theories of postmodernity to evince Kerouac's antecedence.

Kerouac's celebrity has negated him as writer and replaced him. In a way that surpasses or bypasses his books, he is a writer who is famous for being famous. Sound bites and glamor images constitute and commodify his celebrity, such as Truman Capote's catty 1959 quip, "it isn't writing at all—it's typing!" (Clarke 1988, 315).[2] Or the 1993 Gap celebrity ad campaign for khakis that, transposing him from a literary canon to a canon of good taste, transforms Kerouac from writer to fashion icon.[3] Such "put ons" have overwritten his writing since *On the Road* made Kerouac famous in 1957. John Clellon Holmes, author of the first Beat novel *Go* (1952), thought the "image of Kerouac" had so eclipsed his friend's books that "People don't read them. Or particularly literary critics. That's why he remains a best kept secret" (Goldman 1982). Kerouac's writing is "secret" because his immense cultural visibility foregrounds only itself—Ihab Hassan has noted that a literary reputation seduces "readers [to] respond to it and pretend that their response is to the work" (Hassan 1970, 197). Relieved of his work, his reputation relieves us of a Kerouac real, a fundamental postmodern negation in which his fame disappears its source.

Kerouac's iconic mass culture celebrity is signified by the media-driven "image of Kerouac," which is, in Kerouac's hipster argot, a "put on," or, in Jean Baudrillard's media theory, a simulacrum. In Baudrillard's account of postmodern culture, which he sees as a mass media culture, the disappearance of a Kerouac real by the "image of Kerouac" is an effect of simulation. Simulation operates, Baudrillard holds, to structure experience by producing a real according to a model, eroding distinctions between them, and replacing the real with the model (Best and Kellner 1991, 119-20). Simulation's "radical negation of the sign" (Baudrillard 1983, 10) parallels cannibalizing of the kind Fredric Jameson ascribes to postmodern pastiche (Jameson 1988, 16). In this, the sign (the author Kerouac and his art) is negated by the simulacrum (the "image of Kerouac" and his typing) that consumes and annuls its source in the real. Hassan cautions that a writer's reputation has the capacity to "turn cannibal, and devour both Man and the Work" (Hassan 1970, 197), just as the "image of Kerouac" has cannibalized the man and erased his real as writer.

Indeed, in the postmodern media discourses which write and disseminate it, the "image of Kerouac" is more real than the writer's instantiation in the social (Best and Kellner 1991, 119). The "image of Kerouac" is a fluctuating, indeterminate second order signifier, a copy for which no original has ever existed. This contingent figure, which lacks and even refuses any clear positioning with regard to the referent it affects to evoke (Kaplan 1998a, 137), "never exchanges for what is real," in Baudrillard's idea, "but exchang[es] in itself, in an uninterrupted circuit without reference" to author or novels (Baudrillard 1983, 11). In Kerouac's celebrity incarnation, typist exchanges for fashion icon and spirals on to further signifiers, erasing the writer with hyperreal models that stand for him—just as

John Updike's 1959 parodic *The New Yorker* review "On the Sidewalk" copied and erased *On the Road* in a way that meant the novel did not have to be read to be "read."

Kerouac's 1959 appearance on *The Steve Allen Show*—a well-known, widely reproduced piece of Kerouaciana[4]—typifies the commodifying impulses of his celebrity makeover in the wake of the 1957 publication of *On the Road*. This commercial tableau effects the author's transformation to a celebrity, a commodity "Kerouac" deployed to sell other commodities tendered by advertisers sponsoring the show, as well as to sell Kerouac's book, which is essentialized as a product for purchase. The televisual discourse exhibits Kerouac's formation as a postmodern icon by burgeoning mass media communication technologies. It provides a textualized, empirical representation of mass culture commodification practices which produced the "image of Kerouac"—the celebrity simulacrum the writer disavows and deconstructs in *Desolation Angels* and *Vanity of Duluoz*. The kinescope records the process of Kerouac's commodification as it occurs live and as it overwrites his resistance to it. He would subvert operations of simulation, countering his commodification with a real by instantiating his literary acumen and subjectivity as writer.

For this appearance Kerouac was to read from *On the Road* to the accompaniment of Allen's bluesy jazz piano riffs, performing an ersatz Greenwich Village, black-beret-with-poetry-and-jazz spectacle that packaged a bohemian art scene for suburban consumption via television. Allen's interview with Kerouac, which precedes the simulated hipster performance, exposes the discontinuity between Kerouac's self-representation as artist, his claim to literary legitimacy, and his re-representation as "Beat writer," a stereotype produced by Allen's appropriations and transformations of remarks elicited from Kerouac about his writing. Making jokes from Kerouac's literary seriousness, Allen's wordplay sells him as a Beat pinup. Yet Kerouac's resistance, expressed in his clandestine reading of the unpublished masterpiece *Visions of Cody*, could not forestall his transformation into typist, which is overdetermined by operations of media simulation in whose linguistic fields signifiers proliferate unbound to a signified. The disparity between Allen's and Kerouac's discourses marks the erasure of a Kerouac real embodied in his texts; even when

Kerouac reads his work, which instantiates his literary claim and an extant original against the celebrity copy, the commercial venue negates it, disappearing the writer into the entertainment vacuum— into the erasures enacted by his Beat fame.

The celebrity commodification of Kerouac cannibalizes the artistic originality that occasioned his television appearance in the first place. Allen's focus on the teletype roll Kerouac used for novel writing, an invention that gave physical equivalence to his composition techniques (spontaneous prose, sketching) and typing speed (100 words per minute), is repackaged as a Beat cliché akin to Capote's typewriting quip, while Kerouac's literary seriousness—his Whitman reference—is treated as a "put on."

> STEVE ALLEN: I've heard that you write so fast that you don't like to use regular typing paper but instead you prefer to use one big long roll of paper. Is that true?
>
> JACK KEROUAC: Yeah. When I write narrative novels I don't want to change my narrative thought, I keep going.
>
> ALLEN: You don't want to change the pages at the end, you mean. . . . Oh, teletype paper. Where do you get it? Where do you get the paper?
>
> KEROUAC: In a very good stationery store.
>
> ALLEN: I see.
>
> KEROUAC: When I write my symbolistic, serious, impressionistic novels I write them in pencil.
>
> ALLEN: Oh yeah? I've seen a lot of your poetry written in pencil but I didn't realize that's how you worked on the prose stuff.
>
> KEROUAC: For narrative it's good. . . .
>
> ALLEN: Well, about this point actually we planned to have Jack read some poetry, and while looking again through his book the other day it struck me, it occurred to me all over again, that his prose is extremely poetic. I think it's probably more poetic than that of, who else writes poetic type prose, Thomas Wolfe?
>
> KEROUAC: Walt Whitman. . . . in *Specimen Days*. Walt Whitman's *Specimen Days*.
>
> ALLEN: I see. I thought you were putting me on there for a minute.
>
> KEROUAC: No. (*What Happened to Kerouac?* 1987)

This interaction forms over one third of the exchange preceding Kerouac's reading. Allen's questions about the teletype roll—a reference to the manuscript of *On the Road*—emphasize the paper Kerouac uses to compose, a focus that transforms the novel to novelty artifact and the novelist to assembly line hack, recasting Kerouac's literary purpose as commodity production. Interpretive authority ("you mean") lies with Allen the host, whose discourse reduces Kerouac's artistic "narrative thought" to goods—"pages"—even though Kerouac insistently presents himself as an artist: he says he types his "narrative novels" on rolls of paper to permit continuity of composition and writes his "symbolistic, serious, impressionistic novels" in pencil; he compares his prose to Whitman's *Specimen Days*; no, he is not "putting [Allen] on." In *Vanity of Duluoz*, Kerouac rejects the phrase "putting me on." Steve Allen suspects Kerouac is "putting him on" with the reference to Whitman, and then says, "I've got the most tired question of all but everybody always *puts it to you*, I'm sure, or because everybody always *puts it to you*: How would you define the word 'beat'?" (my italics). The locution "everybody always puts it to you" operates in a different register to signify or suggest a different colloquialism, to be shafted—both valences of meaning suggest being tricked, cheated, victimized. "Put it to you" is linguistically and hermeneutically close to "putting you on," the slang for lying Kerouac detested. But the commercial interests of the media venue endorse Allen's dumbed-down revisions because Kerouac's artistic seriousness will not play for the camera—or sell. And since material elicited from Kerouac provides for the jokes, his commodification is effected on the back of his self-representation: the instantiation of his celebrity obliges Kerouac to perform stand-up self-parody.

Thus, the conceptualization and writing of *On the Road* are obscured in a joke about Kerouac's famous speed of composition:

ALLEN: Jack. . . . How long did it take you to write *On the Road*?

KEROUAC: Three weeks. . . .

ALLEN: Three weeks! That's amazing! How long were you on the road itself?

KEROUAC: Seven years

ALLEN: Seven years! I was on the road once for three weeks and it took
me seven years to write about it! . . . (What Happened to Kerouac? 1987)

Ironically, *On the Road*'s success ensured that the writer could be
made to serve as straight man for jokes about his work because it
delivered him to mass culture and television where the novel is
reduced to a formula: three weeks of writing after seven years on
the road. This formula literalizes the signifier "on the road," overwrit-
ing the title's ambiguous existential metaphor with the implication
of a replicable consumer activity, being on the road. Representing
Kerouac's literary labor as the speed of manufacture, the formula
reifies the "typist." Allen transposes the formula's numbers to site
himself/everyman in the inversely analogous position of being on
the road for three weeks and requiring seven years to write about it.
His reversal, a joke, implies that even if less efficient than Kerouac,
anyone could write about being on the road. Or, that what makes
Kerouac the "professional" is that it only takes him three weeks to
write about it. The joke erases *On the Road*, as well as Kerouac as
artist: Tim Hunt has shown that the teletype manuscript of *On the
Road* is the fourth version of the novel Kerouac wrote over several
years. Television's preference for the sound bite formula disappears
Kerouac's considerable work preceding those three weeks of writing because *On the Road*'s actual origins have no entertainment or
commodity value, any more than did Kerouac's account of his art;
neither can serve as setups for jokes.

Allen's lead-in to Kerouac's reading specifies the capital enterprise which television show and host, guest and performance, all are
bound to serve. "Right now we'll look into Jack Kerouac's *On the
Road* and he'll lay a little on you, you know, you have to buy these
pages," Allen jokes (*What Happened to Kerouac?* 1987). Television
entertainment is a vehicle for product commercials aimed at a viewing audience; one product to be sold by the selling of Jack Kerouac
is his novel, a commodity dispensed here in a free sample. Although
Kerouac is made to advertise *On the Road*, he resists his exploitation
as a sales gimmick and reverses the joke made at his own expense
by reading "pages" which could not be purchased: he reads from the
unpublished manuscript of *Visions of Cody*, which he concealed
behind the copy of *On the Road* he holds to the camera.[5] Reading
Visions of Cody, which he composed directly after finishing his

fourth version of *On the Road* in the hopes of improving what he regarded as that book's weaknesses, Kerouac instantiates his literary seriousness and commitment to art. He "secretly" reads for free a text free of commercial value since, unpublished, *Visions of Cody* existed only as a private holding. This hijacked reading inscribes a noncommercial nonprofit Kerouac in place of the commodified "Beat writer" used to sell *The Steve Allen Show*. This is Kerouac's "put on"—not the reference to *Specimen Day*s but his reading of an unpublished, uncommodified book; in this venue, the "put on" is the real.

But the commodifying discourses of the media venue, which is meant to transform the writer into entertainment, overwrite his instantiations of the real. Though Kerouac reads from *Visions of Cody*, his resistance to being a one-man writing factory spewing out book product on paper that never ends is futile: he is perceived to be reading *On the Road*, the best-seller for sale. His identity as artist instantiated in the subversive reading of *Visions of Cody* is paradoxically invisible in its display, least because the book was unpublished. For in celebrity's media venues, simulation is empowered to overwrite primary source knowledge with naturalized constructions; to establish as "real" the second-order signifier, the hyperreal "beatnik" Kerouac. The kinescope shows the simulacrum "Kerouac" established *in vivo* over the author's resistance to the misrepresentations and clichés of media talk. There is ample proof of Allen's esteem for Kerouac; their meetings are widely reported to have been congenial (Allen 1992, Clark 1984). Thus the commodification of Kerouac is a hostile takeover innocent of personal animosity. Enacting its own irrevocably commercial dicta, the entertainment venue negates the artist, the writer of books, and purveys a cult hero/celebrity to sell the show that its corporate sponsors hope will sell soap.

Kerouac's pre-postmodernism takes an exponential leap in his postfame novels *Desolation Angels* (1965) and *Vanity of Duluoz* (1967), which register, resist, narrativize, and subvert his mass media appropriation and transformation by simulation as on *The Steve Allen Show*. These late novels specifically interrogate implications of representation by a media gaze and its impact on the living artist, figuring media such as television, and print and photographic journalism as agents of distorted representation. These novels also attest to a cure for the subject's postmodern fragmentation as a result of being centered in a media gaze and reconstituted as a surveillance object: this status as (media) object of the gaze provides coherence and unity, ameliorating fragmentation, albeit by assuming the form of the positional feminine, as defined by Mulvey (1989, 14–26). The massive media attention fixed on Kerouac after *On the Road*'s publication in 1957 is registered in *Desolation Angels* and *Vanity of Duluoz* as imprisonment by intrusive scrutiny. Kerouac's analysis of his celebrity depicts mass media attention as a surveillance that produces a vertiginous sense of unreality as a hyperreal "Kerouac" model erases and is passed for the writer. At the same time, the texts inscribe resistance to the writer's celebrity, his captivity by reputation, deconstructing his disappearance into the Baudrillardean hyperreal.

An experience of hostile and disturbing celebrity colors Book Two of *Desolation Angels*. Overtly self-referential allusions to unpalatable fame and a misunderstood novel called "*Road*"—a big mad book that will change America! They can even make money with it. You'll be dancing naked on your fan mail" (Kerouac 1965, 260)—evince anxiety of public exposure and the intrusion of autobiography into the fictive discourse. Kerouac composed pensive associational Book One in 1956, before celebrity; in November 1957 he suspended that project to write *The Dharma Bums* and did not return to *Desolation Angels* until 1961. Book Two is a postlapsarian account of the writer-protagonist's descent from retreat on Desolation Peak to the noise and paralyzing exposure of "making it," his already-met doom to "get published, meet everybody, make money, become a big international traveling author, sign autographs" (Kerouac 1965, 259). This fame of movie-star dimensions preoccupies Book Two of *Desolation Angels*, as the protagonst Jack Duluoz endeavors to escape the prison of scrutiny through the liberating act of narrating, ultimately to no avail.

In *Discipline and Punish* Michel Foucault describes the panopticon surveillance mode of carceral institutions as "an apparatus for transforming individuals" into "docile and useful" bodies by employing a "permanent gaze" to control them. A "technique . . . of coercion" (1977, 211–16), panopticism inculcates in the individual himself the surveillance that impels his conformity. As Vaclav Havel wrote from prison in 1981, "It seems to me that even when no one is watching, and even when he is certain no one will ever find out about his behavior" a prisoner is "compel[led . . .] to behave . . . as though someone were observing him" (Lane 1994, 63). Mirroring Foucault's claim that the state transforms individuals through surveillance, *Desolation Angels* recounts the coercive power of media recognition which functions as a regulating agent analogous to the police. The novel depicts the way coercive surveillance—via the mass media—succeeds in the production of a "docile" individual who, internalizing his own surveillance, monitors himself and modifies his behavior "even when no one is watching"; the way Duluoz transforms himself from "dissident" writer to "conformist" citizen.

Representing fame as an invasion of privacy and breach of the chosen austerity of the artist's life, the novel portrays the media's attention to the writer's person in place of his work as an act designed to coerce into conformity subjects who are designated dissident. It posits celebrity, figured as scrutiny by a social gaze, as a reformist, rehabilitative discourse that produces self-regulation from dissidence. In the ruin of the writer's self-sufficiency and privacy, the media-generated gaze of fame effects simulation's transformations; Duluoz sees that the media and police conspiracy enlists him in the work of his own transformation. Under the lights of the interrogation cell cum television studio, the nomadic artist dwindles to a bourgeois:

> the cops stopped me in the Arizona desert that night when I was hiking under a full moon at 2 A.M. to go spread my sleepingbag in the sand outside Tuscon—When they found I had enough money for a hotel they wanted to know why I sleep in the desert—You cant explain to the police, or go into a lecture—I was a hardy son of a sun in those days, only 165 pounds and would walk miles with a full pack on my back, and rolled my own cigarettes, and knew how to hide comfortably in riverbottoms or even how to live on dimes and quarters—Nowadays, after all the horror of my literary notoriety, the bathtubs of booze that have passed through my gullet, the years of hiding at home from hundreds of petitioners for my time (pebbles in my window at midnight, "Come on out get drunk Jack, all big wild parties everywhere!")-oi-As the circle closed in on this old independent renegade, I got to look like a Bourgeois, pot belly and all, that expression on my face of mistrust and affluence (they go hand and hand?)—So that (almost) if it was now the cops were stopping me on a 2 A.M. highway, I almost expect they'd tip their caps—But in those days, only five years ago, I looked wild and rough—They surrounded me with two squad cars.

They put spot lights on me standing there in the road in jeans and work-
clothes, with the big woeful rucksack a-back, and asked: "Where are you
going?" which is precisely what they asked me a year later under
Television floodlights in New York, "Where are you going?"—Just as you
cant explain to the police, you cant explain to society "Looking for
peace." (Kerouac 1965, 230-31)

Kerouac represents fame's alterations through their registration on
the body, literalizing Foucault's "docile and useful" reformed detainee
in his account of the physical deterioration caused by celebrity. The
signifier, the "horror of my literary notoriety," figures public recognition as disgrace, dishonor, and ignominy; as a dreadful fall from
"hardy," "renegade" self-sufficiency to bloated, alcoholic "affluence."
Literary notoriety is writ on the writer's body with intimations of
gout, excess, corpulence, producing a reformed subject whose physical degeneracy ironically signifies the model citizen: his "face of mis-
trust and affluence" is the face of a bourgeois who "cops . . . tip their
hat" to, not arrest. The tightening noose, the "circle closed in on" the
writer, figures a claustrophobic public capture that evokes the
carceral panopticon, which is literalized in the writer's interrogation
by police, when, surrounded by squad cars, he is fixed in the glare of
their crime lights. Like the police lights in the desert, the surveillance of television floodlights robs him of "renegade" subjectivity;
whether vagrant or media object, the famous writer is made the
Foucauldian docile body.

Mirroring the metastructure of the novel, this representation of
celebrity compares the writer before and after fame, but it blurs the
distinctions; except for celebrity's invasive "petitioners" and the
physical deterioration, Kerouac suggests that for the nonconformist,
there is little difference. Held in a punitive gaze, he is both ways vulnerable to surveillance, random stops, questioning, re-representation.
Nonconformity is an apparent offense to the conformist social, but
celebrity also activates its mechanisms for containment. Before fame,
the writer is assailed for ignoring trespass and vagrancy laws; becoming famous, he is assailed for and by celebrity itself. Celebrity—literary notoriety—is figured as punishment for nonconformity. Foucault
argues that the repressive social can transform dissidents to docile
bodies without violence; its panoptic functions "substitute for force . . .
the gentle efficiency of total surveillance" (Foucault 1977, 217). In the

postmodern of advanced communications technology, the media gaze in *Desolation Angels* can re-represent the serious writer as typist, party maven, drunk—a fashion icon in khakis. Deprived of a private life, besieged by fans who mistake his zest for dissipation, Duluoz cannot mediate their power to define him, any more than Kerouac could overwrite Steve Allen's jokes. Laura Mulvey notes that narratives of the "sadistic" social "depend on making something happen, forcing a change in another person"; as in the Foucauldian panopticon, the "sadistic" gaze "ascertain[s] guilt ... assert[s] control; and subjugat[es] the guilty person through punishment" (Mulvey 1989, 21–22). Just so, in the Kerouacian tautology, the celebrity is ultimately guilty of celebrity which is also his discipline.

Desolation Angels' representation of fame depicts the alteration of the artist-body subjected to fame's scrutiny. The power of "literary notoriety" to subjugate, control, and coerce produces the bloated domestication of the bourgeois "typist" from the "wild and rough" writer. In transforming the hobo into bourgeois drunk, fame replaces the real with the hyperreal model. Duluoz observes that the media questioning him under television spotlights pose the same question as the police, "Where are you going?" He offers both the single answer, "Looking for peace," which implies that in a postwar, postmodern social where private property is protected, where the famous are public property, and where public recognition is surveillance, the celebrity can preserve no private self; no real. Moreover, there's nowhere to hide from the coercive social if the subject has been transformed by his capture into the agent of his own captivity. As in the Foucauldian panopticon, the coercive media gaze that disciplines and transforms its object enlists the celebrity in his own surveillance: drinking "bathtubs of booze" to dull the onslaught, the writer turns himself into the dissipated bourgeois; internalizing his reputation, he makes himself the disabled, disreputable drunk, a self-caricature of his own ebullience.

Addressing the same question to the hobo as to the celebrity points to and affects the media's hyperreal blurring of the real and the model—the vagrant writer and the celebrity—that prevents reinscription of the real even by the living subject, as in Kerouac's futile efforts on *The Steve Allen Show*. The erosion of distinctions between the writer and the celebrity empties the real of content, producing a copy for which no original has ever existed. The erasure of content by form—the writer's erasure by the celebrity drunk—is a defining principle of the postmodern art Susan Sontag called "Camp." Sontag's identification of the "artifice" of Camp, its "Being-as-Playing-a-Role" (1969, 280–81), gets at the empty vessel effect of postmodern simulation and Kerouac's transformation by fame from the real of being a writer to the hyperreal of being an icon.

Yet in the same way that Kerouac contested his commodification by his subversive reading of the unpublished *Visions of Cody* on television, *Desolation Angels* deconstructs the media/social gaze that is central to the spectacle of celebrity. Kerouac intervenes in his fame at the metalevel of narration by narrativizing it: holding in *his* narrative gaze the specularizing police and media, he (re)claims the active, masculine position of bearer of the look; in the gaze of his narrating "I" the police and media are assigned the feminine position of bearer of (his) meaning. This maneuver turns the tables on the fame that contains Kerouac by containing fame in a Kerouac narrative, reinstating the "renegade" writer over the drunk bourgeois, achieving restoration, remasculinization—revenge. In narrativizing his own fame, Duluoz works to restore his place as the masculine *maker* of meaning from being the feminine *bearer* of meaning, following Mulvey's analysis of gender in narrative structure (1989, 14–26). But Kerouac's last novel published in his lifetime, *Vanity of Duluoz*, suggests the chronic contingency of this countermove in the high-tech hyperreal of the postmodern social.

Written in 1967, a decade after the onset of fame, *Vanity of Duluoz* appropriates a celebrity Kerouac as a constitutive part of a Kerouac story, a zenith in Kerouac's reflexive reckonings with emerging postmodern phenomena which he anticipated in his earlier books and endured in his life. The novel is both implicit and explicit testament to the continuing depredations of celebrity. That the narration retells stories of growing up recounted in preceding Kerouac novels suggests a fatigue of invention, whose cause, we are invited to conclude, is the occasion for the novel, as stated on the first page: the writer-protagonist Duluoz would gain his wife's understanding via a "recitation of the troubles I had to go through to make good in America between 1935 and more or less now, 1967" to become "a WRITER whose very 'success,' far from being a happy triumph . . . was the sign of doom Himself" (1967, 7). In this construction, success is ruin, the destruction by celebrity of a usable subjectivity ("WRITER"). The narration is plagued by an anti-narrative uncertainty of subjectivity, even if it is documented in primary sources: media attention has made Duluoz feel "that my birth records, my family's birth records and recorded origins, my athletic records in newspaper clippings that I have, my own notebooks and published books, are not real at all . . . that I am not 'I am' but just a spy in somebody's body" (1967, 14). This contingency renders *Vanity of Duluoz* a provisional fictive autobiography of an unverifiable historical self whose experience of his own perspective is as a voyeur; it is a first person account from the position of a pod person, a facsimile self-estranged from his own physicality and secreted in an appropriated, alien corps—as he puts it in *Desolation Angels*, a "hardy son of a sun" trapped in the bloated body of a drunk.

Addressing the author's celebrity simulation, the narration of *Vanity of Duluoz* inscribes Kerouac's media image in the ironic, self-reflexive simulacrum, "this inexistent 'Jack Kerouac'" (1967, 12). The signifier neatly conveys a paradox of simulation, the way a referent is at once refused ("inexistent") and at the same time the requisite evoked or quoted body ("Jack Kerouac"). The "inexistent 'Jack Kerouac'" captures the discursive quality of being disappeared by fame, ironizing the postmodern destabilization of identity and narrative—its fragmentation of subjectivity—in the way the referent Kerouac is there in the phrase and not-there at the same time. The narrative perspective of *Vanity of Duluoz* copies this effect, sliding between the persona Jack Duluoz, and an implied and inscribed Kerouac, a subject who contests his objectification as the "inexistent 'Jack Kerouac'" but who also assimilates this empty model to his tale.

Vanity of Duluoz uses the negation of Kerouac as the premise for a Jack Kerouac narrative. The narration contravenes the assumption that the protagonist is the eponymous Duluoz by invoking the author Kerouac; it presents the ironic paradox of the subject's erasure by simulation when this occurs in his awareness.

> [E]verybody's begun to lie and because they lie they assume that I lie too. . . . Thus that awful new saying: "You're putting me on." My name is Jack ("Duluoz") Kerouac and I was born in Lowell Mass. on 9 Lupine Road on March 12, 1922. "Oh you're putting me on." I wrote this book

Vanity of Duluoz. "Oh you're putting me on." It's like that woman, wifey, who wrote me a letter awhile ago saying, of all things, and listen to this:

"You are not Jack Kerouac. There is no Jack Kerouac. His books were not even written."

They just appeared on a computer, she probably thinks, they were programmed, they were fed informative confused data by mad bespectacled egghead sociologists and out of the computer came the full manuscript, all neatly typed doublespace, for the publisher's printer to simply copy and the publisher's binder to bind and the publisher to distribute, with cover and blurb jacket, so this inexistent "Jack Kerouac" could not only receive two-dollar royalty check from Japan but also this woman's letter. (Kerouac 1967, 12)

The narrative sites the "inexistent 'Jack Kerouac,'" the author's recognition of his disappearance by simulation, in technological advances in commodity production, key factors of the postmodern turn. Ironically writing a book about the impossibility of writing books, the narrator recounts the fall of literature to sociology and computer technology—there are no intellectuals or writers, only hackers or "mad bespectacled egghead sociologists." The writing of literature is replaced by the Orwellian fantasy, which even royalty checks and readers' letters cannot disprove, that "books are not even written." Author and text are endlessly replicable commodities produced by computer and print technology and peddled to consumers: here "typewriting" produces the hypertext. In Kerouac's critique of fame, social, media, technological, and capital discourses conspire to profit all participants in the chain of production—computer hack, publisher, printer, binder, distributor, jacket designer, and blurb writer— a chain that cannibalizes Jack Kerouac to fabricate the profitable commodity "put on" or simulacrum, the "inexistent 'Jack Kerouac.'"

This discourse elaborates the postmodern instability of signification; the repeated phrase "you're putting me on" captures the chronic debasement of the real that echoes with Steve Allen's incredulity at Kerouac's reference to *Specimen Days* which Kerouac repeated and still Allen claimed "I thought you were putting me on." *Vanity of Duluoz* references Kerouac's experience as a celebrity, critiquing the provisional present ("everybody's begun to lie") of the "put on" or simulation, in which even fundamental biographical information— pure census data—(name, and date and place of birth) is contingent.

Holmes thought the "image of Kerouac" evolved from a misleading identification of the writer with the "wild" characters of *On the Road* (Goldman 1982). But here fame's superimposition of the historical figure, the author Kerouac, onto the persona Duluoz is also only provisional, for, absurdly, in the new mass media social "there is no Jack Kerouac" according to the (anti-) fan letter. The "inexistent 'Jack Kerouac'" expresses this erasure, the vertiginous reflexivity of possessing and experiencing a historical identity while simultaneously being experienced and possessed as a simulacrum; as a "put on."

The "inexistent 'Jack Kerouac'" derives its challenge to simulation from its origination by (and in) an existent, original Kerouac. In his nonfiction fiction *The Armies of the Night*, subtitled *History as a Novel the Novel as History* (1968), Norman Mailer, who serves simultaneously as author, narrator, and protagonist, narrates his first-person account in the third person and as "the novelist"; authoring his own simulation, he retains subjectivity. This move captures the fictive position of historical actors in narratives that presume to account for lived events, as well as the necessarily fictional or manufactured condition of historical narratives themselves. So, too, the "inexistent 'Jack Kerouac'" reaches to express the concurrently fictional and factual discursive quality of being disappeared by media discourses. This strategy for preserving subjectivity does not succeed for Kerouac as for Mailer. For not only has Kerouac been the experimenter articulating nascent postmodern tendencies, but as famous Beat writer he has been the laboratory for their cultural practice; as *Desolation Angels* suggests, he has been the anatomized body of Beat embodiment. His celebrity means that *Vanity of Duluoz* cannot be (personal) history as novel, Mailer's solution to contingency, because for the "inexistent 'Jack Kerouac'" history is unverifiable. With primary sources no longer "real," the personal is false consciousness for a "spy in somebody's body."

Yet although Kerouac's late work played on postmodern conditions, that did not forestall or spare him their effects. Both his literature and fame manifest his status as avatar and articulator, object and laboratory of the nascent postmodern. In a nexus of overlapping convergences and interrelations, his work, life, career, and cultural status all register, bear witness to, shape and are shaped by nascent and maturing postmodern phenomena, a multiplicity of tendencies tropified by the celebrity "put on," the simulacrum "image of Kerouac"—what Kerouac formulated as "this inexistent 'Jack Kerouac.'" Kerouac's exposure of the paradox of being the real (body) fame simulates shows the way his late work turned further into the postmodern, an underrated innovation that attests to the writer's uncanny ability to swing with a (postmodern) time he was not born into but anticipated and helped to invent—albeit at his own expense.

Notes

Portions of this essay were presented in a paper at the conference on "The Writings of Jack Kerouac," New York University, June 5, 1995, and are drawn from my book in progress, *Gender and Narrative in Jack Kerouac: Beat Anticipations of the Postmodern*. I am indebted to Maria Damon, Tim Hunt, Albert Sabatini, Jennie Skerl, and Regina Weinreich for their comments on the paper.

1 Those who periodicize the postmodern as emerging during WWII (see Kerouac's "The Origins of the Beat Generation" [1959]), and galvanized by the bombing of Japan and the discovery of the Nazi death camps (see Norman Mailer's "The White Negro" [1957]) confine its etiology to the United States. Europe, recovering from war, did not see a postmodern emergence until May 1968, considerably later than developments in the United States. See Lhamon (1990, 151–2); Huyssen (1986, 179–221).

   However, recognition of the postmodern and theories about its character were most powerfully developed by European, not American, theorists, such as Roland Barthes, Michel Foucault, Jean-François Lyotard, Jean Baudrillard and so on. In the 1960s, U.S. critics Leslie Fiedler, Irving Howe, Harry Levin, and Susan Sontag began to produce essays discussing the end of the modern, or a change they tentatively titled postmodern, but writers and visual artists in the U.S. had been registering and expressing the postmodern emergence for nearly twenty years by then.

   I see the Beat generation writers, the New York School of Abstract Expressionists, and the African-American civil rights movement—all rising during the war and coming to notice in the 1950s—as avatars of the postmodern. See Lhamon (1990, 180).

2 Capote uttered this deathless jibe in his 1959 appearance on the David Susskind television talk show, Open End; see Clarke.

3 A classic postmodern artifact, a campaign that nostalgically and ironically appropriates and pastiches, recycles and refits, images of the 1950s and 1960s to sell khaki trousers in the 1990s, the Gap Ltd. ad series included vintage photographs of such luminaries of cool as Allen Ginsberg, Miles Davis, Andy Warhol, James Dean, and Chet Baker, as well as modernists Ernest Hemingway, Arthur Miller, Pablo Picasso, and Capote himself.

4 See Richard Lerner and Lewis MacAdams, directors, What Happened to Kerouac?

(1987). The audiotape of The Steve Allen Show on which Kerouac appeared is also pastiched into Connie Goldman's 1982 National Public Radio story on Kerouac. I treat the transcription of this appearance as a text in my discussion. I made the transcription I am using; there is no published version of it, to my knowledge.

5 All the Kerouac biographies report that he read concealed pages from the manuscript of the unpublished Visions of Cody first, before reading the last paragraphs of On the Road. This is obvious to those who know the novels and hear and/or watch the kinescope of the reading. See, for example, Clark (1984, 177).

Works Cited

Allen, Steve. 1992. *Hi Ho Steverino*. New York: Barricade Books.

Baudrillard, Jean. 1983. *Simulations*. Trans. Paul Foss, Paul Patton, and Philip Breitchman. New York: Semiotext(e).

Best, Steven, and Douglas Kellner. 1991. *Postmodern Theory: Critical Interrogations*. New York: Guilford.

Clark, Tom. 1984. *Jack Kerouac*. New York: Harcourt.

Clarke, Gerald. 1988. *Capote: A Biography*. New York: Simon and Schuster.

Fiedler, Leslie. 1971. "'The New Mutants' and 'Cross the Border—Close the Gap.'" In *The Collected Essays of Leslie Fiedler*. Vol. 2. New York: Stein and Day.

Foucault, Michel. 1977. *Discipline and Punish: The Birth of the Prison*. In *The Foucault Reader*, ed. Paul Rabinowitz, trans. Alan Sheridan. New York: Pantheon.

Friedman, Ellen G. March. 1993. "Where Are the Missing Contents? (Post)Modernism, Gender, and the Canon." *PMLA*. 108. 2 (month): 240–52.

Goldman, Connie. 1982. National Public Radio story on *On the Road*. Boulder: The Jack Kerouac Conference, Naropa Institute. Author's transcript.

Halberstam, David. 1993. *The Fifties*. New York: Villard.

Hassan, Ihab. 1970. "Focus on Norman Mailer's Why Are We in Vietnam?" In *American Dreams, American Nightmares*. Ed. David Madden, Carbondale: Southern Illinois University Press.

Howe, Irving. 1970. "'The Culture of Modernism' and 'Mass Society and Postmodern Fiction.'" In *Decline of the New*. New York: Harcourt.

Hunt, Tim. 1981. *Kerouac's Crooked Road: Development of a Fiction*. Hamden CT: Archon Books.

Huyssen, Andreas. 1986. *After the Great Divide: Modernism, Mass Culture, Postmodernism*. Bloomington: Indiana University Press.

Jameson, Fredric. 1988. "Postmodernism and Consumer Society." In *Postmodernism and Its Discontents*. Ed. E. Ann Kaplan London: Verso.

Kaplan, E. Ann. 1988a. "Feminism/Oedipus/Postmodernism." In *Postmodernism and Its Discontents*, ed. E. Ann Kaplan. London: Verso.

———. 1988b. "Whose Imaginary? The Televisual Apparatus, the Female Body, and Textual Strategies in Select Rock Videos on MTV." In *Female Spectators*, ed. E. Deidre Pribram London: Verso.

Kerouac, Jack. 1965. *Desolation Angels*. New York: Coward-McCann.

————. 1967. *Vanity of Duluoz*. New York: Putnam.

Lane, Anthony. 1994. "Kafka's Heir." *The New Yorker*, 31 October, 55–71.

Levin, Harry. 1966. "What Was Modernism." In *Refractions: Essays in Comparative Literature*. New York: Oxford.

Lhamon, Jr, W.T. 1990. *Deliberate Speed: The Origins of a Cultural Style in the American 1950s*. Washington: Smithsonian Institution Press.

Lyotard, Jean-François. 1984. *The Postmodern Condition*. Trans. Geoff Bennington and Brian Massumi. Minneapolis: University of Minnesota Press.

Mailer, Norman. 1957. *The White Negro: Superficial Reflections on the Hipster*. San Francisco: City Lights.

————. 1968. *The Armies of the Night: History as a Novel the Novel as History*. New York: New American Library.

Mulvey, Laura. 1989. *Visual and Other Pleasures*. Bloomington: Indiana University Press.

Murphy, Timothy S. 1997. *Wising Up the Marks: The Amodern William Burroughs*. Berkeley: University of California Press.

Sontag, Susan. 1969. "Notes on 'Camp.'" In *Against Interpretation*. New York: Dell.

Updike, John. 1959. "On the Sidewalk: (After Reading, At Long Last, *On the Road* by Jack Kerouac)." *The New Yorker*, 21 February, 32.

What Happened to Kerouac? 1987. Directed by Richard Lerner and Lewis MacAdams. Author transcript.

CHAPTER THREE

Beating Time: Configurations of Temporality
in Jack Kerouac's *On the Road*
Erik R. Mortenson

After World War II, the United States Time Corporation was looking for a new product line. It found it in the Timex watch. In a
market traditionally dominated by the Swiss, this U.S. company revo-
lutionized the field through a twin combination of industrial mechanization and marketing. As David S. Landes notes in *Revolution in
Time*, "United States Time sold these watches in every available retail
outlet . . . a quarter of a million points of sale at the peak . . . selling
not elegance or prestige but cheap time . . . people could afford not
one watch but two or three or more" (1983, 339). United States
Time's success is telling because it demonstrates the degree to which
postwar America was becoming time-conscious. This company's
name alone conjures up images of monolithic proportions, of a standard time that all Americans could set their lives by. In a booming
postwar economy, such an attention to time was indeed necessary to
ensure that everything "ran smoothly." After all, Benjamin Franklin's
dictum still rang true: Time is money. But not everyone welcomed the
idea of a wristwatch on every American arm.

Jack Kerouac's 1957 novel *On the Road* was one such voice of
dissent. Kerouac's novel has long been considered subversive in its

questioning of America's booming postwar economy. Upon its publication it was both lauded as an "authentic work of art" by Gilbert Millstein (Nicosia 1983, 556) and derided by one critic as the quintessence of "everything that is bad and horrible about this otherwise wonderful age we live in" (Tytell 1976, 159). The novel was attacked for both its innovative style and its depiction of marginalized characters, causing one *Time* reviewer to label Kerouac the "Hippie Homer" writing about a "disjointed segment of society acting out its own neurotic necessity" (Charters 1973, 290). Yet for all this controversy, few remarked on the novel's questioning of one of the most fundamental (if often overlooked) underpinnings of any society—its use of time. *On the Road* wages an attack on constraining notions of time that companies like United States Time were so eager to exploit. Repeatedly questioning the accepted concept of temporality defined by the clock, Kerouac's work instead probes for a way to break through this constricting notion of time in an attempt to address the even larger existential problems of temporality.

In its most basic sense, *On the Road* is an attack on the corruption of time by capitalism. In his essay "Reification and the Consciousness of the Proletariat," Georg Lukacs explores capitalism's influence through an analysis of the notion of reification first established by Karl Marx. The central tenet Lukacs derives from Marx is that through reification "a man's own activity, his own labour becomes something objective and independent of him, something that controls him by virtue of an autonomy alien to man" (1968, 86–87). The commodity itself gains ascendancy, subjugating consciousness and establishing itself as the basis of interaction between humans. And the key element that allows this process to occur is time. Through rationalization, time becomes more and more precise, allowing for an ever-constricting set of temporal demands on the worker. Lukacs explains that "the period of time necessary for work to be accomplished . . . is converted, as mechanization and rationalization are intensified, from a merely empirical average figure to an objectively calculable work-stint that confronts the worker as a fixed and established reality" (88). The specificity of "clock time" creates a greater precision that allows demands on time to become increasingly precise. This quantification of time is accompanied by the conversion of time into space. Again drawing on Marx, Lukacs concludes that "time sheds its qualitative, variable, flowing nature; it freezes into an exactly delimited, quantifiable continuum filled with quantifiable 'things'. . . in short, it becomes space" (90). Where work was once an individual craft tied to the organic notion of length of day or season, capitalist mechanization has now rendered production as being in a fixed place for a designated time.[1] The farmer and carpenter have given way to the factory worker, stuck in front of a machine, forced to reproduce the same motions for the length of his shift.

It is not difficult to see how Kerouac's novel *On the Road* is, on its most superficial level, a reaction against the Lukacsian notion of reification. Few characters hold a job, and those who do usually work only temporarily. Even while at work, Sal and Dean often show up late or skip out at various times, unconstrained by schedule or routine. Set against the repetition of mechanistic rationalization, we have an overabundance of idiosyncratic actions and behaviors. Very few actions in this novel are ever repeated exactly. Kerouac seldom gives the exact dates and times of his travels, referring only to months of the year or seasons. Thus reification's insistence on "clock time" is jettisoned in favor of spontaneity. Space in *On the Road* remains equally nebulous. The title itself hints at this; the book is more concerned with movement than with fixed location. In fact, the reader is often surprised by this need to avoid staying in one place, as cross-country trips are undertaken merely to see someone in another city or to stop by for "a few days." Many of the most important events in the novel, for instance, take place in the spaces *between*, while moving from one location to another. If reification congeals fluid temporality into rigid spatiality, Kerouac's insistence on the motion of travel sunders this bond by replacing stasis with flux. Sal's veneration of the "fellahin" is likewise a critique of reification.[2] In *Outline of a Theory of Practice*, Pierre Bourdieu contrasts Western notions of linear "calendar" time with the North African Kabyle idea of "practical time, which is made up of incommensurable islands of duration, each with its own rhythm, the time that flies by or drags, depending on what one is *doing*" (1977, 105). The Kabyle concept of time is personal and idiosyncratic, depending not on an "objective" standard but on where one happens to be and what one happens to be doing. Yet *On the Road* confronts reification in a more specific manner, through the character of Dean Moriarty.

At first glance it seems as though Dean is an example of, rather than an attack against, Lukacsian reification. Early in the novel, Sal travels to Denver to see his friends, and asks Carlo Marx "What's the schedule?" explaining that "There was always a schedule in Dean's life" (Kerouac 1976, 42). Sal then makes it to Dean's apartment, where Dean promptly treats the reader to an example of his schedule-making. Explaining to Camille that he must go, she in turn replies:

> "But what time will you be back?"
>
> "It is now" (looking at his watch) "exactly one-fourteen. I shall be back at exactly three-fourteen, for our hour of reverie together. . . . So now in this exact minute I must dress, put on my pants, go back to life, that is to outside life, streets and what not . . . it is now one-fifteen and time's running, running"—
>
> "Well, all right, Dean, but please be sure and be back at three."
>
> "Just as I said, darling, and remember not three but three-fourteen."
>
> (Kerouac 1976, 43–44)

What is most striking in this passage is the detail in which Dean plans out his actions. Carlo's explanation of Dean's routine is fluid by comparison, rounding off (at most) to the half-hour. Dean himself, however, carries his calculations to the exact minute, insisting on three-fourteen, not simply three p.m. Such detailed division of time seems consistent with Lukacs's notion of an ever-increasing rationalization of time. In fact, Dean's account seems overrationalized, since not even capitalism runs with such minute-by-minute efficiency. Dean's conception of time is hyperrealized. Even as he is exiting the door he realizes that "it is now one-fifteen and time's running, running—." Of course, by taking capitalist rationalization to the next step, he is calling attention to the degree to which "clock time" has gained currency.[3] Yet Dean's antagonism to reification resides not so much in the increasing mechanization of time, but rather in how that time is employed.

By itself, rationalization does not necessarily have to be a limiting phenomenon; even the Kabyle employ a rudimentary calendar. It is only when such rationalization is coupled with a capitalistic mode of production which conflates time and space that the mechanization of temporality becomes pejorative. Drawing on Marx's critique of the idea that "one man during an hour is worth just as much as another man during an hour," Lukacs concludes that "In this environment where time is transformed into abstract, exactly measurable, physical space . . . the subjects of labour must likewise be rationally fragmented" (1968, 89–90). For Lukacs, time becomes a space to be inhabited by equally interchangeable workers who now form just another factor in the workings of the "machine." It is this "machine" that then takes over, subjecting workers to its own set of laws and rules. The Kabyle might operate under a temporal grid, but their temporal paradigm is fluid and open to individual interpretation (Bourdieu 1977, 106). Dean's temporal rationalization also avoids such pitfalls since it is not tied to a capitalist mode of production. While the reification process has perverted time in order to constrict space and dominate the worker, Dean uses time to serve his own ends. Thus Dean is able to retain the agency that is denied the worker; the spaces he will inhabit will be his own. Time may still be subsumed by space, but it is a space that Dean is free to configure according to his own wishes. Time does not employ Dean—he employs time.

The space Dean creates is inhabited by a variety of pursuits that likewise challenge the constricting notion of reification and the capitalistic system that utilizes it. Dean's actions are indeed "rationally fragmented," but this fragmentation is figured in an economy of ecstasy, not of oppression. Finding a girl for Sal, making plans to go to the midget auto races, having sex with various women, and getting drunk with his friends are all activities that focus on the fulfillment of desire rather than materialist production. In fact, this frenetic activity has left Dean broke. For all of his "production," he claims that "I haven't had time to work in weeks" (Kerouac 1976, 45). While it would be wrong to treat Dean simply as a Marxist rebel, he is able to avoid the production of commodities, which ultimately destroys the worker. Because Dean names it, time regains its "variable, flowing nature" (Lukacs 1968, 90) that is denied it by reification, and the space filled for Lukacs with "the reified, mechanically objectified performance of the worker" (90) is replaced by personal experience.

And against Lukacs's notion of time as rigid space, Dean's space is extremely fluid. Running from one place to another, Dean's temporality is inextricably bound up with movement, not stasis. While

Dean may rationalize time, the uses to which he puts it often involve activity and change. If David Harvey is correct in declaring that "those who command space can always control the politics of place" (1990, 234), then Dean's restless itinerary poses a threat to established notions of capitalistic power. Through continual motion, Dean is able to avoid remaining in a fixed place that would render him susceptible to control. As Harvey notes, "The rigid discipline of time schedules, of tightly organized property rights and other forms of spatial determination, generate widespread resistances on the part of individuals who seek to put themselves outside these hegemonic constraints" (238). Dean's rejection of fixed place is emblematic of Beat attempts to escape a spatial control that becomes intertwined with temporal constraint. Rejecting the "spatialization of time" that Harvey associates with "Being," Dean opts instead for a "Becoming" that seeks "the annihilation of space by time" (273). Thus Dean's need to constantly "go," to perform "our one and noble function of the time, *move*" (Kerouac 1976, 133) as Sal says, needs to be understood as a desire for both spatial and temporal movement and flux.[4]

This questioning of conventional notions of time that Dean's tacit rejection of reification involves allows him to inhabit a different temporality, one based completely in the moment. *On the Road* provides ample evidence that Dean's conception of time is shifted away from past and future and towards an ever-changing present. Arriving at the doorstep of Sal's relatives in Virginia, Sal describes an altered Dean:

> "cause now is the time and we all know time!" . . . he roared into downtown Testament, looking in every direction and seeing everything in an arc of 180 degrees around his eyeballs without moving his head. . . . He had become absolutely mad in his movements; he seemed to be doing everything at the same time. (Kerouac 1976, 114)

Dean is frenetically living in the moment, trying to stay within the ever-unfolding horizon of the "now." To "know time" is to engage it both passively and actively. Dean accepts the belief that life must be lived in the present and practices this knowledge by filling each of these moments with as much activity as possible, attempting "to do everything at the same time." For Dean, this idea of life in the present is concomitant with the idea that there is an underlying order that makes worry superfluous. Dean later explains to Sal that "We passed a little kid who was throwing stones at the cars in the road. 'Think of it,' said Dean. 'One day he'll put a stone through a man's windshield and the man will crash and die. . . . I am positive beyond doubt that everything will be taken care of for us" (120). The difficulty in this passage lies in reconciling the idea that if everything will be taken care of, then what about the man with a rock through his windshield? Who took care of him? But notice that Dean does not say everything will turn out safely. Instead, he claims that "everything will be taken care of." And every moment necessarily takes care of itself; it occurs. Dean's faith in the moment is based on a knowledge that past and future are not separate frames of reference, but are instead part of the present itself. There are not separate times, but one time, and that time is "now."

Maurice Merleau-Ponty has offered a similar account of temporality. In *Phenomenology of Perception*, he writes:

> What there is, is not a present, then another present which takes its place in being, and not even a present with its vistas of past and future followed by another present in which those vistas are disrupted, so that one and the same spectator is needed to effect the synthesis of successive perspectives: there is only one single time which is self-confirmatory, which can bring nothing into existence unless it has already laid that thing's foundations as present and eventual past, and which establishes itself at a stroke. (Merleau-Ponty 1962, 421)

For Merleau-Ponty time is a sort of continuum, and to remain fixed on a past and future is to betray the "plenitude of being in itself" (1962, 421). Thus for Dean to fret about a rock through his windshield, or any other calamity which might befall him, is absurd. It may occur, but when and if it does, it is something that must occur and as it does so, it necessarily becomes part of the present. Of course, such an idea sounds disturbingly close to the notion of fate. But Dean's belief in living life in the moment need not mean that life is predetermined. Dean still retains personal agency within the moment; his faith is that his actions will inevitably be the right ones for that particular present. The idea that Dean espouses, then, is to accept this moment, and rather than fighting it with regrets about the past or fears for the future, to revel in it as a type of momentary infinity which encompasses both past, present, and future.

What Dean wishes to avoid in his abandonment to the continual present is what Heidegger refers to as "inauthentic" time. In his work *Being and Time*, Heidegger explains that "The inauthentic temporality of everyday Dasein as it falls, must, as such a looking-away from finitude, fail to recognize authentic futurity and therewith temporality in general" (1962, 477). In order to avoid facing the knowledge of her/his own death, a person will look away from this "finitude," and instead dwell in an "inauthentic temporality" which mistakes time as infinite. As Elizabeth Deeds Ermarth claims in *Sequel to History*, "To exist in historical ('inauthentic') time is to exist as nobody and thence, Heidegger's logic goes, to act like an immortal or at least like someone able to pretend that one's finitude is not absolute and that it can be mediated by various means" (1992, 35). People often attempt to avoid contemplating the final end of their existence by positing that they will somehow "live on" through fame, philanthropic contributions, or amassing wealth. Such attempts, however, distract one from the present, which is the real basis for life. Dean avoids Heidegger's idea of "inauthentic" time in two complementary ways. The most obvious is Dean's attempt to live in the moment. By residing in the present, he locates himself within the Heideggerian notion of "authentic" time. Realizing that life will end, he seeks to make the most of it by maximizing his understanding of every moment. Second, his "Beat" lifestyle disavows fame, fortune, and other attempts at personal aggrandizement that are the "means" to supposedly transcend finite human life. This is the secret of Dean's "Beatness." He realizes that the material and social glories of the world are nothing but obstructions to viewing life. Focusing exclusively on the unfolding moment, Dean avoids the trap of seeing the present as anything but what it really is—the final and ultimate reality.

On the Road is not content to provide Dean as the only example of how life in the present is lived. Kerouac's novel works through contrast as well. On their way from San Francisco to New York, Sal and Dean end up in a car with a man headed for Kansas and a tourist couple. Although it is immediately clear that these passengers are the "square" counterparts to the "Beat" protagonists, Dean goes on to explain the separate notions of time that distinguish the groups:

> "Now you just dig them in front. They have worries, they're counting the miles, they're thinking about where to sleep tonight, how much money

for gas, the weather, how they'll get there—and all the time they'll get there anyway, you see. But they need to worry and betray time with urgencies false and otherwise, purely anxious and whiny, their souls really won't be at peace unless they can latch on to an established and proven worry." (Kerouac 1976, 208)

In attempting to break up duration, to plan and fret about past and future, the passengers "betray time" because they do not allow themselves to be free in the present moment. Dean's knowledge of time is that time will take care of itself, it has to, because each moment must continue on. This fact leaves Dean free to live in the continual present that is always its own horizon. Thus the insistence on action and movement that characterizes Dean and *On the Road* in general: you need to continually move in order to stay in sync with time, to always live on its perpetually unfolding edge. The passengers, by comparison, need worries in order to avoid what life in the present implies. By focusing on future problems, they are able to leave Heidegger's "authentic" time and move into infinity. A worry about the future implies that there will be a future for that worry to materialize in, and thus their soul can be "at peace" with the knowledge that it will exist tomorrow. For Heidegger, anxiety is positive since it helps to bring Dasein to an authentic understanding of its Being, one that is based on the finality of existence. Anxiety "throws Dasein back upon that which it is anxious about—its authentic potentiality-for-Being-in-the-world" (1962, 232). Yet these passengers are evidencing a different anxiety—that of the "they." Heidegger explains that "He who is irresolute understands himself in terms of those very closest events and be-fallings which he encounters in such a making-present and which thrust themselves upon him in varying ways. Busily losing *himself* in the object of concern, he *loses his time* in it too" (463). Fretting about such things as "money," "gas," and "weather," the passengers blind themselves to the one fact which could allow them to live an authentic temporal existence—death. While such a denial is costly since it is bought with anxiety and unhappiness, the present is even more fearful, as it implies uncertainty and an abandonment to time.

It could be argued, however, that Dean too is implicated in an "inauthentic" losing of himself in worldly objects. But while the passengers already alluded to lose themselves in an overidentification

with worldly concerns, Dean might be said to do precisely the opposite—he seeks to escape his ties to the situation around him.
Heidegger contrasts what he terms the "moment of vision" with the
"now," claiming that "The moment of vision is a phenomenon which
in principle can *not* be clarified in terms of the '*now*.'. . . In the
moment of vision nothing can occur; but as an authentic Present or
waiting-towards, the moment of vision permits us *to encounter for
the first time* what can be 'in a time' as ready-to-hand or present-at-
hand" (1962, 387–88). To exist in the "now" is to exist "inauthentically" in a world dictated by the "they." The "moment of vision," by contrast, involves a more primal examination of the world, one that does
away with everyday notions and assumptions. Dean is indeed escaping. But what he escapes is not simply responsibility, but the ordinary conception of things. Rather than seeing the world as others
see it, Dean attempts to "encounter for the first time" what is truly
important in the present moment.

But to what extent has Sal escaped "inauthentic" time? Although
Sal seems to share Dean's ecstatic revelry in the moment, when
expounding his own thoughts, quite a different belief system
emerges, one that focuses not on the fleeting quality of life, but on
death. Early on in the narrative, Sal feels haunted, and ultimately realizes that "Naturally . . . this is only death: death will overtake us
before heaven. The one thing that we yearn for in our living days . . .
is the remembrance of some lost bliss that was probably experienced in the womb and can only be reproduced . . . in death"
(Kerouac 1976, 124). While the passengers use worries and fears to
leave the present, Sal seems to look both backward and forward for
release. Death becomes equated with birth, and life becomes the
proverbial circle. Transcendence for Sal thus becomes a desire for a
death that both replicates some "bliss" while simultaneously remov-
ing the person from time into heaven. Dean, however, remains
unconvinced. Sal relates his feelings to Dean, who "would have nothing to do with it" because "we're all of us never in life again" (124). In
keeping with his Heideggerian viewpoint, Dean realizes that since
death is our final act, it makes sense to enjoy the moments of life
that we are given, a belief that Sal finally admits is correct.

Although he agrees with Dean's admonition to live in the
moment and forget death, Sal cannot escape his fixation. Later in the

novel, alone in San Francisco and hungry, Sal passes a fish-n-chips joint and has a vision:

> And for just a moment I had reached the point of ecstasy that I always wanted to reach, which was the complete step across chronological time into timeless shadows . . . and the sensation of death kicking at my heels to move on, with a phantom dogging its own heels, and myself hurrying to a plank where all the angels dove off and flew into the holy void of uncreated emptiness . . . innumerable lotus-lands falling open in the magic mothswarm of heaven. (Kerouac 1976, 173)

Once again Sal's notion of transcendence involves death. But rather than a Heideggerian acceptance of death as a means to live life, Sal remains focused on death itself. Timelessness is achieved *through* death, not because of it. This conception is likewise firmly rooted in specifically Christian terms. The word "angels" is, of course, laden with religious implications, "mothswarm" evokes images of winged angels flying towards the God-created light at the end of the tunnel, and Sal's final destination is always conceived of as heaven. Heidegger sidesteps the question of eschatology in *Being and Time*, declaring "If 'death' is defined as the 'end' of Dasein—that is to say, of Being-in-the-world—this does not imply any ontical decision whether 'after death' still another Being is possible" (1962, 292). Ontologically, however, it would appear that a belief in the afterlife abstracts the believer out of the world and into a timeless infinity. Yet Sal's vision, despite its apparent "inauthenticity," nevertheless provides a means of escape "across chronological time" and into what he terms "timeless shadows." Sal may attempt to follow Dean's example, but ultimately his Christian belief in the transcendence of death differentiates him from Dean's belief in the sanctity of the moment. Although Sal follows Dean throughout the novel, he never entirely abandons his own moral conceptions. However, despite Sal's failure to emulate Dean, they nevertheless remain united in their mutual attempts to escape oppressive notions of time.

Sal's insistence on death as an element of transcendence can be seen even more starkly when he describes his thoughts on Mexico and civilization. Sal states:

> For when destruction comes to the world of "history" and the Apocalypse of the Fellahin returns once more as so many times before, people will

still stare with the same eyes from the caves of Mexico as well as from the
caves of Bali, where it all began and where Adam was suckled and taught
to know. (Kerouac 1976, 281)

Sal seems to be calling Western notions of time to task in this passage. History is bracketed by quotes, a stylistic move suggesting that
it is suspect. Thus history is what the West deems to be important,
and often excludes such marginalized places as Mexico. This notion,
according to Sal, will be overturned, and real history, rooted in its
"primitive," fellahin beginnings, shall return. Interestingly, the erasure
of Western notions of time is still figured in a Christian economy,
since timeless origins are connected with the suckling of Adam, an
obviously Biblical figure. Yet even more disturbing is that this escape
from an "inauthentic" history that seeks to make easy sense of
humankind's past is rendered as "Apocalypse." This term is Christian
and thus in keeping with Sal's reliance on Biblical concepts, but the
idea that we will end up staring out of caves is highly disastrous.
Once again we see transcendence rendered as death and destruction. Throughout *On the Road* there exists a tension between Dean
and Sal's conceptions of timelessness. Dean's is a life-affirming philosophy, a belief that life should be lived to the fullest in every
moment. Though Sal seems to desire this idea, his notions remain
firmly entrenched in Christian ideals that display temporal transcendence in terms of annihilation. Where Dean sees an infinity in the
moment, Sal sees infinity in the beyond.

Yet Mexico is not always configured as death and doom. In an
attempt to critique notions of time in the United States, the novel
makes numerous references to the less constricting temporal order
of Mexico. The capital, Mexico City, is described as a place without
physical or temporal end. Sal writes "We wandered in a frenzy and a
dream. We ate beautiful steaks for forty-eight cents in strange tiled
Mexican cafeterias with generations of marimba musicians standing
at one immense marimba.... Nothing stopped; the streets were alive
all night...nothing ever ended" (Kerouac 1976, 302). Here temporality is limitless, from "generations" at a single "immense" marimba,
to a city where there is activity "all night." It is no accident that *On
the Road* takes a detour from its east-west travelings and eventually
heads south. Mexico is repeatedly portrayed in obverse relation to an
oppressive America. Things are cheaper, cops are nicer, and time

sheds its constraining feel. This point culminates, perhaps, in Dean's gift of his wristwatch for a crystal. Traveling through the mountains, Dean spots some Indian girls selling crystals by the road. Dean then "went fishing around in the battered trunk in the back—the same old tortured American trunk—and pulled out a wristwatch. . . . Then Dean poked in the little girl's hand for 'the sweetest and purest and smallest crystal she has personally picked from the mountain for me'" (Kerouac 1976, 298). The contrasts generated by this passage are endless. The "American trunk" situates the wristwatch, itself laden with images of time, in a distinctly U.S. context. Its exchange for the native crystal thus signals a swap of constraining, constructed, American temporality for the natural, formless production of the Indian earth itself.[5] The presentation of an alternative temporal universe undermines the idea that time constructed in the U.S. is somehow "natural" and singular.

Though *On the Road* clearly sees Mexican temporality as preferable to that of America, the question as to what time itself means in Mexico remains. If U.S. time is rejected, with what is it being replaced? An answer to this question can be found in Robert Levine's book *A Geography of Time*. Admittedly written some forty years after *On the Road*'s publication, this work is nevertheless a valuable asset in understanding how time is perceived in Mexico. Levine compared thirty-one countries in terms of three factors, walking speed, work speed, and the accuracy of public clocks, in order to determine where the pace of life was fastest. Mexico ranked last (1997, 136). According to Levine, "Slowness is so ingrained in Mexican culture that people who abide by the clock invite insult" (138). Rather than controlling time with clocks and established schedules, Mexico instead tries to mesh with time. Where the U.S. has accepted a Lukacsian rationalization of temporality, Mexico opts for organic notions of time. Quoting a psychologist who commutes from Tijuana to San Diego, Levine writes "In Mexico, we are inside the time. We don't control time. We live *with* the time" (190). Of course Sal had experience with this concept even before his trip to Mexico. In California Sal has an affair with Terry, a Mexican girl who soothes him with "'*Manana*,' she said. 'Everything'll be all right tomorrow.' . . . Sure, baby, *manana*.' It was always *manana* . . . a lovely word and one that probably means heaven" (Kerouac 1976, 94).

Interestingly, the English word "tomorrow" is translated as "*man-ana*," but the dictionary translates "*manana*" as both "tomorrow" and "in the near future" (Castillo and Bond 1987, 161). While the English "tomorrow" can refer to an unspecified future, it appears as though the Spanish "*manana*" contains more temporal ambiguity. Rather than designating a fixed time, the use of the word "*manana*" allows for open-ended possibility in the future, which is precisely why Sal thinks it "means heaven." Time in Mexico is less rigid and fixed than in America.

The attempt to reach a separate temporal order situated apart from confining "clock time" through an appeal to a marginalized community occurs in American jazz clubs as well. In San Francisco, Sal and Dean spent a night in "the little Harlem on Folsom Street," where "colored men in Saturday-night suits were whooping it up in front. . . . A six-foot skinny Negro woman was rolling her bones," and "Groups of colored guys stumbled in from the street" (Kerouac 1976, 196–97). Jazz scenes such as this occur frequently in *On the Road*, and are always depicted as events charged with frenzy and activity. Crowds flow in and out, exhorting the musicians to "Stay with it!" (197) or "Blowblowblow!" (200) while the musicians themselves sweat and strain to reach higher and higher levels of ecstasy. And these characters are almost always African-Americans. Citing the anthropologist Jules Henry, Levine talks about how African Americans "distinguish their own culture's sense of time . . . from the majority standard of 'white people's time'" (1997, 10). Like notions of time in Mexico, African-American time is structured around events, not the clock. But as the sociologist John Horton notes, while this slow tempo exists when money is tight, "time is 'alive' whenever and wherever there is 'action' . . . [it] accelerates exponentially on Friday and Saturday nights" (11). This dichotomy is a coping mechanism. Jazz scenes such as this show the "hot" side to the staid, "cool," beat character on the street. What Sal and Dean find in the African-American community is a different temporal order, one that maximizes joy by slowing when resources are not available and expanding when they are.

Yet this shift in temporal order is not only bound up with the social sphere of African-Americans, but exists within the music as well. The day after this scene takes place, Dean attempts to explain to Sal the different temporality that jazz music inaugurates. He says:

> "Here's a guy and everybody's there, right? Up to him to put down what's on everybody's mind. . . . All of a sudden somewhere in the middle of the chorus he gets it—everybody looks up and knows. . . . Time stops. He's filling empty space with the substance of our lives. . . . He has to blow across bridges and come back to it with such infinite feeling soul-exploratory for the tune of the moment that everybody knows it's not the tune that counts but IT." (Kerouac 1976, 206)

Two points in particular bear comment. The first, and most important, is that "Time stops." At first glance, this seems at odds with the notion that Dean transcends time by living perfectly within each successive moment. If time stops, that would mean that Dean would have to become static in order to stay within the present. There is, however, another way of viewing this statement. The phrase "Time stops" could mean that the authoritative, oppressive "clock time" is what stops. In *The Culture of Spontaneity*, Belgrad discusses the notion of *mitwelt*, defining it as "the coordination of our internal, subjective reality with external processes" (1998, 191). According to Belgrad, "Clock time is the psychological state of mitwelt, reified and given objective status in the culture. . . . Rhythm, by contrast, preserves the sense of mitwelt time as relational and intersubjective" (191–92). Jazz challenges the dominant notion of time, creating instead its own internal temporality. As Belgrad notes, quoting George Lipsitz, such music allows the listener "to think of time as a flexible human creation rather than as an immutable outside force" (192). Clock time stops, but a new temporality, governed by the jazz musician, continues on, allowing him to "fill the empty space with the substance of our lives." It is also worth noting that this tune is finite. As Dean explains, the musician is looking for the "tune of the moment," a sound which is infinitely variable but limited by the audience and the particular present into which it must be meshed. The "IT" Dean refers to, then, is that temporal space chiseled out of capitalism's reified time that always waits in the background for the tune to end. But as Ermarth notes, "the substitution of rhythmic time for historical time has significant and threatening consequences" (1992, 53). This finitude allows listeners access to that plenitude of being in the present that Dean continually tries to achieve, but at the cost of knowing that any transcendence or understanding exists only for that duration. As Heidegger notes, it is this knowledge that things will not last that provides such access to the present. The tune reminds everyone that everything must eventually end.

Jazz improvisation not only provides access to the moment, but access to a community within the moment as well. The jazz musician, though responsible for putting down "what's on everybody's mind," is by no means alone. The audience is likewise involved in attaining the "IT" that is the ultimate goal of the improvisation. When he gets "IT," then "everybody looks up and knows; they listen" (Kerouac 1976, 206). As the tune continues, "everybody knows it's not the tune that counts but IT" (206). "IT" is a connection between the musician, the audience, and individual members of the audience all coming together as a whole.[6] Without the musician, this synthesis would not occur, but without the audience, the musician would be blowing only for himself. As Belgrad observes, the structure of bebop "suggests an intersubjective dynamic, one in which the individual and the community empower one another" (1998, 191). And the participatory nature of the genre, marked by a social and racial blindness, is what allows such a connection to occur. According to Belgrad, "There is no dichotomy pitting the individual against the group. . . . Nor is unity of purpose enforced by a hierarchical authority structure" (191). Jazz's altered temporality is egalitarian and open to all, a joint project where everyone is welcome to participate. Such an idea of community is emblematic of Kerouac's novel as a whole and its attempt to enact change by providing its readers with an altered view of temporality. Belgrad observes that Beat works such as *On the Road* "entailed linking personal experience to a larger social and historical context" (206). Like the jazz musician, Kerouac too is trying to catch the "IT" through his work, trying to catch the words and phrases that will let "everybody know it's not the tune that counts but IT."

But while the tune will end, the written word lives on. Kerouac's investment in the literary places him in the same sort of position as the passengers in the car; he needs writing as a guarantee. But where the passengers' worries generate a future, Kerouac's writings seek to preserve a past. In contrast to Dean's ephemeral life in the moment, Sal insists on the written record as a means to "inauthentically" extend his past experiences into the future.[7] It is no surprise that Dean comes to Sal to learn "how to write" (Kerouac 1976, 5), and that Sal then shambles after him, "because I was a writer and needed new experiences" (9). Sal loses himself in Dean in the same way that he loses himself in his visions, and regains himself only when he returns home at the end of his journeys in order to write. The irony of Kerouac's work is that Sal's adventures with Dean can never be truly recorded, since describing a memory is not the same as being present during it. A book is an ersatz substitute for a lived life, just as a recording of a jazz set will never allow the listener to fully connect with the audience that was actually there. Sal may critique the idea of "history" and seek transcendence in the beyond, but his need to record signals a fear of the chaos occasioned by time's ceaseless flow. By creating his "Duluoz Legend," Kerouac is engaged in a historicizing project that critics such as Julia Kristeva have criticized as a "zeal to master time" (Ermarth 1992, 41).

On the Road's attack on constraining notions of temporality is not without its problems. The novel's critique ultimately remains inconsistent; Sal and Dean's notions of transcendence often differ radically from one another, and these characters' conceptions of time themselves alter throughout the text. On the Road likewise retains a completely modernistic approach to the problem of temporality. Though considered innovative, Kerouac's text seldom challenges temporality in a way we have come to expect in his more experimental novels and in postmodern works in general—through the narrative itself. And by the end of the novel the hero Dean Moriarty is presented as a questionable force, his energy spent and his once-transcendent oratory turned into mumble: "can't talk no more—do you understand that it is—or might be—But listen!" (1976, 307). But despite these considerations Kerouac's work is still effective in introducing its readers to new ways of thinking about time. The first step involves exposing clock time for what it really is—a means of controlling the worker. Only after this oppressive system is abandoned can a quest for an "authentic" way of experiencing time be undertaken. Sal and Dean have certainly left the work-a-day world behind them, and their continual attempt to live time to the fullest becomes an injunction to the reader—question accepted notions of temporality in whatever way you can if you want to reach the infinity beyond time.

Notes

1 In his article "Time Cents: The Monetization of the Workday in Comparative Perspective," Richard Biernacki claims that "the commodification of labor time does not simply mirror the exigencies of the capitalist labor process" but also "depends on cultural assumptions" (1994, 81). Despite this important caveat, the Lukacsian notion of reification does seem an acceptable paradigm for explaining a system where the worker is forced to sell her/his time to a particular firm.

2 While the Oxford English Dictionary defines "fellahin" as "A peasant in Arabic-speaking countries," in her book *Off the Road*, Carolyn Cassady explains that for Kerouac this term represents "a Utopian existence without hassles, a timeless peace" (1990, 166).

3 Dean's exactitude could also be viewed as a form of "camp." Such a formulation would then see Dean as mocking a capitalist system that is so "hung-up" on time that it must account for every minute of it.

4 In *Grace Beats Karma: Letters From Prison,* Neal Cassady, the real-life inspiration for Kerouac's Dean Moriarty, relates that while in San Quentin he attempted to memorize the names and reigns of all the Popes. His space effectively fixed, this enormous task allowed Cassady to continue moving across time, mentally if not physically.

5 In his article "Man Out of Time: Kerouac, Spengler, and the 'Faustian Soul'" Michael D'Orso connects this interest in the "fellahin" with Oswald Spengler's *The Decline of the West*. According to D'Orso, Spengler believed that "primitive man" lived each moment "with no conception of past or future," but "as he became aware of his surroundings . . . man imposed thought on them, gradually . . . losing touch with the rhythm of nature" (1983, 20).

6 Thus Kerouac's insistence on presence. While Sal and Dean listen to the jukebox, records, and radio, it is important for them to actually attend jazz club performances in order to truly gain this sense of mitwelt.

7 While Kerouac has well over twenty books in print, Cassady has only three: a half-finished autobiography and two collections of letters. It is not surprising, then, that although they shared many adventures, Kerouac's writing secured him a place in American history while the name of Cassady languishes in relative obscurity.

Works Cited

Belgrad, Daniel. 1998. *The Culture of Spontaneity: Improvisation and the Arts in Postwar America*. Chicago: University of Chicago Press.

Biernacki, Richard. 1994. "Time Cents: The Monetization of the Workday in Comparative Perspective." In *NowHere: Space, Time and Modernity*, ed. Roger Friedland and Deirdre Boden. Berkeley: University of California Press.

Bourdieu, Pierre. 1977. *Outline of a Theory of Practice*. Trans. Richard Nice. Cambridge: Cambridge University Press.

Cassady, Carolyn. 1990. *Off the Road: My Years with Cassady, Kerouac, and Ginsberg*. New York: Penguin Books.

Cassady, Neal. 1993. *Grace Beats Karma: Letters From Prison*. New York: Blast Books.

Castillo, Carlos, and Otto F. Bond, eds. 1987. *The University of Chicago Spanish-English/English-Spanish Dictionary*. 4th ed. New York: Pocket Books.

Charters, Ann. 1973. *Kerouac*. New York: St. Martin's Press.

D'Orso, Michael. 1983. "Man Out of Time: Kerouac, Spengler, and the 'Faustian Soul'." *Studies in American Fiction* 11: 19–30.

Ermarth, Elizabeth Deeds. 1992. *Sequel to History: Postmodernism and the Crisis of Representational Time*. Princeton: Princeton University Press.

Harvey, David. 1990. *The Condition of Postmodernity: An Enquiry into the Origins of Cultural Change*. Cambridge: Blackwell Publishers.

Heidegger, Martin. 1962. *Being and Time*. Trans. John Macquarrie and Edward Robinson. London: SCM Press.

Kerouac, Jack. 1976. *On the Road*. New York: Penguin Books.

Landes, David S. 1983. *Revolution in Time: Clocks and the Making of the Modern World*. Cambridge: Belknap Press.

Levine, Robert. 1997. *A Geography of Time*. New York: BasicBooks.

Lukacs, Georg. 1968. "Reification and the Consciousness of the Proletariat." In *History and Class Consciousness: Studies in Marxist Dialectics,* trans. Rodney Livingstone. Cambridge: MIT Press.

Merleau-Ponty, M. 1962. *Phenomenology of Perception*. Trans. Colin Smith. London: Routledge and Kegan Paul.

Nicosia, Gerald. 1983. *Memory Babe*. New York: Grove Press.

Tytell, John. 1976. *Naked Angels: The Lives and Literature of the Beat Generation*. New York: McGraw-Hill Book Company.

CHAPTER FOUR

The Author as Spiritual Pilgrim:
The Search for Authenticity in Jack Kerouac's
On the Road and *The Subterraneans*
Steve Wilson

It is quite common for modern student readers, well trained in the virtues of multiculturalism, to accuse Jack Kerouac and his compatriot Beat writers of racism, homophobia, and misogyny. Certainly one can point to numerous instances where Kerouac's views on women, African-Americans and homosexuals (including his close friend, Allen Ginsberg) are less open-minded than we might imagine from the "King of the Beats"—a group thought to be radically liberal. However, such a view overlooks Kerouac's many painful attempts— attempts recorded with brutal honesty in his books—to confront and challenge his prejudices. Thus, although teaching the Beats will surely lead to questions about Kerouac's character as a liberal, it will more importantly provide concrete evidence to students that the road to multiculturalism was far from smooth. Indeed, one can see that Kerouac battled between his need for embracing openness and his need for writing through the fracturing of his prejudices, between *being* and *writing about*. To teach the Beats, then, is to explore a central issue of modern America, cultural diversity, as it was first given voice by an Anglo writer unafraid to explore his very American mind.

***

Near the end of *Siddhartha*, his novel on Buddhist enlightenment, Herman Hesse describes how his main character has come to both understand and embody Nirvana. When Siddhartha's lifelong friend Govinda asks him the way to truth, Siddhartha urges him to look into his face. What Govinda sees there are the images of people Siddhartha encountered in his journeys through life: "he saw faces, a long series, a continuous stream of faces—hundreds, thousands, which all came and disappeared and yet all seemed to be there at the same time, which all continually changed and renewed themselves and which were yet all Siddhartha" (1971, 150). What he sees in Siddhartha's face are the outcasts of the "refined" world—criminals, victims, women and men engaged in passionate sex, corpses (150). Siddhartha has reached Nirvana because he has embraced that which others seek to avoid: the dispossessed, the outsiders.

On a similar quest for spiritual enlightenment, Beat author Jack Kerouac sets out at mid-century to surround himself with the lives of those beyond the bounds of "normal" American society. Fictionalized in *On the Road* and *The Subterraneans*, his quest leads him to live with hobos, befriend criminals and drug users, and have interracial affairs with Mexican and Native American women—all this in the confining social environment of late 1940s America, when conformity was seen as a civic good. While most Americans in the postwar decades sought comfort and security, Kerouac and his fellow Beat writers would reject those desires as artificial. The life of the outsider was for them the last place where authenticity survived in the manufactured world of America. The Beats argued that outsiders such as Mexican migrant worker Terry in *On the Road* and Mardou—mentally unstable and half Cherokee, who appears in *The Subterraneans*—could not fit into mainstream America because of their race, their criminal records, their economic status, their sexual orientations. Far from being a difficulty, though, this was a benefit to their spiritual development; for example, Kerouac felt that African-American culture—jazz, for instance—encouraged the enlightenment of the individual because it valued the intense moment over tradition, intuition over reason shaped by education. He and other Beats believed that Black culture revered these things because a life lived outside an Anglo worldview (stressing the evils of the body) ensured Blacks would stay in touch with a certain essential human-ness Anglos had lost. As a result of these opinions, Kerouac's search for truth would involve "digging" the lives of the dispossessed—not merely studying Blacks, Mexicans, criminals, but attempting to *become* them for a time, as Buddha sought to contain all walks of life within the Self.

Kerouac's interest in the "outsider" is itself an intriguing and complicated tangle of emotions for him as he sets out on his quest for authenticity. As biographer Ann Charters notes, by birth Kerouac was himself something of a cultural outsider in America:

> Kerouac drew upon his ancestral heritage as the descendant of French Canadian immigrants. Even when his books weren't specifically about his Franco-American experience growing up in Lowell, he emerges as a dynamic human being in his narratives largely because he is self-conscious that he was a man with a past, a writer deeply marked by a different cul-tural background of his family, never completely assimilated into American life. From Kerouac's early childhood, he was well acquainted with the feeling of being an outsider. His roots were solidly planted in working class, immigrant soil. (Ginsberg 1990, 181)

Indeed, Kerouac's narrators in both *On the Road* and *The Subterraneans* reveal their immigrant backgrounds, but only in pass-ing. Sal Paradise (Salvatore), from *On the Road*, is Italian-American. Leo Percepied, early in *The Subterraneans*, notes that, similar to Kerouac himself, he is "a Canuck, [he] could not speak English till [he] was 5 or 6, at 16 [he] spoke it with a halting accent" (1989, 3). Even so, these narrators, mirroring Kerouac's own attitudes, align themselves time and again with the white mainstream of America. Sal Paradise bemoans suffering for his "white ambitions," going through life a "white man disillusioned" (180). Percepied struggles throughout *The Subterraneans* with the social implications of enter-ing into an interracial relationship (as we shall explore later), reveal-ing the foundation of that struggle as his "awful American as if to say white ambitions. . ." (45). Kerouac's conflict, then, is between the reality of his French-Canadian background, often reinforced for him by Gabrielle Kerouac, whom scholar Clark Blaise describes as a "corrosively ignorant and loudly bigoted mother" (2000, 2); and his white-skinned ability to blend into the 1940s and 1950s American Dream of security and suburb, where he "tried to be as American as apple pie" (Ginsberg 1990, 184). His outlook as a "white man disillusioned" may explain in part the romanticizing of outsider life, as well as the ways Kerouac often stereotypes the lives of minorities in his works. Jon Panish argues that "the African American characters and art forms that are depicted in Kerouac's novel are not substantially different from the 'Negro symbols' used by the romantic racialists over a century earlier to help eradicate slavery" (1993, 107). Willing himself to forget his own immigrant background, I would argue, Kerouac defines his life as one filled with "white ambitions," since he can assume the appearance of mainstream America and holds— albeit uncomfortably—its social values of success and acceptance (see Nicosia 1983, 593). He realizes the emptiness of the values promoted by mainstream America, but he sees himself as embodying those values, and so seeks in the lives of people prohibited by skin color from assimilation that authentic existence earned through the suffering of "real," unavoidable outsider status in America.

Further complicating his quest, what Kerouac will discover in the course of reinventing his searches as literature is that the writer, through the act of making art, removes himself from the very experiences/suffering he seeks to embrace, and indeed, from the enlightenment he had hoped to find. He learns that art requires distance, sacrifice of one's life to creating rather than experiencing. In the end, then, Kerouac's direction in these two early autobiographical works will be to trace his increasing awareness, and deepening despair, that life as a writer will make him only at best a Boddhisatva—one guiding others to possible enlightenment— always describing what he can never himself obtain. Moreover, he will come to believe that there is something artificial in the very act of going out into the world as a writer; he will by the time of *The Subterraneans* question his own motives for the relationships and lifestyles he enters into.

***

When *On the Road* achieved the status of a holy book for disaffected youth in the mid-1950s, many readers assumed that freewheeling car thief and philosopher Dean Moriarty, the king of the American road, was in fact a fictionalized version of the author. Joyce Johnson, whose *Minor Characters* recounts her life with Kerouac at the beginning of his fame, notes that Kerouac was almost immediately set upon by young people wanting to tap into Dean's boundless energy. Men wrote to him sharing their exploits with the law. Women threw themselves at the man they thought to be the sexual dynamo represented by Dean. Within weeks of a glowing review of *On the Road* in *The New York Times*—a review that called the book's author the voice of a new generation—Kerouac was complaining about all the fan mail from readers who seemed to miss the spirituality of his book while focusing on the kicks of Dean Moriarty (1992, 477-81). In fact, readers were correct to assume that Kerouac's book was drawn heavily from real life; as Edward Foster asserts in *Understanding the Beats*, Kerouac's "works depend on perfect honesty" (1992, 77). In reality, though, Kerouac's alter-ego in the novel is not Dean but the narrator, novelist Sal Paradise, a somber outsider in the lower middle-class world of his family as well as among the group of bohemian friends whose characters would eventually shape the public's sense of the Beat Generation. Paradise is on a search for authenticity in a mid-century America bent on conformity and convenience. He is mesmerized by but wary of Dean's manic drive for experience. Kerouac, too, would spend his life trying to clarify his search for the authentic—attempting to distance himself from the mindless fashion, drug use, and violence that came to be popularized in "Beatnik" culture.

The fundamental irony of the quest recounted in *On the Road*—an irony Kerouac himself expressed—was that he was a writer, to most working class sensibilities a questionable occupation at best, at worst comfortable and lacking hardship. His father Leo regularly berated Jack for having no "real job," and noted eloquently, "artist shmartist, ya can't be supported all ya life" (Watson 1995, 64). To prove—to himself and his working class relatives—the validity of his vocation, Kerouac repeatedly referred to writing as "his work," and set goals for himself that required physical and psychological sacrifice for his art: drinking to excess, taking speed to fuel three-day writing orgies, developing his technique of trancelike composition, abandoning relationships that might lead to stability. He sought to create real suffering in a life that seemed sheltered.

***

From the opening lines of *On the Road*, when Sal Paradise reveals himself as "having just gotten over a serious illness that I won't bother to talk about, except that it had to do with . . . my feeling that everything was dead" (Kerouac 1976, 3), Kerouac establishes that his narrator is on a quest for enlightenment—a search for a spiritual cure. As I mentioned earlier, this quest will take the form of a search among the people on the fringes of society for signs of authenticity. One could examine numerous instances reflecting Kerouac's equating of outsider status with authenticity: his descriptions of the farmers, waitresses, and hobos he meets on his first trip west; his trip to Mexico with Dean, where he finds a poor society that relies on trust and openness rather than the repression he feels in the United States. Throughout the novel, though, the central element in Sal's exploration is his friend and road-buddy Dean Moriarty, modeled closely after Kerouac's real-life friend Neal Cassady.

Paradise is intrigued by the boundless energy—both psychological and sexual—he finds in Moriarty because Dean has had a life that should have extinguished his joy for living. In this contradiction— the embodiment of suffering and honest love of life in one man— Paradise finds a guide for his own journey toward meaning:

> [Dean's] dirty workclothes clung to him so gracefully, as though you couldn't buy a better fit from a custom tailor but only earn it from the Natural Tailor of Natural Joy, as Dean had, in his stresses. And in his excited way of speaking I heard again the voices of old companions and brothers under the bridge, among the motorcycles, along the wash-lined neighborhood and drowsy doorsteps of afternoon where boys played guitars while their older brothers worked in the mills. . . . And his "criminality" was not something that sulked and sneered; it was a wild yea-saying overburst of American joy; it was something Western, the west wind, an ode from the Plains, something new, long prophesied, long a-coming (he only stole cars for joy rides). . . . Dean just raced in society, eager for bread and love; he didn't care one way or the other, "so long's I can get that lil ole gal with that lil sumpin down there tween her legs, boy," and "so long's we can eat, son, y-ear me? I'm hungry, I'm starving, let's eat right now!" (Kerouac 1976, 10)

We learn immediately prior to this passage that Dean has a long history of jail-stays, and as a young boy lived on the streets of Denver
with his alcoholic, drifter father. He has been a resident of skid row
from his early youth. As Paradise tells us, Dean is "starving" for the
essentials of existence, but this has turned not into bitterness but an
unbridled, essentially early-American appetite for life. More to our
point, Dean has learned about Natural Joy from "his stresses," rather
than the sanitized life being sold by American mainstream society.
Perhaps, Paradise thinks, Dean can teach me to understand and par-
take of the purity of his authentic existence won by hardship.

What is it that Dean discovers in his frantic existence? "It." The
essence of human existence: to be in the moment and living without
the need for what John Keats called "reaching irritably after facts and
reason" (1993, 831). Although Dean cannot put "it" into clearer terms
when Sal tells him he "wanted to know what 'IT' meant" (Kerouac
1976, 106), he does know the feeling when he sees it in others or
experiences it himself:

> Time stops. He's filling empty space with the substance of our lives, con-
> fessions of his bellybottom strain, remembrance of ideas, rehashes of old
> blowing. He has to blow across bridges and come back and do it with
> such infinite feeling soul-exploratory for the tune of the moment that
> everybody knows it's not the tune that counts but IT. . . . (Kerouac 1976,
> 106)

Dean and Sal part ways by the end of *On the Road*, after an
intense and intimate friendship and several wild trips across the
United States and into Mexico. One important lesson Paradise learns
from his tutelage under Moriarty is that authenticity in life requires
abandoning our need for personal ties. We must focus our energies
on obtaining our own kicks, and mustn't let any obligations to others
get in our way. This philosophy is shown to Paradise in clearest
terms when late in the story Dean leaves him seriously ill in Mexico
City. As Dean says, he's "gotta get back to his life" (Kerouac 1976,
302). This is a turning point in the relationship, with Sal acknowledging that Dean cannot commit to a true, long-term friendship: "When
I got better I realized what a rat he was, but then I had to understand
the impossible complexity of his life, how he had to leave me there,
sick, to get on. . . . 'Okay, old Dean, I'll say nothing'" (303).

Thus, Sal assigns Dean's shirking of responsibility not to a lack of caring but to the life he has led. Suffering may lead to self-realizations, but the journey is, in the end, a focus on the *self* over others. This is a lesson Sal finds difficult to adopt; throughout the novel, Kerouac uses the image of Sal looking longingly at the past and friends disappearing in the car's rear-view mirror as a way of showing Paradise's romance for the people and places he experiences. Dean never looks back; his eyes are always on the road ahead. But nostalgia is for Kerouac the necessary burden of the writer—especially a writer such as himself, who relies so completely on the powers of his memory and the experiences of his life to create art. No surprise, then, that at the close of *On the Road* Sal leaves Dean standing alone on a street in New York City, but remembers his friend with a mixture of love and sadness.

One other relationship in *On the Road* is worth examining as it relates to our topic: the love affair between Sal and Terry, the Mexican girl he meets in a bus station in Bakersfield, California. Sal is at first attracted to Terry because she was "the cutest little Mexican girl in slacks" (Kerouac 1976, 81). His two-week affair with her allows him access to a life among migrant farm workers, the outcast, and the destitute. With sincere affection, Terry and Sal settle into what becomes a sort of marriage; and Sal is introduced to Terry's world, at the center of which is her brother, Ricky: "a wild-buck Mexican hotcat with a hunger for booze" (91) whose philosophy of work was to do it "manana." Kerouac writes that "Ricky always had three or four dollars in his pocket and was happy-go-lucky about things" (91). And like Dean, Terry, and Ricky come from the lowest of economic backgrounds. Terry's sister's house was a "sliverous Mexican shack" on a "little rat alley" (87). Terry's hangouts were on LA's Central Avenue, which, Sal explains,

> is the main drag of LA. And what a wild place it is, with chickenshacks barely big enough to house a jukebox, and the jukebox blowing nothing but blues, bop, and jump. We went up dirty tenement stairs and came to the room of Terry's friend. (Kerouac 1976, 87)

To support his newly acquired family, Sal obtains a job picking cotton, something he has never done before. They live in a tent beside the fields, beside other migrant families, and though the work is backbreaking and the pay abysmal, Sal thinks he has "found [his] life's work" (96).

During this experience, a transformation in Sal occurs, through which he comes to see himself as one of the social outcasts whose group he has joined:

> Sighing like an old Negro cotton-picker, I reclined on the bed and smoked a cigarette.

> I was a man of the earth, precisely as I had dreamed I would be, in Paterson. There was talk that Terry's husband was back in Sabinal and out for me; I was ready for him. One night the Okies went mad in the road-house and tied a man to a tree and beat him to a pulp with sticks. I was asleep at the time and only heard about it. From then on I carried a big stick with me in the tent in case they got the idea we Mexicans were fouling up their trailer camp. (Kerouac 1976, 97)

This is far more than mere identification with an outsider group. Here Sal sees himself as one of the dispossessed, calling himself a Mexican when he is closer culturally to the Okies and their views on his adopted race.

Even so, Sal soon realizes that his life as a migrant worker cannot be permanent. Within days of the above-stated epiphany of his "Mexicanness," Sal says that he "[is] through with my chores in the cottonfield. I could feel my old life pulling me back" (Kerouac 1976, 98). Borrowing a phrase from Hemingway's *The Sun Also Rises*, Sal says that "everything was collapsing" (99), which Hemingway used to signal the end of the fiesta. As Kerouac renders it, Sal's life with Terry and her friends is idyllic, harsh, unforgiving and comforting all at once—authenticity that, like Dean's, is born of hardship and the prejudices of mainstream Americans. Sal, the writer, also illustrates that a writer's place may not be within such a life, but removed from it and back in front of the typewriter, sifting through experiences to put into words the truths of human existence.

In the novel published one year after *On the Road*, *The Subterraneans*, Kerouac once again submits himself to the difficulties of an outsider existence, this time when he enters into a passionate but short-lived affair with Mardou Fox, a half-Black, half-Cherokee woman with a history of mental instability. Although Kerouac through his protagonist will again explore and search for authenticity in the same sorts of places and people he did in *On the Road*, he will also struggle with a nagging suspicion that as a writer he consciously seeks out suffering as material for his writing. Is this another, and also necessary, layer to the distancing from life that a writer must face?

As is the case in *On the Road*, the novel's narrator, Leo Percepied, as well as the novel's story of a doomed love affair, are patterned closely upon real events in the author's life. Foster notes that "Kerouac chose Percepied as his own name in the novel because the book does not present an objectively detailed sequence of events but rather a record of his often very subjective percep-tions" (1976, 57). In other words, *The Subteranneans* is a recounting of Kerouac's emotional/psychological reaction to actual events. However, although Percepied, like Sal Paradise before him, is drawn to the downcast of American society, he approaches life and his quest for authenticity with a cynicism that is only hinted at by Kerouac in *On the Road*. Many readers may find the calculating Leo a questionable character for his willingness to seek out—even fuel— suffering, but one could argue based upon the novel that the writer Kerouac, who is even closer in personality to Leo than to Sal, now believes the writer's true role to be that of extracting meaning from those who live it, because as a writer he cannot live authenti-cally himself. In a sense, then, the emotional detachment Dean advocates as necessary in a quest for truth is artificially created by Kerouac when he chooses to use his owned failed relationships in his art. By betraying his relationships, he is then able to recreate them as literature.

Written in just seventy-two hours soon after the breakup of the affair upon which *The Subterraneans* is based, Kerouac's Benzedrine-driven novella explores the tense love relationship between Percepied—a brooding writer who, like Kerouac at the time, has one published book under his belt—and Mardou Fox. Mardou is the love-object of most of the straight men in the group of bohemians Kerouac calls "the subterraneans." They are serious, intel-lectual, dark and ascetic, whereas Percepied—out of place just as Sal was—seems to them a New York hoodlum who might beat them all up. Leo wanders through their nightly parties with a studied world-weariness, leaving periodically for his home, security, and a return to "his work": writing.

Mardou attracts Leo from the first moment he sees her, and as he reveals, "'By God, I've got to get involved with that little woman' and maybe too because she was Negro" (Kerouac 1989, 2). Elsewhere in the novel, Percepied explains that his having an affair with a Black woman would be a scandal in his family, suggesting just how far from the world of his upbringing he is venturing:

> Doubts, therefore, of, well, Mardou's Negro, naturally not only my mother but my sister whom I may have to live with some day and her husband a Southerner and everybody concerned, would be mortified to hell and have nothing to do with us—like it would preclude completely the possibility of living in the South . . . what would they say if my mansion lady wife was a black Cherokee, it would cut my life in half, and all such sundry awful American as if to say white ambition thoughts or white daydreams. (Kerouac 1989, 45)

This is brutally honest because the sentiments, though expressed by Kerouac's narrator, come straight out of the author's own lower middle-class background as a youth in Lowell, Massachusetts. The author's relatives, and indeed most of the mid-century American society, "would be mortified to hell and have nothing to do with" an interracial couple. Why, then, does Leo pursue an affair with Mardou? Because she, as did petty thief and drifter Dean Moriarty, holds some clue to the essence of life, and because the writerly Leo sees in and explores through Mardou not an individual finally but an embodiment of the philosophy we have discussed thus far: that the suffering of the outsider's life leads to authenticity. Certainly, Mardou— Black, Cherokee, and fragile—is very different from what most middle-class Americans of the 1950s would have seen as "normal." For this very reason, to Leo—who sees himself as a descendant of the white oppressors—she holds an essential key to existence. In spite of the economic struggles Leo has seen in his life, his whiteness offers him the possibility of assimilation, but may also bar him from the authenticity Mardou has gained from living life on the fringes of American society. Recall the way in which Dean Moriarty became a symbol of the Western/early-American love of life as you listen to the way in which Leo paints Mardou's past as an allegory of the American outsider:

> But they were the inhabitors of this land and under these huge skies they were the worriers and keeners and protectors of wives in whole nations gathered around tents—now the rail that runs over their forefathers'

> bones leads them onward pointing into infinity, wraiths of humanity
> treading lightly on the surface of the ground so deeply suppurated with
> the stock of their suffering you only have to dig a foot down to find a
> baby's hand. (Kerouac 1989, 20–21)

What makes Mardou of interest to Leo is that she has gained access
to understanding through pain—generations of oppression. Coming
from a people whose history is "so suppurated with the stock of
their suffering you only have to dig a foot down to find a baby's
hand," she holds within her psyche and her body the roots of suffering in America as one of the abused "Original Americans." This has
not led to her collapse but to the insight that living is a painful journey toward enlightenment and acceptance. What Leo only understands intellectually Mardou has lived and knows viscerally because
of her social status and ties to a history of oppression. Her life is
filled with the essences of the earth: "juices"; "the ground filled with
. . . bones"; "her wild now-Indian eyes now staring into the Black
with a little fog emanating from her brown mouth, the misery like
ice crystals on the blankets on the ponies of her Indian ancestors"
(25). Such earthy images remind us that Mardou's life is truth incar-
nate rather than knowledge as thought only. Like Hesse's Siddhartha,
Mardou *contains* authenticity. In the 1950s culture of conformity,
such ethnic differences as Mardou's also insured one's outsider status. Mardou's very appearance made it impossible for her to fit into
the white world of Ozzie and Harriet. Thus, she and others like her
had to undertake a lifelong struggle to survive in a society that
would rather forget them.

Leo's love affair with Mardou, then, gives him what must have
been remarkable access to a way of life most Americans in the 1950s
had never seen. What he finds there is elemental, harsh, and challenging. As a writer Leo is able to share this experience with his readers. If we wonder at his conscious choice to enter into a romance
knowing it was doomed to fail by society's prejudices and his
always present duties to his writing, if we are taken aback by the
racist overtones of Leo's ideas, we must remember that he knowingly endured the pain and recounted his prejudiced feelings as a way
to generate a book that might open up others' eyes to the realities of
life in America, as well as suggest a path to understanding. Beat poet
Gary Snyder, who served as the inspiration for Japhy Ryder in
Kerouac's *Dharma Bums*, explained to me in a recent interview

that the Beats were not perhaps as open about women and race as we today would like to think, but they were probably the most open-minded people of their day. Kerouac conveys in his novels that the Beats' respect for the authenticity of outsider life led them to explore previously ignored sections of American society. Still, while the author's close friends found themselves actually living lives beyond the norms of society—Allen Ginsberg a gay Jew with a paranoid-schizophrenic mother, William Burroughs a criminal and inveterate drug user—Kerouac was always able to (and often did) return from his wild escapades to his doting mother. Perhaps when we consider these facts of the author's life, conflicted and enlarged by his philosophy of suffering and spirituality, we can understand the reasons Kerouac/Leo entered into a relationship with a woman such as Mardou, why he drank himself into rages, and why as a writer he always questioned his place in the world.

***

As did Dean's in *On the Road*, Mardou's journey through poverty, prejudice, and madness leads to an embracing of life and its possibilities rather than a crippling cynicism. She explains that

> [being in the asylum] made me see the preciousness of really being out of there and out on the street, the sun, we could see ships, out and FREE man to roam around, how great it really is and how we never appreciate it all glum inside our worries and skins, like fools really, or blind spoiled detestable children because . . . they can't get . . . all . . . the . . . candy . . . they want. . . . (Kerouac 1989, 35)

Clearly, the characters of Leo and Sal represent those people walking about "all glum inside [their] worries and skins." As I mentioned earlier, Kerouac comes to see that the writer's life creates a barrier between him and the joy in existence expressed here by Mardou. In *The Subterraneans*, this barrier is described with great insight by Mardou rather than Kerouac's alter-ego, who is still trying to convince himself there may be some way to write and live authentically. Leo tries to argue that he has always wanted a pure and sweet existence, much as Kerouac does throughout his life:

> it was [Mardou] who later said "Men are so crazy, they want the essence, the woman is the essence, there it is right in their hands but they rush off erecting big abstract, constructions."—"You mean they should just stay home with the essence, that is lie under a tree all day with the woman but

Mardou that's an old idea of mine, a lovely idea, I never heard it better
expressed and never dreamed." (Kerouac 1989, 16–17)

However, even though he has thought about such an idyllic life, he
in the end returns to his work: "And so having had the essence of
her love now I erect big word constructions and thereby betray it
really ... (16–17). Thus, Leo/Kerouac/Sal is destined to spend his life
"creating big word constructions" rather than surrendering himself
to the rush of existence that is carrying Dean, Terry, and Mardou
along. Abandoning Mardou, all he can do is "write this book" (111).
Still, Kerouac gains suffering through his work, in which he betrays
the most intimate of secrets about himself, his prejudices, his friends
and his lovers. These betrayals bring him shame and pain, but as he
says in *The Subterraneans*, "work was my dominant thought, not
love—not the pain which impels me to write this even while I don't
want to, the pain which won't be eased by the writing of this but
heightened, but which will be redeemed ..." (18).

***

Art can never be a replacement for authenticity, but perhaps it
can give us the outlines of the path we are to follow. One could con-
vincingly argue that Kerouac romanticizes the life of the downtrod-
den, as well as his own life, but of course this may be the very point.
Creating fiction from autobiography is an act of conscious myth-
making. Sadly, for Kerouac, writing the meaning of life came at the
loss of fully experiencing it; yet, through this act of sacrifice to art
the writer may find his redemption.

Reading Kerouac and the Beats allows students an insight into
the opening up of American literature to new ethnic voices at mid-
century. Too, it reminds us that the movement from Anglo homo-
geneity in our country's literary tradition was a challenge to
American writers. Not always as "liberal" as we might wish today, the
Beats nevertheless voluntarily cast themselves into the vortex of cultural diversity long before it became socially acceptable. For this
they deserve our attention, our patience, and our gratitude.

Note

An earlier version of this essay was published in the April 1999 issue of *The Midwest Quarterly*.

Works Cited

Bartlett, Lee, ed. 1981. *The Beats: Essays in Criticism*. Jefferson, NC: McFarland.

Blackburn, William. 1977. "Han Shan Gets Drunk with the Butchers: Kerouac's Buddhism in *On the Road*, *The Dharma Bums*, and *Desolation Angels*." *Literature East and West* 21.1–4 (January-December): 9–22.

Blaise, Clark. 2000. "Kerouac in Black and White." *Ishmael Reed's Konch Magazine*, 2 March. Online. http://www.ishmaelreedpub.com/blaise1.html.

Charters, Ann. 1972. *Kerouac*. San Francisco: Straight Arrow.

Clark, Tom. 1984. *Jack Kerouac*. San Diego: Harcourt Brace Jovanovich.

Donaldson, Scott, ed. 1979. *On the Road: Text and Criticism*. New York: Viking.

Foster, Edward Halsey. 1992. *Understanding the Beats*. Columbia: University of South Carolina Press.

Ginsberg, Allen. 1990. "The Past Is the Root of the Future." In *Un Homme Grand: Jack Kerouac at the Crossroads of Many Cultures*, ed. Pierre Anctil, Louis DuPont, Remi Ferland, Eric Waddell. Ottawa: Carleton University Press.

Hesse, Herman. 1971. *Siddhartha*. New York: Bantam Books.

Johnson, Joyce. 1992. "from *Minor Characters*." In *The Portable Beat Reader*, ed. Ann Charters. New York: Penguin Books.

Keats, John. 1993. "To George and Thomas Keats." In *The Norton Anthology of English Literature*, vol. 2, ed. M.H. Abrams. New York: W.W. Norton.

Kerouac, Jack. 1976. *On the Road*. New York: Penguin Books.

———. *The Subterraneans*. 1989. New York: Grove Weidenfeld.

McNally, Dennis. 1979. *Desolate Angel: Jack Kerouac, the Beats, and America*. New York: Random House.

Nicosia, Gerald. 1983. *Memory Babe: A Critical Biography of Jack Kerouac*. New York: Grove.

Panish, Jon. 1993. "Kerouac's *The Subterraneans*: A Study of 'Romantic Primitivism.'" *Melus* 19 (3): 107–29.

Snyder, Gary. 1997. Personal interview. 21 February.

Stephenson, Gregory. 1979. *The Daybreak Boys: Essays on the Literature of the Beat Generation*. New York: Morrow.

Watson, Steven. 1995. *The Birth of the Beat Generation*. New York: Pantheon Books.

Weinrich, Regina. 1987. *The Aesthetics of Spontaneity: A Study of the Fiction of Jack Kerouac*. Carbondale: Southern Illinois University Press.

CHAPTER FIVE

A White Man in Love: A Study of Race, Gender, Class, and Ethnicity in Jack Kerouac's *Maggie Cassidy*, *The Subterraneans*, and *Tristessa*
Nancy McCampbell Grace

Jack Kerouac is generally not thought of as a writer of love stories, his name more readily evoking images of jazz, poetry, Buddhism, the boy gang, and cars zooming along the omnipresent road. But a considerable portion of his Duluoz legend is devoted to representations of women he loved. *Maggie Cassidy*, written in 1953, introduced the portrait of Mary Carney, an Irish girl who was his high school sweetheart. Later that same year he used *The Subterraneans* to record his brief but intense relationship with Alene Lee, an African-American woman whom he renamed Mardou Fox for purposes of publication. In 1955–56, he wrote *Tristessa*, a reflection upon Esperanza Tercerero, an Aztec-Hispanic morphine addict. Significantly, their stories are not road stories. All are set in spaces defined by corporation limits and the walls of tenement houses and Beat pads. Safe within domestic spheres and linguistic artifice, Kerouac dared to do what he dared not do elsewhere: masquerade as a *dark* female, the ultimate white male experimentation with forms of identity challenging the regulatory character of self as cultural formation.

This focus on color should not surprise readers of the Duluoz legend. As Kerouac wrote in *Lonesome Traveler* (1989, 39), the African-American was "the essential American." In many respects, Kerouac's fascination with race and ethnicity, conjoined with gender and class codes, addresses what Toni Morrison describes in *Playing in the Dark* (1993) as the white writer's expression of his/her dream through the presence of the black character. According to Morrison, the white writer throughout American literary history has used the story of the "Africanist presence," a black person as bound and/or rejected, to reflect on humanity, specifically the risky venture of exploring "one's own body in the guise of the sexuality, vulnerability, and anarchy of the other" (1993, 53). Kerouac engaged in this process through ficto-autobiography—repetitively confessing and reconstructing his own history through the imaginative rendering of memory.

In the love stories, this attention to color works not only to accentuate the black presence but also to conflate racial categories so that Kerouac's creation of dark characters not explicitly black, such as Maggie and Tristessa, encodes a subtext of "otherness" that speaks of the black experience as well as that of other marginalized groups. These forms complicate the story of race in America, demarcating and blurring boundaries of human cast and producing imbrications that defy our efforts to separate them. By so doing, the darkness of the Kerouacian female and her allegorical Africanist heritage become the allegory of Kerouac's own condition as a marginalized male, a masculine hybrid.

It's critical that we not lose sight of Kerouac's hybrid status. The commercialization of his image, especially his recent elevation to white-collar advertising icon, has all but erased his history as the French-speaking son of working class, French-Canadian Catholics in ethnically diverse Lowell, Massachusetts. But it's a history that bequeathed him a complicated identity, one which transformed his own Caucasian heritage into something of a sinister monolith, a force to be feared and shunned but nonetheless revered.

"White" has never been essentialist. It is an unstable historical and social category characterized by particular groups moving in

and out of its boundaries through the vagaries of legal codification.[1]
In the Lowell of Kerouac's youth, French-Canadians were more privileged than some who could not have the same "purity" of lineage. It
was a heritage Kerouac remained proud of all his life. But French
Canadians were also considered by many to be stupid and lazy. As a
result, they bore the brunt of a prejudice that labeled them *les
blancs negres* (Nicosia 1984, 15).[2] Complicating matters, Kerouac
claimed Irish and Native-American descent, an ancestral mix that,
whether actual or a product of family lore, aligned him with peoples,
long-denied personhood. Kerouac then grew up an ambivalent amalgamation, the maligned and homeless "Canuck," a hybrid of hybrids.

It is this identity, a paradoxically unstable and rigid formation,
that to a great extent propels the movement of his love stories. His
engagement with the Africanist presence fuels the project of self-
construction, drawing upon a host of linguistic strategies to flesh out
a consciousness that expresses distrust of all color markers, especially the label "white male." In particular, we find those strategies that
Toni Morrison identifies: economy of stereotype, metonymic displacement, metaphysical condensation, fetishization of race, dehistoricizing allegory, and patterns of disjointed, repetitive language
(1993, 67–69). All converge in images of the conflicted white man in
love with the dark woman.

To portray this female, Kerouac relied upon three character
types: the white goddess, the fellaheen, and the grotesque. The goddess appears as the "White American Woman," or "The Good Blonde"
as he named her in a short story of the same title. She is the founda-
tional block of his protean self, that which he must deify, reify, and
vilify as he wrestles with identity. Pure and beautiful, a trophy wife
or girlfriend signifying economic, social, and spiritual success, the
White American Woman is the converse of the blemishes and orifices of the (dys)functioning sexual and social body, negating the
mid-twentieth century American fear of corruption represented by
loose and domineering women, homosexuals, blacks, and other
"deviants." Her powers are illusionary, however. A pastiche of religious iconography and Hollywood celluloid, she reflects the antithetical cultural paradigms with which he existed: the pure asexuality of
the Virgin Mary merged with the more open and attainable sexuality
of the female movie star.

Kerouac juxtaposed the White American Woman with the fella-heen, or "wailing humanity" as he called them in *On the Road* (1979, 280). The fellaheen is a subset of the primitive, a category to which Western culture has historically relegated blacks, women, and the feminine. Presented discursively, the body of the primitive, particularly the female, is often constructed as oversexed, devious, diseased, irrational, voiceless, fit only to breed or labor. This is the subjected body, created through systemic practices of violence and ideology. In this respect, Kerouac's attraction to it replicates a Western pattern of using the primitive body to encode desires that we seek to repress, to sustain practices of domination and subordination. Specifically, Kerouac used the fellaheen to negotiate what he understood as the natural and supernatural. The interplay is complicated, the female fellaheen becoming the earthly substance with which, and the surface upon which, his narrators recognize their own flawed character. This includes their inability to actualize personal and cultural definitions of self as well as their attempts to resolve perceived disjunctions between hegemonic cultural practices and the nature of self, spirit, and world.

These images are conjoined with a pattern of structures known as grotesque realism, a social and literary phenomenon rooted in European folk culture. As a bodily category, the grotesque embraces the despised, exoticized, irregular, and incomplete. It also defines the body as a site of ideological codification. As Mikhail Bakhtin argues in *Rabelais and His World*, grotesque realism of the Renaissance period is identified with the "low" culture of carnival, comedy, and social rebellion and conceives of the body not as an individual unit but as a social body. Drawing upon metaphysical condensation to destroy the human oppressor, it blends with the world, animals, and objects, stressing the human mouth and the lower body parts which are open to the outside and undermine body/world dualism (1984, 27, 317). Later during the Romantic period, the grotesque as a literary phenomenon viewed the world as alien and terrifying. Reconciliation with the body occurred in a "subjective, lyric, or even mystic sphere" (1984, 39) stressing the triumph of the individual. Kerouac had a deeply felt propensity for both forms, perhaps a legacy of his Catholic Breton heritage nurtured through folk customs in French-speaking Lowell.

The grotesque, in combination with the fellaheen and the White American Woman, provides an ideal mechanism to create indeterminacy, open-endedness, counter-identification, and disidentification— all key elements in Kerouac's love stories. As the remainder of this discussion demonstrates, his ficto-autobiography, focused on the generating power of the dark female, adjusts the belief that he extolled white masculinity at the full expense of women and minority males. While his prose tends to commodify people of color and white women, it is simply too easy to label him racist and misogynist. The Duluoz legend presents a much more complex mapping of the human project.

Maggie Cassidy

Maggie Cassidy is the story of Kerouac's high school romance with a 17-year-old, working class, Irish girl. Told through the tightly woven perspectives of three Jacks (16, 20, and 32 years old), the book chronicles his courtship of Maggie from 1939, his last year at Lowell High where he is a star athlete, to 1943, the year he ships out as a merchant marine. Kerouac's Maggie is his first and purest love, a variant of the white goddess. While their story features no fellaheen women *per se*, his account of the relationship establishes imaginative patterns of the fellaheen and the grotesque that lay the groundwork for Mardou Fox, and Tristessa. *Maggie Cassidy* also exemplifies his ability to control the discipline of ficto-autobiography to such an extent that his conclusions about the social conditions of America surpass as authentic transformative rhetoric those of *The Subterraneans* and *Tristessa.* The book argues that those who refuse to defy the cultural formations of identity participate in the dehumanization of themselves and others.

In the first several chapters, Maggie, whom he meets on New Year Eve 1938, emerges as the sublime antithesis of young Jack's "Canuck half-Indian" gawkishness (1993, 30). Orchestrating the majestic language of romance, Jack presents a Janist-faced Maggie surviving in his memory as saintlike whiteness and ancient female darkness. He venerates her godlike whiteness, but it is her freckled ethnic body, her dark agrarian Irish ancestry which Jack believes he shares, that allows him freer play. Imagining himself inside her darkness, he discovers the possibility of potentialities which he expresses as a Whitmanesque catalogue of masculine roles. Some beautiful, some ugly, all the selves that he desires and despises—"her brother, husband, lover, raper, owner, friend, father, son, grabber, kisser, keener, swain, sneaker-upper, sleeper-with, feeler, railroad brakeman in red house"—he maps out on the dark interior of her body (1993, 77). This darkness, evoking the primitive exotic, is a force of beauty and elegance for Jack, the promise of self-knowledge and self-definition, a sign of maturity and manhood.

But the image of classic beauty quickly breaks down. Jack revises his initial impression of Maggie, remembering that she had appeared "small, thin, dark, unsubstantial" (1993, 36), thereby creating a desexualized female body, somewhat like, but a distorted form of, the saintly white body. The shape of sex, which threatens classical perfection, gives way to the body of the child. This manipulation has disturbing connotations (hints of the pedophile), especially because Maggie is so clearly a sexual being who attracts Jack just when his own sexuality is awakening. The image of the childlike dwarf may well reflect Jack's deflated sense of himself projected onto Maggie, a device to bond them in memory. It may also act as a barrier to protect them, at least in Jack's mind, from sexuality, the full expression of which was thwarted by pervasive courtship customs of the day and the doctrine of Irish and French-Canadian Catholicism, both of which conflate sex and love, allowing limited expression of love and demanding sexual abstinence by "good" girls and respect for this abstinence by "good" boys.

Consequently, the only recourse Jack and Maggie have when they begin to date is to neck and pet, integral components of the dating system when Kerouac was a teenager (Bailey 1998, 81). But their behavior is by no means chaste. Their response to the body and to the social codes controlling that body suggests a subterranean system defying mainstream tenets of identity. They practice a strange kissing ritual that involves chewing on each other, interchanging spittle, and sustaining the kiss until their muscles cramp and their lips crack and bleed (Kerouac 1993, 37). This grotesque image records an act of cannibalism, the acting out of the stereotypic "black" (i.e., sexual, sinful, immoral, lower class) to counter the "white" (i.e., nonsexual, good, moral, middle class), a socially acceptable way of having sex and not having sex.

Jack notes that neither he nor Maggie know why they do this, although they've heard that other teens do the same. He also speculates that the kisses are fueled by a "gigantic sexual drive" as well as "the fear of the world" (1993, 37). His hypothesis, a product of maturity and hindsight, is astute. When sex is subsumed by the romantic concept of love as holy, as it is for Jack and Maggie, when religious rites and class consciousness codify sex, we render the body something to be feared, especially the sexually awakening body. The world itself, which is their future represented through the body, also becomes an object of fear. Disfiguring the lover's perfect, untouchable mouth, consuming bits of each other, the young couple symbolically, and largely unwittingly, negate the culturally mandated restrictions of gender and sex roles, the isolation and impotence that accompany such restrictions. In other words, they coax each other into the world.

For Maggie, this means pleading with Jack to marry her and live with her in Lowell, a request that is not unreasonable. Maggie, who failed to complete junior high, has few opportunities other than that faced by generations of poor Irish girls: marry and have children, a condition upon which her own success as a woman depends. A part of Jack desperately wants to accept this future. Maggie's darkness, like the brown fellaheen glow that he associates with Lowell and uses as a watercolor wash throughout the book, is the aura of his ethnicity and working-class identity that he values and seeks to preserve. In this respect, his feelings are not unlike those of many ethnic individuals, whose intense desire to retain the heritage of family and country is buttressed by the fear of the larger "foreign" world in which the vulnerable ethnic group exists as a subpart, a component that faces diminution or obliteration through Americanization.

But Jack also associates marriage to Maggie with personal and cultural stagnation. If he marries her, he loses his childhood, family security, status as a star athlete, and freedom to hang out with his gang and to date other girls. Then, too, remaining in Lowell negates the middle-class aspirations of his parents, who, like millions of working-class Americans, plan a better life for their son, including the furthering of his education. Maggie's darkness, akin to the Lowell tenements stained with ethnicity and working-class identity, threatens this future. Paradoxically, then, Maggie comes to signify the absence of movement, of progress, of becoming.

As Maggie's world rushes in on him, Jack seeks to seal off the orifice through which it pulses, transforming her saintly darkness into the bestial grotesque: "a little darklashed lowered disbelief and nay, loose ugly grin of self-satisfied womanly idiocy-flesh, curl of travesty-cruelty" (1993, 92–93). He contemplates "ripping her mouth out," that is, denying her the world and life and then of murdering her which he admits wanting to do. But Jack can't kill Maggie. Hatred is converted into tenderness, which opens the door to the life-affirming, lower stratum of society, enabling him to both affirm Maggie's goodness and nullify her presence through imaginative reflection on their love. Conflating the temporality of his 16-year-old memory with the present, the narrator constructs a visionary tableau conjoining Christ's feet nailed to the cross and those of poor fellaheen workers who stand with "one foot on the other to keep warm" (1993, 41). This double image transmutes into Maggie and Jack himself. Ecce homo! Maggie, Jack, and the fellaheen become the grotesqueness of Jesus, his mutilated body, destroyed by human sin, embracing the depravity (grotesqueness) of the human condition and the potentiality (perfection) of redemption. Maggie, the horrific female, is subsumed into the gentle masculinity of the crucified Christ. This configuration is not the strict social life of the Renaissance grotesque as Bakhtin presents it but a rendering of the grotesque as a generative form pulling the supernatural down into the natural realm.

The passage positions Kerouac as a self-perceived outcast who cannot participate in the American dream of economic plenty, someone so marginalized, and fatalistically so, that he huddles outside the economic spectrum. This is a terribly bleak vision of the immigrant future and a sharp criticism of American political and economic beliefs. It also prompts us to question the processes by which a culture stratifies itself, certain subsets nurturing amongst other subsets feelings of inferiority through institutional practices (such as church doctrine) to maintain the hierarchy. However, legitimate as it may be, Jack's critique of American culture is somewhat disingenuous. Unlike the fellaheen, he has chosen to opt out of the dominant culture and can move back into it whenever he desires, a pattern in Kerouac's fiction for which he is legitimately criticized. Ironically, he is his most vocal critic, his narrators chastising themselves for lacking the strength to live as a fellaheen. But despite such self-awareness, he affirms his and his nation's own whiteness, i.e., the freedom to move at will, each time he rejects the fellaheen, which must be denied if others are to survive.

To this point, *Maggie Cassidy* reflects the narrator's polarized consciousness: his desire to distinguish himself as a white male from all other human beings and his need to eschew belief in the supremacy of the white male. However, the novel argues that both are possible, and may even work in concert, because of the African presence. This dynamic is revealed in the book's most dramatic episode, the 30-yard dash that Jack runs against an African-American male from nearby Worcester North High School. Significantly, the meet appears in the text soon after Jack contemplates killing Maggie. Social codes and his feelings for her prohibit direct attack, so he must find a surrogate whipping boy. The young man is John Henry Lewis, a name that evokes the fellaheen railroad worker of folk legend, John Henry. Throughout most of the episode, however, he is called "the Negro" or "the colored boy."

The track episode appears to be an amalgamation of two high school meets in which Kerouac participated in January 1939. The Lowell team competed against Worcester North on January 14. Kerouac set the pace for a team victory by winning the 30-yard dash, but he did not compete against an African-American runner. No African-Americans attended Worcester North at the time, and Kerouac's opponents in the dash were white students from Lowell. The second event, Lowell v. Worcester Commerce, was held on January 7 in Lowell. The Commerce team, which beat Lowell, included one African-American, Matthew Jenkins, a junior who ran the 30-yard dash, soundly beating Kerouac who placed third.[3] These events, as Kerouac restructured them, transform his defeat by an African-American into a victory signifying personal and cultural aggrandizement. Understandings of manhood, success, acceptance, and the future are all worked out by demonizing, glorifying, and humanizing this young black runner.

Jack fears being beaten by a black man, an event that would signal Jack's inferiority. He also wants desperately to protect his white city from invasion by the black foreigner, likening himself and Lewis to "warriors of two nations." To this end, his father encourages him. Emil Duluoz calls Lewis a "bastard" and denigrates him with racial stereotypes—"they're supposed to run like damn streaks! the antelopes of Africa!," instilling in Jack the mandate that he must beat back the terrifying presence of the dark continent, prove his manhood, and by implication legitimize his birthright as Emil's son and an American. Jack participates in this thinking, imagining Lewis as a grotesque lion with a reptilian head and "venom tiger eyes" (1993, 97, 101).

The race itself is a Homeric feat. Like Ulysses, Jack wins with physical skill and cunning. He beats the gun, just barely and legally (he believes) and just enough to fly past Lewis. As he does, he takes ownership of him, thinking of him as "my Negro, my Jim," an act of psychological enslavement created by fear of the black other. As slave master, he beats "his Negro," he recalls, not with muscle (or the body) but with the mind (the not-body) (1993, 103), emerging as a world conqueror, even surpassing, as his father tells him, the triumphs of another black man and national hero, Olympic gold-medallist Jesse Owens (1993, 111).

The process obliterates the life-threatening grotesque, maintains the status quo, and glorifies individual achievement. As the African presence, Lewis embodies the enslavement and degradation from which Jack must run if he is to escape Lowell. Then, too, as the grotesque as cultural symbol, Lewis personifies the threat of anarchy, the destruction of the known social order, and the immanent breakdown of the separation of the individual (white) ego from the body of low (black) culture. A subpart of this dynamic also amplifies sexuality, the competition metaphorically suggesting that white male conquest of the white woman, that is, Jack's power over Maggie, is propped up by his conquest of the black man.

But the narrative resists the false ideology of separating the body from the world. Although Jack says that he legally beats the gun, a reader might suspect that the white youth had an unfair advantage. We also know that Maggie does not witness the race; she's across town at a dance with another man. Without her presence and knowledge of his victory, Jack's defeat of Lewis fails to defeat Maggie. In addition, the implied narrator denies racial essentialism, acknowledging that his youthful concept of race has been fed in part by the "circuses and unclean magazines" (1993, 98) of popular culture. "[Y]our exotic is just a farmer," the older, wiser narrator tells his younger self, "he goes to church . . . has a father, brothers as well as you . . ." (1993, 103).

If the book were to stop here, we could declare that the African presence as literary device envisions the real lives of African-Americans. It doesn't, however. The narrator returns John Henry Lewis to the status of a channel for self-expression, likening the runner's physical gestures to those of early bop musicians. Lewis becomes the older Kerouac's personal iconography, the embodiment of revolutionary, hip, and ultramodern art. The image of creativity, rebellion, and heroism in the face of social denigration is more positive than that of the slave, but it is still romantic racism dehumanizing Lewis. As such, it illustrates what Morrison sees in the tortured conclusion of *The Adventures of Huckleberry Finn*, the simulation and description of the parasitical nature of white freedom (57).

Kerouac sustains his literary meditation on white and black in the remainder of the novel through memories of the disintegration of Jack's relationship with Maggie. Three key scenes emerge: Jack's 17th-birthday party, the Horace Mann prom, and the couple's last meeting in 1943. Elements of the grotesque dominate each, but it is the birthday party that incorporates the carnival aspect of the grotesque as one of the most powerful critiques of dehumanization. A form of spectacle commemorating official celebratory days, carnival sits on the border between art and life and is shaped by patterns of play, such as laughter, clowns and fools, equalization, and temporary liberation from prevailing truth and established order (Bakhtin 1984, 7). The party, taking place on March 12, the cusp of winter/death and spring/life, encompasses all of these. There's game playing, gift giving, drinking, sexual foreplay, and the raucous sounds of French *joual* mixing with English. Everyone is in high spirits except Jack who cannot accept Maggie's flirting with his friends and father. He becomes a jealous anticlown, his illusions—personal, social, and relationally bound—barring him from renewing life with Maggie through spectacle.

To illuminate the process, Kerouac used phenomena in his own life, two newspaper photographs documenting his party exposing them as devices by which culture constructs restrictive templates of self-identity. The camera, as Kerouac shows us, is used to manipulate a reality grounded not in objectivity or an *a priori* essence but in the narratives we use to make meaning—and thus the self. Aware of this, Jack refuses to smile for the camera, but the resultant images are no less false. In *The Lowell Sun*, he looks like "a moronic . . . unnamably abnormal beast of a boy" surrounded by family members sentimentally arranged to protect him. In *The Evening Leader*, he stares at the world like a "Greek athlete hero with curly black locks, ivory white face" (1993, 142). Neither is an impartial reflection of reality nor a purely subjective impression of reality. Both represent a self based on a complex tapestry of public discourses prescribing masculinity, each reflecting identities recognizable to Jack. Together they speak to the fluid and fragmentary nature of subjectivity.

Upon seeing the photos, Jack prefers classical beauty to the grotesque because it better suits his dream of wealth and fame. But he also senses that the classic image is falsely grounded in ego and isolation, thereby prohibiting him from enjoying life-affirming carnival and acting like his pal Iddyboy, another French-Canadian youth who without Jack's dreams of masculine greatness punctuates the party with a cry of "lifeloving girlhugging fencecrashing hungry satisfaction . . ." (1993, 143). Iddyboy's outburst is a trademark signal of Kerouac's affinity for the fellaheen. It compels him to seek time and again those who defy the determinacy of a future structured through economic success, family, and dour regimentation—those with "the biggest laugh" he'd ever heard. Carnival, after all, doesn't happen just once; it must be ritually repeated.

Awareness is no guarantee of action, however, and Jack's failure to embrace carnival signals his decision to leave Lowell and Maggie to seek his future at the Horace Mann School where he's to play football and prepare to enter Columbia. His first night in the city, he contemplates what he calls his "post-Iddyboy" future, an idiomatic expression for postgrotesque, postethnic, and post-Maggie. He sees himself as an "American Super Dream Winner, Go Getter, Wheel," wearing a snow-white scarf, conversing in white dialogue balloons, and married to a sexy blonde of "starry perfection." The whiteness of American masculinity and superiority introduces his ultimate fantasy: his desire to rewrite the history of two dark worlds—Africa and Spain (1993, 166–68). It's not by chance that his vision unites sexual and economic success and dominance over the African. In the American imagination, these are necessary for freedom and self-hood, concepts built upon the systemic and institutionalized belief in the inferiority of women and people of color, especially African-Americans. But it is also significant that Kerouac places himself in a cartoonish, Hollywood scenario, thereby sustaining his critique of the dream as shallow and artificial.

The conclusion of the book relentlessly pursues the shattering of American whiteness. The process is set in motion when Jack invites Maggie to his spring prom. Kerouac's telling of the event accurately portrays the commodity-driven character of middle-class dating in the late thirties and early forties. He bluntly recounts that wealthy white fathers buy the accoutrements of beauty so their white daughters can be "purchased," or dated, by white men (1993, 180). Maggie and Jack, described as darker-skinned, contrast sharply with the sophisticated city couples whose class is encoded in color: masculine whiteness by the urbane language of Horace Mann's Jewish crowd, feminine whiteness by powder and jewels. Plainly, Jack and Maggie are out of their league, and, equally as plain, the whiteness of Jack's chosen world is false.

The text fails to present a meta-discursive analysis of how language perpetuates patterns of domination, but the brief linking of whiteness and Jews suggests that Jewish whiteness is a construction like other forms of race and that Jack harbors feelings of inferiority and resentment toward Jews. The text also hints that Jack's own non-whiteness, a bright red face created by his egotistical misuse of a sunlamp, may be false as well, a sign that he remains ambivalent about both his white and non-white identities.

Unable to fully use his own body to confront oppressive cultural formations of identity, Jack claims Maggie's naturally tawny body as the symbol of social and racial inequity. As Jack explains in perhaps the book's most perceptive passage, Maggie can't compete with the Horace Mann women because the interplay of class and color keeps her from knowing "it was done or how to do it or *how to know* [emphasis mine]" (1993, 180). Forms and practices of knowledge are denied her. The union of class, race, and ethnicity creates a glittery white costume masking natural "blemishes and freckles" (1993, 180) and exists as the pinnacle of a human hierarchy only because others are denied access through disadvantage and ignorance, falsely led to believe that their economic and racial/ethnic identity imply innate moral deficiency and personal failure. Whiteness becomes a class charade; race is nothing more than class in fancy dress.

Maggie intuits this and urges Jack to return to Lowell. But her speech, less that of a working-class Irish girl than it is Kerouac's own language, is laced with a rush of lyrical images and elliptical syntax characteristic of Jack's self-reflexivity. Appropriating her mouth, creating her voice, he prophesies his own future: "O Jacky come home have Christmases with me"; if not, "[y]ou'll burn yourself out like a moth jumping in a locomotive boiler looking for light" (1993, 184). The warning goes unheeded. As the narrative advances three years, we learn that Jack has left school, is working in a Lowell parking garage while waiting to ship out with the merchant marines, and has become mean-spirited. He meets Maggie and tries to have sex with her, but he's too drunk to perform. The scene, a pathetic reversal of the earlier one in which he imagined her body as a fecund text from which he can become everyman, signals the falsity of his decision to privilege the white, middle-class, masculine world. He is left bereft. Life, the dark woman, laughs at him and walks away.

The Subterraneans and Tristessa

Despite the grim conclusion of *Maggie Cassidy*, Kerouac held onto the possibility of finding the dark woman. Rather than succumb to the role of passive, cynical spectator, he retained a more romantic belief in the power of self-agency and the dream of a classless America. In *The Subterraneans* and *Tristessa*, this vision is strengthened as the white American woman fades into the background, replaced by the fellaheen woman and race mixing. This focus is especially noteworthy considering that Kerouac wrote both books in the early fifties, a time when anti-miscegenation laws still existed in more than fifteen states. Even California, the setting for *The Subterraneans*, had not overturned its law until 1948 and upheld a firm invisible social code against interracial relationships, as did the rest of the country.

The Subterraneans is a gnarled and naked confessional centered on the intersection of race, class, and personal autonomy. It is more complex and self-aware than *Tristessa*, a short, bifurcated story favoring elliptical lyricism rather than self-reflection. But both share themes and formal structures, including first-person narrators who are again thinly veiled avatars of Kerouac, now a middle-aged writer riddled with self-loathing and disenchanted with the narrow-mindedness of white, middle-class, postwar America. Each narrator appears plagued with "sin," and while the specific sin remains unclear, it is evident that each believes his gender, race, and ethnicity to have left him much for which to atone. He is faced with a choice: elect a life of hatred and self-disgust or act to redeem himself and his nation. Each chooses the latter, acting on the critique of American culture that is the legacy of *Maggie Cassidy* by taking to the road in search of a new home and a new woman.

Leo Percipied settles with Mardou in the Beat underground of San Francisco; Jack Duluoz meets Tristessa in the slums of Mexico City. As the stories unfold, the fellaheen woman becomes the conduit through which the narrators find respite from obligation, regimentation, routinization, and inequality, acting as a metaphor for democracy, offering the gift of personal and social progress through the image of the embracing lovers. Love is not enough, however, to transform both the narrator and America. Leo and Jack cannot move beyond the nuanced consciousness with which Jack Duluoz concludes *Maggie Cassidy*, and they ultimately disconnect from the embrace to reestablish the supremacy of the white male and his predominance as a writer, in the process acting out Kerouac's understanding of the self as both fluid and centered.

Initially, Mardou and Tristessa represent the covenant of social regeneration through the social body, acquiring this power through membership in the "low" culture of the grotesque. Ostracized from family and friends, rejected as inferior because of their race and sex, they live on the borderland with deviants, clowns, and the unwanted. Their very bodies are the badge of membership. Mardou's is black and small, wracked by drug and alcohol use, psychic breakdown, male violence, and sexual excess. Tristessa's is even more distorted. Her Aztec ancestry is the brown veneer for a sarcophagus of rotting flesh housing the bones of a woman so addicted to morphine she can barely walk or talk. Their faces are dark flat screens upon which Jack and Leo envision a panorama of fellaheen images signifying equality and freedom.

   Both women project a freakish quality, and a reader may have difficulty thinking of them as "grotesque" without substituting the term
"freak." This slip is not inappropriate. "Freak" has a contemporary
social dimension relevant to Kerouac's use of the grotesque. The tradition of the freak as monster has a long history in European culture, but
freakishness, radically democratic and open to individualistic self-
appropriations of class, race, ethnicity, gender, and sexuality, is a distinctly U.S. style of social dissent, manifesting itself most distinctly in
the fifties as the Beat underground and then finding full form in the
1960s (Russo 1994, 75). This tradition of freak encompasses both the
"freak of nature" and the "freak of culture." Mardou and Tristessa are
born to the narrator as "freaks of nature," physically different from
what he has known. Because they are part of the Beat culture ("beat"
as Herbert Hunke used it, meaning "beaten down," and "beat" as
Kerouac defined it, signifying "beatific"), they are also "freaks of culture," lonely, despised, and misunderstood by a society that denies
them a legitimate place at its table. Relegated to the periphery, their
beauty and humanity are visible to only a few truth seekers, in particular, the Kerouacian narrator who thrills at the sight of "actual" freaks,
women unlike any other he has every seen, envisioning himself as
them or in solidarity with them. Through their excesses—their
criminal behavior, sexual promiscuity, flips, vulnerable childlike bodies, even the strangeness of Mardou's intelligence—Kerouac builds
the body of his own mind, one so "criminal" that he cannot reveal it
except through feminine masquerade.
   Of the two, Mardou is the more complex and therefore her role
as grotesque social body more complicated. Intelligent, well read,
independent, perceptive, feisty, and physically strong, she is as tangible as Leo, and he respects her as much as he does his male friends
and heroes who have suffered and endured. He perceives her as a
redeemer, a young, "cool," black subterranean symbolizing his entry
into San Francisco's intellectual, jazz-oriented *avant garde*. This
"coolness" is a modern version of the stereotype of black women as
exotics: Mardou as a beautiful yet distorted female blends elements
of the masculine and feminine, the forbidden and the desired, into an
exciting curiosity. When he begins to date her, possessing her body
and appropriating her "otherness," he joins a younger, hipper group,
shedding a self that he defines as aging and isolated; a dumb "Canuck"

who can barely control the English language, his sexuality, or his huge ego; a marginalized ethnic racist with no self-confidence. In this respect, Leo fetishizes Mardou's blackness, not in the sense defined by rigorous psychoanalytic theory but rather as a magical device that will transfigure him into his vision of the essential American.

As much as he would like to decenter whiteness and replace it with blackness, however, he remains a white male seeing others from this standpoint. His entry into the hip underground is conditioned by at least a slim tether connecting him to the white world of his ethnicity and the fantasy of the White American Woman. From the moment he meets Mardou, he whitens her. She reminds him of a white girl he knew in high school and about whom he had sexual fantasies. He also finds charming her new bop generation language which he describes as part "Negro highclass," part white, educated, beautiful rich girl language (Kerouac 1958, 10). This speech, also fetishized in her tiny, crooked front teeth through which she makes a "gleeful little shniffle" (1958, 37), establishes Mardou's race and sex as a magical bridge of carnivalesque rebirth between white and black cultures.

Consistent with this connection is the code whereby he enters the underground: he must establish himself as a sexually dominant white male. He first competes for Mardou with two white male friends, Julian Alexander (Kerouac's friend Lucian Carr) and Adam Moorad (the poet Allen Ginsberg). If he wins her love, he has defeated them (1958, 19). Second, he competes with a black male, effecting a defeat as grand as young Jack Duluoz's defeat of John Henry Lewis and Jesse Owens—he beats the black bop genius Charlie "Bird" Parker. Leo achieves victory through parasitic subordination and humiliation of the black man, remembering Parker "distinctly digging Mardou several times" (1958, 19) at a club where they go to see him perform. Leo notes that Bird's look is not challenging, but the explanation implies that in his own mind a battle has taken place, and the white man has won, wresting away the black man's property: the body and love of a black woman. Leo, however, can't live as this kind of oppressor. Highly conscious of America's history of racial conflict—and of his own uneasy position as a white man in a racially divided society, he experiences racial guilt which he struggles to placate. Quickly erasing his domination of Bird, he images him as a gentle god with the power to foretell the demise of Leo's relationship with Mardou (1958, 20). While still a dehumanizing act (Bird as god is just as much a mechanism for Leo's new identity as is Bird the defeated lover), the image assuages racial guilt and restores to Bird a kind of power that the latter denied him.

Leo is well aware that by dating Mardou he breaks a social taboo, one so powerful that even some of his hip friends, such as Adam, choose not to violate it. The consequences are high. White America has long perpetuated potent romantic narratives founded on racial prejudice, and Leo has a great deal invested in such narratives. If he marries Mardou, his dream of living the Faulknerian life of a great white gentleman writer in the South will be destroyed. So will the romance of his own family. His mother, to whom he is deeply attached and for whom he feels responsible, will reject a black Cherokee daughter-in-law (1958, 62). So too will his sister and her Southern husband, with whom Leo may have to live. Unable to give up these particular dreams, he is, nevertheless, brave enough to break the taboo in part because of the benefits accrued by being with Mardou. Not inconsequentially, one of these is the opportunity to deal with his "race problems." In this respect, Kerouac's use of Mardou's body, the physical signifier of the human creation of (dis)privilege, functions as an intimation of human regeneration and social progress, a personal example of the larger civil rights movement gaining momentum in the fifties. His acceptance of her body, which an apartheid-based society has designated grotesque, as well as all else that constitutes her, professes faith in the human power to overcome prejudice and recognize our common human face.

Most dramatic is the way Leo deals with his fear that blacks are sexual mutants, manipulating the grotesque image of the regenerating social body to illustrate its more modern alienating form. For example, he imagines that her genitals are "a black thing ... hanging" (1958, 63), a grotesque illusion with its hint of the hermaphrodite that repulses him. He confesses his fear, and although his articulation of it brings her pain (and, admittedly, to many readers as well), the risk pays off. She allows him to examine her, and by challenging the stereotype, they destroy the myth of black biological inferiority, concluding that black women are not pernicious (1958, 63). Unfortunately, Kerouac fails to treat black males the same. Those few who appear in the narrative are described as sexual perverts who expose themselves to Mardou (1958, 45–46). These images remain unexamined, standing as a grave injustice to black men in general and underscoring the cultural practice of hiding prejudice in the guise of "unbiased" reporting of someone else's experiences. But to his credit, Leo remains sensitive to Mardou's race-based experiences, enabling her to teach him about the perverse webbing that binds gender, skin privilege, and social codes of behavior.

Unbeknownst to Mardou, however, Leo also relies upon her body, voice, and personal history to achieve a complex dissolution of his consciousness producing a fusion with all life forms and a sermon on the condition of the American fellaheen. Reporting stories Mardou has told him about her past, he creates subnarratives tightly woven throughout the central narrative of their affair. The subnarratives are composed of Mardou's quoted speech, Leo's third-person paraphrases, and his own rhapsodic improvisational monologue. At times, the voice he creates for her is distinctly Kerouacian. As in *Maggie Cassidy*, Kerouac makes little effort to distinguish the vocabulary and syntax of the female from his own. For instance, when Mardou wonders why anyone would want to harm her, it is unquestionably Leo's (or Kerouac's) poetic voice shaping this fear: "I quaked when the giver creamed, when my father screamed, my mother dreamed—I started small and ballooned up and now I'm big and a naked child again and only to cry and fear" (36). This is not to negate Mardou's feelings of vulnerability. Rather it underscores the tendency of the narrative to displace the dark female with the narrator's own psychological state. This predisposition produces a doubling effect, confirmed when Leo realizes that he and Mardou are so alike that she is his sister (1958, 71).

Critical to this process is Leo's understanding that since Mardou never knew her parents she grew up with "no belief and . . . no place to get it from" (Kerouac 1958, 22). Mardou, however, projects beliefs with each word she speaks, so it is not difficult to infer what Leo has done: interpret her past to license himself to write his own version of her history. Her oppression and liberation become his, and he is free to play with them at will. His imaginative encounter with her body comprises a metaphysical journey highlighting the impermanence of self and other. This theme dominates the narrative. Mardou as individual gives way to Mardou as racial and historical concept, warping into Mardou as surrogate male of color and then Mardou as white male Canuck Leo. The result is what Toni Morrison calls dehistoricizing allegory: the civilizing process as vast and indefinite, something "taking place across an unspecified infinite amount of time" (1958, 68) thus excluding history, both personal and cultural, as a process of becoming.

Two passages illustrate this most clearly, both relying upon forms of the Romantic grotesque locating regeneration in a space both private and sublime. In the first, Leo focuses on Mardou's accounts of her history and suffering. As he listens, her contorted frame grows into "the background for thoughts about the Negroes and Indians and America in general but with all the overtones of 'new generation' and other historical concerns" (Kerouac 1958, 27). Situating the hipsters of the fifties against the huge canvas of the oppression of people of color in the United States, he contemplates the significance of the new underground and his own place in it. Mardou dissolves into the panorama of the American West, framing Leo's vision of the horror of white America's destruction of its own dark people, the nameless "wraiths of humanity treading lightly the surface of the ground so deeply suppurated with the stock of their suffering you only have to dig a foot down to find a baby's hand" (1958, 29). Pulling himself out of the reverie, he refocuses on the immediacy of her small body, the momentary destruction of time and space, through vicarious terror and redemption, bringing them closer together.

Leo depends upon this process which we see again when he retells Mardou's story about a shop where she encounters a man in a wheelchair surrounded by animals. The story delineates the life-affirming grotesque transformation down into the not human and the subsequent generation up into the *spiritus mundi*. Most of the passage appears as choppy verbatim quoting of Mardou, the twisted language an analogue of her physical and psychic grotesqueness. Punctuating the narrative are long asides in which Leo improvises upon the story. The first parenthetical contains a magical point of liminality portending a mystical denouement: Mardou passes through a doorway into a room filled with caged birds. She wants to stand in the cool green jungle of the story and communicate with the birds through their "birdy terror, the electric spasms of their . . . squawk, lawk, leek" (Kerouac 1958, 40–41). Mardou's proximity to their life-

filled mouths prepares her to talk with the man, which facilitates her
connection to the ethereal expanse of human wisdom. At this point,
she ceases to exist as an individual for Leo who in response spins out
a rhapsodic vision of her as a holy Negro Joan of Arc, who on a fine
Easter day, the promise of resurrection in the air, mutates into the city
of San Francisco, its history and multicultural citizenry. Her blackness,
and thus her martyrdom, becomes a mystical force balanced with the
whiteness of the city. Together, they empower Leo to call forth the
specter of her father, a fellaheen shadow of himself (1958, 44). The
possibility of social reformation, the destruction of the barrier
between Leo and the world of the oppressed, the eradication of his
and his nation's racial guilt, becomes actualized truth for him.

Two years later, living in Mexico City and writing *Tristessa*,
Kerouac remained transfixed with this concept of truth. It is not
insignificant that the narrative, highly confessional with little plot or
character development, is set outside the United States in a place
where racial distinctions appear less prevalent. Jack's Mexico City is
the heart of fellaheen country, a land cut off from the social hierarchy dominating the United States. In *On the Road*, he calls Mexico
the place where we "will finally learn ourselves" (1979, 280), and in
Tristessa, one of those lessons seems to be that since America has
failed its own people a classless society is possible only where the
illusions of black and white blend and are negated by brown.

Tristessa, presented as the brown fusion of Maggie and Mardou,
the amalgamation of Billie Holliday, Ava Gardner, and the Viennese
actress Louise Rainer (Kerouac 1960, 8), embodies this exotic ideal,
which is rooted in the grotesque negation of the pristine and sanitized. Everywhere he looks, Jack sees the despised and deviant. All
live on the streets or in tiny, filthy rooms. Tristessa's home is no different. It's littered with garbage and inhabited by her pimp El Indio, her
sick sister, a dove on the mantelpiece, a cat, a hen, a rooster, and a
howling Chihuahua "pooch bitch" (1960, 14). The mouth and the genitals form the center of this grotesque world. The kitten mews and
pees; the dove makes leery human teeth-grins; the dog yelps in heat;
the cock screeches; the sister moans and vomits; El Indio jabs needles
into gaping holes in his arms; and Tristessa pleads for sex. It is a hellish zone into which the refuse of the "straight" world has been
poured, and Tristessa's body is the dark hole around which the debris

swirls, including Jack himself. Jack gives himself up to the dark vortex, believing that in the very pit of human misery there resides the truest form of human life. At first, he perceives it as a "golden movie" of his own creation, an illusion of no substance. But by giving himself up to it, accepting its "inside-outness," he opens the way for rebirth through the destruction of illusion. Participation in the social world is possible because he can imagine Tristessa's hellish room not simply as dark, desperate, and evil but tinted with Rabelasian comedy, especially self-mockery and animal/human transfusion.

The latter is expressed most consistently through Jack's association of Tristessa with the kitten in her room whose tiny, flea-bitten body encapsulates her goodness and suffering. As Jack thinks about and cares for the kitten, he does the same for Tristessa. The boundaries between her body and the kitten's vanish, the distance between Jack and Tristessa melts away. But he also mocks himself as a clown whose silly earnestness and naiveté convince him to make friends with all these creatures with whom Tristessa lives. He negates his own high-mindedness in a comic scene in which Tristessa's rooster and hen are metamorphosed into a cartoonish human couple, Mr. and Mrs. Gazookas. The "Mr." chuckles and yells; the "Mrs." wears an adjustable hat draped over her beak (Kerouac 1960, 20). In both cases, animal, woman, and man become consubstantial, the shade of death mutating into birth. Life and joy pour in.

These visions hold all that the Kerouacian narrator has searched for, but couldn't find, in other places and with other women, and in one of Kerouac's most exalted examples of grotesque metamorphosis, Tristessa transcends them all, rivaling Christ himself. Struggling to make Jack understand that she prefers friendship to money, she pantomimes sex by crudely pumping her loins in the air. The act is a sign of sterility, a sad reminder that the only love she has known is that of a man who "give[s] it to her in the bed" (Kerouac 1960, 53). But as Jack watches, her pathetic gesture emerges as an image of the Annunciation. Standing with her legs spread, her vagina covered by her skirt but implicitly open to the world, Tristessa extends herself to the spirit of life which fills her being and radiates out from the crown of her head in the shape of innumerable hands (1960, 57). At that moment, she is a bodhisattva and an angel.

This passage, typical of Kerouac's maneuvering of the female body throughout his fiction, illustrates his inability to sustain the earthly exuberance of the Renaissance grotesque and his tendency toward the Romantic lyricism of spiritual fulfillment. Pulled by the forces of a Catholic mentality and his study of Buddhism, his narratives resist the physicality of the body, and thus his own humanity. Of special repugnance is his sexuality which for both Jack and Leo is a prehistoric, masculine menace to themselves and others. The tendency to seek escape from the body and sexuality is channeled primarily through images of Mardou and Tristessa as the Virgin Mary. The dark woman is elevated into the realm of classical perfection where she exists as the very source of the *mysterium tremendum*, the pure and suffering Stabat Mater weeping at the sight of her crucified son. But this same fantasy also magnifies and sustains her grotesqueness. Even in virginal glory, Tristessa and Mardou remain pastiches of female ideals holding within themselves the destruction of the sublime. Their otherness, as black and Mexican, drug addict and psychotic, as womb and vagina, is so antithetical to the classic, asexual female iconography of the Virgin Mary that the narrator is repulsed by them. The fantasy of the Madonna imparts but momentary salvation, and he is left imprisoned and isolated, cut off from any woman with whom he can establish community.

The fragility of Kerouac's connection to the social body of equality is underscored by his manipulation of Tristessa's behavior after her apotheosis. At this point, she declares them nothing, pointing a finger at Jack and saying "you." Kerouac records a phonetic representation of her Hispanic accent that renders "you" as "Jew." In other words, you/Jew who are outcast, you/Jew who are despised, you/Jew who are condemned to wander the earth in search of a home. Jack faces himself as the dark-skinned Jew and sees "two empty phantoms of light . . . ghosts in old haunted-house stories . . . white and not-there" (1960, 57). This white nothingness is a specter of self-negation, the emptiness of not only the calm Buddhist mind but also the white Catholic self who fears damnation and annihilation. In this sense, *Tristessa* becomes an extension of Jack's psyche, an expression of his abjection, his self-loathing, and his condemnation of American culture.

Such darkness cannot long withstand the light of day. In both books, the blurring of the body politic, the fluidity and fragmentation of the grotesque, the possibility of equality and democracy itself, terrify the narrators, threatening their desire for a unified self and the cultural milieu in which that self exits. The white, masculine writer faces extinction if he sustains identification with the freak and female. The dark female must be obliterated if the narrators are to be reborn and to survive.

In *The Subterraneans*, Leo begins the process by returning Mardou to that which he had initially feared: the evil black female. Leo knows it's wrong, but he can't stop himself from thinking of her as a "Negress" thief, a sexual deviant bent on destroying all men (Kerouac 1958, 104). The sad irony here, which Kerouac recognizes, is that Leo's identity as a white male depends upon the demonization of the black woman. As long as she remains human, he remains enslaved. His fear of her, which he correlates with emasculinization, is so exaggerated that at one point he compares them to characters in Tennessee Williams's "Desire and the Black Masseur," a grisly story about race and sadomasochism. Leo identifies with Anthony Burns, the white, child-like homosexual in the story who, as a way of atoning for feelings of inferiority and racial guilt, becomes erotically addicted to beatings by a nameless Negro masseur, who harbors free-floating hatred of all whites. The masseur, whom Leo likens to Mardou, finally kills Burns, eats his flesh, and then drops a bag filled with his bones into a lake (1958, 68). The significance of this allusion cannot be underestimated. Leo, by transforming Mardou into a nameless, faceless, black man of unrestrained brutality, eradicates all that is real and good about her, exposing his deep fear that white heterosexual masculinity will be annihilated through intimacy with a black woman. He will die if he does not subdue this dark "unnatural" presence, if he cannot find a way to return to the asexual and isolating world of white masculine work (1958, 57).

The destruction of Mardou as an object of love is completed in the comic pushcart episode which begins with a nightmare Leo has in which Mardou cuckolds him with his friend Yuri Gligoric (the poet Gregory Corso). In the dream, the whole world, including the living and the dead (Kerouac 1958, 85), surrounds their bed where Leo lies naked, stinking fish heads besieging him and gigantic big blue flies biting him. Yuri and Mardou make love, and Leo wakes up just as he hits Mardou and tackles Yuri. The images of alienating grotesqueness, especially his battering of Mardou, foreshadow the night when Yuri steals a pushcart, uses it to taxi them home, and leaves it in front of Adam's apartment. Comedy quickly erupts. Adam and Leo overreact, lecturing each other in self-impressed style on the morality of the act, and slapstick breaks out as they throw their keys at each other. But in this case, comedy does not produce social transformation. The dream and the pushcart theft trigger in Leo deep feelings of jealousy. His fear, an extension of his fantasy that Mardou is a sexually perverted destroyer of white men, compels him to push her away. He unjustly blames her femaleness and blackness for his own inadequacies, until she and Yuri finally "make it together," the coupling of their bodies signifying the final betrayal. When Leo learns about the cuckolding, his own body becomes terrifying: "the lower part of my stomach sagged into my pants or loins and the body experienced a sensation of deep melting down—going into some soft somewhere, nowhere—" (1958, 148). Mardou's body of betrayal renders Leo's own body a parallel grotesque and their relationship impossible.

In *Tristessa*, Jack's relationship with the fellaheen woman is doomed long before he ever meets her. Metaphorically, the text suggests that democracy and self-improvement cannot be achieved in a place apart. The farther one goes from the social body of one's origin, the farther one gets from meaningful progress, certainly from the symbolic fecundity of love. Tristessa's sordid history, especially the abuse of her body, signifies that she is incapable of loving anyone. Jack has no control over her addiction which destroys her mind to the point where he likens her to an Aztec witch threatening to kill him. His deification of her and his belief that he loves her are worthless anodynes, and as she becomes more maniacal, her body begins to implode. In Part 1, she has convulsions, and in Part 2, her entire body, particularly the lower stratum, becomes ghastly: her arms covered with cysts and one leg completely paralyzed (Kerouac 1960, 65). She eventually collapses, her head crashing against the ground, blood trickling out of her nose and mouth. The head, carrying the essential grotesque orifice of the mouth, moves downward past the womb and anus to the very ground from which the body springs.

The collapse is unquestionably a symptom of the physical death that she carries within her body. Symbolically, this linking of life and death signals the Renaissance rejuvenation of the social body and/or the Romantic transcendence of the individual into the sublime. Jack now rejects both. Tristessa doesn't literally die, but he manipulates her body so that in a metaphoric sense she does die, or more accurately, he kills her. First, he observes that Tristessa "has no body at all, it is utterly lost in its skimpy dress." Then he reports that Tristessa declares that she doesn't want love (Kerouac 1960, 91). The combination of his vision and Tristessa's words effectively negates her presence. Orifices through which the world can enter the body no longer exist, since the narrator has obliterated the body through his presentation of it. Jack cuts himself off from the social body promising redemption, freedom, equality, and communal acceptance.

Jack and Leo finalize their escape from the redemptive body of the female by transforming themselves into a grotesque. Each becomes a freak of the freaks, a paranoid and hypermasculinized buffoon who abuses and abandons his love, condemning himself as unworthy and berating himself for not loving them enough. Returning to self-loathing and passivity, he falls into the role of a spectator watching his own orchestration of his own destruction. The pattern is introduced in *Maggie Cassidy* when Jack as a callous merchant seaman attempts to force sex on Maggie who rejects him. It is extended in *The Subterraneans* and *Tristessa* as the narrator is rejected by the freaks themselves, who in turn, pursue and torment him: Mardou and Yuri have an affair, and Mardou chooses independence over Leo. Tristessa also rejects Jack for another addict, choosing impotence and drugs over love.

But unlike *Maggie Cassidy*, which leaves Jack with only his own disgusting behavior, *The Subterraneans* and *Tristessa* present the narrator's freakishness as a self-constructed device for change and growth. Each concludes with the narrator newly formed as an agent of creation: Leo goes home to write the story of his love for Mardou, and Jack heads to Sicily and Arles to rewrite the legend of his life. Both are left alone in the freak show audience where they view the female as a celluloid sideshow, the illusion of freedom and equality which they look upon with a certain degree of sadness and guilt and then discard. With relief, the white male narrator takes off his mask as woman of color and exposes the face of a new man. With all its blotches and blemishes, inadequacies and infirmities, it's by no means perfect. But it's all he has. And it's enough with which to write a book.

Notes

1   For example, the 1705 Virginia "act concerning servants and slaves" stated that "no negroes, mulattos and Indians or other infidels or jews, Moors, Mahometans or other infidels shall, at any time, purchase any christian servant, nor any other except of their own complexion" (Rothenberg 1998, 102). In 1938, the Louisiana State Supreme Court ruled that "Negro" was the only definition of color and that Filipinos were not colored but white (Fuchs 1990, 140). A much less visible form of the mercurial definition of "white" appears in Al Hinkle's account of finding Allen Ginsberg a job on the railroad in San Francisco in 1952: "They wouldn't hire Allen as a brakeman at that time because they wouldn't hire any Jews as brakemen. At that time there was, actually, in the union, a clause that you had to be white—and that [didn't] include Jews, too" (Gifford and Lee 1994, 165). For a comprehensive discussion of the legal construction of race, consult Lopez (1996).

2   In correspondence with me, Gerald Nicosia explained his sources for this:

> When I did my interviews in Lowell in 1977-1978, many of the French Canadians and others told me of the pejorative use of the term "les blancs negres" to refer to French Canadians, though I gathered the term was more in use early in the century, when the French Canadian ghettos were more clearly defined. . . . Part of that came from the fact that the French did not generally push their kids academically, toward college, etc., as the Greeks and Irish did, but took the lowest-paying, back-breaking jobs, like blacks in other big cities. Also, some of the French neighborhoods really were run-down, trashy tenements, which could easily suggest an inner-city ghetto. On top of that, many of the French had language problems, . . . and I was told that French people would often be teased about their inability to pronounce the word "three," (t'ree). (Nicosia 1998)

3   Evidence indicating that these are the two meets includes Kerouac's specific reference to Worcester North as the team against which young Jack's team was competing and his use of "WC" for the race results as reported by *The Lowell Sun* reporter. See *The Lowell Sun* (1939a, 13), and (1939b, 15). Information about the Worcester North in-door track team came from Lynn Couture, library media specialist at Worcester North High School, and from *Northern Lights*, the Worcester North High School yearbook (1939). I obtained information on Matthew Jenkins with the assistance of Theresa Davitt, Worcester Historical Museum librarian, who consulted *Caduceus*, the Worcester Commerce yearbooks (1938–40), as well as *The Commerce Mercury* (November 10, 1938; January 13, 1939).

Works Cited

Bailey, Beth L. 1998. *From Front Porch to Back Seat: Courtship in Twentieth-Century America*. Baltimore: Johns Hopkins University Press.

Bakhtin, Mikhail. 1984. *Rabelais and His World*. Trans. Helene Iswolsky. Bloomington: Indiana University Press.

Fuchs, Lawrence H. 1990. *The American Kaleidoscope: Race, Ethnicity and the Civic Culture*. Hanover: University Press of New England.

Gifford, Barry, and Lawrence Lee. 1994. *Jack's Book: An Oral Biography of Jack Kerouac*. New York: St. Martin's Press.

Kerouac, Jack. 1958. *The Subterraneans*. New York: Grove Press.

———. 1960. *Tristessa*. New York: McGraw-Hill Book Co.

———. 1979. *On The Road: Text and Criticism*. Ed. Scott Donaldson. New York: Penguin Books.

———. 1989. *Lonesome Traveler*. New York: Grove Press.

———. 1993. *Maggie Cassidy*. New York: Penguin Books.

———. 1994. *The Good Blonde and Other Stories*. San Francisco: Grey Fox Press.

Lopez, Ian F. Haney. 1996. *White by Law: The Legal Construction of Race*. New York: New York University Press.

The Lowell Sun. 1939a. 9 January, 13.

———. 1939b. 16 January, 15.

Morrison, Toni. 1993. *Playing in the Dark: Whiteness and the Literary Imagination*. New York: Random House Books.

Nicosia, Gerald. 1994. *Memory Babe: A Critical Biography of Jack Kerouac*. Berkeley: University of California Press.

———. 1998. "Re: Kerouac Questions." Personal e-mail. 10 April.

Rothenberg, Paula, ed. 1998. *Race, Class, and Gender in the United States: An Integrated Study*. 4th ed. New York: St. Martin's Press.

Russo, Mary. 1994. *The Female Grotesque: Risk, Excess and Modernity*. New York: Routledge.

Williams, Tennessee. 1985. "Desire and the Black Masseur." *Tennessee Williams Collected Stories*. New York: Ballantine Books.

CHAPTER SIX

Reconceiving Kerouac: Why We Should Teach *Doctor Sax*
Fiona Paton

> Despite all confusion to the contrary, now that time's passed, I think the best poet in the United States is Kerouac still. Given twenty years to settle through. The main reason is that he's the most free and the most spontaneous. . . . I think he's stupidly underrated by almost everybody. (Ginsberg, 1999)

In his 1966 *Paris Review* interview, Allen Ginsberg acknowledges influences as diverse as Christopher Smart, Lester Young, William Blake, and Louis-Ferdinand Céline, but he concludes "Kerouac, most of all, was the biggest influence I think—Kerouac's prose" (1999, 36). He elaborates on this a few pages later: "Like one long sentence page of his in *Doctor Sax* or 'The Railroad Earth' or occasionally *On the Road*—if you examine them phrase by phrase they usually have the density of poetry, and the beauty of poetry, but most of all the single elastic rhythm running from beginning to end of the line and ending 'mop'!" (40). I want to draw attention to the fact that Ginsberg cites *Doctor Sax* and "The Railroad Earth" as his primary examples of Kerouac's "long prose line," with *On the Road* only "occasionally" demonstrating the same "density of poetry" and "single elastic rhythm." Ginsberg's prediction that Kerouac's reputation would take twenty years "to settle through" was astute, yet still overly optimistic: despite the recent upsurge of interest in Kerouac, *Doctor Sax* continues to go in and out of print, while *On the Road* continues to monopolize the attention of both students and scholars (Swartz 1999). I believe that *On the Road* is not Kerouac's most important work; that, in fact, the "settling through" of his reputation will not happen until we begin to teach and research novels like *Doctor Sax*, which brilliantly demonstrates Kerouac's jazz aesthetic without itself being a jazz or "beat" novel. In this essay, I will discuss both the stylistic and the thematic aspects of the novel in some detail, providing both a general context and specific pointers for teaching it to either graduate or undergraduate students.

Doctor Sax is one of Kerouac's earliest mature novels, written in 1952 shortly after he had discovered the sketching technique that was to form the basis for his spontaneous prose method.[1] On one level, the novel is a recreation of Kerouac's boyhood in Lowell, Massachusetts: the adult narrator, Jack Duluoz, looks back with nostalgia and affection at a pre-WWII world characterized by B-movies, vaudeville shows, pulp magazines, and radio shows. Much of the novel consists of descriptions of family and school life, poignant yet humorous, with adult and child perspectives merging in a narrative voice that makes frequent departures into the French-Canadian *joual* of Kerouac's childhood. But despite the obvious warmth and security of this Pawtucketville community, young Jacky is haunted by intense fears of death and evil, fears engendered largely by the emphatically dark Catholicism of his upbringing. Hence Jacky creates an imaginary superhero called Doctor Sax based on the Street and Smith radio and magazine character The Shadow. Doctor Sax, simultaneously fearful and paternal, helps Jacky negotiate his way from childhood to puberty, replacing religious nightmares with the more manageable fantasies of pulp fiction. Through Doctor Sax the novel develops a supernatural subplot involving an evil wizard and his cohort of vampires, gnomes, and assorted monsters who are in the process of freeing the Great Snake of World Evil from a cavernous pit beneath a castle in Lowell. Only Jacky Duluoz knows that Armageddon is being staged in his hometown, and as this subplot gradually unfolds, the line between reality and fantasy grows ever more uncertain. Ultimately, the novel suggests that the battle between good and evil is being forever waged in each individual soul. This religious subtext, along with the underlying Cold War political allegory represented by the satanic inhabitants of the castle, makes *Doctor Sax* an ambitious and profound novel. But it is also a work of tremendous humor and exuberance, and once students adjust to the anarchic nature of the prose, they have a good time reading it.

Given the challenges of both subject matter and style, I have found it useful to frame the novel with two other Kerouac texts, his 1959 essay "On the Origins on a Generation," and his 1957 *ars poetica* "Essentials of Spontaneous Prose," both available in *Good Blonde and Others* (Allen 1993; "Essentials" is included here in an Appendix). I assign the "Origins" essay first because it addresses three issues that are crucial for this novel and Kerouac's work in general: religion, popular culture, and jazz. Prior to beginning the novel, I have students list all the associations or ideas they have about "beatniks" and what it meant to be "beat" in the late fifties. Then, after they have read the "Origins" essay, I ask them to compare their associations with Kerouac's own statement. Does he define "beat" in the same ways? What definitions is he resisting? Students should be encouraged to voice any concerns they may have, whether about the romanticizing of marginality or drug taking, or about the very masculine ethos of the Beats. Such issues can be contextualized by a short lecture on the prevailing cultural atmosphere of 1950s America, an atmosphere that relentlessly enforced middle-class mores, affirmed material consumption, and valorized domesticity as part of a propaganda campaign designed to promote the American Way of Life over Soviet Communism.[2] The Beats, interestingly, while challenging many of the social norms of their time, also reproduced certain social norms, the most troubling perhaps being an inherent chauvinism that defined the beat experience in primarily male terms. Students should be made aware of the alternative perspectives presented in, for instance, Joyce Johnson's *Minor Characters* or Hettie Jones's *How I Became Hettie Jones*. But alongside the essay's cultural limitations, students should note the larger spiritual concerns that Kerouac addresses, as his emphasis on Christianity and Buddhism and his insistence that "beat" encompasses "beatitude" as much as "down and out." Kerouac writes about visiting his Lowell church and having "a vision of what I must have really meant with

'Beat' anyhow when I heard the holy silence in the church" (1993b, 63). Discussing this connection with both Lowell and Catholicism helpfully corrects the typical misconceptions that Kerouac's work naively celebrates hedonism and rootlessness. Kerouac is better understood as a spiritual seeker with a deep attachment to place and community.

The essay also contains Kerouac's most direct statement on popular culture, which he connects explicitly with the Beats. The Beat sensibility, says Kerouac,

> goes back to the wild and raving childhood of playing The Shadow under windswept trees of New England's gleeful autumn and the howl of the Moon Man on the sandbank until we caught him in a tree (he was an older guy of fifteen), the maniacal laugh of certain neighborhood madboys, the furious humor of whole gangs playing basketball till long after dark in the park, it goes back to those crazy days before World War II when teenagers drank beer on Friday nights at lake ballrooms and worked off their hangovers playing baseball on Saturday afternoon followed by a dive in the brook—and our fathers wore straw hats like W.C. Fields. It goes back to the completely senseless babble of The Three Stooges, the ravings of the Marx Brothers (the tenderness of Angel Harpo at harp, too). (Kerouac 1993b, 57)

Some consideration of this topic will lay important groundwork for the students' encounter with *Doctor Sax* by inviting them to consider the thematic significance of The Shadow/Sax and pop culture generally in the novel. For Kerouac, popular culture is associated with "the glee of America, the honesty of America," with "wild self-believing individuality" that "had begun to disappear around the end of World War II" (1993b, 59). The character of Doctor Sax, like the comic strips, movies, and pulp fiction referred to throughout "Origins," is part of Kerouac's nostalgic affirmation of a prewar America that for him embodied everything that had since been lost: creative energy, spontaneity, humor, optimism, and a certain affinity with uncomplicated pleasure. Of course, Sax also represents much more than this, but at this stage one point should be emphasized: for Kerouac, popular culture was quintessentially American at a time when disillusionment with Europe was at an all time high. While the Beats paid homage to European writers such as Joyce, Kafka, Mann, Baudelaire, and Rimbaud, they also felt that Whitman and W.C. Williams represented more authentic models for American literature. Both Whitman and Williams had sought to establish a native literary tradition, and this was a cause that the Beats embraced wholeheartedly. Hence in "Aftermath: The Philosophy of the Beat Generation," Kerouac identifies the Beats as "subterranean heroes . . . prophesying a new style for American culture, a new style (we thought) completely free from European influences (unlike the Lost Generation), a new incantation" (1993a, 47).

Students should come to *Doctor Sax* with some sense of Kerouac's aesthetic agenda and should be aware that his "new style" was deeply influenced by movies, pulp fiction, comic strips, and jazz. It is the jazz influence that I want to focus on here,[3] because, despite its crucial importance, the subject has not yet been fully explained in relation to Kerouac's spontaneous prose style. In "Origins," Kerouac describes his instinctive connection with bebop musicians like Charlie Parker and Dizzy Gillespie: "they kept talking about the same things I liked . . . night long confessions full of hope that had become illicit and repressed by the War, stirrings, rumblings of a new soul" (1993b, 60). The reference to "rumblings of a new soul" connects with Kerouac's insistence on "a new style for American culture" and brings out the oft-noticed but underappreciated connection between Kerouac's writing style and jazz—or, more accurately, bebop. Bebop *was* something new in the late 1940s and early 1950s, and Kerouac was excited and amazed by the combination of improvisational freedom and technical virtuosity that he heard in musicians like Charlie Parker. He developed his spontaneous prose method partly to try and capture a similar effect in writing. A little time spent on this topic considerably enhances the students' understanding and appreciation of Kerouac's technical innovations, so I will spend the next few pages outlining my own approach to teaching this aspect of *Doctor Sax*.

Most students are initially rather frustrated by the idiosyncrasies of Kerouac's language, which they find difficult to read because of the unconventional punctuation and the descriptive digressions that replace a more conventional plot structure. One useful in-class activity is to play a few of the excellent recordings of Kerouac reading, especially those that are accompanied by Steve Allen's jazz piano.[4] Hearing Kerouac read teaches students to listen for the inherent rhythm in the language, helps them to enjoy the play of sound effects in his phrasings, and increases their sensitivity towards the range of tone he employs. But listening to jazz music is also extremely helpful, for this teaches students to recognize the structural principles underlying his apparently unstructured work.

Jazz improvisation develops from the melody and chord progressions of the song and takes place within a recognizable form that is reproduced in most jazz tunes. The melody (A) is repeated twice, followed by a bridge section (B), after which the melody (A) is again repeated. Then come the solo improvisations, which recreate the melody by recombining individual notes from the song's chord progressions. After each instrument has soloed, the musicians return to the original melody (A). This AABA structure is relatively easy to illustrate with any number of classic jazz tunes—for instance, Benny Goodman's "Stompin' at the Savoy" or Duke Ellington's "Cottontail." At this point, turn to Kerouac's "Essentials of Spontaneous Prose" (see Appendix). Originally written in 1953 to explain his three-day execution of *The Subterraneans* to Ginsberg and Burroughs (Charters 1987, 189), the "Essentials" was later published by *Black Mountain Review* in 1957. Too easily dismissed as impressionistic romanticism, the "Essentials" actually provides important insight into Kerouac's method, foregrounding concrete connections between this method and the jazz structure outlined above.

Kerouac's emphasis on sketching a "definite image-object" at the beginning of "Essentials" alludes to the breakthrough in writing style that occurred in 1952 when artist friend Ed White advised him to "just sketch in the streets like a painter but with words" (Kerouac 1996, 355). In doing so, Kerouac discovered the almost limitless potential of an ordinary object or scene that "is set before the mind" (either in reality or memory) and explored on two levels simultaneously—those of objective description and subjective association. The idea of a "definite image-object" is later restated as the "jewel center of interest": "Begin not from preconceived idea of what to say about image but from jewel center of interest in subject of image at *moment* of writing" (1993b, 70). The writer should focus on that which is most compelling in the scene or situation, and from that central image or idea "write outwards swimming in sea of language to peripheral release and exhaustion" (70).

Kerouac's desire to represent the workings of the artistic imagination in the moment of creation has clear affinities with Jackson

Pollock's action painting, but also, of course, with jazz improvisation. He makes this connection explicit when describing the "undisturbed flow from the mind of personal secret idea words, *blowing* (as per jazz musician) on subject of image." But note that Kerouac is not advocating completely random or "automatic" writing: "blowing . . . on subject of image" posits an affinity with the jazz musician who improvises around particular chord progressions. Tim Hunt has already noted the equivalence between the melody in jazz and Kerouac's 'image-object' (Hunt 1996, 146). What needs to be emphasized, however, is the way Kerouac returns to that image-object—or melody—once his improvisation has run its course. This is suggested in the "Structure of Work" section: "Follow roughly outlines in outfanning movement over subject, as river rock, so mindflow over jewelcenter need (run your mind over it, once) arriving at pivot, where what was dim formed 'beginning' becomes sharp necessitating 'ending'. . ." (1993d, 70). For all its metaphoric density, this description strongly suggests the jazz structure outlined above, whereby improvisations develop outwards from a basic melody in the moment of playing until fulfillment (or exhaustion) is reached, at which point the soloist, "arriving at pivot," returns to the melody and concludes the number.

Before having students analyze any given passage in depth, it is helpful to point out the regularity with which Kerouac repeats this structure in *Doctor Sax*. See, for instance, Chapter 20, which begins with a meditation on "The underground rumbling horror of the Lowell night," a meditation that is then brought to a close on the next page with the repetition of "underground rumbling horrors of the Lowell night" (1987, 44–45). Other sketches do not repeat exact phrases but rather central images or feelings. In Chapter 5, for instance, the short opening paragraph begins and ends with the association between Doctor Sax and the woods (9). Similarly, the next paragraph begins and ends with reference to the Merrimac River (9–10). Some sketches are short; others extend over several pages. Many observe paragraph breaks; others overlap within the same paragraph and sometimes narrative development takes the prose in a more linear direction. Kerouac's jazz aesthetic is never formulaic or mechanical, but it is repeated consistently enough to demonstrate a conscious underlying rationale.

This basic structural connection between spontaneous prose and jazz provides the foundation for students' understanding of Kerouac's achievement as a stylist. However, they should also understand that Kerouac's closest affinity is with the bebop musicians of the postwar period, and that his prose innovations come out of the same intense mood of experimentation that produced bop legends like Charlie Parker, Dizzy Gillespie, and Thelonius Monk. Historian Alan Pomerance provides a useful summary of this postwar mood:

> The perfectly-blended sax section of Glenn Miller as it pulsed and throbbed through "Moonlight Serenade" had been in harmony with the ensemble effect and precision teamwork required for successful pinpoint bombing teams, or the launching crews on aircraft carriers. But with peace came a need to get out from under the mechanized regimentation necessary for victory. The year 1946 brought an intense desire for individuality of thought, action, dress, comportment, and music.
>
> For jazzmen, especially the blacks, it meant a rejection of the ensemble and a return to the solo, but a solo so personal that nothing from the past could provide a guideline or pattern for the sound or feeling as you blew it. It was eccentric, it was non-conformist, it was bop. (Pomerance 1991, 185)

Although the term "bop" was considered inadequate and even trivializing by some (including Ralph Ellison and Charlie Parker), its onomatopoeic aspect was actually quite fitting, for bop did *sound* radically different from the big band jazz that preceded it. Bop was played by small combos, and it had a faster tempo and more agitated style. The emphasis was on improvisation rather than arrangement, and these improvisations were more complex, with more themes per solo. With this emphasis on solo improvisation, technical virtuosity was absolutely crucial, and the musicians had to be innovative and ambitious enough to create unusual and unpredictable melodies and harmonies. The element of surprise, always valued in jazz music, now became more important than ever (Gridley 1994, 140). That Kerouac identified with this new sound is clear from a 1954 letter to Alfred Kazin: "I've invented a new prose, Modern Prose, jazzlike breathlessly swift spontaneous and unrevised floods" (1996, 449). By calling his approach "Modern Prose," Kerouac directly references bebop, which, when it emerged in the mid-1940s, was called Modern Jazz (Gridley 1994, 139).

Of all the great and innovative bop musicians, alto saxophonist Charlie "Bird" Parker is generally acknowledged as the greatest and most innovative. In fact, musicologists now view him as one of the most important figures in twentieth-century music as a whole (Gridley 1994, 143). Parker's ability to improvise at high speed and with great melodic inventiveness stunned his audiences (and fellow musicians). Using double and quadruple time figures even when playing slow ballads, Parker basically played more notes in his solos, and played them faster, than jazz audiences had ever heard before.[5] He was also humorously eclectic, borrowing phrases not just from earlier jazz musicians like Louis Armstrong, but also from popular songs, traditional folk melodies, classical music and opera: "His favorites were the opening of the clarinet descant of *High Society*, the opening phrase of the *Haba–era* of Bizet's opera *Carmen*, and the opening of Grainger's *Country Gardens*" (Owens 1995, 34). Parker epitomized most brilliantly all the defining characteristics of bop, its speed, its unpredictability, its rhythmic complexity, and its humor. That Kerouac admired Parker greatly, and understood the technical significance of his playing, is clear from his novels, letters, and the poems he wrote about Parker.[6] Hence students should be aware that the many idiosyncrasies in Kerouac's style are not gratuitous liberties but premeditated attempts to capture the fluidity and intensity of bop music in writing.

Below is a two-page extract from *Doctor Sax* (Book Three, Chapter 2) that illustrates the structural affinity between Kerouac's spontaneous prose method and jazz music. It is useful to take students through a line-by-line reading of at least one sketch, considering the development of ideas, stylistic features, and broader thematic issues. I will address all three of these levels on a line-by-line basis, although my analysis will be by no means exhaustive.

> The very skeletal of the tale's beginning—The Paquins lived across on Sarah in a Golden Brown House, a two-story tenement but with fat owf-porches (piazzas, galleries) and purty gingerbread eaves and Screens on the porches making a dark Within . . . for long flyless afternoons of Orange Crush. . . . Paquin brothers were Beef and Robert, Big Beef of the ass-waddling down the street, Robert was a freckled earnest giant good intentioned with all, nothing wrong with Beef, freckled too, goodnatured, my mother says she was sitting on the porch one evening and Beef came out with the moon to talk to her, told her his deepest secrets about how he wanted to just go out and enjoy nature as far as he was concerned—or

some such—she my mother sat there reigning over wild conversations, Jean Fourchette the idiot came stompin by with his firecrackers and google giggled in the late sun afternoon streets of Fourth July Lowell 1936 and made monkey ginsy dances for the ladies whose children most likely by this time were all downtown disbanding among crowds of the Fourth July Common Fireworks and Carnival, great nights—tell you about it— Jean Fourchette saw my mother sitting on the porch in a scrape of eve and asked her if she was lonely would she like to be entertained by some fireworks, she said okay, and old mad Jean set everything-he-had-in-his-pocket-off—plop plow, scatter, zing; cross—he entertained the ladies of Sarah avenue not twenty minutes before the opening bomb gong down at the Common across the soft July rooftops of Lowell clear from white tene-mental creameries of Mt. Vernon porch to crazy rick-ass Bloozong Street across the river over by the dye works, over by the tanners, over by your Loo-la, Lowell—over by your long hoo-raws, rorar old old rohor—rohor motor clodor closed door—on the pajama leg hanging, ding, with the white hoozahs flangeing right, they made left on a wide swing, beat the time with every wing, the ring, saw nothing in the heaven eyes but silver-star-bells, of all descriptions, saved but never knew it, he tried every means to explain to the odd festival of types gathered around his shoe-horn, 'Looka here ladies and genelmen,—'as me and G.J. and Vinny and Scotty are scuffling around at the Carnival—(my mother is smiling at Jean Fourchette) (Boom!) the fireworks are beginning, the whore-caster by the stream is showing you how the horses race in wild hullah, they had— There were races run with wooden flap-horses leaping ahead on the turn of a dice—they spun the dice so fast (in cages) you could see the horses leap ahead in their win—a crazy inanimate wild living race like you'd imagine angels run.......when they feel—X was the mark where the bing-lights played, in the night mist a top hatted clown presided over the tote-board—Further on we smelt shit in the grass, saw cameras, ate popcorn, blew the string balloons to heaven—Night came shrouding bluely with flap off arms in the hiarzan—Hanging moss (like the moss in the Castle hanging as you hear a kid whistle for his balloon) (in the grass the littler kids are wrestling in a Tiny Tim Din you can hardly see—big souls from lit-tle acorns—Wrangling toots on all sides of pipe streams, furt-fut peanuts for sale, furtive hipsters of the time, underfoot shammysoft dusts)—Beef Paquin, now, years later, I see huddled in a football hood coat heading home from the mills in mid December, bending to the wind around Blezan's corner, advancing homeward to hamburger supper of the upper clime, the golden rich consistency of his mother's kitchen—Beef is going into Eternity at his end without me—my end is as far from his as eterni-ty—Eternity hears hollow voices in a rock? Eternity hears ordinary voices in the parlor. On a bone the ant descends. (Kerouac 1987, 103–04)

As we know, much of *Doctor Sax* is comprised of sketches from memory, and many sketches follow the structure set forth in the

"Essentials." Here, the "narrator"[7] is describing his childhood friends, the Paquin brothers, and they constitute the jewel center of interest. Their "Golden Brown House" suggests the gingerbread house of fairy tales, and it acquires a symbolic resonance through capitalization. This association with fairy tales is then made explicit in "purty gingerbread eaves." But here we have an interesting tonal shift: the ironic "purty" implies a certain simplicity and sentimentality, so that ironic distance is created even while evoking the golden days of childhood. With humorous wonder the narrator recalls the "*Screens*" around the porch (a decidedly middle-class addition) that allowed for the bliss of "long flyless afternoons of Orange Crush." But these screens also created "a dark Within," and again capitalization creates a symbolic resonance. If we recall that at least one fairy-tale house of gingerbread contained an evil witch (i.e., "Hansel and Gretel"), then this Golden Brown House carries mixed associations of mystery and danger. This ambivalence very much characterizes the novel overall and is, I think, one of its great achievements. The wonder and the apprehension that so defines childhood experience finds expression through the fantasy world of Jacky, whose inner life is permeated with images from Catholicism, fairy tales, movies, and pulp magazines. And, of course, *Doctor Sax* is very much a novel of psychological and spiritual development. The "dark Within" is also the mysterious depths of the individual psyche, into which Jacky will journey at the end of the novel.

The next segment of the sketch describes the Paquin brothers in the comic-strip style that Kerouac uses so exuberantly throughout *Doctor Sax*: "Big Beef of the ass-waddling down the street." Arthur Asa Berger, author of *L'il Abner: A Study in American Satire*, places comic strips within the literary tradition of the grotesque, noting their shared emphasis on "distortions, caricature, and overstatement, incongruity, unnaturalness, and ugliness" (1994, 65). Comic strip artists often simplify and exaggerate one aspect of physical appearance; here, Beef Paquin is defined by his huge behind, and the image given comic immediacy by the compound noun-gerund "ass-waddling." But Beef is also a poignant image in the sketch. The brief anecdote that follows describes a moment of tender communion with another person—the narrator's mother—which is presented in almost romantic—and Romantic—terms: "Beef came out with the moon to talk to her, told her his deepest secrets. . . ." The mother, meanwhile, sits "reigning over wild conversations," the tone of celebration here characteristic of Kerouac's tendency to imbue the mundane with an almost mythic significance.

At this point in the sketch, "following free deviation [association] of mind," the narrator shifts to his mother's conversation with Jean Fourchette on the Fourth of July, 1936. The mentally retarded Fourchette also has an air of comic strip grotesquesness about him ("google-giggled" references the comic strip character Barney Google), but, once again, human connectedness is emphasized—asking if Jacky's mother is lonely, Jean offers to set off his fireworks for her entertainment. This particular segment is stylistically the most unorthodox. Kerouac's love of comic strip onomatopoeia is given free rein in "plop plow, scatter, zing," and as he follows the motion of the fireworks "over by the dye works, over by the tanners, over by your Loo-la, Lowell," description yields to the pure play of sounds. The stalled incomprehensibility of "rohor motor clodor closed door" shifts into a series of rhyming phrases: "the white hoozahs flangeing right, they made left on a wide swing, beat time with every wing, the ring. . . ." Students will, of course, find such passages difficult to read. What is going on? On the level of narrative action, Jean is letting off his fireworks, watching them in amazement, and slapping his pajama-clad leg in time to their explosions. Stylistically, Kerouac is both mimicking the random motion of the fireworks and enacting the creative play of the jazz soloist, particularly the bebop soloist, by pushing spontaneous experiment to the very edge of control. The absence of regular punctuation in some of these clauses and the density of images reproduces the intricate speed of bop improvisation, with Parker's double and quadruple timing suggested by hyphenated constructs like "old mad Jean set everything-he-had-in-his-pocket-off" and "silver-star-bells." Gridley's description of Parker could apply equally to Kerouac: "During his improvisations, his mind seemed to be bubbling over with little melodies and paraphrases of melodies. It was as though he had so much energy he could barely contain himself" (1994, 143).

The next segment offers a series of jumbled vignettes of the Carnival itself, where Jacky and his pals are "scuffling around." Students may feel that Kerouac's conversational tone, so much a part of his spontaneous prose method, becomes at this point somewhat gratuitous. Why include false starts such as "they had—there were races run . . ."? Again, it is important to connect Kerouac with both the abstract expressionists and bebop musicians of the early fifties. The process of recording the creative mind in action, and the accompanying associations of authenticity and life-energy that this process suggested, was the defining element in America's postwar cultural renaissance. Bum notes and stray splotches of paint have their equivalent in Kerouac in typos and incomplete utterances, and yet, for all the casualness of the diction, the prose is often strikingly original and the ideas are always complex.

One pattern to direct students toward, here and elsewhere, is the constant tension between the physical and the spiritual. The realm of the body is powerfully present throughout the novel—here we find "whore-caster" substituted for "forecaster"; the boys smell "shit in the grass." At the same time, the wooden horses race "like you'd expect angels run." The boys blow "the string balloons to heaven." The wrestling children are "big souls from little acorns." But Kerouac is not opposing the realm of the body and the realm of the spirit in orthodox Christian terms of sin and redemption. His vision is much more Blakean: the created world and the physical body are infused with life-energy, and hence are themselves divine. In an interview, Kerouac described sexual intercourse as "the gateway to paradise" (Allen 1993, 53), and *Doctor Sax* as a very Rabelaisian celebration of the body. Innocence, for Kerouac, is not freedom from sin so much as freedom from the concept of sin. His recreation of childhood is in many ways idyllic, but he is also pointedly frank about the child's fascination with bodily functions and bodily pleasure. Like both Rabelais and Blake, Kerouac celebrates everyday life and the physical body as holy, and, like them, imparts intensity to his vision by always reminding us that all is transitory. Mortality is a pervasive presence in all Kerouac's writing: in this sketch, for instance, night is described as "shrouding bluely," and, indeed, it is the awareness of death that turns the sketch back toward the jewel center of interest, Beef Paquin.

The turn occurs after the phrase "underfoot shammysoft dusts"; "dust," with its associations of physical death, acts as the pivot whereby "what was dim formed 'beginning' becomes sharp-necessitating 'ending.'" The narrator now thinks about Beef "years later . . . heading home from the mills in mid December." At the end of the sketch, childhood innocence is replaced by an adult knowledge of mortality:"Beef is going into Eternity at his end without me—my end is as far from his as eternity—Eternity hears hollow voices in a rock? Eternity hears hollow voices in the parlor. On a bone the ant descends." Death is that moment of pure isolation, the journey that all must take alone, and it is within this context that we should understand Kerouac's emphasis on moments of human connection. The intuitive tension between "child" Beef and "adult" Beef is what contains the "jewel center of interest"—the tragic transience of life. In fact, students might notice that mortality is implied in the opening phrase of the sketch,"The very *skeletal* of the tale's beginning," which is echoed in the closing phrase,"On a *bone* the ant descends" (emphases added).

Yet despite this preoccupation with mortality, we still find Kerouac's characteristic tone of celebration as he describes Beef's "hamburger supper of the upper clime, the golden rich consistency of his mother's kitchen." "Golden," which so often denotes divine immanence for Kerouac, combines with "upper clime," the heavenly realm within the everyday, the sacredness of family and human connection. Kerouac's dense conflation of two T.S. Eliot poems in "Eternity hears hollow voices in a rock?"[8] is countered by "Eternity hears ordinary voices in the parlor." Redemption is always part of Kerouac's vision, but it is redemption here on earth, in the holiness of life. He posits a heavenly realm beyond life, the realm of "eternity," but he also insists on the sacredness of the here-and-now. It is through the joy of living that we are redeemed. The mentally retarded Jean Fourchette, who, when he lets off his fireworks, sees "nothing in the heaven eyes but silver-star-bells" is "saved but never knew it."

The close reading of a particular passage provides a valuable framework for analyzing the rest of the novel, especially if Kerouac's spontaneous prose method is discussed in some depth. If students understand that Kerouac is drawing on jazz, comic strips, pulp fiction, and movies in order to create "a new style for American culture" (1993a, 48), they respond much more positively to the challenges of his non-linear, iconoclastic prose style. Kerouac has been characterized as anti-intellectual because of his impatience with "gray faced academic quibbling" (1993c, 76), but he was certainly not *un*intellectual. His writing performances were spontaneous in the same way that jazz improvisations are spontaneous: much careful thought and disciplined experimentation lay behind them. As he explained to Ted Berrigan: "You think about what actually happened, you tell your friends long stories about it, you mull it over in your mind, you connect it together at leisure, then when the time comes to pay the rent again you force yourself to sit at typewriter, or at the writing notebook, and get it over with as fast as you can . . ." (1999a, 121). This point needs to be emphasized—the speed of writing does not at all imply absence of intellectual reflection. *Doctor Sax*, for all its linguistic playfulness, is a deeply intellectual book. It is now time to take students through some of the major symbolic patterns of the novel, the central one being, of course, Doctor Sax, Kerouac's affectionate parody of The Shadow.

Who was The Shadow? In 1930, pulp giants Street and Smith sponsored a Thursday night radio program based on their *Detective Story* magazine. Each show was introduced by an other-worldly announcer who called himself The Shadow, and who began each broadcast with some variation of the chilling words, "Who knows what evil lurks in the hearts of men? *The Shadow knows! . . . Ha ha ha ha ha! . . .*" Although The Shadow didn't appear in any of the actual stories, his popularity quickly grew so great that Street and Smith launched the pulp thriller of that name (Tollin 1996, 4–7). Written by the amazingly prolific Walter Gibson, *The Shadow* combined hard-boiled detective fiction with supernatural mystery, and more than fulfilled the sinister promise of its original disembodied voice. Needless to say, The Shadow also got his own radio program, and the original broadcasts are now available on CD and cassette (*The Shadow Chronicles* 1996). But it was the pulp magazine that captured the young Kerouac's imagination, and it was the magazine version of The Shadow that would provide the template for his own superhero.

The similarities between the two are integrated into the narrative on a number of levels, the most basic being that of appearance. Both wear a long black coat and black slouch hat, both have hawkish noses and blazing eyes, and both emit the famous laugh. Both can also be quite terrifying in appearance: The Shadow has "a solemn, monkish profile that shone a ghastly green as the light revealed it!"

("Hands in the Dark" 1932, 34), while Doctor Sax is "all greenfaced and leering" (33). In their fight against evil, both concoct various powders in their respective laboratories, and both scale sheer walls with rubber suction cups. Here is a representative passage from *The Shadow Magazine*:

> A few minutes later, momentary clearing of the clouds showed a black form clinging to the sheer wall of the great gorge! Suspended over noth-ingness, The Shadow was creeping along the cliff, past the projection of the barring fence!
>
> The moonlight passed. The only sign of The Shadow's progress was the slow, squidgy sound of the rubber suction cups that he had attached to his hands and feet ("The Creeping Death" 1933, 64).

Kerouac's version is decidedly more apocalyptic, but the debt is clear: "The Parapet heaved up further, it was about to gulp itself up, rocks and dust and sand flew, Doctor Sax took his suction cups and climbed the sheer wall of the Parapet and came to the edge howl-ing" (1987, 234). Stylistically, too, Kerouac draws on *The Shadow Magazine*, echoing its constant use of certain words like "ink" and "shroud." Here, for instance, is Walter Gibson: "The light clicked out. A low, mocking laugh swept through the inky room. Its tones were answered by the shrouding walls" ("The Romanoff Jewels" 1932, 23). And here are some of Kerouac's variations on these motifs: "he looks across the wide dark towards Snake Hill behind the wet shrouds" (1987, 21); "a blue smoke shroud castle" (143); "he vanishes like ink in inky night" (155); "a cape of ink furls upon the waters" (170); "he put a shroudal hand on my shoulder" (197).

Clearly, Kerouac integrated a great deal of the original *Shadow* material into his novel, but such borrowings would not necessarily be apparent to a reader without the necessary background knowl-edge to recognize them. Interestingly, though, Kerouac chooses to make the connection explicit, as when Duluoz says, "Doctor Sax was like The Shadow when I was young, I saw him leap over the last bush on the sandbank one night, cape a-flying" (1987, 33). And at times the two merge into one in their symbolic representation of night and dark mystery: "it might have been the arrangement of the shadows.—Ah Shadow! Sax!—" (35). Hence, while Duluoz often describes Doctor Sax as a real personage, he just as often empha-sizes his fictionality and makes clear the process of his evolution from *The Shadow Magazine*. By doing so, he reminds the reader that Doctor Sax is a fictional construct not only of the author but also of the narrator, and so undermines one of the crucial aspects of fantasy literature—that its alternative world be consistently maintained.

A similar device is the hyperbolic language used throughout to describe both Sax and the evil denizens of the Castle. The effect is often one of pure grotesquery. Far from being the dignified, charismatic crime fighter with nerves of steel and lightning reflexes, Doctor Sax is a maniac who "comes striding with his stick, blowing snot out of his nose, casting gleeful crazy glances at frogs in mud puddles" (1987, 28). Kerouac even includes a direct parody of Walter Gibson's style in Sax's own narrative, "DOCTOR SAX, AN ACCOUNT OF HIS ADVENTURE WITH THE HUMAN INHABITANTS OF SNAKE CASTLE." The effect of this inserted narrative is to further burlesque Doctor Sax and the pulp fantasy genre itself. But isn't Doctor Sax the hero of the novel? If so, why make fun of him? What Doctor Sax actually represents in the novel is a crucial question, and provides a good starting point for a consideration of the novel's themes.

Duluoz tells us at the start of the novel that "Doctor Sax I first saw in his earlier lineaments in the early Catholic childhood of Centralville—deaths, funerals, the shroud of that, the dark figure in the corner when you look at the dead man coffin in the dolorous parlor of the open house" (Kerouac 1987, 4). This connection of Sax with death, Catholicism, and childhood nightmares is important: Sax embodies the same sublime fears represented by his mother's "phosphorescent Christ on a black-lacquered Cross" (44) and the family's statue of Saint Thérèse, which Jacky has seen turn its head in the dark (4). Duluoz recalls that "my whole death and Sax is wound in satin coffins" and states "I gave up the church to ease my horrors—too much candlelight, too much wax" (68). Doctor Sax functions for the young Jacky as an alternative to the sublime horrors of Catholicism. Sax takes on those horrors, but in a more manageable form. He is a mediating figure who both embodies the fear of darkness and death and offers protection from it. "I sensed he was my friend," says Jacky in Book One, "my old, old friend . . . my ghost, personal angel, private shadow, secret lover" (34).

Sax's explicit fictionality is further emphasized through the distinctly psychological status accorded him. Sax is associated with

Jacky's unconscious mind in decidedly Jungian terms, and therefore is often associated with forbidden knowledge, particularly sexual knowledge. Of Zaza the "moron" Duluoz says, "along the dump he'd drooled since childhood, spermatazoing in all directions . . . they'd seen him try it under a porch. . . . Doctor Sax lurked under porches watching these operations, from the cellar, made notes, sketched" (Kerouac 1987, 69). Duluoz's description of his idyllic childhood is constantly intersected by references to his own growing awareness of sex and his own sexual experimentation, and so statements such as "there is evil in the flashing green round of brown night—Doctor Sax was everywhere in this" (57) are not as contradictory as students might at first think. "Sax" is certainly intended as a pun on "sex" as well as "saxophone," and if his nature seems contradictory, it is because he represents the transition from Innocence to Experience. This transition is psychological as well as physical: sex is associated with sin for Jacky, but it is also the source of intoxicating pleasure and energy. That Sax represents unconscious desires and forbidden knowledge is strongly implied in "Doctor Sax hides around the corner of my mind" (11). Like Jung's "shadow," Doctor Sax represents repressed impulses that stand in opposition to the conscious ego.

Doctor Sax, we are told, "had knowledge of death" (Kerouac 1987, 43), and it is this association with forbidden knowledge that connects him to the Faust legend. In describing Sax as Faustian, Kerouac is tapping into a myth that has become embedded in both popular and literary culture. The historical personage is usually identified as the early sixteenth-century necromancer Georg Faust from the small German town of Nittlingen. Although by reputation a flamboyant braggart, Georg Faust did have wide knowledge of medicine, alchemy, and magic; after his death around 1540, fantastic rumors flourished about his supernatural powers (Smeed 1987, 1–2). These rumors were given a more permanent form by the anonymous chapbook, *Historia von D. Johan Fausten*, published in Germany in 1587, which depicts Faust as the arrogant scholar who sells his soul to the Devil in return for unlimited knowledge (Smeed 1987, 3). But Faust is punished for his presumption by a gruesome death, and hence this first printed version of the Faust story established the moral lesson that would dominate the many subsequent retellings: intellectual curiosity has God-given limits that should not be violated. Of these many retellings, Goethe's *Faust* is the most relevant for our purposes: in his "Origins" essay, Kerouac writes, "my hero was Goethe and I believed in art and hoped someday to write the third part of *Faust*, which I have done in *Doctor Sax*" (1993b, 62). I will consider what Kerouac meant by this later. Few students will be familiar enough with Goethe's *Faust* to interpret *Doctor Sax* within its framework; however, given a brief overview of the Faust legend, they should be able to identify the Faustian aspects of Doctor Sax's character.

Like Goethe's Faust, Sax is associated with alchemy and arcane knowledge: "Sax worked on his herbs and powders for a lifetime. He couldn't rush around like The Shadow with a .45 automatic battling the forces of evil, the evil that Doctor Sax had to battle required herbs and nerves . . . moral nerves, he had to recognize good and evil and intelligence" (Kerouac 1987, 32). The preparation that Sax is working on is comprised of "spider-juices and bat powders" (155) as well as a special herb that "the Monks of the Rooftop Monastery" have sent to him tied to the leg of a dove (169). The Noah allusion is reinforced by the "ark shack" (135) where Sax lives, and these are important details, for Sax is in the service of God, not the Devil. He is described as "the King of Anti Evil" (169) and has devoted his life to studying his lifelong enemy the Snake, in preparation for the final apocalyptic battle against the forces of evil. Yet Sax, like Goethe's Faust, is an ambiguous character whom Kerouac describes as "a mad fool of power, a Faustian man" (43). This phrasing evokes the misguided striving after supreme knowledge that characterizes so many versions of Faust. Why emphasize these negative associations in a character who is also portrayed as the savior of mankind and the protector of children? This question takes us into the heart of the novel's theological framework.

I earlier asked why it is that Doctor Sax, the titular hero of the novel, is so often burlesqued by the writer. In part, the satiric tone reflects the fusion of perspectives in the narrative voice: the imaginative intensity of the twelve-year-old boy combined with the wry detachment of the older Duluoz. But Kerouac is also signaling right from the start that Sax's stature is limited. When contained within the world of Jacky's boyhood imagination, Sax is a superhero indeed. But when that fantasy world of pulp fiction is placed within a larger religious framework, Sax's powers are rendered negligible. Note that his vial of magic powders turns out to be useless against the Snake. After his failed attempt, Sax takes off his hat and cape and stands revealed as an ordinary man, saying, "'Funny thing is, I never knew that I would meet Judgement Day in my regular clothes without having to go around in the middle of the night with that silly cape, with that silly goddam shroudy hat, with that black face the Lord prescribed for me'" (Kerouac 1987, 240). Sax, the King of Anti Evil, strives for the supreme knowledge that will allow him to defeat the Snake, but he can never attain that knowledge, for he is merely a servant of a higher power.

Sax, then, is Faustian, but in an altruistic way that is quite different from the Faust of legend. There is, however, another more traditionally Faustian character in the novel: the Wizard. It is the Wizard who is bringing the Great Snake of World Evil up from the depths of the earth "a hundred years before its time" (Kerouac 1987, 222), and he rejoices in the destruction he and the Snake will wreak: "We will darken the very sun in our march" (227). In his power-mad hubris, the Wizard evokes the original Georg Faust (and also Goethe's Faust) much more strongly than does Sax. In fact, the Wizard is actually called Faustus (50) and is identified with Nittlingen (the birthplace of the original Georg Faust) several times; his wife is called "Mrs. Wizard Nittlingen" (24), and Sax refers to "'The Wizard of Evil with his Nittlingen pain-gnomes'" (208). Kerouac, showing a familiarity with Faust stories other than Goethe's, even describes the Wizard as still bearing "the horrible marks of his strangulation and occupation by the Devil" (52)—a fate that was said to have befallen Georg Faust (Palmer and More 1965, 121). Thus we can see that the Faust legend is operating thematically in Doctor Sax on a number of different levels. Sax is Faustian in his striving for knowledge. But Sax also plays Mephistopheles to Jacky's Faust. Just as Mephistopheles transports Faust around the world on his magic cloak, Sax magically transports Jacky around Lowell (210) and enfolds him in his "Shroudy Cape" (201). Sax is also associated with the Devil through the description "like a Goethe witch" (212), an allusion to the "Witch's Kitchen" scene in *Faust*. Jacky, a young boy on the verge of Experience, is also seeking knowledge, and like Goethe's Faust, turns from Christianity to the supernatural for solace. And the Wizard, too, is Faust in his most sinister form—a mortal who has sold his soul to the Devil in return for unlimited power. What unites these different embodiments of the Faust character is the common theme of human striving, and this is also the central theme in Goethe's *Faust*.

Goethe's Doctor Faust, as a young man, had, through asceticism and prayer, sought from God the power to dispel the ravages of the plague amongst his community. Disillusioned by his failure, Faust rejected Christian dogma and instead adopted a pantheistic humanism that included alchemy: "So I resorted to Magic's art, / To see if by spirit mouth and might / Many a secret may come to light" (1.377–79). Middle-aged at the play's opening, and driven almost to suicide by his frustrated desire for intellectual and spiritual fulfillment, Faust readily enters into a wager with Mephistopheles: "If the swift moment I entreat: / Tarry a while! you are so fair / Then forge the shackles to my feet" (2.1699–1700) In other words, if Faust should ever reach a moment of true contentment, then the Devil may take him. The remainder of the play follows Faust from this pact to his old age and death, and includes his youthful regeneration by the Witch's potion, his seduction and abandonment of the innocent Gretchen, his interaction with sundry demons and spirits, his collaboration with the Emperor of the Imperial Court, his physical union with the conjured spirit of Helen of Troy, and his vast land reclamation project, over which he presides at the end. Having wrested an empire from the sea, and thus having triumphed over nature, Faust at the end of his life calls for one last project, a huge canal that will drain an unhealthy marsh. It is at this point, with a legacy of brutal exploitation and sorcery behind him, that Faust experiences the altruistic vision that offers him contentment at last: "I'd open room to live for millions / Not safely but in free resilience. . . . Such teeming would I see upon this land, / On acres free among free people stand" (2.11563–580). Now he utters the words previously stated in his wager with Mephistopheles: "I might entreat the fleeting minute: / Oh tarry yet, thou art so fair!" (2.11581–582).

Perhaps it is because true contentment comes from the knowledge of having benefited humankind as a whole that Faust's soul is saved at the end. The Heavenly Host appear in brilliant radiance and distract Mephistopheles with their beauty while throwing roses down upon his minions, roses which, as the pure embodiment of divine grace, burn the "hellish host," causing them to "hunch and

flinch" (Goethe 2.11710). Faust's soul is carried up to Heaven, and
Mephistopheles is left to bemoan the "wretchedly mishandled" cul-
mination of his labors (2.11836). It is, ultimately, the mystery of
divine grace that Goethe is celebrating at the end, for Faust has been
no paragon of virtue. Yet he has exhibited the potential for good, too,
both in his early life and even just before his seduction by
Mephistopheles, when the sound of Easter church bells filled him
unexpectedly with joy and love (1.780–84). His striving to be always
more, to know always more, even if through forbidden means, articulates the dilemma of human existence. For in the "Prologue in
Heaven" human striving is presented negatively as the source of
error: "Man ever errs the while he strives," says the Lord (1.317). Yet
at the end, the angels who carry Faust to Heaven proclaim,
"'Whoever strives in ceaseless toil/Him we may grant redemption'"
(2.11936). The question then becomes, what is one striving for, good
or for evil?

Adam McLean has suggested that Goethe's *Faust* can be read as
an allegory of the tension between good and evil in the individual
soul, with Gretchen and Mephistopheles representing the good and
the evil aspects of Faust (McLean n.d., 1). Faust does, after all, at one
point say, "Two souls, alas, are dwelling in my breast" (Goethe
1.1112). Kerouac has a similar design in mind, for Sax and the
Wizard, in Duluoz's inner spiritual drama, represent the good and
evil potentialities of the human soul. Sax, the altruistic embodiment
of Faust, is, like Faust, defeated at the end by the forces of evil, and
yet, like Faust, is saved through the grace of a higher power. The
Wizard, the evil embodiment of Faust, is annihilated, disappearing in
the conflagration of his own making. And, like Goethe, Kerouac uses
the image of the rose at the end of the novel to represent divine
grace. Jacky, having witnessed the destruction of the Snake by the
Great Bird, heads for home, gathering roses as he goes: "I found
another rose, and put another rose in my hair, and went home. By
God" (1987, 245).

The rose is an important repeated symbol in the novel; it does
not appear gratuitously as a mere echo of Goethe. But, like Goethe,
the symbolism often seems ambiguous. On the one hand, the rose is
connected by Sax with the power to overthrow evil: "'roses know
herbs better than you'" (Kerouac 1987, 208). But the rose is also asso-

ciated with the river in flood, and the river in flood is associated
with the Snake and with the convergence of evil. Hence Chapter 4
of Book 4, "The Flood," begins "Mell, river rose, mell" (148). The play
on words evokes both the river rising and the flower. "Mell," a British
dialect word that comes from the French "mêler," means to blend or
mix. As so often in *Doctor Sax*, the meaning is oblique and com-
pressed. But one of Kerouac's central concerns is necessary coexis-
tence of opposites. The melding, or mixing, of good and evil in the
novel (note, for instance, that Sax's dove is also an albino bat) is suggested in this poetic opening phrase. Then, when Jacky stands looking down at the "carnage of huge rains in a snow flood" in Part 5 he
cries, "'Oh rose of the north, come down!'" (156). Duluoz then contemplates the source of the Merrimac in the fairy-tale north where "a
lover boy in a Hans Christian Anderson fairytale dropped a rose into
the stream" (156). Jilted by his "little Gretchen," this boy throws away
the rose meant for her, and so it finally reaches the Merrimac. To say
that the rose symbolizes spiritual rather than sexual love is rather
too easy a reading of this oblique passage, but we can certainly say
that the rose symbolizes the redemptive power of love, for, we are
told, "The rose was meant for mary" [sic] (156). The rose as a symbol
of the Virgin Mary is most famously represented in Dante's *The
Divine Comedy*, where she is described as "The Mystic Rose" whose
snow-white petals are the souls of the blessed (*Paradiso* 31.1–3).
Kerouac's "rose of the north" is probably intended to suggest the
"dazzling white" (31.15) of Dante's Mystic Rose.

But the rose is also associated with Saint Thérèse of Lisieux, she
who is mentioned several times in *Doctor Sax* as the source of various religious nightmares and visions (Kerouac 1987, 4, 34, 145). Also
known as the Little Flower of Jesus, Thérèse had her calling from
God when still a child, and entered the Carmelite Convent of Lisieux
when only fifteen, hence her particular association with children
(*The New Catholic Encyclopedia* 1967, 14: 78). On her deathbed in
1897, Thérèse had said, "After my death I will let fall a shower of
roses" (Society of the Little Flower, website); Kerouac refers to this in
Visions of Gerard (1976, 129), the novel he wrote in memory of his
older brother, who died aged nine. The rose thus represents tenderness and compassion, and it is significant that the novel ends with
Jacky Duluoz joyfully gathering roses as he passes by the Grotto

(245), previously a scene of such dark foreboding [i.e., "Everything there was to remind of Death, and nothing in praise of life" (125)]. By the end of the novel, the religious images that have previously been so terrifying and resonant of death have become powerfully affirming. And Doctor Sax, the mediator between Innocence and Experience, the embodiment of supernatural powers, becomes just an ordinary guy when viewed in the context of a larger religious scheme. Thus the novel represents the passage from childhood to adulthood and the replacing of religious fear with religious faith.

This is an important point for students to grasp. The novel is so unconventional in style and structure that it is initially difficult for students to accept that it has a serious religious content. A few key passages should be pointed out. For instance, Book Six, entitled "The Castle," begins with an explicitly religious reference: "A strange lull took place—after the Flood and before the Mysteries—the Universe was suspending itself for a moment of quiet" (Kerouac 1987, 183). In Catholic Doctrine, mysteries are revealed truths that surpass normal understanding and through which God makes himself known to the limited human mind (*The New Catholic Encyclopedia* 10:157). This sense is reinforced by Doctor Sax's words to Jacky shortly afterwards, when they finally meet face to face: "'The understanding of the mysteries,' he said, 'will bring forth your understanding of the maples'—pointing at the air" (1987, 194). That Jacky's entering of the Castle is meant to represent self-knowledge has already been suggested in Duluoz's description of the Castle as "wild, noble, baronial home of the soul" (191). And this suggests that as well as Saint Thérèse of Lisieux, Kerouac was also thinking of Saint Teresa of Avila, the sixteenth-century Spanish Carmelite nun and Doctor of the Church represented so famously by Giovanni Bernini in *The Ecstasy of Saint Teresa*. Teresa of Avila's most famous work is *The Interior Castle*, a series of meditations arising from her vision of the soul as a castle comprising many rooms "some above, others below, others at each side; and in the center and midst of them all is the chiefest mansion where the most secret things pass between God and the soul" (1990, 19). As Doctor Sax leads Jacky further and further into the Castle, they witness all kinds of monsters that have run straight off the pages of the lurid pulps devoured by Kerouac in his boyhood. But once deep inside the castle, Jacky has a vision that is unambiguously Christian in nature:

> But even as I looked everything trembled to turn white. The milky moon was first to send the radiant message—then the river looked like a bed of milk and lilies, the rain beads like drops of honey. Darkness shivered white. Ahead of me in snow white raiment Doctor Sax suddenly looked like an angel saint. Then suddenly he was a hooded angel in a white tree, and looked at me. I saw waterfalls of milk and honey, I saw gold. I heard Them singing. I trembled to see the halo pure. (Kerouac 1987, 223)

Doctor Sax then leads Jacky to the edge of the Pit, where far below he sees the huge mountain-head and lake-eyes of the Great World Snake (226). Having known good, Jacky must also know evil; moreover, in keeping with the theme of *The Interior Castle*, he must recognize that evil as part of himself, his soul as already fallen: "I leaned on a stone, The Pit yawned below, I looked down to face my horror, my tormentor, my mad-face demon mirror of myself. . . . I found myself looking into the horror, into the void, I found myself looking into the Dark, I found myself looking into IT, I found myself compelled to fall. *The Snake was coming for me!*" (238).

The Biblical dimensions in this final section of the novel are unmistakable. We are told that "The Angels of the Judgement Day were making great tremendous clang across the way" (Kerouac 1987, 227), and Sax himself says, "'My son, this is judgement day'" (236). The Great Snake clearly represents the Biblical Satan: the description of it emerging "from the unspeakable central dark depths to which originally he had been hurled" (234) and now appearing in "full flaming fury of the dragon" (234) echoes the vision of John in The Book of Revelation (12:7). The Snake also clearly references Virgil's description of Satan at the end of *The Inferno* as "The Great Worm of Evil/which bores through the world" (34.108-09).

When the Snake emerges, despite the best efforts of Sax, it seems as though the end of the world is indeed nigh:

> Showers of black dust made a shroud of wings and a droop-drape bierlike background in the clear sky like a thundercloud without sense, in the center of its darkness darkly and more high rose the Mysterious Head. . . . Into the beautiful glary pale of giant massclouds that had come to cover the sun, leaving a snow White hole, rose the mighty venom headed Serpent of Eternity—clouds formed at his slowly emerging base. (Kerouac 1987, 241)

As I have noted elsewhere (Paton 2000), the imagery here strongly suggests the mushroom cloud of an atomic explosion. The Soviet atom bomb tests of 1949 and the outbreak of the Korean War in 1950 had so heightened political anxiety about a third world war that President Truman authorized the development of the hydrogen bomb, which was tested on the Eniwetok atoll on November 1, 1952. Oakley describes the effects: "The bomb blast created a fireball 5 miles high and 4 miles wide and a mushroom cloud 25 miles high and 100 miles wide, completely destroyed the mile-wide island, left a hole in the Pacific floor a mile long and 175 feet deep, and created a temperature at the center of the blast five times greater than the center of the sun" (1986, 45). Kerouac, writing *Doctor Sax* throughout 1952, creates a Wizard whose evil is the unleashing of a destructive force that "will darken the very sun" (1987, 227) and return the earth to fire (228). Like Faust who dreams of harnessing the power of the ocean (*Faust* 2.10219), Wizard Faustus dreams of harnessing the power of the Snake: "I'd rather lead my candle Satan soul with my Promised Snake dragon-ing the earth in a path of slime fires and destruction" (Kerouac 1987, 227).

Lest this seem to be reading too much into the novel (as Kerouac's detractors like to point out, his writing was just "typing"[9]), it might be useful to consider Kerouac's own statement on *Doctor Sax*:

> "Faust Part Three" simply means this: Goethe wrote Faust Parts one and two, ending with dull Canals, and I just wrote Part Three of the Faust Legend about the soul of the West. Faust sold his soul to the devil but Sax rushed in and called Faust a bastard. Consult Spengler on the "Faustian Western Soul" . . . take a look at what Spengler said about Faust, and how Faust led up to Space Missiles because he believed in the "endlessness of the soul." (Kerouac 1999, 298)

Goethe's *Faust* has been read as a Romantic response to the Industrial Revolution. Faust, in his insatiable striving for control over the natural world, can be seen as the ultimate embodiment of technological hubris (Berman 1988, 63). But for Kerouac, perhaps, the atomic age represented a further extension of this hubris, to a degree that Goethe could never have envisioned. A new era of technological mastery over nature perhaps required a further exploration of what Spengler called the Faustian soul of Western Civilization (1986, 1.354). Kerouac, considerably influenced by

Spengler, may have intended *Doctor Sax* to represent the final phase of western culture, a phase dominated by the cult of the individual (Hitler, Stalin, and Mussolini seemed to eerily confirm this) and characterized by successive world wars until finally united under the rule of a Caesar-figure (Spengler 1986, 2.416). Kerouac's Atomic Faustus may hint at the prospect of such political imperialism: with the hydrogen bomb, the idea of ruling the world was not outside the bounds of contemporary political thought.

But Kerouac's vision is by no means nihilistic. True to the spirit of Goethe, although even more unconventional in expression, the mystery of divine grace is given concrete form at the end. A huge Bird of Paradise arrives, "surrounded by a great horde of white doves," with "gorgeous feathers of Heaven" (Kerouac 1987, 242), and "black as Jonah, thunderous-faced" (243). Jonah in the Hebrew means "dove," but the allusion to this Biblical character also implies God's transcendent mercy: in the Bible, the citizens of Ninevah are spared, despite Jonah's insistence that they deserve punishment. His anger, for he was the agent of their reform, is perhaps reflected in the Bird, also the agent of God's mercy (Jonah 4.1). The Bird grabs the Snake in its beak and flies off with it: "The bloody worm was ousted from his hole, the neck of the world was free" (Kerouac 1987, 245). Just Dante and Virgil emerge from Hell just before dawn on Easter Sunday, so do Jacky and Doctor Sax emerge from the Castle at dawn on a Sunday that Kerouac suggests is also Easter: "the bell was clanging with a ding dong, the Lord rose on Easter morning, daisies rejoiced in fields beyond the churches, almighty peaces settled in the clover" (244).

The preceding discussion has emphasized the Christian aspects of *Doctor Sax*. However, when teaching this intricately structured novel, it would be a mistake to leave students with the impression that Kerouac is espousing straightforward Catholic doctrine, especially given a political climate that was fanatical in equating western democracy with God and Soviet communism with Satan. Kerouac's Great Bird may be described in Christian terms, but the eagle devouring the serpent is also the central symbol of Aztec myth and the emblem of the city of Mexico. According to Aztec legend, the vision of eagle with the serpent in its beak would indicate to the wandering Mexica where they should build their capital (Bierhorst

1990, 192). Kerouac's postscript to the novel—"Written in Mexico City, Tenochtitlan, 1952, Ancient Capital of Azteca"—indicates his interest in and knowledge of the culture. The Great Black Bird, while possibly alluding to Dante's Roman Eagle (the Church), more directly evokes the Andean condor, the largest flying bird in the world, which signified to the Inca rebirth and salvation. Sax, when he cries out "'O Palalakonuh Beware!'" (Kerouac 1987, 170), is using a name derived from the Nahuatl word for "very poisonous snake," "Palancacoatl."[10] Sax's invocation to Christ, "Savior in the Heaven! Come and lift me up" (233) is balanced by his later pagan invocation, "Ah the Great Power of the Holy Sun . . . destroy thy Palalakonuh with thy secret works" (238). Like Goethe, Kerouac combines pagan and Christian myth in a vision that emphasizes not one single doctrine but the importance of faith generally, and does so in a form that fuses high and low culture in ways not yet attempted in the novel, whether American or European.

If we keep in mind Morris Dickstein's claim that "nothing was more characteristic of the fifties than its weakness for hard and fast cultural distinctions, exclusions, hierarchies" (Dickstein 1977, 4), then we can better appreciate Kerouac's achievements in *Doctor Sax*, a novel that actively and exuberantly seeks to bring together different literary, cultural, and religious systems. For Kerouac, as for Blake, "All religions are one" (1984, 5) and, like Blake, he viewed the imagination as holy. For Blake, "This world of Imagination is the World of Eternity; it is the divine bosom into which we shall all go after the death of the Vegetated body" (358). In *Doctor Sax*, Duluoz, recalling his "innocent book-devouring boyhood immortal night" (Kerouac 1987, 203), tells us, "I lay in my white sheets reading with cat and candy bar . . . that's where all these things were born" (43). Jacky's suffering, his fall into Experience, and his ultimate salvation take place within his own consciousness. And Doctor Sax, like Virgil guiding Dante, functions as a mediator for Jacky between the temporal and the sacred realms. Doctor Sax, in all his lurid, hyperbolic verbosity, ultimately represents the creative force of the imagination. The novel overall is a testament to that which is holy and redemptive in all of us: the power to believe.

APPENDIX
ESSENTIALS OF SPONTANEOUS PROSE

SETUP. The object is set before the mind, either in reality, as in sketching, (before a landscape or teacup or old face) or is set in the memory wherein it becomes the sketching from memory of a definite image-object.

PROCEDURE. Time being of the essence in the purity of speech, sketching language is undisturbed flow from the mind of personal secret idea-words, blowing (as per jazz musician) on subject of image.

METHOD. No periods separating sentence-structures already arbitrarily riddled by false colons and timid usually needless commas—but the vigorous space dash separating rhetorical breathing (as jazz musician drawing breath between outblown phrases)—"measured pauses which are the essentials of our speech"—"divisions of the sounds we hear"—"time and how to note it down."

SCOPING. Not "selectivity" of expression but following free deviation (association) of mind into limitless blow-on-subject seas of thought, swimming in a sea of English with no discipline other than rhythms of rhetorical exhalation and expostulated statement, like a fist coming down on a table with each completed utterance, bang! (the spacedash)—Blow as deep as you want, satisfy yourself first, then reader cannot fail to receive telepathic shock and meaning-excitement by same laws operating in his own human mind.

LAG IN PROCEDURE. No pause to think of proper word but the infantile pile-up of scatological buildup words till satisfaction is gained which will turn out to be a great appending rhythm to a thought and be in accordance with the Great Law of timing.

TIMING. Nothing is muddy that runs in time and to laws of time— Shakespearean stress of dramatic need to speak now in own unalterable way or forever hold tongue—no revisions (except obvious rational mistakes, such as names or calculated insertions in act of not-writing but inserting).

CENTER OF INTEREST. Begin not from preconceived idea of what to say about image but from jewel center of interest in subject of image at moment of writing, and write outwards swimming in sea of language to peripheral release and exhaustion—Do not afterthink except for poetic or P.S. reasons. Never afterthink to "improve" or defray impressions, as, the best writing is always the most painful personal wrung-out tossed from the cradle warm protective mind—tap from yourself the song of yourself, blow!—now!—your way is your only way—"good"—or "bad"—always honest, ('ludicrous') spontaneous, "confessional" interesting, because not "crafted." Craft is craft.

STRUCTURE OF WORK. Modern bizarre structures (science fiction, etc.) arise from language being dead, "different" themes give illusion of "new" life. Follow roughly outlines in outfanning movement over subject, as river rock, so mindflow over jewel-center need (run your mind over it, once) arriving at pivot, where what was dim formed "beginning" becomes sharp-necessitating "ending" and language shortens in race to wire of time-race of work, following laws of Deep Form, to conclusion, last words, last trickle—Night is The End.

MENTAL STATE. If possible write "without consciousness in semi-trance" (as Yeats' later "trance writing"), allowing subconscious to admit in own uninhibited interesting and so "modern" language what conscious art would censor, and write excitedly, swiftly, with writing or typing cramps, in accordance (as from center to periphery) with laws of orgasm, Reich's "beclouding of consciousness." Come from within, out—to relaxed and said.

Notes

1 Students should be made aware that *On the Road* is not spontaneous prose. One version of it was, indeed, written in a three-week period, but Kerouac discovered his sketching method after this famous scroll experiment, and the version of *On the Road* that was finally published in 1957 had been carefully revised and edited. By far the best discussion of this matter is Hunt (1996). For a shorter overview, I recommend Charters (1991).

2 A particularly useful source is Whitfield (1996).

3 I have discussed the stylistic effects of movies, pulp fiction, and comic strips in Paton (2000, 166–94).

4 I especially recommend the first album, *Poetry of the Beat Generation*, in the boxed set, *The Jack Kerouac Collection* (1990).

5 Parker's double-timing is wellillustrated in his 1949 version of "Perdido"; an added bonus is Ella Fitzgerald's inspired scatting on the same track, which is a wonderful illustration of the kind of playful experimenting with sound and rhythm that Kerouac explored in his prose.

6 For instance, the 240th Chorus of *Mexico City Blues* begins, "Musically as important as Beethoven/Yet not regarded as such at all" (242).

7 It is very easy for students and scholars alike to conflate Kerouac and his various personae, whether Paradise, Percepied, or Duluoz. The latter is Kerouac's most transparent fictional identity, and Kerouac himself often conflated the two: "My name is Jack ('Duluoz') Kerouac and I was born in Lowell Mass. on 9 Lupine Road on March 12, 1922" (1982, 14). He has also simply used his own name, as in "October in the Railroad Earth." Nonetheless, when teaching *Doctor Sax* it is important to distinguish between author and narrator so that students remain aware that it is a carefully structured novel in which the author has made certain choices in order to create certain effects. Kerouac is not simply retelling incidents from his childhood as they occur to him, casually and indiscriminately, but creating a literary text that layers meaning into a conscious design.

8 In "The Hollow Men" (1925), Eliot portrays with frightening starkness the spiri-

tually bereft condition of contemporary humanity and emphasizes the irrevocable distance between the human and the divine, interestingly through the metaphor of "The Shadow." In "The Rock" (1934), he represents the founding of the Church (the rock), its degradation through human apathy, and its ultimate triumph. While no doubt sympathetic to Eliot's sense of the "perpetual struggle of Good and Evil," Kerouac seems to reject his emphasis on "the Visible Church" as the necessary site for communion with God. For Kerouac, "Eternity hears ordinary voices in the parlor."

9 This infamous putdown originated with Truman Capote (Charters 1991, viii).

10 I am indebted to Dr. Susan Toby Evans of The Pennsylvania State University for this information.

Works Cited

Allen, Donald, ed. 1993. *Good Blonde and Others.* San Francisco: Grey Fox Press.

Berger, Arthur Asa. 1994. *L'il Abner: A Study in American Satire.* Jackson: University Press of Mississippi.

Berman, Marshall. 1988. *All That Is Solid Melts into Air: The Experience of Modernity.* New York: Penguin.

Bierhorst, John. 1990. *The Mythology of Mexico and Central America.* New York: William Morrow & Co.

Blake, William. 1984. *Poems and Prophecies,* ed. Max Plowman. London: Everyman's Library.

Charters, Ann. 1991. Introduction to *On the Road.* New York: Viking Penguin.

———. 1987. *Kerouac: A Biography.* New York: St. Martin's Press.

"The Creeping Death." 1933. *The Shadow Magazine,* 15 January, 1–80.

Dante Alighieri. 1977. *The Divine Comedy.* Trans. John Ciardi. New York: W.W. Norton.

Dickstein, Morris. 1977. *Gates of Eden: American Culture in the Sixties.* New York: Basic Books.

Douglas, Malcolm. 1999. "'Jazz America': Jazz and African American Culture in Jack Kerouac's *On the Road.*" *Contemporary Literature* 40.1: 85–110.

Ellington, Duke. 1997. "Perdido." In *Duke Ellington's Greatest Hits.* Columbia.

Ginsberg, Allen. 1999. "Interview with Thomas Clark (1966)." In *Beat Writers at Work.* New York: The Modern Library.

Goethe, Johann Wolfgang von. 1976. *Faust: A Tragedy.* Trans. Walter Arndt, ed. Cyrus Hamlin. New York: W.W. Norton.

Gridley, Mark C. 1994. *Jazz Styles: History and Analysis.* 5th ed. Englewood Cliffs, NJ: Prentice Hall.

"Hands in the Dark." 1932. *The Shadow Magazine,* May, 1–82.

The Holy Bible. 1989. New Revised Standard Version. Nashville: Thomas Nelson Publishers.

Hunt, Tim. 1996. *Kerouac's Crooked Road: Development of a Fiction.* 2nd ed. Berkeley: California University Press.

"The Isle of Doubt." 1933. *The Shadow Magazine,* 15 August, 7–85.

The Jack Kerouac Collection. 1990. CD. Los Angeles: Rhino Records.

Johnson, Joyce. 1983. *Minor Characters*. London: Picador.

Jones, Hettie. 1996. *How I Became Hettie Jones*. New York: Grove Atlantic.

Kerouac, Jack. 1999a. "Interview with Ted Berrigan (1968)." In *Beat Writers at Work*. New York: The Modern Library.

———. 1999b. *Selected Letters, 1957-1969*. Ed. Ann Charters. New York: Viking Penguin.

———. 1996. *Selected Letters, 1940-1956*. Ed. Ann Charters. New York: Penguin Books.

———. 1993a. "Aftermath: The Philosophy of the Beat Generation." In *Good Blonde and Others*, ed. Donald Allen. San Francisco: Grey Fox Press.

———. 1993b. "On the Origins of a Generation." In *Good Blonde and Others*, ed. Donald Allen. San Francisco: Grey Fox Press.

———. 1993c. "The Origins of Joy in Poetry." In *Good Blonde and Others*, ed. Donald Allen. San Francisco: Grey Fox Press.

———. 1990. *Mexico City Blues*. New York: Grove Weidenfeld.

———. 1987. *Doctor Sax: Faust Part Three*. New York: Grove Press.

———. 1982a. "October in the Railroad Earth." In *Lonesome Traveller*. London: Granada.

———. 1982b. *Vanity of Duluoz*. London: Granada.

———. 1976. *Visions of Gerard*. New York: McGraw-Hill.

McLean, Adam. n.d. "The Alchemical Drama of Goethe's *Faust*." <http://www. levity. com/alchemy/faust.html. 31 May 2000.

The New Catholic Encyclopedia. 1967. 17 vols. New York: McGraw-Hill.

Oakley, J. Ronald. 1986. *God's Country: America in the Fifties*. New York: Dembner Books.

Owens, Thomas. 1995. *Bebop: The Music and Its Players*. New York: Oxford University Press.

Palmer, Philip Mason, and Robert Pattison More. 1965. *The Sources of the Faust Tradition: From Simon Magus to Lessing*. New York: Haskell House.

Parker, Charlie. 1993. "Perdido." In *Charlie Parker 1949: Jazz at the Philharmonic*. Polygram.

Paton, Fiona. 2000. "Beyond Bakhtin: Towards a Cultural Stylistics." *College English* 63 (November): 166–94.

Pomerance, Alan. 1991. *Repeal of the Blues: How Black Entertainers Influenced Civil Rights*. New York: Citadel Press.

"The Romanoff Jewels." 1932. *The Shadow Magazine*. 1 December, 1–83.

Rosenthal, David. 1992. *Hard Bop: Jazz and Black Music, 1955–1965*. New York: Oxford University Press.

Saint Theresa of Avila. 1990. *The Interior Castle*. Trans. and ed. E. Allison Peers from the Critical Edition of P. Silverio de Stanta Teresa. C.D. Christian Classics Ethereal Library. http://www.ccel.org/t/teresa/castle.html. 15 June 2000.

The Shadow Chronicles: Original Shadow Broadcasts. 1996. CD. Carrolltown, GA: GAA Corporation.

Smeed, J.W. 1987. *Faust in Literature*. Westport, CN: Greenwood Press.

Society of the Little Flower. 2000. <http://:www.littleflower.org/therese/index. html. 13 June 2000.

Spengler, Oswald. 1986. *The Decline of the West*. 2 vols. Trans. Charles Francis Atkinson. New York: Alfred A. Knopf.

Swartz, Omar. 1999. *The View from On the Road: The Rhetorical Vision of Jack Kerouac*. Carbondale: Southern Illinois University Press.

Tollin, Anthony. 1996. "The Shadow: The Making of a Legend." In *The Shadow Chronicles: Original Shadow Broadcasts*. CD. Carrolltown, GA: GAA Corporation.

Whitfield, Stephen. 1996. *The Culture of the Cold War*. 2nd ed. Baltimore: Johns Hopkins University Press.

CHAPTER SEVEN

Word Begets Image and Image Is Virus: Undermining Language and Film in the Works of William S. Burroughs

Douglas G. Baldwin

> An essential feature of the Western control machine is to make language as non-pictorial as possible, to separate words as far as possible from objects or observable processes. (Burroughs and Odier 1989)

> I can feel a probing insect intelligence behind the camera. (Burroughs 1992c)

For two of my semesters as a graduate student, I had the privilege of teaching in Yale University's College Seminar program. These are small classes—enrollment is limited to 18 students—designed to offer undergraduates various "innovative and experimental" curricula not available through the mainstream course catalogue (I remember for instance that one especially popular seminar studied the philosophy of Chinese gardens). My own, in fact relatively traditional and dissertation-based, class was titled "Postmodern American Fiction and Film." Over the course of thirteen weeks, we read eleven novels and (evenings before the once-a-week seminar met) viewed the eleven adaptations of these works. What made the class "non-mainstream" was both the interdisciplinary film-literature approach, not common

at Yale, and the selection of many authors one might roughly associate with the zeitgeist of the 1960s—Vladimir Nabokov, Ken Kesey,
Philip K. Dick, Kurt Vonnegut, Joseph Heller, E. L. Doctorow, et al.—a
period whose authors are neither traditional enough to be taught as
canonical, nor new enough to be taught as "contemporary." Our larger theoretical focus was on the narratological interrelationships of
prose and film within the narrower context of concerns with theories of adaptation and postmodernism. Perhaps inevitably, most of
the classroom dialogue concentrated on the former of these
approaches. "How has the novel influenced its own adaptation?" and
"How has the director responded to and imitated the novelist's writing?" were the questions most often asked, even though I tried to
focus some of our discussions in part on how these contemporary
novelists themselves were self-consciously writing in a world
increasingly dominated by visual, rather than verbal, narration. Both
times that I taught this seminar our discussions of one pair of
works—William S. Burroughs's 1959 *Naked Lunch* and the 1991
David Cronenberg (very loose) adaptation—generated an interesting
and obverse approach from the norm. We became especially concerned with how film specifically—and technologies of the moving
image generally—seemed to have influenced Burroughs's writing
both stylistically and thematically, rather than studying how
Burroughs's prose had influenced Cronenberg's adaptation. It is this
approach—starting from what André Bazin has usefully termed the
"cross-breedings" of the two media of film and prose as twentieth-
century novelists gained a "new way of seeing things provided by
the screen" (1967, 61)[1]—that informs my current work.

Briefly, I wish to argue that all of Burroughs's writing reveals his
bipolar response to the rapid cultural ascendancy of the uniquely
twentieth-century media of, primarily, film but also the subsequent
medium of television and video. The bipolar response is, on the one
hand, a fascination with narrative methodologies developed along
with the growth of various technologies of the moving image as they
suggest potential "cinematic storytelling" that he could imitate in language, and, on the other hand, an increasing suspicion of the potential societal "control" technologies of the moving image may have
over the individual. One may argue that this ambivalent response to
such media as film, television, and video—a desire to imitate media

one intrinsically suspects—informs the work of many of the post-modern novelists of post-1945 America, and, further, that this general distrust of technologies of mass culture and media is especially problematic for those very *avant-garde* writers who are likely to experiment with narrative strategies inspired by new technologies of representation.[2] However, with Burroughs the approach is specifically complicated by his analogous fascination with, and simultaneous suspicion of, the very verbal medium he uses to express his anxiety about alternate and competing technologies of discourse. For Burroughs, *both* visual and verbal narratives traditionally fail to mimic real processes of perception; they instead redefine how people "see." For Burroughs, this "redefining" becomes a trope for how perception—individuals' "narrative self-fashioning," as it were—is controlled by outside forces. Thus, I will argue, while Burroughs's aleatory fiction conflates the techniques of the initially disparate media of visual imagery and prose, it also simultaneously seeks to challenge the traditional narrative common to both and to offer in a rebellious stance an alternative narrative style that promises to free readers from social, aesthetic, and political forms of "control" represented by society's "normal" visual and verbal storytelling.

In a 1976 interview, Burroughs pronounced, "I think that writing *is* a transcription of a film. And so I've used a lot of film techniques. I see something, and I say, 'Well, this is a film, so this is take so-and-so, and we see it from this viewpoint'" (1980a, 164). This "transcribing of a kind of film in the mind"—and the subsequent aesthetic tension between the competing media of film and prose fiction—informs all of Burroughs's writing. In this essay, my analysis of film's contrasting narrative and thematic influence on Burroughs's early fiction frames comparative "readings" of Burroughs's two filmscript novels (the 1969 *The Last Words of Dutch Schultz: A Fiction in the Form of a Filmscript* and his 1979 *Blade Runner: A Movie*) and three experimental films Burroughs helped Antony Balch make in the early 1960s (*Towers Open Fire*, *The Cut-Ups*, and *Bill & Tony*). I am interested in how each work develops Burroughs's thematic focus on all forms of mass media as the locus of a virus like societal threat. In a Burroughsian world, film parallels language as it operates as aesthetic and social metaphor: the visual becomes the viral in a world where video technology merges with, then usurps, prose as the site of narrative authenticity in a world of socially constructed images. In Burroughs's fiction, drug addiction mirrors image addiction, and that, in turn, functions as a trope for State control of the individual. Burroughs thus offers a strongly cinematically informed prose as a way to "storm the reality studio" in both aesthetic and social rebellion, breaking through the traditional novel's (and society's) narrative discourse in order to offer alternative modes of what initially appear to be mere anti-narratives.

In Burroughs's first novel, the 1953 *Junky*, narrator Bill Lee describes his "first experience with junk." To combat the initial onslaught of nausea and fear, Lee lies down, and a "series of pictures passed, like watching a movie" (1977, 7).[3] The rapid, non-diegetically linked images that "Lee" then "sees" under the influence of his first shot of heroin subsequently describe the kind of cinematic montage we find in Burroughs's major fiction, where seemingly disparate scenes, images, and ultimately even individual words are thrown with what Burroughs has defined as "randomized montage" against the reader's imagined narrative screen (1991, 53ff). From the mosaic of these juxtapositions the reader must structure not so much a plot as an abstract painting, a visual sensibility formed from spattered bits of language.[4] Explaining the anti-novelistic form of *Naked Lunch*, Burroughs later stated:

> I think that the novelistic form is outmoded and that we may look forward to a future in which people do not read at all or read only illustrated books and magazines or some abbreviated form of reading matter. To compete with television and photo magazines writers will have to develop more precise techniques producing the same effect on the reader as a lurid action photo. (Burroughs and Odier 1989, 27; italics added)[5]

For Burroughs, writing a "lurid action photo" will mean restructuring his prose fiction to match cinematic and painterly expressionism, and, eventually, experimenting literally with mixed media as his "prose fiction," his "screenplay novels," and his "illustrated books" attempt to "compete" with all visual media—and to break free of the "representational straitjacket of the novel" (1991, 55)—while still insisting upon resisting the implicit societal control such media can have.[6]

In *Naked Lunch*, the "Atrophied Preface" (which appeared in the last twenty pages of the original Paris 1959 edition, before Burroughs added the "Deposition" and "Appendix" to the American

Grove Press edition) randomly repeats scenes ("shuttle pictures" and "[t]entative half impressions," says the narrator [1992a, 198]) as well as characters culled from the novel's narrative threads in a style that recalls the briefly fashionable Hollywood movies that would flash scenes from the already-viewed film during the closing credits. This filmic sensibility complements the novel's opening *film noir* parody where the narrator offers the nerd "Ivy League advertising exec-type fruit" a scene from an imagined Hollywood "B production": a drug pusher fleeing a narc in New York's subway system. *Naked Lunch* prominently foregrounds references to film jargon; such terms as "cut," "fadeout," "flashback," and "play it back on the screen" recur even in scenes outside the formally evoked movie sequences. This early, seminal Burroughs work also features the famous Burroughsian advice on how to read the text: "So instead of yelling 'Where Am I?' cool it and look around and you will find out approximately. . . . You were not there for *The Beginning*. You will not be there for *The End*. . . . Your knowledge of what is going on can only be superficial and relative . . ." (1992a, 199; Burroughs's italics and ellipses). In Burroughs's explanation of his reordering of the novel—"I do not presume to impose 'story' 'plot' 'continuity'" (1992a, 200)—and in his depiction of a fictional world freed from "space-time" continuities, the postmodernist novel *Naked Lunch* does not aim even for the kind of potential narrative linear structure readers might pull from the stream of consciousness prose associated with the high modernists. Rather, the readers are in effect "seeing" an experiment in visual/verbal expressionism, Burroughs's initial attempt to merge two media. Later, in such works as *The Book of Breeething*, *The Third Mind*, *Cobble Stone Garden*, and *Ah Pook Is Here*, Burroughs will literally blend illustrations with prose in an analogous attempt to mix media and to demonstrate his principle, "Remember that the written word is an image" (1991, 55).[7]

Burroughs's aesthetic, I would argue, from his earliest writing is primarily one of image-in-flux, motion created in effect from scattered verbal images, what he terms "pinpoint photos of arrested motion." His intent is to create the literary equivalent of being able to see an entire painting or a photographed tableau, at once. These individual "photographed" images are then in effect sped across the reader's imagined eye in a recreation, as it were, of the film's origins

in "persistence of vision" or "phi effect"—the physical and psychological phenomena whereby the movement of, for instance, twenty-
four photographic stills per second creates "moving pictures" in the
viewer's eye. Burroughs's prose forces the viewer-reader to create
the sense of a moving picture from the rapidly presented still
images.[8] Burroughs's verb-truncated prose splatters broken narratives, sentences, and even words into "units which be all in one
piece and should be so taken, but the pieces can be had in any order
being tied up back and forth, in and out fore and aft like an innaresting sex arrangement . . . [a] kaleidoscope of vistas, medley of tunes . . .
[as] I, William Seward, will unlock my word horde" (1992a, 207–08).
Burroughs conflates ("non-normal") sex, language, and "kaleidoscop-
ic" vision as early prose protest against society's controlling definitions of sexuality, narrative, and visual perception. In Burroughs's
world view, "the virus in both male and female precipitates sexual
frenzy" (Burroughs and Odier 1989, 12). Burroughs first displays his
problematic correlation of sexuality and illness in *Naked Lunch*,
which includes within its narrative the infamous "Blue Movie"
sequence, directed by "The Great Slashtubick," an *artiste* ironically
devoted to "real" not faked Hollywood effects. This section of *Naked
Lunch*—"A.J.'s Annual Party"—has received perhaps more critical discussion than it merits for its so-called "Swiftian" satire of capital punishment, a simplistic reading I would argue that Burroughs tossed
out as a short-term placebo to validate the obscenities for what he
considered a naive American readership. For the purpose of this discussion, however, what interests me is not the issue of pornography
in its evocation of the Burroughsian images of homosexuality and
hanging, orgasm and death (although he shares with Bataille a fascination with these doublings); rather, it offers a way into understanding Burroughs's efforts to blur film and prose fiction. In *The Job*,
Burroughs presents a bizarre example of a "sex virus [that] so
inflames the sex centers in the back brain that the host is driven
mad from sexuality, all other considerations are blacked out. Parks
full of naked, frenzied people, shitting, pissing, ejaculating and
screaming" (Burroughs and Odier 1989, 188). Burroughs uses this as
a lead-in to a discussion of aural and visual mass media initially figured as social virus but then turned on those in control to under-

mine state authority: Burroughs's media "cross-breeding" thus leads to revolution.

Burroughs's use of a film-within-a-novel in *Naked Lunch* also foreshadows his subsequent efforts to write actual films, to write formally filmic novels, and to write seeming "filmscript novels" (or, more precisely, what Bruce Morrissette has usefully termed *ciné-romans*). In *Naked Lunch*, the "blue movie" sequence is, furthermore, part of what Brian McHale in *Postmodernist Fiction* has defined as an element of the "postmodern dominant," in which prose narratives use scenes from fictionally created films to generate ontological slippage in the diegesis: both the "real" narratives and the "fictional" films are narrated confusingly on the same ontological level, a "world-within-the-world, often one in competition with the primary diegetic world of the text, or a plane interposed between the level of verbal representation and the level of the 'real' . . . further destabiliz[ing] an already fluid and unstable fictional reality" (1987, 128).[9] Thus in *Naked Lunch* it becomes difficult to discern precisely where the "blue movie" sequences are separate from the framing fictional world in which they supposedly occur; the blurring narrative levels undermine the reader's safe role as a member of an uninvolved audience. Similarly, the increasingly pornographic passage underscores the reader's complicity as sexually embodied participant, not merely intellectually distant spectator, at a level of obscenity one did not initially intend to be involved in, as the "movie" shifts from "societally acceptable" pornography to a kind of *reductio ad nauseam* display of the perverse underlying truth its audience would wish to deny. Burroughs thus restructures the very terms of spectatorship as the visually inscribed prose forces a readerly involvement in the construction of narrative levels of representation of sex as metaphor of both illness and control (as early as *Junky*, Burroughs's metaphors relate "waves of hostility and suspicion" to "some sort of television broadcast" [1977, 5]).[10]

In the trilogy that follows (and derives from) *Naked Lunch—The Soft Machine, The Ticket That Exploded*, and *Nova Express*—film plays an increasingly thematic as well as stylistic role in Burroughs's narratives. Cameras as representative of all society's media become weapons of both State repression and organized rebellion as the science fiction tales detail Burroughs's themes of control and freedom, what McHale has usefully described as

> the thematic function of the interposed ontological level of the film. Reality in Burroughs is a film shot and directed by others; we are actors in the movie, our lives scripted and fixed on celluloid . . . the ontological level of the movies, interposed between reality and its textual representation, functions as a global metaphor for Burroughs's master-theme of control. (McHale 1987, 129–30; McHale's emphases)[11]

For Burroughs in *Nova Express*, the fight is seemingly hopeless: "'. . . those dumb rubes playing around with photomontage—Like charging a regiment of tanks with a defective slingshot'" (1980b, 44),[12] hopeless, that is, unless both the artist and the art "consumer" renegotiate the aesthetic terms of narrative with an anti-viral serum of rebellious storytelling. Burroughs's statement in *The Job* that "Image and word are the instruments of control" (Burroughs and Odier 1989, 59) becomes a Burroughsian leitmotif: "Image"—as created visually with video technology and verbally with metaphor—is the virus and the addiction central to the fictional world described in randomized juxtaposition of scenes, sentences, and individual words. Burroughs offers such readings in both his interviews and his fiction. "I predicate that the word is an actual virus," he has said to Robert Palmer, "and a virus that has achieved equilibrium with the host, and therefore is not recognized as a virus. . . . They replicate themselves with the cells but they don't harm the cells" (1972, 50); five years earlier, he had told Conrad Knickerbocker "[a]ddicts would do their work and come home to consume the huge doses of images awaiting them in the mass media" (1967, 149). Burroughs develops this motif in *Nova Express* where the "death-dwarf" is literally hooked on images, as this following passage suggests: "image *is* junk. . . . 'Reality' is simply a more or less constant scanning pattern—The scanning pattern we accept as 'reality' has been imposed by the controlling power on this planet, a power primarily oriented towards total control" (1980b, 51–52). But, we are told by the narrator of *The Ticket That Exploded*, the weapons of control can be turned against the controllers in a reiteration of Burroughs's "storm the reality studio" leitmotif: "A camera and two tape recorders can cut the lines laid down by a fully equipped film studio" (1987, 111). Burroughs here argues that his visually informed and fragmented narratives function as potentially successful revolution by using the very same controlling narrative methodologies against the society that relies on the addictive and viral mass media to placate and control its citizens.[13]

Thus, I would argue, Burroughs's aesthetics parallel his ideological rebellion. In *Nova Express*, apomorphine, the drug that in *Naked Lunch* Burroughs proposes as the only viable cure for addiction to heroin, is figured as an anti-viral agent, one designed to break lines of social control, just as Burroughs's random cut-ups are designed to break free from the control of the Word.[14] Working with ideas suggested by the painter Brion Gysin, Burroughs in his early trilogy increasingly uses the "cut-up" or "fold-in" aleatory style that challenges the representational authority of both written language and filmed image to narrate "history." In *The Job*, Burroughs explained his use of Hassan i Sabbah's "Nothing Is True—Everything Is Permitted" in terms of social representation: "If we realize that everything is illusion, then any illusion is permitted. As soon as we say that something is true, real, then immediately things are not permitted" (Burroughs and Odier 1989, 97).[15] Chance juxtapositions of images or words create their own reality, one as viable as societally constructed narratives (especially as generated by the media). "Implicit in *Nova Express* is a theory that what we call reality is actually a movie," Burroughs further told Knickerbocker: "It's a film—what I call a biologic film . . . for 'Nova Police,' read 'technology'" (1967, 159). The battleground is one of competing narrative strategies and media.[16] *Nova Express* describes itself as in effect a "war of images"; for the Nova Police, Nova Mob, and Nova Criminals, media and video imagery are the weapons of choice.[17] In *The Ticket That Exploded*, film is figured as the dominant monopolistic tool of State authority: "The reality film has now become an instrument and weapon of monopoly. The full weight of the film is directed against anyone who calls the film in question, with particular attention to writers and artists" (1987, 151). In Palumbo's reading of what he terms Burroughs's "science fiction tetralogy": "Contemporary existence is seen as a film that is rerun again and again, trapping the human soul like an insect imprisoned in amber, negating any possibility of real freedom" (1979, 326). Characters are caught in movies scripted by outside forces that wish to control them. At the same time, Burroughs's stylistics represent his efforts to seek to break free of these narrative bonds by evading linear structure: the books themselves participate in the rebellion they describe. At this stage in his artistic development, Burroughs is beginning to see how the synergistic merging of cinematic and prose storytelling offers an escape from the controls of literary and social structures.

During this decade Burroughs also works with Gysin and experimental filmmaker Antony Balch on four short films that feature the same stylistic approach to narrative that Burroughs is using as the controlling narrative methodology in his prose fiction: *Towers Open Fire*, *The Cut-Ups*, *Bill & Tony*, and *William Buys a Parrot*.[18] We see here Burroughs's one brief foray into working within the film medium itself (not counting, of course, such later involvement as his brief appearances in cult film cameo roles, Nike commercials, *Saturday Night Live*, and the like). Burroughs's films are as experimental in their narrative strategies as is his coeval fiction. Circumventing "classical Hollywood narrative," these Balch-Gysin-Burroughs collaborations explore the narrative potentials of the film medium. Burroughs is interested in the power of the image—like the word—as it can be manipulated and restructured in order to suggest not so much alternative narratives as anti-narratives free from the constrictions of socially constructed language and image. In his essay "Screenwriting and the Potentials of Cinema," Burroughs explains, "We were trying to expand the awareness of the audience by experimenting with the film medium. . . . What we were trying to do was jar people into an awareness [of the unconscious mind] by actually showing them mechanisms of perception that, of course, go on all the time" (1991, 79). Imitating that postmodern architecture that displays normally hidden structural mechanisms, simply by exposing the literary architectonics of both media—film and prose fiction—Burroughs hopes to teach his audience how to break free from controlling narratives and media.

Burroughs's consistent method is to underscore the potentially filmic in his prose and, at the same time, to bring to traditional filmic narrative the kind of radical narrative restructuring suggested by film but, ironically, developed in postmodernist prose. Burroughs has argued in *The Job* that film alters and falsifies reality, that, as Barthes might argue, photographs have less representational validity than memory, and that they can replace "real" memory with "false" (if seemingly "authentic") representation (Burroughs and Odier 1989,

35ff).[19] In *Chaos in the Novel: The Novel in Chaos*, Alvin Seltzer describes all of Burroughs's fiction as having a cinematic effect: "the imagination receives a series of images which the mind does not have time to cope with" (1974, 343). The rapid juxtaposition of seemingly unrelated images into an Eisensteinian dynamic montage that informs Burroughs's first five novels becomes the central methodology of his first work in the medium of film itself. He and Balch challenge narrative linearity with the kind of rapid cuts that will come to define current video narrative in everything from MTV to Oliver Stone's *Natural Born Killers*. Writing on film, Burroughs has indicated that this use of montage in film and literature more closely matches human perception (especially urban perception) than ideologically inspired linear narrative with its satisfying closure (1991, 54-5).

Burroughs's and Balch's eleven-minute 1963 collage *Towers Open Fire*—part of the script of which appears in related forms in *Nova Express* and *The Ticket That Exploded*—is thus less a story than a series of flashed images, a montage of flickering scenes the viewer must (try to) link into a resemblance of narrative. Balch describes it as a "straightforward attempt to find a cinematic equivalent for Burroughs's writing: an 11-minute collage of all the key themes and situations in the books, accompanied by a Burroughs soundtrack" (1972, 8). The film stars Burroughs as, for example, a CEO sonorously intoning at the British Film Institute board room in front of hand-copied hieroglyphs from the *Egyptian Book of the Dead*; as a combat soldier in an "orgasm attack" firing Ping-Pong balls at framed family photographs; and as a stoned drug addict zoo visitor staring down a vulture. Other prominent scenes include the following: old news footage from the 1929 Stock Crash (what Balch claims represents a symbol of society crumbling)[20]; a "Gysin flicker-dream-machine"; Balch himself masturbating; and numerous disjointed intercut scenes that defy diegetic description (1972, 8-9). The soundtrack meanwhile features Burroughs's infamously stentorian voice reading passages culled from his science fiction trilogy. Echoing the "storm the reality studio motif," the central image of *Towers Open Fire* is of "breaking through the gray room," which Burroughs has described as representing the "photography dark room where reality photographs are actually produced."

Burroughs's and Balch's collaboration, the aptly titled *The Cut-Ups* (first released in a twenty-minute-long version in 1966, then subsequently shortened by Balch to twelve minutes), plays even more so with film as a medium created from linked but discrete images. Its non-diegetic soundtrack played over repetitively flashed scenes consists of four constantly repeated sentences read over film footage created from double and triple superimpositions of sections of film. The original film was literally "cut up" into four equal pieces in the lab and then recombined in a precise pattern taking one foot of film from each of the four rolls and splicing it in turn to pieces from the other three rolls. The mechanical visual and verbal ordering produces what I find to be a fascinatingly engrossing and mesmerizing short work, if one that many early audiences found to border on the unwatchable or, interestingly, aggressively assaultive on the viewer. This latter sensation may well be Burroughs's intent, representing aesthetically his thematic concerns with words and images as weapons: "By making explicit the fragmentary nature of consciousness, we managed to arouse and upset the audiences, just as viewers were upset by the first exhibitions of abstract paintings" (1991, 79).[21] Those willing to stay with the film find themselves instinctively trying to find, and then superimpose, linear narrative onto the "randomized montage."[22]

In their 1963 *Bill & Tony*, voice and image are reversed so that the nature of filmic identity is interrogated by the medium itself as Burroughs's voice is played to Balch's face and vice versa. They read alternately from a Scientology Auditing manual (a recurrent motif in Burroughs's fiction) and a selection from the script to Tod Browning's cult film *Freaks* (distributed by Balch in Britain and shown as part of a double-bill with *Towers Open Fire*). Here Burroughs's script offered an early postmodernist undermining of film's claims for authentic representation and the subsequent paranoid fear of film replacing the individual's identity. In his *Rolling Stone* interview, Burroughs describes their project: "Balch and I did an experiment with his face projected onto mine and mine onto his. Now if your face is projected onto someone else's in color, it looks like the other person. You can't tell the difference; it's a real mask of light" (1972, 49). At least part of the intended effect is what in *The Ticket That Exploded* Burroughs calls a "strong erotic effect" (1987, 18). Burroughs also describes an even eerier experiment, to "record

and photograph very friendly and very unfriendly faces and words
and then alternate them 24 frames per second. That should have
quite an upsetting effect, I think; you don't know until you actually
do it" (1972, 49).[23] Burroughs's "experiments in deliberately upsetting and deranging the audience" (1991, 60) effectively restructure
audience perception. Image and word both lose stable, representational value. In the same year, Balch and Burroughs made the short
(about a minute and a half) *William Buys a Parrot* which also
undermines visual and verbal narrational validity. Although one
would expect some play on the conceit of the parrot—a "verbal"
bird that can meaninglessly echo human speech (Burroughs's image
of all speech, one might claim)—here, ironically, the Burroughs-bird
encounter is filmed in silence. Language has been circumvented, as,
in the brief and inconclusive series of shots, has narrative.

Following the experimental fiction and films of the 1960s comes
Burroughs's shift towards a more controlled, coherent narrative
voice in two self-consciously filmic novels: in 1969, *The Last Words
of Dutch Schultz: A Fiction in the Form of a Filmscript* (Burroughs's
first *ciné-roman*) and, the following year, *The Wild Boys*, a novel that
from its opening metaphor directly describes itself in terms of a film:
"The camera is the eye of a cruising vulture" (1992b, 3). Burroughs
here returns to what he himself earlier termed "nineteenth-century
style writing," while using twentieth-century film narrative as his
metaphorical medium; thus, the novel features both a more clearly
linear narrative and, ironically, a more self-consciously classic
Hollywood genre of filmmaking as opposed to the experimental
work in actual film Burroughs had already done with Balch. Film,
however, remains the major motif. In Jennie Skerl's summary of *The
Wild Boys*: "The novel is like a film theater for an audience of one,
showing several narratives simultaneously on several viewing
screens surrounding the viewer. At times the viewer observes the
narratives (which he can perceive only one at a time); at times he
enters one of them as a character (actor)" (1985, 81).[24] The language
of *The Wild Boys* blurs technical filmscript description with traditional novelistic narrative. Burroughs seems to co-opt for his own
use the medium that he'd figured as social threat in his science fiction trilogy. As in *Blade Runner: A Movie*, written at the other end of
the decade in 1979, Burroughs controls the randomized photomon-

tage that marks his work during the 1960s as he now experiments with writing actual film-novels.

Both *The Last Words of Dutch Schultz* and *Blade Runner* feature a narrative self-consciousness that recalls "The Great Slashtubick's" role as director in *Naked Lunch*. That is, both filmscripts include within their narratives specific self-referential descriptions of themselves *as* films.[25] Thus in *The Last Words of Dutch Schultz*, the narrative describes Dutch Schultz' memories as early silent Hollywood movies, so that we have an *mise en abîme* effect, a gangster's filmic nostalgia as the primary visuals of both the interior and framing film narratives.[26] The imagined film is in turn itself formed from uses of fragmented "stock footage 1920s film" that is constantly intercut with the main narrative film: "The loop turns, wheels interlock and the character is drawn out. . . . Passage of time is indicated by a loop repeating daily sale of junk and sex" (1970, 5-6). (Similarly, the screenplay includes references to a separate "junk loop" and "sex loop" that play "over and over" throughout the text.) Burroughs in "The Retreat Diaries" describes the narrative technique of this *ciné-roman* as: "The *structure* is that a man is *seeing a film* composed of past present and future, dream and fantasy, a film which the reader cannot see directly but only infer through the words" (1984, 192; Burroughs's italics). This "filmscript novel" includes actual news photos; the pages are split down the middle with narrative on the left and "soundtrack" on the right: the effect thus forces the reader to combine the descriptions into his or her own privately imagined film, while simultaneously "reading" the images taken from the "historical record," a concept Burroughs's script itself repeatedly interrogates.[27] Burroughs here privileges the synergistic blending of film and prose narration, demonstrating how the *ciné-roman* format allows an author the freedom to exploit the postmodernist restructuring of both media. Eric Mottram's description of an earlier edition of *Dutch Schultz*—"making the connections simultaneous to perception between newspaper, portrait and book, and between newsprint-image, drawing on canvas, and book-cover introduction" (1977, 239)—points to Burroughs's efforts in this work to blur the normal distinctions between novel and film.[28] Burroughs also, in effect, uses the screenplay medium of *Schultz* for what appear to be imaginative "filmings" of typical scenes from *Naked Lunch*: Scenes

181 and 183 feature grotesque, satiric restaurant scenarios that directly recall the 1959 novel, as if Burroughs were trying to merge his earlier novelistic prose into a scenarist's text (1993, 72-73); in a similar
vein, Burroughs's carnival motifs from his earlier work appear in
Schultz in the persona of the "Whisperer," whom gangster Dutch
Schultz hires to spread rumors on his behalf—the Whisperer's voice
filters through subsequent crowd scenes as if part of the "film's"
soundtrack (1993, 80-86).[29]

Similarly, *Blade Runner: A Movie* is created from Burroughs's
experiments with merging, or conflating, the discrete genres of
prose fiction, film, and filmscript, again featuring the Burroughsian
leitmotifs of sex, drugs, addiction, and (inter)national conspiracy.
Blade Runner opens *in medias res* with a writer/director describing the "film we're about to see" to his potential producer: "Now B.J.
you are asking me to tell you in one sentence what this film is
about?"[30] As in *Naked Lunch*, we are in the "film within a film" world
of ontological confusion as the narrative spirals downwards towards
a Conradian layering (although here it is forms of media as well as
narrative frames that dominate). In the course of the filmscript-novel
the narrator offers alternate possibilities for the imagined film, possibilities suggesting what is now being explored in hypertext fiction
(e.g., "From this point on there are two story lines that can run alternately or on two screens. The story that we have been following up
to this point becomes increasingly bizarre, dreamlike and episodic.
The other story, played out in linear future set, is real and logical
within the limited framework" [1990, 50-51]). The dialogically figured narrative voice suggests a producer-director story-table discussion in a Hollywood studio with the reader thus a participant in the
creation of a film he originally was merely observing, a sensibility
echoing the viewer/actor role in *The Wild Boys*.[31] The narrator tells
B.J., "Now here are a few sample shots" to introduce his descriptions
of possible scenes to the proposed film, a line followed by a "higher-
level" narrative voice stating, "*He riffles through stills from the
movie like a deck of cards* ..." (1990, 7; author's emphases and ellip-
sis): what follows is a collage of descriptive scenes (many seemingly
isolated, discrete scenarios) from what appears to be a proposed
futuristic dystopian "film" about an America without adequate medical
technology or insurance and the medical underground that subse-

quently appears. The printed text itself indicates breaks in the narrative with images of film stock (one thinks of the Viking Press edition of *Gravity's Rainbow*, with similar filmstrip icons between "scenes" of the novel); the text uses these images of film stock intercut with the stripped-down screenplay like prose to suggest how traditional narration is then intercut with filmic descriptions to effect a Burroughsian shift in audience reading expectation—film and novel merge in a challenge to either's hierarchical social status in society's narratives.

Interestingly, both of these two filmscript-novels represent an ironic reversal of Burroughs's movement in his novels from surface incoherence toward seeming linear narrative: the 1969 *The Last Words of Dutch Schultz* reads as a relatively straightforward Hollywood production, while *Blade Runner* ten years later features the rapid and often unexplained juxtapositions of Burroughs's 1960s science fiction trilogy.[32] It's as if Burroughs's experiments with *written* films move toward increased narrative experimentation just as his prose fiction moves towards traditional narrative normalcy. In his *Rolling Stone* interview, Burroughs emphasizes that "the text is still essential . . . and there are things really that there's no point in translating into pictures, since they are much clearer in prose. There's another point where a page of prose can't do what a picture does" (1972, 50). While trying to conflate the two discrete media of visual and verbal representation, Burroughs struggles to create a new form of narrative (akin to the "third mind" leitmotif of his work with Gysin) which privileges neither medium but, rather, interrogates the assumptions of control that underlie both.

In 1964, Marshal McLuhan framed his analysis of Burroughs's work in terms of what Burroughs himself later terms the "electronic revolution": "Burroughs is unique only in that he is attempting to reproduce in prose what we accommodate every day as a commonplace aspect of life in the electric age. If the corporate life is to be rendered on paper, the method of discontinuous nonstory must be employed." For McLuhan, an "evening watching television programs is an experience in a corporate form—an endless succession of impressions and snatches of narrative" (1991, 69). (Of course this vatic image of channel surfing the corporate reality recalls Burroughs's image of a "mosaic of a thousand newspapers" that recurs in *Naked Lunch*.) In McLuhan's "the medium equals the message" paradigm, Burroughs blurs visual and verbal orderings of reality to offer his "readers" a freedom from artistic, ideological, and narrative control. Word and image may each alone be addictive viruses. Traditional novels and "traditional" Hollywood-produced films may be voices of the State designed to limit and control individuals' perceptual understanding. However, combined and then restructured, Burroughs's fiction suggests, narratives formed from these two media together may represent a way to "storm the reality studio" and break free from addiction to traditional storytelling.

It is to this very confluence of prose and visual media in Burroughs's fiction that our Yale College seminar in "Postmodern American Fiction and Film" inevitably returned while we were considering prose works (and their adaptations) as disparate as *Catch-22* and *Short Cuts*, *Do Androids Dream of Electric Sheep?* and *Ragtime*. Initially in this century, it has been the link (and the implied competition) between film and prose storytelling that has informed many of the narratological developments in major American novelists, from the Hollywood-influenced (and financed) modernists to the contemporary postmodernists who attempt to "represent reality" in a world transformed and defined by the electronic revolution in which new modes of communication threaten to leave the novel behind. To "teach" the American post-World War II novel, then, one must look to the influence of competing forms of narrative representation created by this century's technologies of the moving image: film, television, video, and, increasingly, computer-generated and Internet-driven storytelling. As early as 1953, Burroughs's prose attempted to subsume and to challenge alternate narrative forms, and his fiction thus makes for an ideal starting point in any attempt to view contemporary fiction through the lens of visual narrational strategies that contemporary novelists simultaneously both resist and imitate.

Notes

1 In Bruce Morrissette's reading of the same phenomenon alluded to by Bazin, "Just as Eisentstein saw precinema in literature, critics now detect in many novels postcinematic effects; a joint evolution appears to be in progress. For better or worse, the two genres, novel and film, must look to a shared destiny" (1985, 27).

2 My current project traces this ambivalent response to film in the development of the twentieth-century American novel, framing my discussion of post-World War II postmodernists Vladimir Nabokov, Thomas Pynchon, Robert Coover, and Don DeLillo (as well as Burroughs) with close readings of four prominent "Hollywood" modernists, Nathanael West, John Dos Passos, F. Scott Fitzgerald, and William Faulkner. In this work, when I refer to both "technologies of the moving image" and "visual imagery," I am thinking primarily of film, but of course this discussion also relates to the "cinematic" storytelling associated with the media that film engendered—television and video—as well as to Burroughs's fascination with the "still" imagery of paintings. However, for the purposes of this discussion, I do not distinguish between the three primary forms of visual technologies of the moving image as they are reflected in Burroughs's work, and I often in fact use "film" as a kind of synecdoche for all forms of narration via these technologies of the moving image. (Increasingly, American novelists are competing with computer-generated imagery, from CD games to Internet narratives, but Burroughs's work does not reflect a concern with these new media.)

3 Later, in the 1964 *Nova Express*, Burroughs will directly link drugs and visuals: "Junk is concentrated image and this accounts for its pain killing action" (1980b, 49); heroin dealers and Hollywood producers share the desire to control users and viewers with the distraction of surface images. In the "Notes on Last Scene" in the Cape Goliard 1970 edition of *The Last Words of Dutch Schultz: A Fiction in the Form of a Film Script*, Burroughs includes a stage direction parallel to his image of addictive-drugs-as-film from *Junky*: "MORPHINE ADMINISTERED TO SOMEONE WHO IS NOT AN ADDICT PRODUCES A RUSH OF PICTURES IN THE BRAIN AS IF SEEN FROM A SPEEDING TRAIN. THE PICTURES ARE DIM, JERKY, GRAINY, LIKE AN OLD FILM" (1970; author's capitalization). The connection during early modernism between visual perception—as "changed" due to views from "speeding trains"—and the rise of the cinema as well as of modernist, "cinematic" narrative has been made before; for a recent discussion see Kirby (1997).

4 Frederick Dolan makes much of what he sees as Donald Palumbo's misreading— "the spots and blobs of paint in an impressionist painting [which] form a coherent image when viewed from a specific distance" (1994, 322-23)—concluding, "The parts of a Burroughs novel do not take their shape from the whole; the point is rather that the very idea of a larger logic becomes a trope introduced at various moments to produce an effect" (1994, 214 n.16). I would argue that Burroughs wants it both ways: the *effect*, or *sensibility* of a single painting, but that the painting remains entirely abstract: it is the reader's/viewer's efforts to superimpose his or her own individual linearity onto chaos that fascinates Burroughs, what in *The Job* he describes as the "[viewer's] mental process shapes what he sees" (Burroughs and Odier 1989, 173), an image paralleling his repeated idea that "what we see is determined to a large extent by what we hear" (1989, 160; 1987, 215-17). Dolan is correct in concluding that Burroughs "preserves the advantages of conventional narrative while avoiding its ideological traps."

5 Compare, for instance, Don DeLillo's, "The power of the film image seemed to be overwhelming our little world of print" (LeClair and McCaffery 1983, 84–85); Robert Coover's, "[Film's] great immediacy: it grasps so much with such rapidity. Certainly it's the medium par excellence for the mimetic narrative" (LeClair and McCaffery 1983, 69); and E. L. Doctorow's, "I don't know how anyone can write today without accommodating eighty or ninety years of film technology" (LeClair and McCaffery 1983, 99).

6 See Dolan for a useful discussion of Burroughs's work, especially his late trilogy, in terms of his political agenda (1994, 114–37).

7 Burroughs originally intended to include twenty-five ink drawings as part of *The Naked Lunch*, and he did produce "thick black calligraphic gestures on a purple and yellow ground" for the original Olympia Press edition of *The Naked Lunch* (Miles 1993, 230). For a useful discussion of Burroughs and his developing use of purely pictorial media, see Miles's chapter, "Shotgun Art" (1993, 229–41), as well as Burroughs's own *Painting and Guns* (1992b). For an excellent introduction to Burroughs's work across various media, see Sobieszek (1996).

8 Describing his (and filmmaker Balch's) own early efforts in experimental film, Burroughs reiterates this idea: "we also went back to the basic premise of film: the retention of the image. Film is based on the fact that you retain an image in your mind for one-tenth of a second, so that images that are actually still, when presented in sequences, will seem to move. And we attempted to show this by having a delayed image" (1991, 79).

9 Fredric Jameson, discussing a similar narrative phenomenon in Claude Simon's *Les corps conducteurs*, concludes, "Here, then, the materialization of the signified by quotation . . . is replicated diegetically or narratively on the level of the sign as a whole, with new and unexpected results: these passages now lift us from the realm of linguistic problematics and linguistic philosophy into that of image society and the media" (1991, 141).

10 See the early Burroughs image in *Queer*, "A television set which was out of order half the time and which emitted horrible, guttural squawks was the final touch of unpleasantness" (1985, 4). (Although not published until 1985, *Queer* was written in the early 1950s.) In *The Soft Machine*, Burroughs writes, "Antennae of TV suck the sky" (1980c, 10): like Pynchon later in *Vineland*, Burroughs throughout his fiction depicts the medium of (specifically American) television as an especially pernicious and pervasive societal addiction, one distinctly linked to drug addiction: "Addicts would do their work and come home to consume the huge doses of images awaiting them in the mass media. Junkies love to look at television" (1967, 149).

11 McHale further argues that the only escape in a Burroughsian world is "through *metalepsis*: breaching the ontological boundary, walking out of the ontological level of film to some higher (or lower) level" (1987, 130). Characters thus challenge the imprisonment of both visual and verbal narrative, existing in both worlds (and neither world) simultaneously.

12 See Nicholas Zurbrugg: "Burroughs's preoccupation with the ways in which variously sophisticated combinations of recorded words and images might be exploit-

ed as weapons, or means of social control. In this respect, photomontage is but a 'slingshot' in comparison with the potency of the electronic mass media" (1984, 95).

13 As John Vernon puts it: "Burroughs's solution to the repressive control that the image of reality imposes is to fragment it and mix it together, to erase all lines between things. If reality is a film, one loosens its grip by submitting it to a state of explosion, by cutting it up and splicing all spaces and times randomly together" (1973, 98).

14 John Kuehl persuasively argues that Burroughs views the "body physical and the body politic analogously" (1989, 243). For Burroughs, then, addiction and virus are realities for the individual just as they are tropes for society's methods of media control.

15 Here I think Scott Bukatman's reading captures Burroughs's conflation of verbal and visual resistance: "I would further argue that the anxiety surrounding the spectacle is not privileging any specific discursive form such as written or spoken language, but that it is directed at the feared manipulation of representational *truth* at a time when the complex interplay of data and representations have usurped earlier forms of cultural and physical engagement and validation" (1993, 29; author's italics).

16 In Steven Shaviro's reading of *Cities of the Red Night*: "When the police forge evidence, or when Hollywood manufactures images, then the police and Hollywood also fall victim to the illusory power of forged evidence and fascinating images" (1984, 70).

17 See Paul Virilio's discussion of a "war of images": "Narcotics were to become the plague of the U.S. expeditionary corps in Vietnam. From the beginning, they suffered from the hallucination of technological combat-delirium, which blurred the distinction between the real and the imaginary" (1989, 85).

18 Balch, twenty years before David Cronenberg, developed a filmscript from *Naked Lunch*—the one scene I've read comes across as a bizarre Pynchon musical comedy, one in many ways more in tune with a Burroughsian sensibility than is Cronenberg's adaptation. Scenes from an adaptation by Brion Gysin (with Burroughs's input) appear in *The Third Mind* (1978, 150–58) and *Here to Go* (Gysin 1982, 131–57). For a useful overview of Burroughs's work in film, see Murphy (1997, 205–16).

19 In *Camera Lucida*, Barthes argues, "Not only is the Photograph never, in essence, a memory . . . but it actually blocks memory, quickly becomes a counter-memory" (1981, 91). Cf. Coover's artist who concludes that, "Photos . . . did not preserve the past, they only distorted it. Memory, left alone, even as it purged and invented, was always right" (1985, 112–13).

20 Burroughs uses this idea when he later includes "[s]tock footage of 1929 crash" cut-in against background silent films for a historical setting in *The Last Words of Dutch Schultz* (1993, 37).

21 In *The Soft Machine* Burroughs repeatedly compares the Gysin "flicker machine" to an act of aggression.

22 Miles has traced the influence of Balch's and Burroughs's work in experimental film collage on, among others, director Nicholas Roeg (1993, 156).

23 In "How to be Humphrey Bogart," reprinted in *The Job*, Burroughs again describes this filmmaking technique, here fictionalized as a screening-room projection organized by an imagined producer B.J., who himself appears in the opening sentence of *Blade Runner: A Movie* (1990, 211–16). Burroughs has also described a parallel aural experiment where he, Balch, and Ian Sommerville spliced and scrambled a tape recording of his voice in order to create a text in which the "original words are quite unintelligible but new words emerge" (1990, 178); again, the desire is to undermine control through reforming of media, image, language, and, ultimately, narrational representation itself.

24 Cf. Josephine Hendin's reading of *The Wild Boys*: "More than cinematic in style, the novel works toward a statement of life as movie, or people as moviegoers—the spectators of their own lives—and of both life and film as products of Maya, the force of illusion that shapes all forms" (1978, 58). Eric Mottram describes the story from *The Wild Boys* "Tío Mate Smiles" as "told in cinematic methods of metamorphosis (pan, zoom, track and montage) which are developed with new skills here and in *Exterminator!* The camera eye and the cutting, synthesizing editor create a rapid method of shot-by-shot shorthand exemplification of information, in the manner of the metamorphic film tradition from *L'Age d'Or* to the works of Jodorowsky" (1977, 177).

25 Unless otherwise noted, the textual references to *The Last Words of Dutch Schulz* are to the 1993 Arcade edition, based on the 1975 Richard Seaver Book (Viking Press); the Cape Goliard (London) 1970 edition has notable stylistic differences.

26 For a discussion of Burroughs's use of *mise en abîme*, or "infinite regress," in a parallel (verbal instead of visual) scene about a man reading "a magazine story about a man reading a magazine story about a man...." (in the chapter "Wind Die. You Die. We Die." from *Exterminator!*), see McHale (1987, 114).

27 Mottram describes the London Cape Goliard edition of *The Last Words of Dutch Schultz* as a cinematic text beginning with "four full-page images of a man shot in a street, the original movie shot sequence reduced to a minimum graphic immediacy of violence . . . the media of presentation are fully given as an initial proposition of the work. Film analyses the object; reproduction analyses the image; words analyse the image" (1977, 239).

28 In this regard, Cronenberg's 1991 film adaptation of *Naked Lunch* complements Burroughs: Cronenberg's film is novelistic right where the novel is filmic. For an extended analysis of Cronenberg's adaptation in the context of a larger study of Burroughs, see Murphy (1997, 67–73).

29 Burroughs's filmic treatment of the Dutch Schultz story makes for an intriguing contrast with Doctorow's *Billy Bathgate*, which itself becomes a Hollywood film. Where Doctorow romanticizes, Burroughs satirizes.

30 The Blue Wind Press edition of *Blade Runner: A Movie* has no pagination; this quote comes from the first page of the text; other page references will follow from this.

31 The inspiration for the "story-line" discussed in the frame comes in turn from the 1974 Alan E. Nourse novel, *Bladerunner* (nothing to do with either the Philip K. Dick *Do Androids Dream of Electric Sheep?* or the Ridley Scott *Bladerunner* movie Dick's novel engendered), and it is instructive to follow how the relatively didactic and straightforward pulp tale about medicine and law becomes reinscribed within a postmodernist sensibility in Burroughs's screenplay treatment. See McHale for an illuminating discussion of this postmodernist recycling (1992, 229–30). To date, the only film treatment of Burroughs's (or Nourse's) *Blade Runner* is the little-known 1983 *Taking Tiger Mountain* (which I have not seen); directed by Tom Huckabee and Kent Smith, it is, according to *The Motion Picture Guide*, "loosely based" on Burroughs's piece: "In a world devastated by nuclear war, a group of militant women brainwash and gender-shift a young man and send him-her off to Wales to assassinate the operator of a white slavery gang" (Nash and Ross 1987, 3266).

32 In Burroughs's words, describing *Schultz*: "This is a perfectly straight film treatment, quite intelligible to the average reader, in no sense experimental writing" (Burroughs and Odier 1989, 30).

Works Cited

Balch, Antony. 1972. "Interview: Breakthrough in Grey Room . . . Towers Open Fire." *Cinema Rising* 1: 8–11.

Barthes, Roland. 1981. *Camera Lucida: Reflections on Photography*. Trans. Richard Howard. New York: Hill and Wang.

Bazin, André. 1967. *What Is Cinema?* Ed. and trans. Hugh Gray. Vol. 1. Berkeley: University of California Press.

Bukatman, Scott. 1993. *Terminal Identity: The Virtual Subject in Postmodern Science Fiction*. Durham: Duke University Press.

Burroughs, William S. 1966. *Towers Open Fire* (filmscript). *International Times*, 31 October–13 November, 8.

———. 1967. Interview by Conrad Knickerbocker. In *Writers at Work: The Paris Review Interviews*. Third Series. New York: Viking.

———. 1970. *The Last Words of Dutch Schultz: A Fiction in the Form of a Film Script*. 1969. Reprint. London: Cape Goliard Press.

———. 1972. Interview by Robert Palmer. *Rolling Stone* (11 May): 48–53.

———. 1974. *The Book of Breething*. Essex: Ou.

———. 1976. *Cobble Stone Gardens*. Cherry Valley, NY: Cherry Valley Editions.

———. 1977. *Junky*. 1953. Reprint. New York: Viking Penguin.

———. 1979. *Ah Pook Is Here and Other Texts*. London: Calder.

———. 1980a. Interview by J. E. Rivers. "An Interview with William S. Burroughs." *Resources for American Literary Studies*. 10.2: 154–66.

———. 1980b. *Nova Express*. In *Three Novels by William S. Burroughs*. New York: Grove Press.

———. 1980c. *The Soft Machine*. In *Three Novels by William S. Burroughs*. New York: Grove Press.

———. 1984. *The Burroughs File*. San Francisco: City Lights Books.

———. 1985. *Queer*. New York: Penguin.

———. 1987. *The Ticket That Exploded*. 1962. Reprint. New York: Grove Weidenfield.

———. 1990. *Blade Runner: A Movie*. 1967. Reprint. Berkeley: Blue Wind Press.

———. 1991. "Screenwriting and the Potentials of Cinema." In *Writing in a Film Age: Essays by Contemporary Novelists*, ed. Keith Cohen. Niwot: University Press of Colorado.

———. 1992a. *Naked Lunch*. 1959. Reprint. New York: Grove Weidenfield.

———. 1992b. *Painting and Guns*. New York: Hanuman.

———. 1992c. *The Wild Boys*. 1971. Reprint. New York: Grove Weidenfield.

———. 1994. *The Electronic Revolution*. 1976. Reprint. Bonn: Expanded Media Editions.

Burroughs, William S., and Antony Balch. 1989. *Towers Open Fire and Other Films*. Montauk, NY: Mystic Fire Videos. Videocassette.

Burroughs, William S., and Brion Gysin. 1978. *The Third Mind*. New York: Viking Press.

Burroughs, William S., and Daniel Odier. 1989. *The Job: Interviews with William S. Burroughs*. 1974. Reprint. New York: Viking Penguin.

Coover, Robert. *Gerald's Party*. 1985. New York: New American Library.

Dolan, Frederick M. 1994. *Allegories of America*. Ithaca: Cornell University Press.

Gysin, Brion, and Terry Wilson. 1982. *Here to Go: Planet R-101*. London: Quarter.

Hendin, Josephine. 1978. *Vulnerable People: A View of American Fiction Since 1945*. New York: Oxford University Press.

Jameson, Fredric. 1991. *Postmodernism, or, The Cultural Logic of Late Capitalism*. Durham, NC: Duke University Press.

Kirby, Lynne. 1997. *Parallel Tracks: The Railroad and Silent Cinema*. Durham, NC: Duke University Press.

Kuehl, John. 1989. *Alternate Worlds: A Study of Postmodern Antirealistic American Fiction*. New York: New York University Press.

LeClair, Tom, and Larry McCaffery, eds. 1983. *Anything Can Happen: Interviews with Contemporary American Novelists*. Urbana: University of Illinois Press.

Lydenberg, Robin. 1987. *Word Cultures: Radical Theory and Practice in William S. Burroughs' Fiction*. Urbana: University of Illinois Press.

McHale, Brian. 1987. *Postmodernist Fiction*. New York: Routledge.

———. 1992. *Constructing Postmodernism*. New York: Routledge.

McLuhan, Marshall. 1991. "Notes on Burroughs." In *William S. Burroughs At the Front: Critical Reception, 1959–1989*, ed. Jennie Skerl and Robin Lydenberg. Carbondale: Southern Illinois University Press.

Miles, Barry. 1993. *William Burroughs: El Hombre Invisible—A Portrait*. New York: Hyperion.

Morrissette, Bruce. 1985. *Novel and Film: Essays in Two Genres*. Chicago: University of Chicago Press.

Mottram, Eric. 1977. *William Burroughs: The Algebra of Need*. London: Marion Boyars.

Murphy, Timothy S. 1997. *Wising Up the Marks: The Amodern William Burroughs.* Berkeley: University of California Press.

Nash, J. R., and Stanley R. Ross. 1987. *The Motion Picture Guide.* Chicago: CineBooks Inc.

Palumbo, Donald. 1979. "William Burroughs' Quartet of Science Fiction Novels as Dystopian Social Satire." *Extrapolations* 20.4: 321-29.

Seltzer, Alvin J. 1974. *Chaos in the Novel, The Novel in Chaos.* New York: Schocken Books.

Shaviro, Steven. 1984. "Burroughs' Theater of Illusion: *Cities of the Red Night.*" *Review of Contemporary Fiction* 4.1: 64-74.

Skerl, Jennie. 1985. *William S. Burroughs.* Boston: Twayne Publishers.

Skerl, Jennie, and Robin Lydenberg, eds. 1991. *William S. Burroughs At the Front: Critical Reception, 1959-1989.* Carbondale: Southern Illinois University Press.

Sobieszek, Robert A. 1996. *Ports of Entry: William S. Burroughs and the Arts.* Los Angeles: Los Angeles County Museum of Art.

Vernon, John. 1973. *The Garden and the Map: Schizophrenia in Twentieth-Century Literature and Culture.* Urbana: University of Illinois Press.

Virilio, Paul. 1989. *War and Cinema: The Logistics of Perception.* Trans. Patrick Camiller. 1984. Reprint. New York: Verso.

Zurbrugg, Nicholas. 1984. "Burroughs, Barthes, and the Limits of Intertextuality." *Review of Contemporary Fiction* 4.1: 86-107.

CHAPTER EIGHT

Intersection Points: Teaching
William Burroughs's *Naked Lunch*
Timothy S. Murphy

The experimental novels of William S. Burroughs, including his
most famous work, *Naked Lunch*, are rarely taught to students of
any level, for two related reasons: their relentless scatology and their
nonlinear structure. If the former difficulty, which no doubt attracts
many casually prurient readers, has lessened in the years since the
books' publication thanks to the stand-up comedy of Lenny Bruce,
Richard Pryor, and their imitators, video pornography, shock radio,
and other widespread cultural phenomena, the latter one has continued to distract readers, both casual and professional, from a comprehensive appreciation of these texts. This situation is obviously unfortunate, since it prevents Burroughs's works from taking their rightful
place among the conflicting traditions that constitute the expanding
"canon" of American literature,[1] but it is also unnecessary because
Burroughs himself offers a straightforward, practical pedagogy of his
writing within *Naked Lunch* itself, in the "Atrophied Preface" that
follows the body of the novel. This pedagogy, conscientiously
applied, can bring any careful reader to a comprehensive understanding of the stakes and gambits of Burroughs's enterprise, as my
experience teaching *Naked Lunch* has shown.[2]

"The word," Burroughs tells us, "cannot be expressed direct. . . . It can perhaps be indicated by mosaic of juxtaposition like articles abandoned in a hotel drawer, defined by negatives and absence. . . " (1990, 105). This is the most succinct description he provides of the compositional method of *Naked Lunch*. I take this to mean that the power of language as an instrument of control, one of the central themes of the novel, cannot simply be asserted in a direct statement, since such a statement would itself be another example of that control; it must instead be insinuated, implied in such a way that the reader can see through not only the forms of verbal control that the novel *depicts* but also the powerful verbal control gesture that the novel itself *is*. This is also the central conundrum of the *Naked Lunch* reading experience: "the novel's paradoxically enabling gesture is to create readers capable of rejecting its most seductive overtures" (Hilfer 1980, 265). Burroughs goes on: "The Word is divided into units which be all in one piece and should be so taken, but the pieces can be had in any order being tied up back and forth, in and out fore and aft like an innaresting sex arrangement" (1990, 207; 1995, disc 3 track 8).[3] The units of the Word that make up *Naked Lunch* are indeed "all in one piece," arranged in a fixed but apparently arbitrary order, but there are many different ways for a reader to fold and weave them into an "innaresting" text arrangement or reading.

"You can cut into *Naked Lunch* at any intersection point," Burroughs claims; it is "a blueprint, a How-To Book," though not a systematic one, that demonstrates "How-to extend levels of experience" (1990, 203; 1995, disc 3 track 8). But it does have a modicum of structure to which inexperienced students can cling: the semi-autobiographical frame-tale of junky William Lee's run-ins with the police, comprising the untitled first section (1990, 3-20) and the "Hauser and O'Brien" section (1990, 189-97) that concludes the main text. Between these bookends, the novel presents the reader with an apparently random sequence or mosaic of juxtaposed scenes, which Burroughs calls "routines" (1990, 10), that forms a fantastic panorama of coercion, distortion, and betrayal. This mosaic, Burroughs suggests on pages 51, 59-60, 99, and elsewhere, can best be grasped as a series of drug- and withdrawal-induced hallucinations that pass through Lee's mind, presented through a kind of radically disjunct stream-of-consciousness technique in which the subjective perspective is often distorted beyond easy recognition.

Like the junky narrator, the student who embarks on a reading of *Naked Lunch* will find herself in a constantly mutating textual space-time continuum that lacks the usual reference points of linear fiction: "I . . . suddenly don't know where I am. Perhaps I have opened the wrong door and at any moment the Man In Possession, The Owner Who Got There First will rush in and scream: '*What Are You Doing Here? Who Are You?*' And I don't know what I am doing there nor who I am" (Burroughs 1990, 199). But the student, again like the junky, should not demand to speak to the management, that is the author, about this: "I decide to play it cool and maybe I will get the orientation before the Owner shows. . . . So instead of yelling 'Where am I?' cool it and look around and you will find out approximately. . . . You were not there for *The Beginning*. You will not be there for *The End*. . . . Your knowledge of what is going on can only be superficial and relative. . . ." (Burroughs 1990, 199). This is the key to reading, and thus teaching, *Naked Lunch*: use your superficial and relative knowledge, work from the middle where you are, draw together what strands of meaning you can, not according to the linear logic of causality and plot, but according to the intermittent, recursive logic of jazz improvisation ("metallic cocaine bebop" [1990, 84]), poetic refrain and recurrent thematic accretion.[4] At least four axes of structural regularity, which Burroughs might call "intersection points"—points in the middle, superficial (that is, surface) points to be threaded by reading—offer themselves to the novice reader of *Naked Lunch*: narrative self-reflexivity, character recurrence, thematic continuity, and the repetition of specific verbal motifs. "The way OUT," we learn, "is the way IN" (1990, 208; 1995, disc 3 track 8).[5]

But perhaps the most fundamental preparation for the study of *Naked Lunch*, for both literature instructors and students, is contextualization.[6] Before turning to the details of Burroughs's novel, let us briefly consider in turn the two situations in which it is most likely to be taught: a general survey of the twentieth-century American novel and a more focused survey of Beat literature. In the first case, Burroughs's formal experimentation will appear less radically alien if it can be compared with one of Gertrude Stein's permutational nar-

ratives, Faulkner's *The Sound and The Fury*, Dos Passos's *USA*, or
Nabokov's *Pale Fire*.[7] Likewise, Burroughs's scatology will appear
less shocking and unprecedented if it can be juxtaposed to the carnivalesque sexuality of Djuna Barnes' *Nightwood* or the heterosex-
ism of Henry Miller and Norman Mailer. In the second case, the
acidic *Naked Lunch* can provide a necessary formal and thematic
counter balance to the spontaneous, bebop-influenced romanticism
of Kerouac's novels and Ginsberg's early poetry. An account of
Kerouac and Ginsberg's roles in assembling the text of *Naked Lunch*
might be assigned to demonstrate the collaborative nature of the
Beats' aesthetics.[8] If the course is designed to allow study of more
than one text by the major Beat figures, then attention to Ginsberg's
most important late sequence, *The Fall of America*, will reveal its
clear debt to the discontinuous compositional method and paranoid
style of *Naked Lunch* and Burroughs's later cut-up novels. To aid the
historical contextualization effort in either of these pedagogical situations (and to acknowledge the resistance that many readers will no
doubt feel toward the text's scatology, as a step toward achieving a
critical perspective on it), the instructor might also consult or assign
an account of the *Naked Lunch* obscenity trials.[9]

In both cases, however, Burroughs's novel can serve best as a
transitional text, suspended between the elegant artificial mytholo-
gies of high modernism and the frenetically paradoxical fabulations
of postmodernism that have come to dominate recent discussions of
the American novel. As I have argued elsewhere,[10] Burroughs's work
as a whole constitutes an alternative to both modernism and postmodernism as those categories are normally defined. The imperative
of modernism, as its ideologues like T.S. Eliot claimed, was to find an
aesthetic replacement for the lost social ordering principles and
structures of the past (in the extended Homeric parallels and formal
encyclopedism of Joyce's *Ulysses*, in the rejuvenated High-Church
Anglicanism of Eliot's *Four Quartets*, or in the ironic redeployment
of Frazer's fertility myths in Woolf's *Mrs. Dalloway*), but by
Burroughs's day the impossibility and even undesirability of this
project had become obvious: the idea of replacing the exploitative
traditional orders of class, nation, and race with the no less threatening models offered by Yeats's eugenic interests or Pound's Fascism
seemed to augur no possibility of progress at all. Yet despite his

refusal of these replacement myths, Burroughs remained committed to the modernist idea that literature could make a difference, could have meaningful social effects.

In Burroughs's work the dissatisfaction with modernism manifests itself most clearly in his rejection of the controlling role of the artist over his material. The first steps toward this rejection can be seen in the mosaic structure of *Naked Lunch*, which was created, according to Beat legend, when the routines were simply sent to the printer in the order that they were typed up by Kerouac and Ginsberg. The rejection reaches its most extreme form in Burroughs's aleatory cut-up trilogy of the sixties, *The Soft Machine*, *The Ticket That Exploded*, and *Nova Express*. The "anti-form" of *Naked Lunch* and the later books is an implicit reproach to the hypertrophy of form characteristic of modernist monuments like *Ulysses* and might be considered evidence of the postmodernism of Burroughs's work according to Jean-François Lyotard's influential model:

> The postmodern would be that which, in the modern, puts forward the unpresentable in presentation itself; that which denies itself the solace of good forms. . . . A postmodern artist or writer is in the position of a philosopher: the text he writes, the work he produces are not in principle governed by pre-established rules, and they cannot be judged according to a determining judgment, by applying familiar categories to the text or to the work. Those rules and categories are what the work of art itself is looking for. (Lyotard 1984, 81)

In *Naked Lunch* the form is not something chosen in advance and imposed upon the raw material, but a fragile local structure that arises from the immanent relations that appear within the material itself, and demands actualization by the reader, as I will argue in more detail below.

However, there is more (or less, depending on your point of view) to postmodernism than mere formal discontinuity. It also involves what Lyotard calls "skepticism toward grand narratives" (1984, 31-38) that claim to explain the movement of history: Christianity, Marxism, scientific progress. These grand narratives act like the rules or categories which dictate and prejudge works of art, reductively interpreting and arbitrarily limiting the possibilities of action available to social agents. In *Naked Lunch* Burroughs does demonstrate considerable skepticism toward these grand narratives: he ridicules not only Christianity but also Buddhism and Islam as

campaigns of manipulation (1990, 102-105), borrows Marxist rhetoric without borrowing the concomitant liberatory ideology (1990,
xix), and viciously lampoons the intentions of supposedly disinter-
ested, "pure" scientists (1990, 20-42 and *passim*). But for Lyotard and
other advocates of postmodernism, this skepticism has the additional consequence of rendering progressive social and political action
virtually unimaginable, and certainly unrealizable at a mass level,
since it must be based on one or another of the now-discredited
grand narratives. This is where Burroughs parts company with the
postmodernists: even though he implicitly criticizes the excesses of
modernism, he continues to imagine and work toward social and
political progress on a mass scale and refuses to be confined to the
"prison-house of language" that postmodernists like John Barth glee-
fully inhabit. This is the hybrid position, critical of both modernism
and postmodernism, that I call "amodernism" (Murphy 1997, 23-25).
Burroughs is by no means the only literary embodiment of this aesthetic perspective, but he is certainly one of the most important[11];
and critical and pedagogical attention to his work will not only illuminate it, but may also contribute to a more nuanced, comprehensive
and adequate understanding of postwar American fiction in general.

***

A productive way of making initial contact with *Naked Lunch* is
to approach it as a do-it-yourself tapestry (with design by Bosch or
Brueghel). At many points the novel itself self-consciously encourages different ways of folding and weaving its constituent elements
into intelligible large-scale structures. This is the first intersection
point. The first suggestion to this effect comes on the first page of
the introduction, when the author glosses his title: "The title means
exactly what the words say: NAKED Lunch—a frozen moment when
everyone sees what is on the end of every fork" (1990, ix). As Allen
Ginsberg has argued, this "relates to nakedness of seeing, to being
able to see clearly without any confusing disguises, to see through
the disguise" (Burroughs 1959, xxii). Burroughs goes on to align his
enterprise with the satire of Jonathan Swift (1990, xv-xvi), though I
would suggest that Burroughs's work more accurately resembles the
radical critique of ideology undertaken by Marx and Nietzsche.
Burroughs's method, surrealistic exaggeration, forms part of the tra-

ditional repertoire of the political satirist, but his goal of "nakedness of seeing" emphasizes the disturbing revelation of obscured truth (though that truth may turn out to be paradoxical or ambiguous) rather than the pointed irony of overstatement and reversal that we find in "A Modest Proposal."[12] In any case, his critical project aims at a practical political effect, demystification, and this alone is sufficient to distinguish it from postmodernism. A bit further on the author returns to this self-reflexivity when he alters the title to "*Bill's Naked Lunch Room*" and asks the prospective reader if s/he wants "to take a look around with Honest Bill" (1990, xvii). This tactic of direct address to the reader is not limited to the introduction. As Anthony Channell Hilfer has argued, "The action of *Naked Lunch* is, quite simply, the moment by moment relation of narrator and reader" (1980, 253). From the very first page of the novel, the narrator importunes the reader. A young "advertising executive type fruit" assists the narrator in escaping from the police; the narrator insists that "You know the type," insinuating common judgment if not outright complicity between himself and the reader (1990, 3; 1995, disc 1 track 1; Hilfer 1980, 252-53). But shortly thereafter the narrator offers a trio of explanatory notes to the reader (intended to clarify slang) implying a greater difference between them than he previously suggested (1990, 4-5). This alternately insinuating and alienating narrative voice will act as Virgil to the reader's Dante on the novel's journey through a modern hell.

The clearest statement of the narrator's intent and the reader's responsibility comes in the "Campus of Interzone University" routine in the form of a mock-academic lecture on the "symbolism of the Ancient Mariner *himself*" in Coleridge's famous poem (Burroughs 1990, 78). The "Prof" asks the reader to

> consider the Ancient Mariner without curare, lasso, bulbocapnine or straightjacket, albeit able to capture and hold a live audience. . . . What is his hrump gimmick? . . . He does not, like so-called artists at this time, stop just anybody thereby inflicting unsent for boredom and working random hardship. . . . He stops those who cannot choose but hear owing to already existing relation between The Mariner (however ancient) and the uh Wedding Guest. (Burroughs 1990, 79)

The Mariner's words "may be rambling, irrelevant, even crude and rampant senile" as *Naked Lunch* itself may appear to be, yet they connect to something substantial, though unacknowledged, in the

Guest or reader. "But something happens to the Wedding Guest like happens in psychoanalysis when it happens if it happens." The upshot of this idea is that "*You can find out more about someone by talking than by listening*" (Burroughs 1990, 79-80). This means that the reader will learn more about him/herself in reading *Naked Lunch* than s/he will learn about the narrator (or the author). The novel's success, as it itself insists, depends on the reader's active, shaping involvement in the process of reconstruction and interpretation.

The "Atrophied Preface" confirms this irregular balance of responsibility by placing the burden of narrative continuity upon the reader:

> Why all this waste paper getting The People from one place to another? Perhaps to spare the Reader stress of sudden space shifts and keep him Gentle? And so a ticket is bought, a taxi called, a plane boarded. . . . I am not American Express. . . . If one of my people is seen in New York walking around in citizen clothes and next sentence Timbuktu putting down lad talk on a gazelle-eyed youth, we may assume that he (the party non-resident of Timbuktu) transported himself there by the usual methods of communication. (Burroughs 1990, 197–198; Burroughs 1995, disc 3 track 8)

Despite the avoidance of the second person in this passage, it is clearly the reader, the "you," who must assume responsibility for the narrative by assuming that standard connective devices have simply been left out as redundant. "I am a recording instrument," Burroughs writes shortly thereafter; "I do not presume to impose 'story' 'plot' 'continuity.' . . . Insofar as I succeed in *Direct* recording of certain areas of psychic process I may have limited function. . . . I am not an entertainer. . ." (1990, 200; 1995, disc 3 track 8). Since the author (and the narrator) does not so presume, it is up to the reader to discover or "impose 'story' 'plot' 'continuity,'" all in quotation marks because these can be at best provisional, local orderings that are made possible by the discontinuous text of the novel but can never be fully validated by it. To misquote Derrida and the postmodernists, we might say that in the case of *Naked Lunch* there *is* something outside the text: the necessary subjective dimension in which it is read, not as a passive unfolding of pre-established forms but as an active weaving of elements into a comprehensible (yet unprivileged) pattern.[13]

The simplest form of continuity to impose or pattern to weave, from the point of view of readers most at home in the traditional novel, is one based on the recurrence of characters (see Table 2).

This is intersection point number two. As these characters reappear throughout the novel, some (like Dr. "Fingers" Schafer) are consistently associated with certain dominant themes (like economic and scientific control of individuals), while others (like A.J.) develop more ambiguous identities that cut across the book's already unstable epistemo-ethical categories. The narrator, William Lee, is the most often encountered character, and to the extent that the novel can be naturalized as his drug- and withdrawal-induced hallucinations his perspective and voice may be said to underlie every routine in the book. But a large part of Burroughs's fame as a writer rests on his creation of subordinate characters or caricatures like Dr. Benway, the control consultant whose nefarious activities are introduced in the first routine after the frame tale, the one that bears his name (1990, 20-42; 1995, disc 1 track 2). This is one of the most heavily analyzed passages in all of Burroughs's work because it states overtly many of the themes of personal and social control to which he regularly returns in all his writings, including the use of scientific conditioning to force subjects to internalize control (1990, 21; 1995, disc 1 track 2) and the avoidance of overt brutality in order to minimize organized resistance (1990, 23; 1995, disc 1 track 2). Benway is also the narrator of the Talking Asshole routine (1990, 119-122; 1995, disc 2 track 4), unquestionably the most famous routine in the book,[14] which appears at the conclusion of a conversation between Benway and his control-minded colleague Dr. Schafer about redesigning the human body for greater "efficiency." Benway broaches this same theme in one of his other appearances in the book (1990, 109-10), and elsewhere displays a remarkably unsettling bedside manner (1990, 55-56, 130). Indeed, Benway's behavior can stand for the ambiguous status of all Burroughs's doctor characters who fight disease (like addiction) but also earn their livings from it and thus have some interest in preserving disease. The police are in a parallel situation with regard to the crime of drug addiction, as the case of Bradley the Buyer (1990, 15-18) demonstrates.

If Benway's appearances in the novel all seem to add up to a consistent if distasteful characterization, then the development of the other most commonly recurrent character, A.J., provides a sharp contrast. Like Benway, A.J. appears in many of Burroughs's later novels as well as in *Naked Lunch*, but unlike Benway A.J. does not seem to act in a completely consistent way. Behind the mask of "an international playboy and harmless practical joker" (Burroughs 1990, 133), A.J. finances Islam Inc., the absurdly diabolical cartel that operates out of the political no man's land of Interzone (1990, 131), but he also antagonizes other members of the cartel like Salvador Hassan O'Leary, the Liquefactionist tycoon and international stool pigeon (1990, 74-76). A.J. is the most important example in *Naked Lunch* of the ubiquitous double agent, whose allegiance, like that of the doctors and the police, cannot be determined with certainty: "A.J. is an agent like me," says the narrator, "but for whom or for what no one has ever been able to discover. . . . I believe he is on the Factualist side (which I also represent)" but "of course he could be a Liquefaction Agent. . . . You can never be sure of anyone in the industry" (1990, 133).

Indeed, you can never even be sure that the characters you encounter are actually characters, since they are certainly not characters of the sort associated with the realistic novel. Late in the book the narrator reveals that his "present assignment" is to

> Find the live ones and exterminate. Not the bodies but the "molds," you understand—but I forget that you cannot understand. We have all but a very few. But even one could upset our food tray. The danger, as always, comes from defecting agents: A.J. . . and Lee and the Sailor and Benway. And I know some agent is out there in the darkness looking for me. Because all Agents defect and all Resisters sell out. (Burroughs 1990, 186)

These defecting agents are "molds," character templates or types (whether arche- or stereo-), like Clem and Jody who "sweep in dressed like The Capitalist in a communist mural" (Burroughs 1990, 129). They are prefabricated images rather than individuals, and what gives them their interest and complexity is not their realistic psychological depth but the disturbing ambiguity of their intentions and commitments. No character in the novel remains consistent: "*all* Agents defect and *all* Resisters sell out." This fundamental inconsistency runs even deeper at some points as when Lee hallucinates, "In his place of total darkness," that "mouth and eyes are one organ that leaps forward to snap with transparent teeth . . . but no organ is constant as regards either function or position . . . sex organs sprout anywhere . . . rectums open, defecate and close . . . the entire organism changes color and consistency in split-second adjustments" (1990, 10). The intent of this systematic inconsistency, however, is not to suspend the reader in interminable reflection on the vertiginous undecidability of binary oppositions but to encourage the reader's attention and skepticism toward institutions of control and the sub-ject-positions that carry out the imperatives of those institutions.

> Once the reader recognizes that all of the characters are such unstable "molds," a symbolic or allegorical reading of the novel becomes possible. This kind of reading, via the third intersection point, can most clearly and fruitfully focus on the theme of addiction, both literal and figurative, which is the thread that stitches the routines together, as it does "the world network of junkies, tuned on a cord of rancid jissom, tying up in furnished rooms, shivering in the junk-sick morning" (Burroughs 1990, 7). The literal and metaphorical economies of addiction, called by Burroughs the "Algebra of Need" (1990, ix-xvi), have been extensively analyzed in Burroughs criticism (see especially McConnell 1967 and Mottram 1977). The upshot is contained in the oft-repeated rhetorical question "Wouldn't you?" (see Table 5). "In the words of total need: 'Wouldn't you?' Yes you would. You would lie, cheat, inform on your friends, steal, and do any-thing to satisfy total need. Because you would be in a state of total sick-ness, total possession, and not in a position to act in any other way" (Burroughs 1990, xi). Total need may be biologic need in the case of liter-al heroin ("junk") addiction (which Burroughs describes clinically and autobiographically in the appendix to Naked Lunch [1990, 216-32]) or something more abstract and metaphorical in the case of the "control addicts" whose "naked need . . . must be decently covered by an arbitrary and intricate bureaucracy" (1990, 21; 1995, disc 1 track 2).

The novel contains a number of very precise and accurate descriptions of literal heroin addict behavior, from the pyramidal organization of drug trafficking (Burroughs 1990, x-xi) to the lack of affect characteristic of many junkies (1990, 32-33, 209). Many of the routines narrated by Lee are extremely naturalistic accounts of addict activity, including judgments on different drugs and directions on how to give oneself a shot (1990, 59-62). The penultimate routine in the book, which is actually called "The Algebra of Need," tells the story of "Fats" Terminal who is born a "translucent-grey foetal mon-key" (standing for heroin as the "monkey on your back") but soon grows a "fat aquarium of body" by pushing junk: "it all drained back into 'Fats' so his substance grew and grew filling plazas, restaurants, and waiting rooms of the world with grey junk ooze" (1990, 187; 1995, disc 3 track 6). The process of extending the logic of addiction leads Burroughs to describe a number of science-fiction addictions like "Mugwump jissom" and the "Black Meat" (1990, 49-51), but the bulk of the novel is focused not on imaginary addictions but on metaphorical ones.

Addiction as theme and metaphor plays itself out in two primary registers: the organization of the human body and political organization (see Tables 3 and 4). Indeed, in *Naked Lunch* politics articulates and inscribes the body as object, while the range of bodies constitutes the range of political subjects or agents at the same time. The best example of this dialectic can be seen in the exposition of the political Parties of Interzone, all of which are based on incompatible totalitarian projects for the human body. The Liquefactionists' program involves "protein cleavage and reduction to liquid which is absorbed into someone else's protoplasmic being" (Burroughs 1990, 75); "It will be immediately clear that the Liquefaction Party is, except for one man, entirely composed of dupes, it not being clear until the final absorption who is whose dupe . . ." (1990, 147). Ginsberg has likened the Liquefactionist methods to Fascism or Stalinism, especially to the "liquidation policies spoken of by Stalin" (1959, xxvi). Alternately, the Divisionists "cut off tiny bits of their flesh and grow exact replicas of themselves in embryo jelly. It seems probable, unless the process of division is halted, that eventually there will be only one replica of one sex on the planet: that is one person in the world with millions of separate bodies" (1990, 149). The third party is the Senders who make use of "one-way telepathic control" of their subjects, "one-way telepathic broadcasts instructing the workers what to feel and when" (1990, 148; 1995, disc 2 track 5). All three parties attempt to eliminate difference and impose absolute uniformity upon society by scientifically manipulating the human body.

Correlatively, society itself is often presented as a diseased body. At the conclusion of the Talking Asshole routine, Dr. Benway suggests that

> The end result of complete cellular representation is cancer. Democracy is cancerous, and bureaus are its cancer. A bureau takes root anywhere in the state, turns malignant like the Narcotics Bureau, and grows and grows, always reproducing more of its own kind, until it chokes the host if not controlled or excised. . . . Bureaucracy is wrong as a cancer, a turning away from the human evolutionary direction of infinite potentials and differentiation and independent spontaneous action, to the complete parasitism of a virus. (Burroughs 1990, 121–22)

If bureaucracy is really a cancer on democracy, then Burroughs would have us "Read the metastasis with blind fingers" (1990, 210) as we work our way through *Naked Lunch* to its conclusion in which Lee finds himself "occluded from space-time like an eel's ass occludes when he stops eating on the way to Sargasso." In his final, allegorical hallucination he is "clawing at a not-yet of Telepathic Bureaucracies, Time Monopolies, Control Drugs, Heavy Fluid Addicts" (1990, 197), a vision of political and bodily control that goes beyond even the frightening images of addiction and manipulation that are presented in the novel.

This outline hardly scratches the surface of Burroughs's interlocking treatment of the body and politics, addiction, and control. These passages link up, directly and indirectly, with dozens of others scattered among the routines that constitute the book. Any of these references can be a point of departure or arrival for class discussion because they are first of all thematic intersection points. Other significant lines of reference, for example mass media (film, radio, television, journalism, etc.), function in a similar way and to a similar extent. From the mock-Hollywood "B production" the narrator offers to the advertising executive (1990, 3; 1995, disc 1 track 1) to the "Revelation and Prophecy of what I can pick up without FM on my 1920 crystal set with antennae of jissom" (1990, 208; 1995, disc 3 track 8), Burroughs constantly associates all human relationships, even the narrator's relation to his own body and the author's (and reader's) relation to his text, with the subtly coercive structure of one-way communications technology. Like the Ancient Mariner and the Senders, the administrators of the media command those who cannot help but listen since they can neither turn away nor talk back.[15] These thematic or symbolic lines, as well as others that cannot be addressed adequately here, do not reduce political struggle or individual autonomy to mere metaphor but instead allow Burroughs's powerful images to "spill off the page in all directions" (1990, 207).

Once the student has acquired a reasonably extensive grasp of the metaphorical and critical/satirical bent of the novel's recurrent character and thematic elements, she may also begin to develop an appreciation of its regular formal elements, the fourth intersection point. Many passages recur in the course of the book, accreting force like incantations or musical refrains (see Table 5). Some, like the one-line advice "As one judge said to another, 'Be just and if you can't be just, be arbitrary'" (Burroughs 1990, 6, 67; 1995, disc 1 track 1), comment on the organization of the novel as well as on its control theme. The most evocative of these images achieve a level of purely linguistic intensity comparable to that of imagist poetry, as do many unrepeated passages (for example the extended description of the "U.S. Drag" [1990, 12-14; 1995, disc 1 track 1] and the storm of uncoordinated images that concludes the novel [1990, 204-13; 1995, disc 3 tracks 8-9]).

The first of these extended refrains, a description of suicide by drowning, appears on page 5 (see also Burroughs 1995, disc 1 track 1) during Lee's performance for the advertising executive:

> The Rube flips in the end, running through empty automats and subway stations, screaming: 'Come back, kid!! Come back!! and follows his boy right into the East River, down through condoms and orange peels, mosaic of floating newspapers, down into the silent black ooze with gangsters in concrete, and pistols pounded flat to avoid the probing finger of prurient ballistic experts. (Burroughs 1990, 5)

This juxtaposition of consumer society's detritus and the concealed evidence of crime establishes symbolically what Burroughs's ambiguous characters establish narratively: the instability of accepted social/political oppositions. In the "mosaic of floating newspapers," we may see an association with the "mosaic of juxtaposition like articles abandoned in a hotel drawer" (Burroughs 1990, 105) that we discussed earlier as a microcosm of the novel itself. An extended reiteration of the passage appears on page 69, in the "Hassan's Rumpus Room" routine:

> [Naked Mr. America] plummets from the eyeless lighthouse, kissing and jacking off in face of the black mirror, glides oblique down with cryptic condoms and mosaic of a thousand newspapers through a drowned city of red brick to settle in black mud with tin cans and beer bottles, gangsters in concrete, pistols pounded flat and meaningless to avoid short-arm inspection of prurient ballistic experts. He waits the slow striptease of erosion with fossil loins. (Burroughs 1990, 69; additions italicized)

In this version Mr. America, who has just proclaimed that "I fart ambrosia and shit pure gold turds," replaces the Rube, Lee's onetime junky partner, and thus heightens the satiric identification of mainstream society with its criminal counterpart. It is no accident that this reiteration interrupts and thus punctuates the eroticized hanging of a youth by a Mugwump under Hassan's watchful gaze, one of Burroughs's central images of the sexuality of domination.

There are several other reiterated passages of similar length, complexity, and force: the "followers of obsolete, unthinkable trades" passage, which achieves a profoundly incantatory momentum in its listing of the anachronistic inhabitants of the Meet Café, and the "races as yet unconceived" passage, which presents one of the few potentially affirmative images in the novel, are chief among them. These passages and the shorter ones that Burroughs more commonly employs serve to knit the novel together at the level of its language and provide a means for readers to establish connections among the fragmentary routines. But such connections are more poetic or even musical than novelistic in that they operate through evocative, impressionistic, or imagistic intensity rather than logical or causal extension. Ginsberg was not wrong when he claimed, on the witness stand in the Boston obscenity trial of *Naked Lunch*, that "there is a great deal of very pure language and pure poetry in this book that is as great as any poetry being written in America" (Burroughs 1959, xxxiii). Like much of Ginsberg's own verse, the poetry of *Naked Lunch* is poetry of disjunction, reiteration, and heightened consciousness of intensity rather than the more familiar poetry of coherent conceit, metrical regularity and symbolic argumentation that students may find easier to approach, but *Naked Lunch*'s poetry rewards the committed reader in ways that traditional poetry simply cannot.

Thus Burroughs's novel, like the similarly forbidding works of Joyce, Woolf, Faulkner and Nabokov, must teach the careful and committed reader how to read it, but unlike their works *Naked Lunch* doesn't offer a single coherent linear reading but an irreducible multiplicity of lines that "spill off the page in all directions, kaleidoscope of vistas, medley of tunes and street noises, farts and riot yipes and the slamming steel shutters of commerce, screams of pain and pathos and screams plain pathic" (Burroughs 1990, 207; 1995, disc 3 track 8). It is up to the determined reader to decide which of those lines and directions to follow from the text out into the world.

Table 1: Table of Contents for Naked Lunch (1990 edition)

Table 2: Recurrence of Characters in Naked Lunch

A.J.: 74–76, 80, 101–02, 108, 131–41, 146
Benway, Dr.: 20–35, 55–56, 109, 111–12, 119–22, 130
Clem and Jody: 101, 129, 143–47
County Clerk, The: 114–15, 153–61
"Fats" Terminal: 47–48, 122, 186–87
Lee, William: 3–20, 51–55(?), 57(?), 59–63(?), 63–67, 99(?), 153–61, 179,
    181, 189–97, 212–13
O'Leary, Salvador Hassan: 67, 75–76, 132, 141–43
Sailor, The: 47–51, 67, 179–80, 181–86, 210
Schafer, Dr.: 94–95, 119
Technician, The: 57-59, 124–27, 138–39

Table 3: Addiction of the Body

5 junk as embalming
6 junk as triumph of the body
8 Willy the Disk
10 organ flux of withdrawal

Table 3 continued on
page 195

11 dropper injection: illusion and reality
15-18 Bradley the Buyer
23 thinking machines
24-25 drugs as control mechanisms
33 junk suspends tension/release cycle = death [cf. xvii-xvii: COLD]
38 male & female both castrated
39–40 viruses
40 symptomatic treatment (also 171)
48–51 science-fiction addictions
52–53 two forms of life: addicted v. normal
55–57 surgery routines
57–59 male birth routine
61–62 the junky's body as an instrument
63 the new body of withdrawal
65 bodily extremes
91 plants growing from genitals
94–96 the deanxietized man = centipede
96 potential human hybrids
105 the flesh corset
109 Iris: Benway's experiment on the body
115 the prolapsed asshole: autonomous organ
119–21 the Talking Asshole sequence
122 the boy with the flute-playing ass
147–51 biologically based Parties
153 the Human Virus can be treated
186 the Exterminator attacks not bodies but molds
188 bodily codes: secrets
210 metastasis

Table 4: Politics of/as Addiction
x junk as monopoly, money (xi), big business (xv)
xix Marx/Engels parody
12–14 the U.S. drag
20–27 Benway's control techniques
34 a functioning police state needs no police
62–63 the President's oblique habit
72, 75 the Liquefactionists mentioned
100 magic and ideology
101 Clem and Jody's anti-native routine
110–12 the Nationalist party—manipulate anti-colonial sentiment
121–22 the space between; democracy as cancer
129 Clem and Jody again (143-45)
131–32 Islam Inc. (from 20; 145-47)
132 A.J.'s shifting allegiances

Table 4 continued on
page 196

147-53 the Parties of Interzone: the Liquefactionists, the Senders, the
   Divisionists (all forms of fascism/control), the Factualists (libertarians)
165-66 Island government; presidency as punishment
169-70 administration as control; the state as tool
186 all Agents defect, all resisters sell out
197 telepathic bureaucracies, time monopolies, etc.
212 they are always rebuilding the city

Table 5: Refrains in Naked Lunch
Wouldn't you? xi, xiii, xvii-xvii, 186, 197, 203
pistols pounded flat: 5, 69
just or arbitrary judges: 6, 67
coughing and spitting junky: 6, 7, 50, 188, 198
selling is more of a habit than using: 15, 210
Irene Kelly routine: 18, 181
morphine v. cocaine: 23, 59
treatment is symptomatic: 40, 171
obsolete, unthinkable trades: 49, 98
races as yet unconceived: 96, 99
soundless hum: 99, 189
the subway: 179, 183, 205

Notes

1 Kathy Acker, hardly a "canonical" figure in the restricted sense of the term, sees
   Burroughs as a central figure in what she calls variously "the other tradition,"
   "the non-acceptable literary tradition," "the black tradition," "the tradition of
   political writing as opposed to propaganda" (1997, 6-7), in any case a tradition
   with which she herself is closely allied. My point is that despite Burroughs's hostility toward all institutions, including the institutions of literary study, his work
   has served as an important point of departure or reference for many other writers and thus deserves to be studied with that continuity in mind.
2 I have taught the novel three times in advanced undergraduate courses (junior
   or senior level), and I base the suggestions that follow on that experience. I
   have not yet had the opportunity to teach Burroughs to graduate students, but I
   believe my suggestions would also apply in that context with only a few alterations.
3 A recording of Burroughs reading this passage, and many of the other passages
   cited in this essay, has recently been released by Warner Brothers. Burroughs
   was an exceptional performer of his own work, and his readings often clarify the
   meaning, tone or characterization of difficult passages, so I will include track references to this recording in my text along with page references to the text of
   Naked Lunch in the hope that these recordings might enrich some instructors'
   and students' reading experiences.
4 Sometimes an additional critical or theoretical reading, like Deleuze and
   Guattari's "Rhizome" (from *A Thousand Plateaus*), can assist students in recognizing the specific attributes of this "reading from the middle." Unlike some

teachers of Burroughs's work, I do not find Deleuze and Guattari's model of "minor literature" to be particularly useful in this context because, like Mikhail Bakhtin's dialogic model, it is too broad to provide precise insights into Burroughs's specific techniques of defamiliarization and demystification. The three fundamental characteristics of minor literature (deterritorialization of language, immediate political valence, collective agency) can certainly help students to situate Burroughs's work *vis-à-vis* mainstream trends in narrative, however; see Deleuze and Guattari (1986, 16-19).

5 Some readers might object that the "Atrophied Preface" should not be taken as a privileged account of the method or meaning of *Naked Lunch*; after all, it is called an "atrophied" preface, one of "many prefaces" that "atrophy and amputate spontaneous" (Burroughs 1990, 203). In light of this it might be claimed that Burroughs is parodying the explanatory preface much as deconstructive critics do (see Derrida 1981b, 1-59). I would resist such a reading, as I believe Burroughs himself would, because it implies that the author's only weapon against addiction and control is ungrounded, non-satirical (that is, postmodern) irony. Burroughs never accepted such misreadings of his work. Responding to a similar misreading of his article on the 1968 Democratic convention in Chicago, Burroughs takes a reviewer to task for assuming that Jean Genet's statements of political commitment, reported by Burroughs in that article, must have been "camping" (1986, 194). Indeed, if we assume that the "Atrophied Preface" is a case of completely ironic "camp," then we must also assume that every similar claim of subversive intent or political commitment Burroughs ever made in interviews and journalistic texts is also ironic. This would lead, I believe, to the impoverishment of both his work and the reader's experience of it.

6 Another very simple device that can help the reader keep the book's structure more clearly in mind while reading is a table of contents (see Table 1), which has not been included in any English-language edition (though the French translation, for one, does contain a table of contents [Burroughs 1964, 257]).

7 I have found that the crystalline formal elegance of *Pale Fire* makes a very useful didactic contrast to what I see as the discontinuous "anti-form" of *Naked Lunch*. The novels' contrasting treatments of homosexuality also create many discussion opportunities.

8 See Miles (1992, 89-109), and Morgan (1988, 272-326).

9 There are two brief accounts of these trials: the out-of-print Black Cat edition of *Naked Lunch* contains transcripts of Norman Mailer's and Allen Ginsberg's testimony from the Boston trial (1959, vii-xxxvi), and Burroughs's defense attorney, Edward de Grazia, includes a digest of documentary sources related to the case in his book (1992, 343-65, 384-97). The most comprehensive examination of the *Naked Lunch* obscenity case is *Contemporary Literary Censorship* (Goodman 1981), though this may be too long to assign as supplementary reading in an undergraduate course.

10 In *Wising Up the Marks*; see especially the introduction and chapter one.

11 Other writers I would consider to be amodern are Acker, Robert Coover, Toni Morrison and Thomas Pynchon.

12 For a more detailed account of this claim, see Murphy (1997, 74–80).

13 This is the point Roland Barthes has argued in his influential essay "The Death of the Author," included in Barthes (1977).

14 For a useful critical perspective on the Talking Asshole routine, see Chapter 2, "Notes from the Orifice: Language and the Body in *Naked Lunch*," in Lydenberg (1987).

15 A useful additional reading that can help clarify the terms of Burroughs's critique of the media as it appears in *Naked Lunch* is the "Culture Industry" chapter of *Dialectic of Enlightenment* (Horkheimer and Adorno 1972, 120–67. See also Murphy (1997, 76–95).

Works Cited

Acker, Kathy. 1997. *Bodies of Work: Essays*. New York: Serpent's Tail.

Barthes, Roland. 1977. *Image-Music-Text*. Trans. Stephen Heath. New York: Hill and Wang.

Burroughs, William S. 1959. *Naked Lunch*. New York: Grove Press/Black Cat.

———. 1964. *Le Festin nu*. Trans. Eric Kahane. Paris: Gallimard.

———.1986. *The Adding Machine: Selected Essays*. New York: Seaver Books.

———.1990. *Naked Lunch*. New York: Grove Weidenfeld.

———.1995. *Naked Lunch, Read by William S. Burroughs*. 3 CDs. Los Angeles: Warner Brothers Records.

De Grazia, Edward. 1992. *Girls Lean Back Everywhere: The Law of Obscenity and the Assault on Genius*. New York: Random House.

Deleuze, Gilles, and Félix Guattari. 1986. *Kafka: Toward a Minor Literature*. Trans. Dana Polan. Minneapolis: University of Minnesota Press.

———. 1987. *A Thousand Plateaus: Capitalism and Schizophrenia*. Trans. Brian Massumi. Minneapolis: University of Minnesota Press.

Derrida, Jacques. 1981a. *Dissemination*. Trans. Barbara Johnson. Chicago: University of Chicago Press.

———. 1981b. "Outwork, Prefacing." In *Dissemination*, trans. Barbara Johnson. Chicago: University of Chicago Press.

Goodman, Michael B. 1981. *Contemporary Literary Censorship: The Case History of Burroughs's "Naked Lunch."* Metuchen, NJ: Scarecrow Press.

Hilfer, Anthony Channell. 1980. "Mariner and Wedding Guest in William Burroughs's *Naked Lunch*." *Criticism* 22: 3 (Summer): 252–65.

Horkheimer, Max, and Theodor W. Adorno. 1972. *Dialectic of Enlightenment*. Trans. John Cumming. New York: Continuum.

Lydenberg, Robin. 1987. *Word Cultures: Radical Theory and Practice in William S. Burroughs's Fiction*. Urbana: University of Illinois Press.

Lyotard, Jean-François. 1984. *The Postmodern Condition: A Report on Knowledge*. Trans. Geoff Bennington and Brian Massumi. Minneapolis: University of Minnesota Press.

McConnell, Frank D. 1967. "William Burroughs and the Literature of Addiction." In *William S. Burroughs at the Front: Critical Reception, 1959-1989*, ed. Jennie Skerl and Robin Lydenberg. Carbondale: Southern Illinois University Press.

Miles, Barry. 1992. *William Burroughs, el hombre invisible—A Portrait*. New York: Hyperion.

Morgan, Ted. 1988. *Literary Outlaw: The Life and Times of William S. Burroughs*. New York: Henry Holt.

Mottram, Eric. 1977. *William Burroughs: The Algebra of Need*. London: Marion Boyars.

Murphy, Timothy S. 1997. *Wising Up the Marks: The Amodern William Burroughs*. Berkeley: University of California Press.

CHAPTER NINE

Allen Ginsberg's Urban Pastoral
Terence Diggory

Exhibits

What does Allen Ginsberg want? The question persists in his poetry, where it has acquired something more of a literary emphasis now that the poet himself is dead. Without insisting too rigidly on the boundary between art and life that Ginsberg delighted in crossing, I want to propose the literary concept of "pastoral" as a useful means for exploring the question of Ginsberg's desire. Taken together, the following three exhibits will suggest what I mean by "pastoral" in this connection and how complex a tradition conveys the concept to Ginsberg.

Exhibit 1: In 1977, the poet Kenneth Koch asks Ginsberg, "What would you consider an ideal existence for yourself as a poet?" Ginsberg replies: "Retiring from the world, living in a mountain hut, practicing certain special meditation exercises half the day, and composing epics as the sun sets" (Ginsberg 1977, 9).

Exhibit 2: In 1954, the San Francisco psychiatrist Philip Hicks asks Ginsberg: "What would you like to do? What *is* your desire, really?" Ginsberg replies:

I really would like to stop working forever—never work again, never do anything like the kind of work I'm doing now [market research]— and do nothing but write poetry and have leisure to spend the day outdoors and go to museums and see friends. And I'd like to keep living with someone—maybe even a man—and explore relationships that way. And cultivate my perceptions, cultivate the visionary thing in me. Just a literary and quiet city-hermit existence. (Kramer 1969, 42)

Exhibit 3: In 1948, Ginsberg has an "auditory hallucination" of "Blake's voice" in his East Harlem apartment, while feeling "cut off from what I'd idealized romantically" and reading Blake's "Ah! Sunflower!" (Ginsberg 1967, 302-03):

Ah, Sun-flower! weary of time,
Who countest the steps of the Sun:
Seeking after that sweet golden clime
Where the travellers journey is done.

Where the Youth pined away with desire,
And the pale Virgin shrouded in snow:
Arise from their graves and aspire,
Where my Sun-flower wishes to go. (Blake 1970, 25)

Each exhibit emphasizes an attribute traditionally associated with pastoral: withdrawal from society to a simpler existence in accord with nature (the "mountain hut" in Exhibit 1); the desire "to stop working forever" (Exhibit 2), the classical *otium* (Alpers 1996, 22-25); idealization of nature (the "sweet golden clime" in Exhibit 3). At the same time, it is evident that Ginsberg is drawing on other traditions besides that of Greek and Latin poetry, which has assigned pastoral its conventions as a genre in Western literature. For instance, in the interview from which I have extracted Exhibit 1, Ginsberg looks to Tantric Buddhism rather than Western literature as the source for the "special meditation exercises" he would practice in his retreat. His specific literary goal of "composing epics" probably looks to Blake, within the Western tradition (1967, 317), in opposition to "the Greek & Roman Classics" that Blake regarded as "the Antichrist" (1970, 656).

Through his affiliation with Blake, Ginsberg engages in opposition not only to literary tradition but also to existing social structures, in a way that distinguishes his version of pastoral from the dominant and essentially conservative "post revolutionary" mode that scholars such as Annabel Patterson have traced from the nineteenth century to the present day (Patterson 1987, 266-68). Patterson's willingness to grant artistic form some measure of independence from historical forces enables her to identify "a wider range of responses" among the practitioners of pastoral than follows, for instance, from Raymond Williams's reduction of pastoral to ideological mystification (Patterson 1987, 139; Williams 1973). Thus, in Blake's illustrations for Virgil's first Eclogue, a surprising undertaking in light of Blake's general antipathy to the Classics, Patterson discovers shepherds serving the ends of political radicalism (Patterson 1987, 252-62). They are the close ancestors of "the crazy shepherds of rebellion" in Ginsberg's "Footnote to *Howl*" (1984, 134). In turn, the prophetic image of the Lamb of God that Blake derived from Biblical tradition supplies, with reinforcement from Christopher Smart's *Jubilate Agno* ("Rejoice in the Lamb"), the mystical protagonist that Ginsberg cast in the drama of "Howl" (1955-56): "Part I, a lament for the Lamb in America with instances of remarkable lamblike youths; Part II names the monster of mental consciousness [Moloch] that preys on the Lamb; Part III a litany of affirmation of the Lamb in its glory" (1994, 636). From the children of Israel in the Bible to the "Lamb in America" of "Howl," this tradition envisions redemption as a collective enterprise, in marked contrast to the individualistic "post revolutionary ideology" that, according to Patterson, "substitutes introspection for social analysis, and imaginative and spiritual advances for institutional change" (Patterson 1987, 267).

Nevertheless, as Patterson demonstrates in her own practice, a degree of introspection is inevitable for the scholar or poet who engages with pastoral, because the suspension of physical labor in pastoral, the fulfillment of Ginsberg's desire to "never work again" (Exhibit 2), becomes a means of highlighting what Patterson calls "imaginative work" (Patterson 1987, 214), such as Ginsberg envisions in his project of "composing epics" (Exhibit 1). As we will see, Ginsberg ultimately diverges from Blake and remains a more purely pastoral poet in the sufficiency Ginsberg ascribes to the work of vision alone, apart from the work of hands. To follow Ginsberg along this path requires, in turn, shifting the critical terms applied to pastoral itself, from the critique of ideology pursued from Raymond Williams through Annabel Patterson to the critique of consciousness pursued from William Empson through Paul Alpers. As Terry

Eagleton has argued (1986), Empson's formulation of "the pastoral process of putting the complex into the simple" (Empson 1974, 22) lays down as a premise the complicated relation of the intellectual worker to social forms that only gradually emerges in Patterson's refinement of the Williams tradition. Even more important, for our purposes, Empson makes the crucial move of defining pastoral according to "inner" rather than "outer" form (Alpers 1996, 47). Looking for work as "outer" form, Raymond Williams does not see the complex "double attitude of the artist to the worker" that Empson, taking "attitude" as a mark of "inner" form, sees in pastoral (Empson 1974, 14). Looking for shepherds as conventional guides to the "outer" form of the pastoral genre, literary critics may not even recognize the existence of "urban pastoral," which requires an understanding of pastoral as mode rather than genre (Alpers 1996, Ch. 2).

Recognizing the mode of urban pastoral is crucial for understanding the connection between the retreat to "a mountain hut" that Ginsberg imagines in Exhibit 1 and the "city-hermit existence" he proposes in Exhibit 2. The "city-hermit" has withdrawn from society in attitude as much as the mountain hermit has withdrawn physically. Even when the "city-hermit" withdraws into behavior that society condemns as criminal, his sensibility is as innocent as that of the shepherd, hence the figure of "the sympathetic criminal" that Empson finds in the novels of Céline and Dostoevsky (Empson 1974, 10-11, 17)—both important authors for Ginsberg (Schumacher 1992, 67,107, 114, 286-87)—but analyzes most extensively in the "Newgate pastoral" of Gay's *Beggar's Opera* (Empson 1974, Ch. 6). Remembering his involvement with Herbert Huncke, Little Jack Melody, and Vicki Russell, who were using his apartment for a stolen goods racket while Ginsberg completed his college degree, Ginsberg reflected, "it was like a whole *Beggar's Opera* scene at my house" (Kramer 1969, 125).

The lens of urban pastoral provided by Empson brings into focus some unexpected alignments for Ginsberg, such as the one with Gay just cited. While it tends to separate Ginsberg from the simple "primitivism" of other Beat writers (Snyder 1985), it highlights his affinities with the New York School poets, despite his own early distinction between "hiptalk" and "queertalk" (Ginsberg 1984, 3). The tradition of homosexual love in pastoral increases the inflection of "queertalk" we hear in Ginsberg's voice the more we recognize his vision as that of pastoral. Notice Ginsberg's shy admission to desiring "maybe even a man" in Exhibit 2. And the more we identify Ginsberg's vision as specifically urban pastoral, the more likely we are to hear echoes of Frank O'Hara, the poet to whom Ginsberg paid the telling compliment, "I see New York through your eyes" (1984, 459). Helen Vendler has applied the concept of "urban pastoral" to place O'Hara in a tradition extending back through William Carlos Williams to Walt Whitman, two forerunners whom Ginsberg was also happy to claim (Vendler 1990, 245). However, since Blake provided Ginsberg's point of entry into this tradition, consideration of Ginsberg's urban pastoral should start from the occasion of Exhibit 3, when Ginsberg learned to see New York through Blake's eyes.

Blake

Throughout his career Ginsberg made reference to his "Blake visions" (1967, 291, 312) in 1948 as his initiation into poetry as a sacred vocation. They began as an "auditory hallucination" (1967, 303) Ginsberg experienced while simultaneously masturbating—a typical Ginsbergian detail—and reading Blake's "Sun-flower" (Exhibit 3). However hallucinated his hearing may have been, or however adolescent his sexuality, his reading of Blake's poem demonstrates mature intelligence. While strongly identifying with the innocent desire for "a sweet golden clime," he is able to criticize that desire and redirect it by repositioning himself in relation to it. This is the sort of reading "Ah! Sun-flower" seems to be designed to elicit (Bloom 1963, 139-40).

In Blake's view, natural desire is cyclical, like "the steps of the sun," because, like the sunflower, it is "vegetated," a term Blake used in other contexts to mean "bound by natural law." Human desire is truly progressive, Blake believed, only when the distinctively human condition of freedom from law is recognized. The proper setting for that freedom is not the garden, where the sunflower grows, but rather the city, where the Lamb of God presides.[1] Urban and pastoral imagery thus combine in Blake's later work to depict a higher, or "organized," innocence (Lincoln 1995, 192, 200-11), as Jerusalem and Eden combine in this description of the Lamb in "Night the Eighth" of *The Four Zoas*:

He stood in fair Jerusalem to awake up into Eden
The fallen Man but first to Give his vegetated body
To be cut off & separated that the Spiritual body
    may be Reveald. (Blake 1970, 363)

Ginsberg experienced such an awakening through his reading of "Ah! Sun-flower" in 1948: "my body suddenly felt *light* . . . it was a sudden awakening into a totally deeper real universe than I'd been existing in" (1967, 304). His experience began with a recognition of his fallen state, "cut off from what I'd idealized romantically" (1967, 302), and thus already a step ahead of Blake's Youth and Virgin, who feel cut off, but show no awareness that the "sweet golden clime" to which they aspire is a romantic idealization. To the extent that that awareness is in the poem, it can only belong to Blake himself— hence Ginsberg's hallucination of actually hearing Blake's voice. The next step was to see with Blake's eyes. Having turned his gaze from an illusory paradise "elsewhere," Ginsberg was prepared to see the reality in front of him: "I suddenly realized that *this* existence was *it*!" (1967, 303). But "it," in this statement, refers to "the sweet golden clime," now relocated. In other words, Ginsberg is claiming that, like the fallen Man awakened by the Lamb in Blake's *Four Zoas*, he has awakened into Eden as a present reality. However, since his present reality, in non-visionary terms, is East Harlem, he envisions Eden in urban form, as the New Jerusalem.

Needless to say, finding imagery that can communicate a view of East Harlem as the New Jerusalem poses a considerable challenge, so it is not surprising to find Ginsberg struggling toward that imagery, even as late as the 1965 interview that I have been drawing on for his recollection of his Blake visions. In that recollection, Ginsberg first overlooks the city altogether: "looking out at the window, through the window at the sky, suddenly it seemed that I saw into the depths of the universe, by looking simply into the ancient sky. The sky suddenly seemed very *ancient*. And this was the very ancient place that he [Blake] was talking about, the sweet golden clime, I suddenly realized that *this* existence was *it*" (1967, 302). Despite Ginsberg's emphasis on the immediate presence of "*this* existence," the temptation to displace Edenic reality "elsewhere," which Blake criticizes in "Ah! Sun-flower," is still evident in Ginsberg's description, in both its spatial (up there in the sky) and temporal ("very *ancient*") detail. Nevertheless, a connection between this "ancient sky" and Ginsberg's sense of having heard the voice of "the Ancient of Days," a Creator figure (1967, 303),[2] suggests that Ginsberg is trying to humanize the sky by depicting it not merely as a natural phenomenon but as a product of art, something created. The Blakean analogue here is the imaginative reclaiming of the world of experience at the end of *Milton*, Book 1: "The Sky is an immortal Tent built by the Sons of Los" (Blake 1970, 126).

Blake's own imagery becomes more humanized in his last epic, *Jerusalem*, where the buildings he depicts are not merely figurative, like the sky, but actual, like those of London, though they are reenvisioned as "Labour of merciful hands" to pre-figure the arrival of the New Jerusalem (Blake 1970, 154). In Ginsberg's second attempt to describe what he saw when he looked out of his window in Harlem, the buildings come into focus as the "solidification" of human imagination, a City of Art after the manner of Blake's Jerusalem (Bloom 1963, 380). "What I was speaking about visually, Ginsberg resumes,

> was, immediately, that the cornices in the old tenement building in Harlem across the back-yard court had been carved very finely in 1890 or 1910. And were like the solidification of a great deal of intelligence and care and love also. So that I began noticing in every corner where I looked evidences of a living hand, even in the bricks, in the arrangement of each brick. Some hand placed them there—that some hand had placed the whole universe in front of me. (Ginsberg 1967, 304)

There is still some displacement in this vision. Ginsberg is seeing the buildings as they were conceived "in 1890 or 1910," not as they appeared to the ordinary eye in 1948, when his vision occurred, or in 1965, when he recollects it. Some of the pastoral mood, therefore, may be due to nostalgia, but a much larger part must be credited to the sensation of being at one with the environment. Most important, that sense of oneness is achieved through identification not with nature's creatures, like "The Lamb" of Blake's *Songs of Innocence*, but rather with the Creator, in the person of the Son, the Lamb of God. In his own words, Ginsberg had experienced "this vision or this consciousness, of being alive unto myself, alive myself unto the Creator. As the son of the Creator—who loved me, I realized, or who responded to my desire, say. It was the same desire both ways" (1967, 303).

> In his effort to emphasize the closeness of his identification with the Creator, Ginsberg moves toward traditional pastoral, but away from Blake.

As he speaks, Ginsberg progressively revises his claim to have seen evidence of the Creator's hand, and claims instead to be in the immediate presence of the Creator: "not that some hand had placed the sky but that the sky was the living blue hand itself. Or that God was in front of my eyes—existence itself was God" (1967, 304). With the erasure of the creating hand, any impression of the "terrible eternal labour" (Blake 1970, 154) Blake thought necessary to build the New Jerusalem has also been erased. For Ginsberg, who upholds the classical ideal of otium, as we have seen, pastoral is defined by the absence of labor. Beulah, a place of temporary rest for Blake (1970, 299; Lincoln 1995, 201), is for Ginsberg "the Great Place" itself ("Falling Asleep in America" 1984, 517). "Jerusalem pillars" are not to be built with the hand but seen with the eye, as shafts of sunlight play upon a windowpane at a rural retreat ("Easter Sunday" 1984, 516).

This attitude extends to the making of verse, the one activity that might appear as labor that Ginsberg, again following classical tradition, admits into his pastoral world. After all, the songs of classical pastoral are sung while the shepherds are resting from their labor as shepherds. Because we never see a shepherd working to compose his song, it appears to arise spontaneously, as both Blake and Ginsberg believed true poetry should arise (Ginsberg 1984, xx, 595). But Ginsberg is confident that it is true poetry as soon as it arises— "first thought, best thought" (1984, xx)—whereas Blake distrusts any material that has not been carefully worked over by hand, as his laborious method of printing his books implies.

The American Tradition

Although I have just measured the divergence between Blake and Ginsberg by the standards of classical pastoral, I do not mean to suggest that the divergence was caused by any observance of classical standards on Ginsberg's part. Rather, the voice of Blake takes on an American accent in Ginsberg's East Harlem apartment because Ginsberg had been training himself in that distinctively American tradition of urban pastoral sketched by Helen Vendler (1990, 245) and traced through the nineteenth century by James Machor (1987). Whitman's view of the city assigns the same privilege to the observer's eye over the laborer's hand that we have seen in Ginsberg's vision of Harlem:

All architecture is what you do to it when you look upon it,
(Did you think it was in the white or gray stone? or the

lines of the arches and cornices?)
(Whitman, "A Song for Occupations" 1968, 215)

In a letter sent to William Carlos Williams in 1956, Ginsberg confessed to "a whitmanesque mania & nostalgia for cities" (Williams 1992, 210), recalling his own nostalgic transformation of Harlem into the city of "1890 or 1910," and recalling also, at least to the readers of Williams's long city poem, *Paterson*, a particularly "pastoral" evocation of the early years of that city in Book 4 (Riddel 1974, 94-97), into which Williams had inserted another letter from Ginsberg (*Paterson* 4 [1951]; Williams 1992, 193).

The version of pastoral that Ginsberg derived from Williams is as much a mode of activity as of imagery. If Blake went beyond pastoral in his insistence on "terrible eternal labour," Williams reaffirms pastoral in his idealization of laborers at rest. Like the singing of the idle shepherds in classical pastoral, their resting signifies the work of the artist as a kind of non-activity, a point that Williams sometimes underscores by explicitly drawing his models from works of art: the "Heavenly man" of *Paterson* 2 (1948) from an Eisenstein film (Williams 1992, 57-58), or the "young/reaper enjoying his/noonday rest" among the *Pictures from Brueghel* (Williams 1988, 389). More pertinent to urban pastoral, because their work is industrial rather than agricultural, are the roofers of "Fine Work with Pitch and Copper" (1936; Williams 1986, 405-406). According to Williams, this poem "is really telling about my struggle with verse" (Williams 1978, 57). Though the term "struggle" hardly seems to apply to the roofers, "resting / in the fleckless light" during the last moments of their lunch hour, we can get some idea of what Williams means if we approach his poem by way of Whitman, and look for the work of the eye rather than the hand. Thus, the poet's work, the effort to see with precision, is revealed in the final image of Williams's poem, as one of the roofers,

> still chewing
> picks up a copper strip
> and runs his eye along it

This is the work that Ginsberg represents in "The Bricklayer's Lunch Hour," one of the poems that Ginsberg "discovered" when Williams told him some of the prose passages in his journals already were poems.[3] "The Bricklayer's Lunch Hour" seems to derive directly from "Fine Work with Pitch and Copper," except that Ginsberg's bricklayer, "gazing uninterestedly," is as idle of eye as he is of hand. In this case, the resting laborer offers a contrast to the poet, whose eye is felt to engage each detail of this scene observed "on a shady street in Denver." Because the poem consists of nothing but details, without interpretive commentary, its mood seems very different from Ginsberg's apocalyptic visions of Harlem, with its "buildings standing in Eternity" (Ginsberg 1984, 595). But to Ginsberg, the scene in Denver still offers "a little shiver of eternal space" (Ginsberg quoted in Schumacher 1992, 81), because fixing the eye on "minute particulars"—a concern for Blake (e.g., Blake 1970, 249) as much as for Williams (Williams 1992, 5), as Ginsberg knew (Breslin 1985, 90)—produces the impression of stopping time.

Having trained his eye in this discipline, Ginsberg was predisposed to see New York through Frank O'Hara's eyes, though in a way that we might not at first associate with O'Hara, and certainly not with pastoral. If the defining moment of pastoral is the moment of rest, such as we have just examined in Williams and Ginsberg, O'Hara's mode, in contrast, is characterized by the impression of speed. "If we contrast O'Hara with Williams," James Breslin argues, "we see how steadfastly O'Hara refused to eternalize his objects"; "they go by too quickly to yield meanings," Breslin elaborates (Breslin 1985, 218, 217). Nevertheless, the objects that speed by O'Hara's gaze frequently converge on a "resting/center," as Williams referred to the young reaper in Brueghel's painting (1988, 390), and that point implies a meaning, more often than not having something to do with mortality. The paradigm is "A Step Away from Them" (1956; O'Hara 1995, 257-58), the occasion for Breslin's comments quoted above, and, I believe, the poem that initiated Ginsberg into O'Hara's way of seeing the city. Like the poems by Williams and Ginsberg we have just been considering, O'Hara's poem is set during lunch hour, but the pace of observation hardly seems leisurely, an impression heightened by the sudden shifts among the sights observed: women on the sidewalk, taxis in the street, watches in shop windows, "cats playing in sawdust." Then abruptly, at the center of the poem, "Everything/ suddenly honks," and things grind to a halt, however briefly.

Ginsberg recalls this "honking" both in "My Sad Self" (1958; Ginsberg 1984, 202), which is dedicated to O'Hara, and in "City Midnight Junk Strains" (1966; Ginsberg 1984, 459), his elegy for O'Hara. The elegiac mood already present in "My Sad Self," as the title implies, may well recall O'Hara's lament for the passing of friends to which he turns after the "honking" moment in "A Step Away from Them." That moment itself extends into eternity in Ginsberg's poem:

> . . . all movement stops
> & I walk in the timeless sadness of existence,
>   tenderness flowing thru the buildings

No doubt Breslin would argue that Ginsberg here proves to be more conventional than O'Hara by restoring what O'Hara was bold enough to do without, the "eternal perspective" in which "thoughts of time and loss" are traditionally "reconciled" (1985, 219). In my view, however, Ginsberg's lines display nothing so fixed as a perspective, but rather a mood holding in fluid suspension two emotions, not thoughts: namely, tenderness and sadness.

This is the mood of pastoral elegy, famously defined by Erwin Panofsky as "that vespertinal mixture of sadness and tranquillity which is perhaps Virgil's most personal contribution to poetry" (1955, 300). In the later English tradition, it descends by way of Shelley rather than Blake. Its arrival in America, by way of Whitman, prepares the ground on which Ginsberg, who quoted Shelley's "Adonais" in the epigraph to "Kaddish" (1959), meets O'Hara, who was too urbane to take seriously Ginsberg's "Blakean mysticism," as James Breslin calls it (1985, 220). Urbanity is a quality not often ascribed to Ginsberg, but it belongs to the complex mood of urban pastoral. Thus, it can be sensed in Ginsberg's ironic comparison of himself, "poking around big history-less Mayan ruins" in the mountains of Mexico, with "Shelley in Italy" (quoted in Kramer 1969, 40), presumably in the act of naturalizing the ruins of Rome by comparing them to "shattered mountains," as he does in "Adonais" (Shelley 1970, 442). O'Hara applies the same principle of comparison but in the opposite direction, from the mountains to the city, when he claims that the sort of "insight into nature" once offered by "the hills outside Rome" is now more likely to be found in the sight of "a woman stepping on a bus" (1954; O'Hara 1975, 42). Observing that "nature has not stood still since Shelley's day," O'Hara argues that technology, in both its scientific and artistic extensions, has made all of nature into a human construct. The ancient division between city and country, a defining feature of traditional pastoral, has been erased.

Ecologues

O'Hara's redefinition of nature provides a useful clue to understanding one of the most significant yet also most puzzling expressions of Ginsberg's urban pastoral, the sequence of "Ecologues of These States 1969-1971" that continues an even longer "Poem of These States" that Ginsberg had begun in 1965.[4] Although Ginsberg's classifying term alludes directly to Virgil's eclogues, it is easy to take the term as wholly ironical, since Ginsberg's "ecologues" invert the "sweet golden clime" of Blake's "Sun-flower" into imagery of ecological disaster:

> Philadelphia smoking in Gold Sunlight, pink blue
>   green Cyanide tanks sitting on hell's floor,
> Many chimneys smoldering, city flats virus-linked
>   along Delaware bays under horizon-smog— (Ginsberg 1984, 514)

However, Ginsberg has been granted this particular vision by going up in an airplane. On the whole, his "Poem of These States" celebrates modern means of transportation, which he took pains to represent in their full range (Schumacher 1992, 475), as much as it condemns industrial pollution. If "the machine in the garden," as Leo Marx established (1964), represents the tension between pastoralism and industrialism in America, Ginsberg enters the garden riding on the machine.[5]

Of all the modern extensions of technology, those of transportation and communication, which also feature prominently in Ginsberg's imagery, have done the most to erase the boundary between city and country and establish the new sense of nature-as-artifice observed by Frank O'Hara. In that sense, Ginsberg appears as natural as O'Hara's "woman stepping on a bus," as Ginsberg does to survey America in the second section of "Iron Horse" (1984, 449-56), or to work among "the poor shepherds" "In the Baggage Room at Greyhound" (1956), an earlier poem (1984, 153-54). The outstanding example of communications technology employed in the work of the sixties is the tape machine on which Ginsberg recorded his impressions as he rode along in an automobile, producing what he called "auto poesy": poetry as "automatic" as that proposed by the surrealists, or as spontaneous as the songs of the shepherds in classical pastoral.

Having thus "pastoralized" certain aspects of industrial production, Ginsberg occupies a middle position from which he satirizes traditional pastoral ideals as well as industrial pollution. It is typical of urban pastoral to reject the traditional ideal of "the return to nature" as a refuge from city problems: "the country will bring us/no peace," says Williams (1988, 88-89); "the country is no good for us," echoes O'Hara (1995, 476). Ginsberg makes himself the object of such critique in "Ecologue," the only poem specifically so titled, and the one poem in the group of "Ecologues of These States" that most clearly employs the title term ironically. Identifying Virgil's eclogues as the poetry of a civilization's end, when "life on a farm" seemed "safer, healthier" than in "garbage-filled Rome" (1984, 545), Ginsberg describes a farm he purchased in 1968 in Cherry Valley, New York, 200 miles from New York City's "suffering millions" (1984, 544). Retreating to the farm does not permit him to escape suffering, however. It is not just that he is pursued by news of the outside world, the war in Vietnam and the domestic war to enforce state control of drugs, but in the daily life of the farm itself, broken bodies and run-down machinery serve as a constant reminder of both individual mortality and universal entropy. The dream of a "safer, healthier" place is exposed as an illusion: "The Farm's a lie!" (1984, 547). At the conclusion of "Ecologue," farmer Ginsberg stares in mock-horror—that is, with the mockery turned on himself—at "bottles & cans piled up in our garbage pail" (1984, 552), just as in "garbage-filled Rome."

There are many poems in which Ginsberg himself asks the question I asked at the outset, "What does Allen Ginsberg want?" "Ecologue," read as part of the larger "Poem of These States," demonstrates how the topic of pastoral enables the poet to refine that question into a critique of desire. The "States" that Ginsberg is exploring, as he makes clear in his cover blurb for *The Fall of America*, are as much "States of consciousness" as they are political entities (1984, 815). What spoils the pastoral dream for farmer Ginsberg is that he has entered the state of possession by actually purchasing a farm, "buying into" a deception as if it were a reality. "Dangerous to want possessions," Ginsberg reminds himself in "Iron Horse," as he contemplates a newspaper ad for "113 acres/of woodland" (1984, 454). A series of quotations from one of Ginsberg's gurus toward the end of "Iron Horse" points to the alternative of total dispossession, rejection of all images, those of poetry as well as those of war, and even that of the self, in favor of "pure Consciousness": "Buddha's Nameless/Alone is Alone" (1984, 455-56).

This ideal is the key to "Wales Visitation," a text that is unique within the "Poem of These States," and indeed within Ginsberg's total oeuvre, because it is almost pure pastoral in the traditional sense and apparently without irony. Although it invokes both Blake and Wordsworth by name, it pretends to reject even the name of Ginsberg, who has been exposed as mere image through "TV pictures flashing bearded your Self" (1984, 480). In place of that personal illusion, the poem assumes the voice of a "Bard Nameless as the Vast." The pastoral imagery that follows this assumption is very beautiful and has received much praise from critics (e.g., Moramarco 1982, 13-14; Schumacher 1992, 486-88), but it is no less a lie than the dream of the farm that Ginsberg mocks in "Ecologue." In fact, it is a worse lie, since in "Wales Visitation" Ginsberg is lying to himself. By the terms he acknowledges in "Iron Horse," the Nameless condition he assumes at the beginning of "Wales Visitation" could be followed by no images, pastoral or otherwise. It is not the Bard who achieves the Nameless condition, but the Saint.

"Iron Horse" is a more honest poem than "Wales Visitation" because, while it honors the Saint's path toward the Nameless, it recognizes the divergence of the Bard's path and commits Ginsberg to it and to his ordinary self, as he returns by Greyhound bus to his home in the city at the poem's end. By naming the city "Mannahatta," Ginsberg acknowledges Whitman as the Bard whose path he is following (1984, 456 and n. 782). O'Hara is not far away, in the poem that immediately follows "Iron Horse" in the arrangement of the *Collected Poems*, where Ginsberg says, "I see New York thru your eyes." We can hear an echo of O'Hara in the casual notation of desire at the conclusion of "Iron Horse"—"taxi-honk toward East River where / Peter waits working" (1984, 456). Earlier in the poem, we can see the influence of Williams in the precise observation of particulars that discovers beauty in the industrial landscape Ginsberg passes through on his way to New York:

Brilliant green lights
   in factory transom windows.
         Beautiful! (Ginsberg 1984, 452)[6]

However, when Ginsberg sees through these particulars to open a series of challenging questions, he is seeing through Blake's eyes:

Why do I fear these lights?
   & smoking chimneys' Industry?
Why see them less godly
       than forest treetrunks
       & sunset orange moons?
Why these cranes less Edenly than Palmfronds?
(Ginsberg 1984, 453)

These questions go to the heart of Ginsberg's urban pastoral. His ability to see even the possibility of equating "smoking chimneys" and "forest treetrunks" shows that he has left behind the state of innocence parodied in "Ecologue" and, more gently, within "Iron Horse" itself. As he resists the invitation to purchase the "113 acres / of woodland" offered for sale in the newspaper, Ginsberg acknowledges:

In my twenties I would've enjoyed running around these
                  green woods naked.
In my twenties I would've enjoyed making love naked
               by these brooks
(Ginsberg 1984, 454)

—but no longer. He has seen death, he has fallen from innocence, and having fallen into "experience," as Blake called it, Ginsberg has progressed to the knowledge not only that "The Farm's a lie," as he declares in "Ecologue," but that "All landscapes have become Phantom," as he concludes in "Iron Horse" (1984, 455).

Ginsberg does not mean to deny that industry can be genuinely destructive any more than Blake would deny that the "marks of woe" he perceived in "London" were genuinely felt (1970, 26). From the standpoint of experience, Ginsberg knows there is good reason to fear the factory more than the forest: "my countrymen make this structure to make War" (1984, 453). But because war is "made," the landscape it produces is a Phantom—a fiction, something made—as much as any landscape, including the natural one. All landscapes ultimately reflect a state of consciousness (Schama 1995); they are "mind-forg'd," as Blake would say (1970, 27). But only those states that deny having been made, that present themselves as an unconditional reality, are "forged" in the sense of being "lies," like Ginsberg's farm in "Ecologue," or like war in "Iron Horse":

              all screaming of soldiers
                                    crying on wars
                    speech politics massing armies
                                    is false-feigning show
              (Ginsberg 1984, 456)

Although this sounds like the guru's too easy dismissal of the phenomenal world as mere "Appearances" (Ginsberg 1984, 455), Ginsberg's simultaneous acknowledgment of the real suffering that Appearances entail suggests that his deeper source is Blake. You "are led to Believe a Lie," Blake warned, "When you see with not thro the Eye" (1970, 484, 512),[7] precisely the diagnosis that Ginsberg assigns to the diseased state of consciousness he calls "war." War's ecological consequence is, so to speak, an inability to see the forest for the lies. However, seen through the eye of Blake's higher, organized innocence, the trees of the forest reappear as having been made, like the rest of the phenomenal world. Thus, Ginsberg's vision of the "spiritual labor" (1967, 306) that produced the buildings of Harlem reappears in "Iron Horse" in the equation of urban pastoral:

                    all these places millions of trees' work
                                    made green
              as millions of workmens' labor raised the buildings of NY
              (Ginsberg 1984, 454)

Notes

1 For the interrelationship of garden and city in Blake's image of Paradise, see Frye (1975, 62), Bloom (1963, 37), and Mitchell (1978, 167).

2 The redeeming connotations of "the Ancient of Days" in Ginsberg are those of the original figure in the Book of Daniel (7: 9–22) rather than in Blake's threatening image, used as the frontispiece to Europe, that critics sometimes refer to as "the Ancient of Days."

3 See Breslin (1985, 89) for Williams on Ginsberg's journals in general; Breslin (1985, 92) for mention of this poem in particular in the context of a "pastoral" tendency in Ginsberg at this time. In Ginsberg (1984, 4) the poem is dated "Denver, Summer 1947," and it appears in verse lineation, but it was first published in the New Directions annual for 1953 (Ginsberg 1953) in prose form.

4 The bulk of the sequence was published in The Fall of America (1973) but it was expanded in the Collected Poems (Ginsberg 1984) through the significant addition of "Wichita Vortex Sutra," "Iron Horse" and "Wales Visitation."
5 See Marx (1964,. 218) for reference to the Beats. In contrast to my emphasis, Marx himself uses a statement by Ginsberg in an interview to categorize his version of pastoral as naive (1988, 199-200). In the poems, Ginsberg's pastoral is usually more complex. Compare Moramarco (1982, 16).
6 Ginsberg's use of the 3-step line also suggests the influence of Williams in this instance.
7 My quotation conflates the wording of similar passages from "Auguries of Innocence" and "The Everlasting Gospel" as Ginsberg does (1967, 296).

Works Cited

Alpers, Paul. 1996. *What Is Pastoral?* Chicago: University of Chicago Press.
Blake, William. 1970. *The Poetry and Prose of William Blake*. Ed. David V. Erdman. Rev. ed. Garden City, NY: Doubleday.
Bloom, Harold. 1963. *Blake's Apocalypse: A Study in Poetic Argument*. Garden City, NY: Doubleday.
Breslin, James E. B. 1985. *From Modern to Contemporary: American Poetry, 1945-1965*. Chicago: University of Chicago Press.
Eagleton, Terry. 1986. "The Critic as Clown." In *Against the Grain: Essays 1975-85*. London, Verso.
Empson, William. 1974. *Some Versions of Pastoral*. New York: New Directions.
Frye, Northrop. 1975. "Blake's Treatment of the Archetype." In *English Romantic Poets: Modern Essays in Criticism*, ed. M. H. Abrams. 2nd ed. New York: Oxford University Press.
Ginsberg, Allen. 1953. "The Bricklayer's Lunch Hour." *New Directions in Prose and Poetry* 14: 342.
———. 1967. Interview by Thomas Clark. *Writers at Work: The "Paris Review" Interviews*. 3rd Series. New York: Viking.
———. 1977. "Allen Ginsberg Talks About Poetry." Interview by Kenneth Koch. *New York Times Book Review*, 23 October: 9+.
———. 1984. *Collected Poems 1947-1980*. New York: Harper and Row.
———. 1994. "Notes for *Howl and Other Poems*." In *Postmodern American Poetry*, ed. Paul Hoover. New York: Norton.
Kramer, Jane. 1969. *Allen Ginsberg in America*. New York: Random House.
Lincoln, Andrew. 1995. *Spiritual History: A Reading of William Blake's "Vala" or "The Four Zoas."* Oxford: Oxford University Press.
Machor, James L. 1987. *Pastoral Cities: Urban Ideals and the Symbolic Landscape of America*. Madison: University of Wisconsin Press.
Marx, Leo. 1964. *The Machine in the Garden: Technology and the Pastoral Ideal in America*. New York: Oxford University Press.
———. 1988. "American Literary Culture and the Fatalistic View of Technology." In *The Pilot and the Passenger: Essays on Literature, Technology, and Culture in the United States*. New York: Oxford University Press.

Mitchell, W. J. T. 1978. *Blake's Composite Art: A Study of the Illuminated Poetry*. Princeton: Princeton University Press.

Moramarco, Fred. 1982. "Moloch's Poet: A Retrospective Look at Allen Ginsberg's Poetry." *American Poetry Review* 11.5 (September-October): 10–18.

O'Hara, Frank. 1975. "Nature and New Painting." In *Standing Still and Walking in New York*, ed. Donald Allen. Bolinas, CA: Grey Fox.

———. 1995. *The Collected Poems*. Ed. Donald Allen. Rev. ed. Berkeley: University of California Press.

Panofsky, Erwin. 1955. "*Et in Arcadia Ego*: Poussin and the Elegiac Tradition." In *Meaning in the Visual Arts*. Garden City, N.Y.: Doubleday.

Patterson, Annabel. 1987. *Pastoral and Ideology: Virgil to Valéry*. Berkeley: University of California Press.

Riddel, Joseph. 1974. *The Inverted Bell: Modernism and the Counterpoetics of William Carlos Williams*. Baton Rouge: Louisiana State University Press.

Schama, Simon. 1995. *Landscape and Memory*. New York: Knopf.

Schumacher, Michael. 1992. *Dharma Lion: A Biography of Allen Ginsberg*. New York: St. Martin's Press.

Shelley, P. B. 1970. *Poetical Works*. Ed. Thomas Hutchinson and G. M. Matthews. London: Oxford University Press.

Snyder, Gary. 1985. "Poetry and the Primitive: Notes on Poetry as an Ecological Survival Technique." In *Poetry and Politics: An Anthology of Essays*, ed. Richard Jones. New York: Quill.

Vendler, Helen. 1990. "Frank O'Hara: The Virtue of the Alterable." In *Frank O'Hara: To Be True to a City*, ed. Jim Elledge. Ann Arbor: University of Michigan Press.

Whitman, Walt. 1968. *Leaves of Grass: Comprehensive Reader's Edition*. Ed. Harold W. Blodgett and Sculley Bradley. New York: Norton.

Williams, Raymond. 1973. *The Country and the City*. New York: Oxford University Press.

Williams, William Carlos. 1978. *I Wanted to Write a Poem: The Autobiography of the Works of a Poet*. Ed. Edith Heal. New York: New Directions.

———. 1986. *Collected Poems 1: 1909-1939*. Ed. A. Walton Litz and Christopher MacGowan. New York: New Directions.

———. 1988. *Collected Poems 2: 1939-1962*. Ed. Christopher MacGowan. New York: New Directions.

———. 1992. *Paterson*. Ed. Christopher MacGowan. New York: New Directions.

CHAPTER TEN

"O fellow travelers I write you a poem in Amsterdam":
Allen Ginsberg, Simon Vinkenoog,
and the Dutch Beat Connection
Jaap van der Bent

In the beginning of September 1957 Allen Ginsberg and Peter Orlovsky, traveling through Europe after having visited William S. Burroughs in Tangiers, arrived in Paris. They were planning to stay with Gregory Corso, who was exploring Europe on his own; in the French capital he had rented a small room in the attic of a nameless hotel at 9 Rue Gît-le-Coeur, the location that in literary history would become known as the "Beat hotel." Always unpredictable, Corso had suddenly left for Amsterdam, however, leaving a note for his two friends which suggested that they join him there for a month, after which the three of them could return to Paris. Ginsberg and Orlovsky did not immediately act upon Corso's suggestion. They explored Paris for ten days, visiting museums and taking in the scenery, but ultimately the lack of money which hounded them throughout Europe forced them to travel north. According to Gordon Ball, who edited Ginsberg's mid-fifties' journals, Amsterdam at the time was cheaper than Paris (1995, 332); it certainly was for Ginsberg and Orlovsky: they could share Corso's room on the

Reijnier Vinkeleskade as well as the proceeds from the stolen books which Corso frequently brought home to pay his way in Holland (Vinkenoog 1998).

Ginsberg's three-week stay in Amsterdam was relatively uneventful. As he had done in Paris, he spent most of his time walking about the city and visiting museums; following in the footsteps of many other Americans he found his way to the Rijksmuseum, where he admired the work of Rembrandt and other Dutch masters. But often he was also plainly bored, again partly because he did not have much money. A poem written in an Amsterdam bar begins like this: "Dumps, nothing to do/I want to be home in bed/with a fiery Book—" (Ball 1995, 376) A few lines further on Ginsberg continues in the same vein: "I got no money/ain't even got the blues/all I got is Amsterdam/and a red lite on the table." (Ball 1995, 377). The poems that Ginsberg, as well as Corso, wrote in Amsterdam are fewer in number and less original than the ones they would write after having returned to Paris. The exception is Ginsberg's "POEM Rocket," written on October 4, the day the Russians launched their first Sputnik, and later published in *Kaddish and Other Poems* (1961).[1] Like its longer companion piece written on the same day, "Moon Prevention" (Ball 1995, 379-85), "POEM Rocket" was partly a collaborative effort of Ginsberg, Corso, and Orlovsky. What is not generally known is that two Dutch writers, Simon Vinkenoog and Adriaan Morriën, were also present when the poem was written and that they, too, contributed to it. Sitting in the rather posh "Café Americain," they answered questions that the three Americans threw at them, and their answers were immediately incorporated into the poem. The writing session ended when both the Dutch and American poets were asked to leave, because they were growing too exuberant (Vinkenoog 1999).

Adriaan Morriën (not Adrian Mourian, as Ball has it) is a Dutch poet (born in 1912), prose writer, and critic who was more than ten years older than Ginsberg and his friends. However, as the editor of a Dutch literary magazine devoted to foreign literature, *Litterair Paspoort* [Literary Passport], he had a nose for what was new and exciting. After having met Corso, and hearing of recent developments in American literature involving the Beats, Morriën immediately asked Corso to contribute an article about these developments to *Litterair*

Paspoort. Corso's loosely written but engaging essay, "The Literary Revolution in America," was published in English in the November 1957 issue; co-authored by Ginsberg but signed by Corso only, it is one of the first essays in which the Beat movement was discussed by two of its own members (1957, 193-96).

Morriën had been put on to Corso, Ginsberg, and Orlovsky by the younger Dutch poet Simon Vinkenoog. Someone had drawn Vinkenoog's attention to the fact that every evening three Americans, "also poets," were to be found in a jazz club called Bohemia, which had recently opened on one of the Amsterdam canals. It was there that Vinkenoog, one evening in October, approached Ginsberg and his friends. Soon the Dutch poet and his American equals were engaged in a lively conversation. Vinkenoog and Ginsberg hit it off in particular: they started visiting each other, sharing an occasional "smoke" (Vinkenoog 1998),[2] and after Ginsberg had left Amsterdam the two always kept in touch. Before very long Ginsberg's poems began to exert a noticeable influence on Vinkenoog's work. A closer look at that influence will not only be revealing of the artistic relationship between Ginsberg and Vinkenoog, but also of the relevance of the Beats to both Dutch literature and European literature in general.

Nowadays a substantial number of American readers will probably be familiar with at least the names, if not the work, of certain Dutch writers. During the last few years books by novelists Cees Nooteboom, Harry Mulisch, and the Flemish author Hugo Claus have all been highly acclaimed by many prominent American critics. Born in Amsterdam in 1928, Simon Vinkenoog belongs to the same generation of writers, but his work lacks the scope and stature of that of his colleagues and has been less widely translated. An anthology of Vinkenoog's poetry was published in Australia in 1990 (Vinkenoog 1990), and two of his longer poems were featured in the 1982 City Lights anthology *Nine Dutch Poets* (Rollins and Ferlinghetti 1982); unfortunately his work was not incorporated in *Living Space: Poems of the Dutch "Fifties"* (Glassgold 1979), an American anthology of mid-century Dutch poetry that is not only larger in scope, but also more informative. Still, English-speaking readers with a countercultural taste could well have heard of Vinkenoog long before they had the chance to come across his ultimately better-known Dutch fellow writers. In the mid-1960s he played a prominent part in Alexander Trocchi's sigma movement, with which at least some American readers became familiar through Lawrence Ferlinghetti's *City Lights Journal*.[3] Together with Trocchi, Ferlinghetti, Ginsberg, Corso, and other poets, Vinkenoog also read in public during the famous June 1965 International Poetry Incarnation at the Albert Hall in London; in Peter Widehead's documentary film about this huge poetry reading, *Wholly Communion* (1966), Vinkenoog makes a spectacular appearance when, trying to elate the spirit of the meeting, he suddenly stands up and, raising his arms, begins to shout "Love! Love!" Two years later, together with George Andrews, Vinkenoog edited a widely read anthology of hemp-related writing which was published both in London and New York, *The Book of Grass: An Anthology on Indian Hemp* (Andrews and Vinkenoog 1967). Vinkenoog's exploits in the subculture of the 1960s are also referred to and described in books like Jeff Nuttall's *Bomb Culture* (1968) and Richard Neville's *Play Power* (1970). More recently A.S. Byatt mentioned Vinkenoog in her "postmodern novel of ideas," *Babel Tower* (1996).[4] Strangely enough neither of the Ginsberg biographies which have been published to date pays much attention to the artistic and personal relationship between the Dutch and the American poet, even though the two met not only in 1957 and 1965 but also during Ginsberg's visits to Holland in the 1970s and 1980s. On each of those visits Vinkenoog served as Ginsberg's translator, after having published the first, and still the only, substantial Dutch translation of Ginsberg's poems, *Proef m'n tong in je oor* (Taste my mouth in your ear; Ginsberg 1966).[5] It was also during one of those visits that Ginsberg found the inspiration for his poem "What the Sea Throws Up at Vlissingen," published in *White Shroud: Poems 1980-1985* and dedicated to Vinkenoog (Ginsberg 1986).

When Vinkenoog met Ginsberg in 1957, he had recently returned to Holland after having lived in Paris for eight years. Feeling stifled by the poverty and, especially, the stuffiness of postwar Holland, he had moved to Paris in 1948. At that time the French capital was of course attractive not only to Vinkenoog and other Dutch poets but also to American writers like Lawrence Ferlinghetti, James Baldwin, Alfred Chester, and Iris Owens; to British writers like Alexander Trocchi and Christopher Logue; and one could extend this list to include the names of literally dozens of other writers and artists who, from various places in Europe and elsewhere, were all drawn to Paris. Vinkenoog was soon on friendly terms with quite a number of French, American, and English writers; in fact, one characteristic he shares with Ginsberg is his openness towards people and new experiences, as well as his ability to put people in touch with each other. After having secured a job as "special requests documents officer" at UNESCO, he began to issue a newsletter called *Blurb*, which he single-handedly typed, stenciled, and sent to people in Holland: to fellow poets and friends, but also to famous writers and intellectuals whom he did not know at all, but who he felt should be aware of his thoughts and experiences in Paris. Again one thinks of Ginsberg who in 1956 wanted copies of the first edition of *Howl and Other Poems* sent not only to thirty-two journals, but also to writers and artists ranging from T.S. Eliot and William Faulkner to Charles Chaplin and Marlon Brando (Ball 1995, 307). When Vinkenoog ended the publication of *Blurb* in 1951, he continued his informative work on the cultural and literary scene in Paris by becoming a regular contributor to *Litterair Paspoort* (from 1952 until 1956). He was for instance one of the first Dutch critics to draw attention to Samuel Beckett's play *Waiting for Godot,* which opened in Paris in January 1953.

As a poet Vinkenoog was part of a postwar movement in Dutch poetry which is usually referred to as that of the "Vijftigers" (the "Fiftiers"). The name refers of course to the 1950s, when a considerable number of usually quite young poets were able to break away from the thematic and stylistic formality which was stifling Dutch poetry in the years that immediately followed the war. As Peter Glassgold appropriately put it in his introduction to *Living Space: Poems of the Dutch "Fiftiers,"* the Fiftiers' movement "had its beginnings in the art world of postwar Amsterdam, among the painters who joined together in 1948 to form the Experimental Group Holland (*De Experimentele Groep Holland*), known internationally as Cobra (*CO*penhagen-*BR*ussels-*A*msterdam)" (Glassgold 1979, ix). Glassgold's characterization of the poetry of the Fiftiers, relating it to the work of the painters, can hardly be improved upon:

> The emphasis was revolutionary, the complete overturning of received aesthetic, social and intellectual standards, with a special stress on the very physicality of art. The young poets attracted to the group–all born

between the two world wars and survivors of the Nazi Occupation–soon applied this attitude to their own, literary art. Without subscribing to fixed goals, they sought to make (paraphrasing one of their number, Gerrit Kouwenaar) not so much a "new" poetry as an "other" poetry – an anitpo-etry, if you like. Or in the words of Lucebert, another of the Fiftiers, they wanted to write experiential poems, unfettered by form and subject mat-ter, that explore "the space of complete living." (Glassgold 1979, ix)

"Experiential poems, unfettered by form and subject matter." Reading a description like this, it is hard not to think of the Beat Generation, of the immediacy of Charles Olson's writing, of Jack Kerouac's "deep form," of Ginsberg's desire (when composing "Howl") not to take into account how his father and other authority figures would feel about what he was writing. In fact, in his introduc-tion Glassgold goes on to mention what he feels to be a number of striking similarities between the Fiftiers and some of the Beats and other "alternative" American poets of the 1950s. After pointing out Bert Schierbeek's indebtedness to Charles Olson, Glassgold refers to the fact that Lucebert, not only because of "his continued association with the art world" but also because of the "[h]ard-boiled, relentless-ly experimental" quality of his work, is strikingly reminiscent of the 1950s poets of the New York School (1979, x). Glassgold also sees a link between Hugo Claus and poets like Robert Duncan and Gary Snyder, because Claus has "moved the Fiftiers' concept of naturalness of expression to the shadowy, primordial recesses touched upon in the early work" of these two American poets (1979, x). Finally, in Glassgold's view, Sybren Polet's "prophetic anarchy" is not unlike "the angry satire of our Beats" (1979, x). Summing up, one can safely say that the physical quality and the social criticism of much Beat and Beat-related writing was also found in the work of the Fiftiers.

However, this very similarity created a problem as far as the reception of Beat writing in Holland was concerned. By 1957 the Fiftiers had succeeded in freeing Dutch poetry from the trammels of convention and formality. Consequently they were hardly on the lookout for any writing that would liberate them even further. In fact, a number of younger writers and even some of the Fiftiers them-selves became increasingly aware that some of the characteristics of Fiftiers' writing that were once new and rejuvenating were gradually growing stale and turning into merely another convention. In the hands of the followers of the original Fiftiers, the Fiftiers' highly imaginal use of language was quickly falling prey to senseless imitation. As a result, many younger Dutch poets by the end of the 1950s distanced themselves from this kind of writing and went in an entirely different direction. They pared down their style and largely did away with imagery and similes, adopting an attitude both towards life and writing that was very sober and down-to-earth. On the whole, they did not respond favorably to the romanticism and the transcendental urgency of a poet like Ginsberg, although some of them were able to draw inspiration from the work of a more mundane Beat-poet like Philip Whalen, at least at first sight.

For a while Simon Vinkenoog was the only Dutch poet who was completely enthusiastic about Ginsberg's work, partly because, not counting the somewhat more objective Adriaan Morriën, he was the only one in Holland who was really aware of what Ginsberg as a poet was up to. When the two met, Vinkenoog was working as a journalist for the Dutch weekly *Haagse Post*. The article which he immediately wrote about Ginsberg, Corso, and other Beats, and which was published while Ginsberg, Corso, and Orlovsky were still staying in Amsterdam, is the first Dutch publication to pay attention to the early achievements of the Beat Generation. Its tone is enthusiastic but at the same time that of an observer, and it is clear that Vinkenoog's personal knowledge of Ginsberg's and Corso's work is still rather limited. Many of the details which are used by Corso in his essay "The Literary Revolution in America" are also to be found in Vinkenoog's article, and Vinkenoog's description of the Beat Generation undoubtedly relies heavily either on Corso's as yet unpublished essay or on what Ginsberg, Corso, and Orlovsky told Vinkenoog about their own work, and that of, for instance, Kerouac, Philip Lamantia, Gary Snyder, and Philip Whalen, who are all referred to in Vinkenoog's contribution. The title of the article was "'Gejank' en 'Benzine'" ("'Howl' and 'Gasoline'"), its subtitle the rather cautious question "New American Generation of Poets?," and it was illustrated by a picture of Ginsberg and Corso that was taken in Amsterdam, as well as by a portrait of rock 'n' roll singer Little Richard; the latter was presented as being able to procure the same ecstacies that, according to Vinkenoog, are characteristic of the work of the Beats.

Before very long Vinkenoog's knowledge of Ginsberg's work increased considerably. When the two met, Ginsberg had handed

Vinkenoog a copy of *Howl*, and at the same time, in Vinkenoog's words, "all his love & knowledge & poetics." (1986, 280) Especially the influence of Ginsberg's poetic theories and practices soon came to be felt in Vinkenoog's work. By the mid-1950s Vinkenoog had become increasingly aware that his poetry lacked the elements of the human voice and breath. In a cycle of poems written in 1956, "Rondom het groene lichaam" ("About the Green Body"), he wrote: "For the heart that writes without measure,/my hand writes a gloomy weather report,/a bottomless song of words/that do not come to life without my voice." (1962a, 30). When Vinkenoog becomes more and more familiar with Ginsberg's poetics towards the end of the 1950s, so do his poems which become increasingly determined by the poet's own spoken voice and by his breath-length. For a series of recordings by poets, brought out by the Dutch publishing house Querido in 1961, Vinkenoog wrote a cycle of poems called "Stem uit de groef" ("Voice from the Groove") which bears the dedication "Voor eigen stem geschreven" (Written for [my] own voice; 1962b, 80). The poem was published in Vinkenoog's collection of poems *Spiegelschrift—Gebruikslyriek* (Mirror Writing—Practical Poetry) which was his first major collection to appear since his getting acquainted with Ginsberg and which contains a number of other poems that also suggest the American poet's influence.

One of those poems is the four-page plus "Royal Saint Germain," written during a visit to Paris in the early sixties. The poem begins with the poet describing how, shortly before midnight, he has just sat down at a café table in Saint-Germain-des-Prés to write down his impressions and to reflect on his experiences of the past day and on what he still wants to accomplish in Paris. He describes how he has roamed the city, "looking for an angry fix" (the quotation from "Howl" is actually in the poem). In Dutch the word "angry" easily leads to an association with "evil," and it is evil which the poet feels he has found in Paris on this particular visit, especially because the friends he had in Paris in the first half of the fifties all seem to have changed:

> They've stopped smoking, they've forgotton how to laugh,
> they've baptized their children Roman Catholic,
> they're doing very nicely—like I do—
> and they know the ropes, they've been around
> and at night they sleep. In order to work during the day,
> in a conservatory, for instance, or in a loft. (Vinkenoog 1962, 99)

Thinking of "Gregory" (Corso, probably), "Hugo" (Claus), (Alexander) "Trocchi" and "Christopher" (Logue), the poet also takes into account the street scenes and the people passing by on the other side of the window. He does so in a relaxed and journallike manner that bears a striking resemblance to the spontaneity that characterizes most Beat poetry. Ginsberg's dictum "first thought, best thought" clearly comes to mind when Vinkenoog writes: "I will not change my words nor take back even one" (1962a, 102).

What "Royal Saint Germain" also illustrates is that it is not just the form of Ginsberg's poems but also their subject matter which struck a chord with Vinkenoog. Although definitely not the first Dutch poet to deal with this particular subject, Vinkenoog stands out among the Fiftiers for his interest in drugs, with which he became acquainted through American friends in Paris in the early fifties, and about which he had also read in the work of French poets he greatly admired, like René Daumal and Henri Michaux. In "Royal Saint Germain" there is reference to the "kif" he is planning to buy the next day, but in a much earlier poem like "Hasjisj" (written in the early fifties) he had already given proof of his keen interest in drugs. The openness with which Ginsberg wrote about drugs and their possibility to transcend the self and to expand the mind clearly had a liberating effect on Vinkenoog. Following in the footsteps of his American example, especially in the early sixties, Vinkenoog experimented feverishly with a number of drugs, from marijuana to LSD-25, taking care to give an accurate account of his experiences (the way Ginsberg also did) in poems, journal entries, as well as in the novel *Hoogseizoen* (High Season), published in 1962.

That novel, Vinkenoog's third, is revealing of the influence which the Beats also had on Vinkenoog's prose style. It features as an epigraph a quotation from Gregory Corso's novel *The American Express* (1961), and the text itself incorporates part of a letter from Ginsberg to Vinkenoog. More importantly, however, Vinkenoog's spontaneous account of bohemian life in Amsterdam in the early sixties is frequently reminiscent of Kerouac, although the events described are less grand than those which are depicted in Kerouac's books: Sal Paradise may be speeding across the American continent in one of Dean Moriarty's fast cars; Vinkenoog's equally autobiographical narrator has to content himself with knocking about pre-Provo Amsterdam on his scooter.

In spite of the relatively small scale in which the events in *Hoogseizoen* are presented, Vinkenoog's novel is a much better example of the influence of Beat writing on Dutch literature than, for instance, a book like Jan Cremer's *I Jan Cremer* which, like in America, has frequently been associated with the Beats (1965). It is true that at-first-sight Cremer's highly autobiographical account seems to place *I Jan Cremer* firmly in a Beat tradition. However, several of the book's "tall tales" were based on stories Cremer picked up from friends and acquaintances, which seems to clash with the autobiographical honesty of most Beat writing; moreover, these stories are told with a straining aftereffect which is untypical of the Beats. And while Cremer may have been stylistically indebted to the Beats (as well as to an older writer like Henry Miller), his iconoclasm seems to be boundless; as a consequence, underground heroes like Vinkenoog and Ginsberg are frequently depicted as figures of fun.

The influence of Allen Ginsberg and other Beat writers on Dutch literature probably reached its pinnacle in the early sixties. Not yet put off by America's interference in Vietnam (the way a few years later Provo would be which led to a rejection of all things American), a number of Dutch writers in the first half of the sixties felt free to experiment with the formal accomplishments of the Beats, as well as with their subject matter. Vinkenoog's fellow-Fiftier Remco Campert, who was close to Vinkenoog both in Paris and in Amsterdam, had already movingly written about jazz (a striking tribute to Charlie Parker, for instance), as well as having written what is considered to be the first Dutch poem about smoking marijuana. His affinity with the Beats revealed itself when, in 1961, he published a Dutch version of Kerouac's "The Beginning of Bop" in *Taboe*, a magazine aimed at Dutch twentiers, to which Campert was a regular contributor (Campert 1961).[6] Having already assimilated the influence of William Carlos Williams and other American poets, a reading of Ginsberg in the early sixties inspired Campert to try out some of Ginsberg's formal experiments in a striking poem entitled "Solo." Together with its "Introductie" ("Introduction"), "Solo" equals "Howl" and "Kaddish" in length if not in emotional scope (1962, 45-93). Taking his cue from Williams's encouragement, "Be reconciled, poet, with your world, it is the only truth!," Campert investigates his personal and poetic universe in a freely associative manner that is reminiscent not only of Ginsberg and other Beats, but also, and perhaps even more so, of jazz. However, in the end Campert was not quite content with what he had achieved in "Solo"; soon after having completed the poem he already looked upon it as an experiment that did not necessarily have to be repeated.

As they did for the Beats in America, for Beat-influenced writers in Holland, writing and jazz frequently went together. Having already picked up on Christopher Logue's jazz and poetry recording *Red Bird* in the mid-fifties (Logue was one of the first to combine poetry and jazz), Vinkenoog was further inspired to combine music and the spoken word after having listened to the several jazz and poetry recordings which accompanied the Beat craze of the late-1950s. Helped out by a number of jazz musicians who were his friends during the last three months of 1963, Vinkenoog organized a series of jazz and poetry evenings in an Amsterdam jazz club called "Sheherezade." These events drew a fair amount of attention and they certainly helped to familiarize Dutch poets, readers, and listeners with a Beat-related poetry in which the poet's voice and performance become integral parts of the written text.

One of the first foreign guests to appear at the jazz and poetry evenings in "Sheherezade," was the African-American Beat poet Ted Joans. On the evening of September 25, 1963, in the company of, among others, Vinkenoog and Campert, Joans helped to further the cause of Beat writing in Holland by reading his highly oral poetry to an intrigued and enthusiastic audience which included several Dutch poets who watched and listened with interest. During the next few decades Joans frequently visited Holland, appearing not only in Amsterdam but also at Rotterdam's Poetry International festival which was called into being in the late 1960s, partly as a result of the increasing popularity of spoken-word poetry that had been initiated by the Beats.

Although Joans never settled in Holland for any length of time, preferring Paris to Amsterdam as his European base, other Americans who were associated with the Beats did in fact take residence in Amsterdam. One of the first to move to Holland was the actor and writer Mel Clay, associated with The Living Theatre of Julien Beck and Judith Malina, who also had a marked preference for Holland.[7] When in late 1964 Allen Ginsberg heard that Vinkenoog was threatened with a jail sentence for possession of marijuana, it was to Mel Clay in Amsterdam that he addressed an open letter appealing to "the common sense of the [D]utch intellectual world, [D]utch journalism, the [D]utch judiciary, the [D]utch police & the [D]utch public to leave Simon Vinkenoog alone to smoke his marijuana in peace," adding that "Earth has more tearful use for Law than this issue."[8]

Clay was later joined by Beat-associated Americans like the filmmaker and poet Piero Heliczer, the poet/publishers Ira Cohen and Eddie Woods, as well as the writer and former *International Times* editor William Levy. For a while Eddie Woods in particular left his mark on the alternative Amsterdam writing scene. In the late 1970s and early 1980s he ran a bookshop called "Ins & Outs Bookstore" on a canal near the red light district; the shop served as a meeting place for American and Dutch Beat-related writers alike, and it also brought out an English-language magazine, *Ins and Outs*, as well as a series of chapbooks and books. While the book publications tended to feature the American expatriates in Amsterdam, the magazine printed not only well-known Americans like Ginsberg, Paul Bowles, Bob Kaufman, and Lawrence Ferlinghetti, but also work by Dutch writers with a Beat connection, such as Vinkenoog, Hans Plomp, and Bert Schierbeek.

This was also the period of the rise (1978) and the fall (1985) of an Amsterdam poetry festival, "One World Poetry" which was the relatively short-lived but impressive countercultural pendant of Rotterdam's more fashionable "Poetry International." In the autumn of eight consecutive years organizer Ben Posset was able to gather in Amsterdam dozens of Beat and Beat-related writers from all over the world (especially from Europe and America). In the peak year 1981, apart from many Dutch and European writers, American Beats like William Burroughs, Michael McClure, Diane Di Prima, Lawrence Ferlinghetti, Ken Kesey, as well as lesser knowns, flocked to Amsterdam where they read to receptive and enthusiastic audiences in countercultural centers like "De Melkweg" (The Milky Way) and "Paradiso." Even when "One World Poetry" was held for the very first time, from 10 to 16 September 1978, apart from William Burroughs many Beats (in this case mostly of the second generation) traveled to

Amsterdam, where they not only read in public, but also participated in a number of workshops. Summing up this festival in 1979, the Dutch literary magazine *Mandala* devoted an entire issue in book form to the event with contributions (in English) from Burroughs, James Koller, Harold Norse, Joanne Kyger, Bill Berkson, Michael Brownstein, Ted Berrigan, and many others (Hoogstraten and Knipscheer 1979).

On the whole the influence of Beat writing on Dutch literature tended to restrict itself to a number of writers who were not only susceptible to the Beats' formal experiments, but also, and perhaps even more so, to their subject matter. At least two reasons can be given why Beat literature did not give mainstream Dutch writing a new look. In the first place the Dutch national character is marked by a matter-of-factness which, in the case of many Dutch writers, is bound to be at odds with the romantic idealism of at least some of the Beats. But the main reason why Dutch literature did not whole-heartedly embrace and incorporate Beat writing has already been hinted at: the literary, social, and spiritual revolution of the Fiftiers had made such a good job of liberating Dutch literature from acad-emism and formalism that by the end of the 1950s most Beat writing came too late in the day for many Dutch writers.

To a large extent this also applies to the reception of Beat litera-ture in France. After the Second World War, French literature was likewise hardly in need of the liberating innovations of Beat writ-ing, having already shaken off its fetters in the time of the surrealists and perhaps even earlier. This does not mean that France was unim-pressed with Beat writing. *Naked Lunch* was not only first published in Paris, Burroughs's experimental writing in general met with much more understanding and serious critical appraisal in France than it was initially accorded in America. And among the still relatively young French writers, a highly popular novelist like Philippe Djian, who has also been translated into English, has inconspicuously but unmistakably incorporated a number of influences from the Beats (Le Pellec 1990, 201-15).

On the other hand, the influence of Beat writing clearly helped to open up and to enliven European literatures that by the late fifties and early sixties were still relatively academic and restrained, such as English and, to some degree, German literature. Around 1960 the

British appearance of two major anthologies, Donald Allen's *The New American Poetry 1945-1960* and Gene Feldman and Max Gartenberg's *The Beat Generation and the Angry Young Men* (titled *Protest* in England), attacked and altered the provincialism of most postwar English writing so successfully that at least British poetry, especially after Ginsberg's stay in London in 1965, has never been able to return to its former stuffiness and self-satisfaction. German literature, which after the Second World War stayed on the safe side of a limited and limiting humanism, was also affected and opened up by Beat writing, especially when in the course of the 1960s a writer like Rolf Dieter Brinkmann, acting in tune with the political unrest among Germany's students, firmly opposed the conventionality of German writing with the immediacy of his own poetry and prose as well as with a flood of translations by Beat and post-Beat writers like Frank O'Hara, Ted Berrigan, and many others.

Now that the Beat Generation is a full-grown literary movement in America and elsewhere, it has clearly and in all likelihood permanently moved into the spotlight in Holland also; younger writers from quite various backgrounds, not just those from the literary fringe, seem only too willing to reveal their affinity with the Beats. As a consequence the beat which since 1960 has added a lively note to Dutch and other European literatures is definitely still to be heard. Perhaps not more loudly, but certainly more widely.

Notes

1 The quotation in the title of this essay is taken from "POEM Rocket."
2 The "smoke" which Vinkenoog refers to is of course not your regular American cigarette.
3 In 1964 Lawrence Ferlinghetti published work by Trocchi in *City Lights Journal* (Trocchi 1964, 14–36).
4 Other publications in English which refer to Vinkenoog include *Esquire* magazine (its June 1965 issue contained an article entitled "The Death of Hip," which includes an account of Vinkenoog's activities), and two books about the Grateful Dead: Harrison (1991), Scully and Dalton (1996). A "voting poem" by Vinkenoog, "To All the Dreary People of Amsterdam," was published in *Bamn* (Stansill and Mairowitz 1971). An English translation of two further poems by Vinkenoog can be found in *Border Crossing* (Behre and Christy 1993).
5 Vinkenoog's only other translation of Ginsberg's poetry that was published as a book is the bilingual *Plutonian Ode/Plutonische Ode* (Ginsberg 1980).
6 Adapted by Remco Campert who, according to an editorial note in the magazine, could not dispose of the printed text of Kerouac's essay and had to base his

translation on Kerouac's "monotonous but fascinating" reading of the essay on the LP *Readings by Jack Kerouac on the Beat Generation* (1959).
7 Vinkenoog's association with The Living Theatre is referred to in *The Living Theatre* (Tytell 1995).
8 Letter from Allen Ginsberg to Mel Clay, December 14, 1964.

Works Cited

Allen, Donald M., ed. 1960. *The New American Poetry, 1945-1960*. New York: Grove Press.

Andrews, George, and Simon Vinkenoog, eds. 1967. *The Book of Grass: An Anthology on Indian Hemp*. London: Peter Owen; New York: Grove Press.

Ball, Gordon, ed. 1995. *Allen Ginsberg: Journals Mid-Fifties, 1954-1958*. New York: Viking.

Behre, Louis, and Dave Christy, eds. 1993. *Border Crossing: An Anthology of Dutch and American Post-Beat Independent Poetry*. New Hope, Pa: Alpha Beat Press.

Campert, Remco. 1961. "Jack Kerouac: Bop onstrond, bop gebeurde." *Taboe* 3: 60-64.

———. 1962. "'Introductie' and 'Solo.'" *Dit gebeurde overal*. Amsterdam: De Bezige Bij.

Corso, Gregory. 1957. "The Literary Revolution in America." *Litterair Paspoort* 12.112 (November): 193-96.

———. 1961. *The American Express*. Paris: Olympia Press.

Cremer, Jan. 1965. *I Jan Cremer*. New York: Shorecrest.

Feldman, Gene, and Max Gartenberg, eds. 1959. *Protest: The Beat Generation and the Angry Young Men*. London: Souvenir Press.

Ginsberg, Allen. 1961. *Kaddish and Other Poems*. San Francisco: City Lights Books.

———. 1966. *Proef m'n tong in je oor*. Trans. Simon Vinkenoog. Amsterdam: De Bezige Bij.

———. 1980. *Plutonian Ode/Plutonische Ode*. Trans. Simon vinkenoog. Heerlen: Uitgeverij 261.

———. 1986. "What the Sea Throws Up at Vlissingen." In *White Shroud: Poems 1980-1985*. New York: Harper and Row.

Glassgold, Peter, ed. 1979. *Living Space: Poems of the Dutch "Fifties."* New York: New Directions.

Harrison, Hank. 1991. *The Dead*. Vol. 1, *A Social History of the Haight-Ashbury Experience*. San Francisco: Archives Press.

Hoogstraten, Harry, and Jos Knipscheer, eds. 1979. *The P78 Anthology*. Haarlem: In de Knipscheer.

Le Pellec, Yves. 1990. "Kerouac lu d' Europe." In *Un Homme Grand: Jack Kérouac at the Crossroads of Many Cultures/Jack Kérouac à la confluence des cultures*, ed. Pierre Anctil, Louis Dupont, Rémi Ferland, and Eric Waddell. Ottawa: Carleton University Press.

Neville, Richard. 1970. *Play Power*. London: Jonathan Cape.

Nuttall, Jeff. 1968. *Bomb Culture*. London: MacGibbon and Kee.

Rollins, Scott, and Lawrence Ferlinghetti, eds. 1982. *Nine Dutch Poets*. San Francisco: City Lights Books.

Scully, Rock, and David Dalton. 1996. *Living with the Dead*. London: Little, Brown.

Stansill, Peter, and David Zane Mairowitz, eds. 1971. *Bamn: Outlaw Manifestoes and Ephemera*. Harmondsworth: Penguin.

Trocchi, Alexander. 1964. "Trocchi's 'A Revolutionary Proposal' and 'SIGMA: A Tactical Blueprint.'" *City Lights Journal* 2: 14-36.

Tytell, John. 1995. *The Living Theatre: Art, Exile, and Outrage*. New York: Grove Press.

Vinkenoog, Simon. 1962a. *Hoogseizoen*. Amsterdam: De Bezige Bij.

———. 1962b. *Spiegelschrift-Gebruikslyriek*. Amsterdam: De Bezige Bij.

———. 1986. "Trust the Word!" In *Best Minds: A Tribute to Allen Ginsberg*, ed. Bill Morgan and Bob Rosenthal. New York: Lospecchio Press.

———. 1990. *And the Eye Became a Rainbow*. Trans. Cornelis Vleeskens. Melbourne: Fling Poetry.

———. 1998. Interview by Jaap van der Bent. Amsterdam, 16 April.

———. 1999. Interview by Jaap van der Bent. Amsterdam, 6 January.

CHAPTER ELEVEN

Mountains and Rivers Are Us: Gary Snyder
and the Nature of the Nature of Nature
Robert Kern

Readers familiar with the overall shape and development of Gary Snyder's poetic career—with its geography and evolution, so to speak—are no doubt also aware of the extensive ground occupied by *Mountains and Rivers Without End* within that career. Published in its final form in 1996, this work, which had been in progress or process for some forty years, is generally regarded as a sort of *summa*, as well as Snyder's major effort in the genre of the "modernist long poem" or "verse epic." Moreover, it should come as no surprise that *Mountains and Rivers*, or at least Snyder's original conception of it as a poetic project, virtually predates his actual career as a publishing poet. It was first mentioned in print in *The Dharma Bums* (1958), Jack Kerouac's fictionalized memoir about Snyder and other figures (Kenneth Rexroth, Philip Whalen, Lawrence Ferlinghetti, Michael McClure) who were (with the exception of the older, already established Rexroth) emerging poets, West Coast cousins of the Beat Generation, whose activities, both literary and otherwise, constituted the San Francisco Renaissance in the mid-1950s. By the time Kerouac's novel appeared, Snyder had already written, but not yet published, the poems that were to make up his first two books—*Riprap* (1959), and his initial attempt at a long poem, *Myths and Texts* (1960). Thus, for the better part of a long, exemplary, and still evolving career—one marked by early involvement with *avant-garde* literary and social movements, by even earlier interests in wilderness experience and the lives and thought of primal or so-called primitive peoples, by serious study of Zen Buddhism in Japan, and by countercultural and environmental activism in the late 1960s, culminating in the development of bioregional theory and practice in the 1970s and 1980s—Snyder has been occupied, on and off, with *Mountains and Rivers Without End*, a poem that reflects all of these interests and that once seemed as if it too might never end.

Snyder himself helps us to contextualize the poem, and to place it within the stream of his experience, with a section of notes at the end of the volume and also with a brief autobiographical essay, clearly meant to set the record straight, called "The Making of *Mountains and Rivers Without End*." Here he pays tribute to certain teachers—those, for example, from whom he learned the discipline of the calligrapher's and painter's brush and pen, a discipline that becomes an important motif in the poem. He also acknowledges the importance to him of certain experiences, primarily of wilderness landscapes—mountains and rivers, in the Pacific Northwest and elsewhere—but also of representations of such landscapes, particularly in Asian art, encountered in books and museums. Referring to the "high snow peaks" he had climbed as a boy, Snyder tells us that he was "forever changed by that place of rock and sky," while it was in Asian paintings that he became aware of "the energies of mist, white water, rock formations, air swirls—a chaotic universe where everything is in place" (Snyder 1996, 153). In this way, his direct experience of the natural world seems to have merged with what he saw in artistic representations of it, and a similar merging of nature and culture takes place in the poem.

In addition to these landscapes, both actual and mediated, which Snyder has sought out in a wide-ranging series of journeys throughout his career, another key element in the gestalt that animates *Mountains and Rivers* is Zen Buddhism, of which he has been a devotee since the early 1950s. This interest originally led him to Allen Watts's Academy of Asian Studies in San Francisco, where, in

the winter of 1955–56, he heard lectures by the Japanese artist
Saburo Hasegawa. As Snyder recalls, Hasegawa spoke of East Asian
landscape painting "as a meditative exercise" (1996, 154). Shortly
thereafter, during his residence at the Rinzai Zen temple compound
of Shokoku-ji in Kyoto, exploring the "local hilly forests" and studying
geology and geomorphology, Snyder himself came to see what he
calls the "yogic implications" of mountains and rivers "as the play
between the tough spirit of willed self-discipline and the generous
and loving spirit of concern for all beings," a "dyad" that was paral-
leled, as he imagined it, "in the dynamics of mountain uplift, subduc-
tion, erosion, and the planetary water cycle" (1996, 155).

What is notable in this essay is not only its survey of the various
interests and experiences that have gone into the "making" of
Mountains and Rivers, but also its display of some of Snyder's characteristic energies and assumptions as a writer, including his tendency to synthesize or to pursue parallels between disparate areas of
experience. Less noticeable but equally typical is the way he down-
plays or simply overlooks the more "literary" aspects of his work.
Although Snyder acknowledges the influence of Japanese Nō drama
and the importance of its aesthetic strategies to his poem, the only
poet he mentions specifically is Ezra Pound, who appears here as a
translator from Chinese, and whose work, Snyder tells us, he was led
to as a student (in a reversal of the usual pattern) by his earlier discovery of Ernest Fenollosa's *Epochs of Chinese and Japanese Art*. For
most twentieth-century poets, arguably, it is Pound who leads to
Fenollosa—particularly to Fenollosa's *Chinese Written Character as
a Medium for Poetry*, as opposed to his less well-known *Epochs*—
and the point here may well be that language and literature per se are
less crucial or determining in Snyder's imagination than direct experience of the world or visual representation of it. Indeed, this possibility is reinforced by Snyder's statement in the "Afterword" to the 1990
reissue of *Riprap and Cold Mountain Poems* that his task as a poet
has often entailed "the work of seeing the world *without* . . . language," and then of bringing "that seeing *into* language"—an effort he
identifies with "the direction of most Chinese and Japanese poetry."
Of course, it is also characteristic of Snyder to align his work, as he
does here, with non-Western poetic traditions, implicitly privileging
those that pursue a self-effacing, disciplined foregrounding of things

themselves, and that have sometimes led him, as he grants, to produce poems that "run the risk of invisibility," their language or textuality upstaged by the sensible world that lies beyond them (Snyder 1990a, 67).

***

The earliest sections of *Mountains and Rivers* began to appear in 1961, and by 1965 Snyder had produced enough of them to bring out the small volume *Six Sections from Mountains and Rivers Without End*. In accord with what is suggested in Kerouac's description of the project (as we shall see shortly), this volume's title implies that the reader is faced here with the first installments of a long work-in-progress, one that, like Pound's *The Cantos* and other modernist epics, promises to unfold serially over time. The reader is informed, in other words, that she or he can look forward to further sections and perhaps even collections of sections of this poem as it wends its way toward coherence, wholeness, and conclusion in the future[1]—although, historically, modernist long poems have been notoriously difficult to conclude and even resistant to closure, ending, in some cases, only with the deaths of their authors. Prominent examples include Whitman's *Leaves of Grass*, in which the origins of the genre can be located, and, in addition to Pound's *Cantos*, William Carlos Williams's *Paterson*.

These are all texts that, for the most part, "include history," or that in some way aim to tell "the tale of the tribe," in Pound's formulations (1954, 86; 1968, 194). But they also include or trace their own history, in the sense that they are published not all at once, at the end point of a process of composition and revision, but as they evolve and expand over the course of their authors' lives, never quite reaching a final or definitive end point. Thus Whitman's career is constituted largely by a series of reincarnations of his great book, each new edition of *Leaves of Grass* offering new poems and revisions of others, as well as altered arrangements of the book as a whole, in a process that continued, more or less, right up until the appearance of the so-called "death-bed" edition in 1891-92. In Pound's case the process was one less of revision than of accretion, insofar as he kept adding new groups of cantos to those already published—until, feeling surrounded by his "errors and wrecks," and convinced that he could not "make it cohere" (Pound 1970, 796), he closed the project down, with "Drafts and Fragments of Cantos CX-CXVII," in 1969, giving himself up thereafter to a self-imposed silence. Williams's *Paterson* followed a roughly similar pattern. Originally projected as a long poem in four "Books" which were published separately in 1946, 1948, 1949, and 1951, at which point the poem appeared to be completed, *Paterson* nevertheless acquired a new fifth Book in 1958, after Williams felt compelled "to recognize that there can be no end to such a story"—a recognition that led him to produce fragmentary notes for a sixth Book in the years right before his death in 1963 (Williams 1963, "Author's Note").

In *Mountains and Rivers*, Snyder replicates but also departs from this general paradigm, the major departure consisting in the fact that the book, published now in what is presumably its final form, has reached a point of closure, and may thus be regarded more as a "work" than a "text" (in Roland Barthes's sense of these terms), fixed and closed off from the fluidity and provisionality of its former status as a text-in-process.[2] At the same time, there is a sense, it seems to me, in which Snyder has been careful to preserve the fluidity and "endlessness" of the poem—thematically if not structurally. In its character as a modernist epic, however, one which for a long time seemed committed to an open-ended and potentially interminable process of development, its thematic interests are closely related to (and were certainly supported by) a structure that, as we might say, had not yet declared itself. This is a poem, after all, which is called *Mountains and Rivers Without End*, in which endlessness is not a problem to be overcome, an occupational hazard for the author of a modernist epic, but a theme, a positive idea, as well as a reality that seems in many ways essential, organic, to a project increasingly focused on the world regarded as a sensible procession of places, a dynamic unfolding of landscapes, both natural and urban, encountered and apprehended by traveling, journeying, mostly on foot, with no end in sight.

During the forty years of the poem's growth, its sections, as they multiplied and appeared in print, could of course be regarded as wholes complete in themselves. The original six sections were all sizable, larger-than-lyric structures, often themselves multi-sectioned, and this has continued to be the case with many of the later additions to the poem, such as "Three Worlds, Three Realms, Six Roads," "The Circumambulation of Mt. Tamalpais," and "The Mountain Spirit." But readers were also reminded, by Snyder's very reference to the parts of the poem as "sections," that they were reading parts of a larger whole still to emerge. Reading them, in terms of this awareness, was necessarily a process of only partial understanding, the reader never knowing fully or precisely where she or he stood with respect to that larger whole, the total landscape or narrative of the still-to-be-completed poem. In many ways, however, this experience of not knowing, of being in the midst of an evolving process, on the way toward some unforeseen end, is an important part of what the poem seeks to convey, as it traces various movements through spaces, times, and modes of experience, including dream and myth, that are themselves unpredictable and changing as they occur—and to some extent this experience is diminished, if not lost, when the poem becomes a finished book, its format or structure laid out in a visible table of contents. Yet it is precisely this experience—which belongs (on an experiential level) to the poem's protagonist and increasingly becomes (on a textual level) the reader's as well—that, I would argue, Snyder is anxious to preserve and project both in the poem's major sections and in the book as a whole. One of the most interesting and telling examples, certainly, is the relatively recent opening or keynote poem of the volume, "Endless Streams and Mountains," first published (prior to its appearance in the book) in 1995.

It is in this text, first of all, that we can see the continuing relevance of Kerouac's 1958 description of Snyder's project, based as it is, no doubt, on Snyder's own original vision of the poem. The passage, in its excited, breathless, run-on fashion, is accurate not only about the general scope of the poem's interests but also about its essential quality of "endlessness," considered both as a structural feature of the text and as part of the reader's experience in reading it. Kerouac's syntax alone tells the story. "Know what I'm gonna do?" asks Japhy Ryder (Snyder) out on a hiking trail one day:

> I'll do a new long poem called "Rivers and Mountains Without End" and just write it on and on on a scroll and unfold on and on with new surprises and always what went before forgotten, see, like a river, or like one of them real long Chinese silk paintings that show two little men hiking in an endless landscape of gnarled old trees and mountains so high they merge with the fog in the upper silk void. I'll spend three thousand years writing

> it, it'll be packed full of information on soil conservation, the Tennessee
> Valley Authority, astronomy, geology, Hsuan Tsung's travels, Chinese
> painting theory, reforestation, Oceanic ecology and food chains. (Kerouac
> 1958, 157)

What marks the passage, by and large, as a reconstruction of Snyder's
own account of the poem is the appearance in it (among other
things) of the term "ecology" which in 1958 was hardly the house-
hold word it was to become a dozen or so years later (although it
was clearly already a part of Snyder's personal lexicon).

To the extent that the poem is now finished, of course, it has
turned out to be less open-ended or interminable than the author of
On the Road envisioned that it would be, and some readers may
even feel that it is not, strictly speaking, a "poem," in the sense of a
single, continuous work, but rather a collection of poems whose
appearance together does not greatly dispel the impression of autonomy or self-sufficiency conveyed by the original six sections and by
later ones as well. Thematically related, the book's sections do not
absolutely require the presence or support of the others in order to
be effective. What may also contribute to a sense that the book is a
collection more than a tightly unified or continuous whole is the
presence within it of a fair number of short, lyriclike pieces for
which there was no precedent in *Six Sections from Mountains and
Rivers Without End Plus One*. Readers familiar with the poems in
that volume, including "Bubbs Creek Haircut," "The Market,"
"Journeys," and especially "Night Highway Ninety-Nine," the ultimate
Beat Generation hitchhiking poem, were led to expect that a
Mountains and Rivers "section," regardless of its content, would be
something akin to a Whitmanian catalogue—inclusive, formally free,
apparently artless and spontaneous, based on natural speech
rhythms, sometimes combining verse and prose, and above all, large,
expansive, a poem that would go on for pages.[3]

Still, what remains important in Kerouac's description is its
implicit analogy between artistic composition or process and *natural* process, both regarded as a sort of endless unfolding, which is
realized in the book largely through its motif of travelling or journeying—and certainly it is to this vision of his project (which is clearly
his own in any case) that Snyder returns, in effect, in "Endless
Streams and Mountains." As we shall see, this poem is a journey for
its readers in the sense that it literally leads us through a landscape

of endless streams and mountains, or mountains and rivers without end, pictured in a Chinese scroll painting. In fact, the compound phrase "mountains and rivers" or "mountains and waters," as Snyder might have explained to Kerouac, constitutes the term for landscape in Chinese (1990b, 102). But the poem is about a journey of Snyder's as well, a sort of research-journey to see the very painting described in the poem, and but one of a series of journeys undertaken to see many of the other mountains and rivers paintings housed in museums around the world (Snyder 1996, 156-57).

***

In "The Making of *Mountains and Rivers Without End*," Snyder not only surveys the various aspects of his experience that underlie the poem but also addresses the issue of its endlessness, telling us, on the one hand, that he never thought it would be endless—that he knew his "time with this poem would eventually end"—and on the other that "Landscapes are endless in their own degree," and that it was, nevertheless, the "form and the emptiness of the Great Basin" that showed him where to close the poem (1996, 158). Snyder's aim, as we might put it, is to approximate the form, which is to say (paradoxically) the endlessness, the uncontainability, of the natural processes that constitute the earth, and this is an aim for which the open-ended and potentially interminable structure of the modernist long poem would seem to be most appropriate. But finally it is not the modernist long poem that is his primary model here. Instead, as the title of the book in its several variations suggests (and as I have just hinted above), it is Asian landscape paintings, and especially hand scrolls (like the one featured in "Endless Streams and Mountains"), that provide Snyder with his most immediate structural format. These hand scrolls are works of art which the viewer unrolls from left to right so that "Place by place unfurls" (1996, 9) in what is, like Snyder's book, a finite representation of endless natural process. Such paintings, moreover, as Snyder points out, are "not fully realized until several centuries of poems have been added" (Snyder 1996, 159). Referring here to the tradition in which owners and viewers of these paintings inscribe them with colophons or seals and poems— additions which make up a running historical commentary, or a set of responses to the paintings that accumulate over centuries—

Snyder seems to conceive of his book, and certainly of particular poems and sections of it, in terms of his own participation in this tradition, one which seems linked to the movement of natural process itself as it is represented in the paintings, and now as it is represented in the book as well.

The sections of *Mountains and Rivers*, that is to say, are further contributions to the realization of the paintings that the book as a whole evokes, and one of Snyder's metaphors for producing them derives, in fact, from the techniques of Asian painting which he first studied as an undergraduate and then took up again when he was working on Oriental languages at Berkeley in the mid-1950s. References to those techniques appear at opposite ends of the book, first near the conclusion of "Endless Streams and Mountains" —

> grind the ink, wet the brush, unroll the
> broad white space:
>
> lead out and tip
> the moist black line (Snyder 1996, 9)—

and then again at the end of the concluding poem, "Finding the Space in the Heart" —

> The space goes on.
> But the wet black brush
> tip drawn to a point,
> lifts away (Snyder 1996, 152)—

suggesting that the book as a whole is not unlike the sort of scroll painting after which it is named, and that both are merely human approximations of the processes outside them which they attempt to portray. "The space" in which those actual processes occur, of course, "goes on." These references, in any case, constitute one way of conferring unity upon the book, explicitly comparing writing with Asian brush painting, or sumi, and implicitly figuring the experience of reading the book as the act of unfurling and viewing a scroll painting—and, in addition, as the activity of walking through a landscape, or many landscapes.

***

> Walking on walking,
> under foot   earth turns.

Streams and mountains never stay the same. (Snyder 1996, 9)

Constituting a sort of motto or leitmotif for the book, these lines appear in the concluding sections of both the first and last poems of *Mountains and Rivers*; they also appear, notably and recurrently, in "The Mountain Spirit," in which Snyder recalls his hair-raising but comic encounter with "old woman mountain," both audience and muse, who challengingly wonders: "But what do you know of minerals and stone. / For a creature to speak of all that scale of time— what for?" (1996, 141). Signifying endless natural process, the lines, in addition, establish the centrality of walking in the book, which for Snyder is always "walking on walking," since "under foot earth turns" or walks also. It is in this sense that streams and mountains never stay the same, and, we might add, never stay, but are always on the way to some other place, some other state of being. "The blue mountains are constantly walking," Snyder writes, quoting Dōgen, the thirteenth-century Japanese Buddhist sage, who also said, "If you doubt mountains walking you do not know your own walking" (Snyder 1990b, 102–03). As Snyder points out earlier in *The Practice of the Wild*, a collection of essays informed as much by Buddhist spirituality as by a deeply informed ecological literacy, places themselves have a kind of fluidity and pass through space and time:

A place will have been grasslands, then conifers, then beech and elm. It will have been half riverbed, it will have been scratched and plowed by ice. And then it will be cultivated, paved, sprayed, dammed, graded, built up. But each is only for a while, and that will be just another set of lines on the palimpsest. The whole earth is a great tablet holding the multiple overlaid new and ancient traces of the swirl of forces (Snyder 1990b, 27).

"Each place," Snyder continues, "is its own place, forever (eventually) wild" (Snyder 1990b, 27), meaning that we cannot own it, and that even when we try to, and attempt to turn it to human purposes, the place's own energies will (eventually) reassert themselves and reclaim it.

This sense of fluidity and movement, of a "swirl of forces" underlying any particular formation or situation in the natural world, no matter how fixed or permanent it may appear to be, informs the

speaker's stream of observations in "Endless Streams and Mountains,"
in which he assumes the perspective of an onlooker viewing the
landscape "from a boat on a lake / or a broad slow river, / coasting by."

> The path comes down along a lowland stream
> slips behind boulders and leafy hardwoods,
> reappears in a pine grove,
> no farms around, just tidy cottages and shelters,
> gateways, rest stops, roofed but unwalled work space,
> —a warm damp climate;
> a trail of climbing stairsteps forks upstream. (Snyder 1996, 5)

While a reader can easily assume that she or he is faced here with a
description of an actual place directly encountered—if for no other
reason than that such descriptions and such encounters are a main-
stay of Snyder's work—what turns out to be the case, of course, is
that the speaker is situated before an ancient Chinese scroll painting
which happens to be housed in the Cleveland Art Museum and
which he is now minutely examining for the reader, having cleared
his mind and slid in "to that created space" (1996, 5)—a gesture
which turns the description of the painting into a form of meditation.
Indeed, even knowing that what we have here is an ekphrastic poem,
or a poem about a painting, such is the force of Snyder's concrete and
disciplined literalism, underlain by his regard not simply for the painting itself but for the ecological accuracy or validity of what it pictures, that it is easy to overlook this fact. The resulting confusion,
however, slight as it is, is both deliberate and productive, since
Snyder is interested in the openness or interchange between art and
nature, the potential equivalence or continuity between looking at a
painting and being in the world. What we may also notice is that all
the action in the description, never mind that we are looking at a
static scene, is attributed to the represented elements or features or
inhabitants of the landscape itself, the speaker who animates it
remaining quite subordinated to what he sees. Thus it is the "path"
that "comes down" and "slips behind boulders," and later it is a "trail"
that "goes far inland" (1996, 5).

Toward the end of the poem Snyder acknowledges that the
Cleveland Art Museum, in which this Sung dynasty painting (A.D.
960-1280) has somehow come to reside, is itself situated in a landscape not unlike the one in the painting—"on a rise that looks out
toward the waters of Lake Erie." In the poem's penultimate section,

he confirms this confusion or identification as he takes one last look at the representation of the land in the scroll and then steps out of the museum:

> Step back and gaze again at the land:
>   it rises and subsides—
> ravines and cliffs like waves of blowing leaves—
>   stamp the foot, walk with it, clap! turn,
>   the creeks come in, ah!
>   strained through boulders,
>   mountains walking on the water,
>   water ripples every hill.
> —I walk out of the museum—low gray clouds over the lake—chill March breeze. (Snyder 1996, 8)

Like the "watching boat" which "has floated off the page" at the end of the poem's first section (1996, 6)—devoted to a detailed tracing of the unfolding landscape from one end of the scroll to the other— Snyder himself here moves away from the painting and leaves the museum, extending his awareness (and the reader's) beyond the represented landscape to the actual one in which he finds himself, the latter reflecting and characterized by the same processes that are depicted in the painting. If ekphrastic poems conventionally attempt to provide access to paintings by means of words and poetic devices, and are often concerned with the adequacy of their efforts to verbally represent what has already been visually represented (not to mention the anxiety that may be occasioned by their awareness of their status as a sort of second-order discourse),[4] Snyder is clearly less interested in such issues of representation and its semiotics than in what he calls "the actual nondualistic world" (1990b, 109), the world beyond and prior to its representations. Referring to the "Mountains and Waters Sutra" by Dôgen, he writes that this text "is called a sutra not to assert that the 'mountains and rivers of this moment' are a text, a system of symbols, a referential world of mirrors, but that this world in its actual existence is a complete presentation, an enactment—and that it stands for nothing" (1990b, 113)— which is to say, presumably, that it stands for nothing but itself.

***

Composed close to the end of his time with *Mountains and Rivers*, and designed, apparently deliberately, to serve as an introduc-

tion or overture to it, "Endless Streams and Mountains," with its sharp
discursive shift from a sort of ecological lyricism in the first part to a
research-based scholarly and historical commentary in the second, is
a curious production for Snyder. The first part is written in his char-
acteristically ecocentric mode, a minutely detailed, outer-directed
style virtually free of subjective reference—although a fair number
of its lines fall noticeably into iambic pentameter, signaling the presence of a craft-conscious, controlling narrator, or what Lawrence
Buell calls a "superintending consciousness" (1995, 144). This part of
the poem, as we have seen, is focused simultaneously on a work of
art, a Sung-dynasty portrayal of the natural world, and, in effect, on
the natural world itself, insofar as Snyder takes the painting's representation of nature seriously, as a naturalistically accurate or environ-
mentally valid rendering—so that it is not simply a great work of art,
or in the words of a commentator writing in 1332, "truly a painting
worth careful keeping" (Snyder 1996, 7) but one that affords some
insight into the reality of nature, as the remarks of another commentator quoted by Snyder suggest:

> The water holds up the mountains,
> The mountains go down in the water . . .
> (Snyder 1996, 7)

As readers familiar with the essays in *The Practice of the Wild*—
especially with its religio-philosophical centerpiece, "Blue Mountains
Constantly Walking"—might recognize, the author of these lines,
which are taken from one of the inscriptions at the end of the scroll,
is writing in accord with a tradition of Chinese thought in which the
phrase "mountains and rivers," or "mountains and waters," functions
as a fundamental philosophical signifier. It refers, as it turns out, not
only to a genre or topos of Asian landscape painting, but equally, as
Snyder suggests, to "the totality of the process of nature" (1990b,
102). Indeed, insofar as "Blue Mountains Constantly Walking" is an
investigation of what Snyder calls the "Chinese feel for land"—
expressed in terms of "a dialectic of rock and water, of downward
flow and rocky uplift," "a dyad that . . . makes wholeness possible"
(1990b, 102, 101)—this key essay can be taken as a useful and
important intertext, an accompaniment to Snyder's project in
Mountains and Rivers that not only illuminates his thinking in its
major sections but that also indicates the extent to which they are

intellectually and thematically continuous with each other over almost the entire course of the poem's forty-year evolution.

"Blue Mountains Constantly Walking," I would also suggest, is a powerful text in its own right, fully worthy of consideration as a central statement by Snyder, one that contains some of his most challenging and assertive writing about what he goes out on a limb here to call "essential nature" or, even more daringly, "the nature of the nature of nature" (Snyder 1990b, 103). What comes across as an aggressive venture into essentialism seems especially provocative in the light of what Snyder has written elsewhere about our equally "essential" ignorance regarding the natural world. In the preface to *No Nature*, for example, his 1992 collection of new and selected poems whose title suggests a cautionary or warning sign displaying the word "nature" circled and crossed out in red, Snyder remarks that:

> we do not easily know nature, or even know ourselves. Whatever it actually is, it will not fulfill our conceptions or assumptions. It will dodge our expectations and theoretical models. There is no single or set "nature" either as "the natural world" or "the nature of things." The greatest respect we can pay to nature is not to trap it, but to acknowledge that it eludes us and that our own nature is also fluid, open, and conditional. (Snyder 1992, v)

In its expression of a positive, if not positivistic, agnosticism, the passage seems motivated by a desire on Snyder's part to keep "nature" free of our definitions and encroaching designs, even to the point of disqualifying the terms that constitute our discourse about nature. Yet, as much as he seeks to keep us at a certain distance from "the natural world," in the interests of allowing it to remain itself, Snyder also acknowledges in the passage that we share with that world qualities of openness, fluidity, and conditionality, and that "our own nature" is inescapably a part of it.

Ultimately, this is the argument, or one of the arguments, that governs both "Blue Mountains Constantly Walking" and *Mountains and Rivers Without End*—the idea, indeed, that mountains and rivers are us, and that we exist in a state of fundamental identity or interchangeability with the physical universe—an extension to the natural world, we might say, of Whitman's radically democratic premise that "every atom belonging to me as good belongs to you" (1986, 63). In the essay Snyder presents this outlook in a number of ways, adopting strategies—oddly enough for a writer who is often hostile to poststructuralist theory and its jargon[5]—that are nothing if not deconstructive in their efforts to dismantle dichotomies, or break down binary oppositions, between art and nature, culture and nature, and humanity and nature. As a way of referring to natural processes in their totality, the notion of mountains and waters, Snyder explicitly tells us, "goes well beyond dichotomies of purity and pollution, natural and artificial. The whole, with its rivers and valleys, obviously includes farms, fields, villages, cities, and the (once comparatively small) dusty world of human affairs." This "whole," of course, is also what is represented in the scroll paintings, some of which, Snyder makes a point of saying, "move through the four seasons and seem to picture the whole world" (1990b, 102).

In another section of the essay, Snyder addresses the Buddhist sense of "homelessness" as one that conventionally signifies a removal from the secular world and particularly from urban life, so that "house" and "home" are opposed, in this Asian version of pastoral, to "mountains" and to a "purity" that transcends ordinary human imperfections. But then, in a characteristic move, he breaks down this opposition, pointing out that, historically, the concept of homelessness undergoes a gradual expansion until, in the work of the T'ang dynasty poet Han-shan, it comes to mean "being at home in the whole universe." Again, but without calling as much attention to the endeavor as I am here, Snyder subtly brings about the collapse of a dichotomy, and homelessness comes to stand for a broader, more inclusive domesticity, one that subsumes both the comforts of home and a natural openness and freedom. As Han-shan himself puts it, in Snyder's own translation:

> Freely drifting, I prowl the woods and streams
> And linger, watching things themselves . . .
> Thin grass does for a mattress,
> The blue sky makes a good quilt. (Snyder 1990b, 104)

"In a similar way," Snyder concludes, giving a bioregional inflection to his argument, "self-determining people who have not lost the wholeness of their place can see their households and their regional mountains or woods as within the same sphere" (1990b, 104).

But Snyder is not yet done with the concept or image of the house, and, reducing it to its most literal status, he takes it further through this deconstructive process, seeing it now "as just another

piece of the world." In this state it is "itself impermanent and composite, a poor 'homeless' thing in its own right. Houses are made up,
heaped together," he goes on,

> of pine boards, clay tiles, cedar battens, river boulder piers,
> windows scrounged from wrecking yards, knobs from K-Mart,
> mats from Cost Plus, kitchen floor of sandstone from some
> mountain ridge, doormat from Longs—made up of the same
> world as you and me and mice. (Snyder 1990b, 105)

In what is essentially a catalogue or congeries of *bricolage*, with the
house analyzed down to its disparate, almost irreducible components, each one linked to its natural or worldly (but ultimately natural) source, the passage itself can be linked to other texts by Snyder,
including "Ripples on the Surface," the final poem in *No Nature*.
Here Snyder concludes with a close-up focus on the house in its natural or wild setting, recalling a classic American frontier image:

> The vast wild
>   the house, alone.
> The little house in the wild,
>   the wild in the house.
> Both forgotten.
> No Nature
> Both together, one big empty house. (Snyder 1992, 381)

The passage provides another example of what Snyder refers to in
"Blue Mountains Constantly Walking" as the possibility of households
and regional mountains or woods existing together "within the same
sphere." Both the house and the wild are viewed here as separate
and the same. The house is alone, set against the vast wild. But the
house is not alone—it is in the wild, and the wild is in the house.
"Both together," finally, make up one large unbounded enclosure—
Han-shan's "spacious home [which] reaches to the end of the universe" (1990b, 104).

Even more telling, and more pertinent to my concern with
Snyder's vision and its persistence in *Mountains and Rivers*, is the
way the passage about the house as "just another piece of the world"
looks back to the following lines from "Bubbs Creek Haircut," which,
written in 1960, is the earliest section of the poem:

> Next door, Goodwill
>   where I came out.
> A search for sweater and a stroll

        in the board & concrete room of
        unfixed junk downstairs—
all emblems of the past—too close—
        heaped up in chilly dust and bare-bulb glare
of tables, wheelchairs, battered trunks & lamps
& pots that boiled up coffee nineteen ten, things
swimming on their own & finally freed
                        from human need. Or?
        Waiting a final flicker of desire
to tote them out once more. Some freakish use.
The Master of the limbo drag-legged watches
                        making prices
        to the people seldom buy.
The sag-asst rocker has to make it now. Alone. (Snyder 1996, 33)

Here is Snyder shopping in the Goodwill, in its lower depths, in fact, encountering all manner of flotsam and jetsam, of cultural debris, of "things" adrift and bereft of their human uses, divorced from their human contexts, and lapsing back into their original identities as anonymous and homeless pieces of the world. Like the "sag-asst rock-er" or the "pots that boiled up coffee nineteen ten," they still retain some traces of their humanization, some personality, some connection to human time, and could conceivably serve some further human purpose, some "freakish use." But that possibility seems to be rapidly fading as they desolately swim "on their own . . . finally freed / from human need."

Just how to evaluate or to regard the entropic condition of what he initially sees as "unfixed junk" in the sad, limbolike emporium of the Goodwill is one of Snyder's concerns in the poem, his version, perhaps, of Frost's "what to make of a diminished thing" (1979, 120). Are these objects in a state of terminal dissolution, returning to the condition of "raw material" whose further use could be nothing but "freakish," or are they, indeed, liberated from the identities and functions imposed upon them by a human appropriation or colonization of the natural? Thinking about the Goodwill itself, and noticing that its basement is an underworld presided over by a "drag-legged" figure, Snyder wonders if it is a kind of hell, a last stop for things on their way to oblivion. Or, alternatively, is it a "paradise of sorts," where things are freed, as he puts it,

        from acting out the function some
                creator/carpenter

thrust on a thing to think he made, himself,
    an object always "chair"? (Snyder 1996, 35-6)

As the image of the decaying "sag-asst rocker" suggests, the arrogance of human invention and definition does not necessarily have
the final word on the ultimate disposition of things. Here, at least, is
an object no longer performing in the capacity assigned to it,
although, in its decay and in itself, like the "chisels, bent nails, wheelbarrows, and squeaky doors" Snyder catalogues in "Blue Mountains,"
it is "teaching the truth of the way things are" (1990b, 105). And in
"Bubbs Creek Haircut," Snyder encounters that truth not only in the
Goodwill but also in the wild, in the mountains, where he discovers,
a bit further on in the poem, what is clearly another version of the
Goodwill. What he sees is

A room of empty sun of peaks and ridges
a universe of junk, all left alone. (Snyder 1996, 36)

Despite the fact that in "Bubbs Creek Haircut" we are virtually at the
beginning of Snyder's career, we nevertheless find him here on the
way toward his later vision of nature and culture as a subsuming
whole, "one big empty house," the dichotomy or difference between
them discovered to be itself a cultural construct or fiction, an idea
subject to the same natural processes as the things that embody
ideas.[6]

***

In his most recent work Snyder addresses more fully his interest
in the emptiness or, to use a Buddhist term, the *thusness* of nature,
regarded as a reality that "stands for nothing." In the terms of his conceptualization, this reality, at its deepest levels, is a swirl of interrelated forces that constitutes wholeness and that stands apart from
human categories and distinctions. It is, to say the least, hard to talk
about. Yet Snyder's effort to encounter or engage with nature at this
level, and to articulate the experience of doing so, has generated
some remarkable poetry and prose, writing which seems calculated
to bring us into the heart of where we are, no matter where we are,
and that conveys something akin to the vision of Wallace Stevens's
snowman, who famously "beholds/Nothing that is not there and the
nothing that is" (1971, 54). In "Finding the Space in the Heart," for

example, the concluding poem in *Mountains and Rivers*, the speaker, "heading for know-not," traversing "mile after mile, trackless and featureless," finds himself in a place, or a space, that is literally "nowhere," unrecognizable and somewhat forbidding:

> Off nowhere, to be or not be,
> all equal, far reaches, no bounds.
>   Sound swallowed away,
>   no waters, no mountains, no
>   bush no grass and
>   because no grass
>   no shade but your shadow.
>   No flatness because no not-flatness.
>   No loss, no gain. So—
>   nothing in the way!
>   —the ground is the sky
>   the sky is the ground,
>   no place between, just
> wind-whip breeze,
>   tent-mouth leeward,
>   time being here. (Snyder 1996, 150-51)

With "all equal" and "no bounds" in sight, how could one not feel disconcerted, disoriented, displaced, ungrounded? Without place, can one *be* at all? Half way through the passage, however, the speaker shifts his ground, so to speak, and an experience that starts out by seemingly recalling some of the more despairing moments of the "What the Thunder Said" section of *The Waste Land* suddenly becomes an intuition of freedom, of limitlessness. There is, for the speaker, in an exhilarating realization, "nothing in the way!"—no obstruction, "no place between" him and where he is, fully present, totally open to the outside, almost purely ecocentric in the moment. Borrowing terms from another poem by Frost ("Directive"), we might say that Snyder's speaker, lost enough to find himself by now, has made himself at home, at least momentarily, in this "no place" (1979, 378).

The passage, in fact, may be regarded as a key example of a verbal representation of the experience of seeing the world (necessarily, in this instance) without language—a text, that is, that creates the effect of a nonverbal awareness of or responsiveness to a place—or a place beyond place—trackless, featureless, and therefore beyond description. What the speaker sees is not nature itself so much as its momentary suspension, or the appearance of it, along with the momentary suspension of the self. With "no waters" and "no mountains" in view, the processes of the earth are out of the picture here, and Snyder, "Off nowhere," between being and nonbeing, seems to have stepped, if not outside the world, then certainly out along its edge, and into a suddenly expanded sense of its limits.[7] At the same time, what he also seems to have stepped outside of is discourse, the world of conceptualization, especially of "nature," and even of "the nature of the nature of nature." Accordingly, the language into which he brings this experience of "heading for know-not" and arriving "nowhere" is virtually a discourse of absence, a language of negation, that can register only the presence (or the absence) of what is not there. This paradoxical effort to respond to nature on its own terms by means, nevertheless, of *our* terms can lead to such a conundrum as "No flatness because no not-flatness"—although the result of the effort is that we find ourselves in a place with "nothing in the way," free, perhaps, of what Lawrence Buell has called "the illusion of mental and even bodily apartness from one's environment" (Buell 1995, 144). This latter possibility is more elaborately suggested in the last passage I want to consider, consisting of a few sternly assertive (and certainly discursive) paragraphs from "Blue Mountains Constantly Walking" which have, nevertheless, something in common with the poetry of "Finding the Space in the Heart."

Snyder begins here with commentary on Dôgen, although the passage slips almost imperceptibly into a virtually sermonic mode of his own:

> Dôgen is not concerned with "sacred mountains"—or pilgrimages, or spirit allies, or wilderness as some special quality. His mountains and streams are the processes of this earth, all of existence, process, essence, action, absence; they roll being and nonbeing together. They are what we are, we are what they are. For those who would see directly into essential nature, the idea of the sacred is a delusion and an obstruction: it diverts us from seeing what is before our eyes: plain thusness. Roots, stems, and branches are all equally scratchy. No hierarchy, no equality. No occult and exoteric, no gifted kids and slow achievers. No wild and tame, no bound or free, no natural and artificial. Each totally its own frail self. Even though connected all which ways; even because connected all which ways.

> This, thusness, is the nature of the nature of nature. The wild in wild.

> So the blue mountains walk to the kitchen and back to the shop, to the

desk, to the stove. We sit on the park bench and let the wind and rain drench us. The blue mountains walk out to put another coin in the parking meter, and go on down to the 7-Eleven. The blue mountains march out of the sea, shoulder the sky for a while, and slip back into the waters. (Snyder 1990b, 103)

Although both here and in "Finding the Space in the Heart" Snyder employs a similar rhetoric of negation, it functions somewhat differently in each text. In the poem it serves to dismiss features of the landscape until the whole environment becomes a luminous symmetry or isotropic unity, so that to be there is to be anywhere or everywhere, at the origin of place. In "Blue Mountains," on the other hand, Snyder dismisses *human* categories and distinctions, whatever *conceptually* inhibits our unity with each other and with the earth, or the unity of being and nonbeing. But the result in both passages is the same. To see directly into essential nature here, as Snyder puts it, is to see that each person or thing is "totally its own frail self," as well as a part of the greater whole. In the striking final paragraph, the surrealistic intermingling of the mythic and the everyday, of the natural sublime of geological evolution and the ordinariness of finite daily human experience (the world of parking meters and the 7-Eleven), expresses Snyder's conviction that mountains and streams "are what we are, we are what they are." At this level, there is no sacred and ordinary. There is no ancient and modern, or Eastern and Western, or natural and human. What counts here, where all boundaries fall away, and what constitutes *thusness*, are solely the processes of the earth, or mountains and rivers without end, forever in motion, wherever and in whatever form they occur. Indeed, as Snyder playfully suggests, bringing "we" and "they," nature and culture, together, even mountains can "park" only for a while, and, as they weather and wash away, must feed the meter with coins before finally slipping back into the waters.

Notes

1 In 1970, in fact, Snyder published an expanded edition of *Six Sections*, containing one additional poem, "The Blue Sky." This new edition is titled *Six Sections from Mountains and Rivers Without End Plus One*. For the final version of the poem, it is worth noting, Snyder has revised the original six sections, quite substantially in the case of "The Elwha River," for example; while the section called "Hymn to the Goddess San Francisco in Paradise" has been entirely excised. For an account of the probable reasons for its removal, see Murphy (1992, 71).

2 In "From Work to Text," Barthes draws a distinction between these two terms on the basis of the closed or fixed nature of the "work" in contrast with the openness of the "text," its permeability to other texts, and its shifting plurality of meanings. Clearly, however, works can also be texts and vice versa. The distinction has less to do with substantive differences between them than with ideologically or critically motivated decisions about how to regard them. See Barthes (1979).

3 For an account of Snyder's work—especially of the section of *Mountains and Rivers* called "Three Worlds, Three Realms, Six Roads"—in terms of a Whitmanian approach to form, see Kern (1977).

4 James Heffernan defines ekphrasis as "verbal representation of visual representation" (1993, 3). With specific reference to the work of the New York School poet Barbara Guest, Sara Lundquist gives an elegant and enlightening account of ekphrasis in terms of the "lively and conflicted emotional, intellectual, and linguistic activity" that the concept subsumes, investigating "the arena of conflict or seduction that a poet enters when she or he represents in words what has already been presented in images" (Lundquist 1997, 264-65).

5 Consider, for example, Snyder's arch suggestion that "there might be a 'narrative theory'" in the world of deer, and that "they might ruminate on 'intersexuality' or 'decomposition criticism'" (1990b, 112).

6 Just as Snyder's reference to "wheelbarrows," in the passage quoted above from "Blue Mountains" (1990b, 105), brings William Carlos Williams to mind, so in "Bubbs Creek Haircut" his thinking seems close in many ways to Williams's slogan "No ideas but in things." Consider especially the lines:

> & make of sand a tree
>   of tree a board, of board (ideas!)
>   somebody's rocking chair. (Snyder 1996, 36)

7 Speaking of the effort "to imagine what the 'objective self' might be," by which he means the philosophical fiction of a decontextualized state of being, one completely removed from place, Lawrence Buell remarks that "We can step out of ourselves if we are lucky; but if we do, we will find no world there." Place-consciousness, as he also points out, is a limitation or constraint that circumscribes our horizons, although it is also salutary in that it "helps to make possible what we can know" (1995, 279). In this sense, however, Snyder's consciousness of "no place" seems greatly, if only momentarily, to expand what we can know, and to allow for access to a more encompassing experience of both environment and self.

Works Cited

Barthes, Roland. 1979. "From Work to Text." In *Textual Strategies*, ed. Josue V. Harari. Ithaca: Cornell University Press.
Buell, Lawrence. 1995. *The Environmental Imagination*. Cambridge: Harvard University Press.

Frost, Robert. 1979. *The Poetry of Robert Frost*. Ed. Edward Connery Latham. New York: Holt, Rinehart and Winston.

Heffernan, James A. W. 1993. *Museum of Words: The Poetics of Ekphrasis from Homer to Ashbery*. Chicago: University of Chicago Press.

Kern, Robert. 1977. "Recipes, Catalogues, Open Form Poetics: Gary Snyder's Archetypal Voice." *Contemporary Literature* 18, 2: 173–97.

Kerouac, Jack. 1958. *The Dharma Bums*. New York: New American Library.

Lundquist, Sara. 1997. "Reverence and Resistance: Barbara Guest, Ekphrasis, and the Female Gaze." *Contemporary Literature* 38, 2: 260–86.

Murphy, Patrick D. 1992. *Understanding Gary Snyder*. Columbia: University of South Carolina Press.

Pound, Ezra. 1954. *Literary Essays*. Ed. T. S. Eliot. New York: New Directions.

———. 1968. *Guide to Kulchur*. New York: New Directions.

———. 1970. *The Cantos*. New York: New Directions.

Snyder, Gary. 1960. *Myths and Texts*. New York: Corinth Books.

———. 1970. *Six Sections from Mountains and Rivers Without End Plus One*. San Francisco: Four Seasons Foundation.

———. 1990a. *Riprap and Cold Mountain Poems*. San Francisco: North Point Press.

———. 1990b. *The Practice of the Wild*. San Francisco: North Point Press.

———. 1992. *No Nature: New and Selected Poems*. New York: Pantheon Books.

———.1996. *Mountains and Rivers Without End*. Washington, D.C.: Counterpoint.

Stevens, Wallace. 1971. *The Palm at the End of the Mind*. Ed. Holly Stevens. New York: Vintage Books.

Whitman, Walt. 1986. *The Complete Poems*. Ed. Francis Murphy. New York: Penguin Books.

Williams, William Carlos. 1963. *Paterson*. New York: New Directions.

CHAPTER TWELVE

Chicanismo's Beat Outrider?
The Texts and Contexts of Oscar Zeta Acosta
A. Robert Lee

I

Beats, The Beat Movement. The key names continue to resonate: Ginsberg, Kerouac, Cassady, Ferlinghetti, Corso, di Prima, Snyder, or Burroughs. Ginsberg's *Howl* (1956) and Kerouac's *On the Road* (1957), likewise, supply the legendary twin anthems, hallucinatory dream poem and road novel of a generational uprising against Cold War "Moloch" and Grey Flannel Suit conformism. Both, too, have passed into history accompanied by their own celebrated aesthetic, "Hebraic-bardic" verse breathline or "bop spontaneity" prose.

Other landmarks add supporting energy and weight. Lawrence Ferlinghetti's *A Coney Island of The Mind* (1958a), in a poem like "Constantly Risking Absurdity" (1958b) catches the then newborn sense of Beat "high theatrics." Gregory Corso's *Gasoline* (1958), with the poems of *Mindfield* (1989) as retrospective collection, in a symptomatic 1960s piece like "Bomb" speaks to the nuclear threat as at once "Death's extravagance" and "Death's jubilee."

Other Beat rallyings would take manifesto form. None has become more influential than Ginsberg's *Notes for Howl and Other*

Poems (1959), with its affiliation to "the visionary" in Whitman and Blake, and Kerouac's "Essentials of Spontaneous Prose" (1958a), with its notion of narrative fed by the speed, the dropout pitch and eventfulness, of American "counter" lives lived always at full tilt. Taken with John Clellon Holmes's "This is the Beat Generation" (1988b) and "The Philosophy of the Beat Generation" (1988b), each in their emphasis upon untrammeled consciousness and the rejection of a "square" world, they have come to serve as a core expression of Beat aim and philosophy.

Matters, however, have long moved on since the heady days when "Howl" could be banned, *On the Road* seized, City Lights taken to court in 1957, a naked Ginsberg or Peter Orlovsky whisked out of view, and high school and college authorities moved to warn American youth against a Beat wave of "sex, drugs 'n rock and roll." An evident measure would be simply to compare the shifts in personnel and focus to have emerged over the thirty-year span between Thomas Parkinson's *A Casebook on The Beat* (1961) or Donald Allen's *The New American Poetry: 1945-1960* (1960), both pioneer volumes, and Ann Charters's *The Portable Beat Reader* (1992), an update as timely and well informed as any.

II

Is it still to be doubted, for instance, that a black, an African-American, Beatdom was not in evidence all along? How, otherwise, to account for LeRoi Jones, albeit in his pre-Baraka phase before the Black Power ethos which underwrites his 1964 "subway" drama classic *Dutchman* (1964) or his clenched-fist poem "BLACK DADA NIHILISMUS"? What of Ted Joans (1969, 1970) as vintage "Afrosurrealist" performance artist and musician, or Bob Kaufman (1965, 1967, 1981) as San Francisco poet-luminary, or A.B. Spellman (1965, 1966) whose jazz credentials led to both verse and musicological writing?[1]

Theirs is a Beat literary seam whose black argot ("Jazz is my religion . . . it alone do I dig" wrote Ted Joans), and whose resorts to rap and blues riffs, could not more bespeak an Afro-America of personally known and lived experience. Their writings throw a necessary contextual, even contrapuntal, light upon the "negro streets at dawn" of "Howl," or Kerouac's attractions to black Denver and to Coltrane and Parker in *The Subterraneans* (1958b) along with his 242-chorus *Mexico City Blues* (1959). They need to be read, also, alongside, and again perhaps against, Norman Mailer's hipster existential credo as set forth in the essay which eventually became the 1956 City Lights pamphlet *The White Negro* ("the Negro's equality would tear a profound shift in the psychology, the sexuality, and the moral imagination of every White alive" [1957]).

Other ethnic takes on Beatdom invite their own kinds of recognition and weighing. In *Griever: An American Monkey King in China* (1987) Gerald Vizenor, Native postmodern, contributes Griever de Hocus, mixed blood Chippewa-Ojibway trickster set down in a puritanic and statist People's Republic of China. In *Trickmaster Monkey: His Fake Book* (1989) Maxine Hong Kingston offers Wittman Ah Sing, her "American Chinaman" hipster-zen figure approximately based on the playwright Frank Chin. Every acknowledgement is due that both are imagined, textual presences, and that they draw upon their begetters's own complex, enraveled Native and Asian American legacies. Allowing that Beat might have been one thing, Hippie a line of succession, could not the case be made that their styles, their stories, ally them, too, with Beat, or at least Beat-related, tradition?

In turn a female literary counterforce to the Beat "fellahin" has rightly, and increasingly, won its recognition. The names grow and multiply from a begetting first presence in Diane Di Prima, author of the gynocentric, fine worked "Loba" poetry sequence (1973, 1978) with its use of wolf goddess myths, and also, and whatever its "made for the trade" commercial haste, of her *Memoirs of a Beatnik* (1969). This Beat-feminine tradition looks to its own varied continuity in poetry like Joanne Kyger's *The Tapestry and the Web* (1965) and *Going On, Selected Poems 1958-80* (1983) and Anne Waldman's *Fast Speaking Woman and Other Chants* (1983).

Memoirists, especially, assume an ever-gathering place. Bonnie Bremser (Brenda Frazer) tells a harrowing drugs-and-destitution story in *For Love of Ray* (1971)—first published as *Troia: Mexican Memoirs* (1969). Carolyn Cassady writes interlinking accounts of a triangle of love and marriage in *Heart Beat, My Life with Jack and Neal* (1976) and *Off the Road, My Years with Cassady, Kerouac and Ginsberg* (1990). Joyce Johnson offers the full rite of passage remembrances of *Minor Characters* (1983). Eileen Kaufman gives her own exhilarated, funny-sad account of a first close encounter with Bob Kaufman in "Laughter Sounds Orange at Night" (1987). Hettie Jones witnesses to a 1960s cross-racial marriage and New York literary life in her warm, unrecriminatory *How I Became Hettie Jones* (1990). Jan Kerouac's *Trainsong* (1988) adds a further increment, a next-generation novel of talented if fatally drug-shadowed Beat womanhood.

No longer, accordingly, can the Beat Movement be thought simply a male court (however gay or pansexual) and whether of literary page, road, boxcar, sex or "speed." Yet nor is that to overlook a whole pantheon of patristic godfathers, mutually unlike as they undoubtedly were. Carl Solomon enters the reckoning as *poète maudit* inspiration for *Howl*. Kenneth Rexroth bills himself as self-vaunting "literary warhorse." Henry Miller greets the Beat generation, Kerouac especially, as not-so-secret sharers in his own unremorseful status as the shock-horror figure of bohemianism, sex, and European expatriation, both in the *Tropics* books (1934, 1939) and *The Air-Conditioned Nightmare* (1945). Chandler Brossard serves as early Village luminary and author of a Beat-allied bohemianism in a novel like *Who Walk in Darkness* (1952). William Carlos Williams, vintage imagist maker of *Paterson* (1946), in his Preface to *Howl* gives license and impetus to literary Beatdom. Herbert Huncke takes on iconic status as Dostoevskian Times Square hustler, thief, and author of *Guilty of Everything* (1990). Above all William Burroughs, "Old Bull," whether as drug veteran, or the dark, vaudevillian master of *The Naked Lunch* (1962), or innovator with Brion Gysin of "cut-up" narrative, from the outset becomes an inerasable Beat mentor.

In his foreword to Anne Waldman's recent anthology, *The Beat Book: Poems and Fictions of the Beat Generation* (1996), Allen Ginsberg (1996) also takes pains to emphasize Beat's affinities with the other arts.[2] He speaks warmly of an "interactive" tradition, a lattice of mutually shared interests and vision. He mentions the film and still photography of Robert Frank and Alfred Leslie; the music of David Amram; the painting of Larry Rivers; and the poetry and art publishing of, besides Ferlinghetti whose City Lights Bookstore/Press began in 1953, Cid Corman, founder of *Origin* magazine, longtime Kyoto resident and publisher of Snyder's landmark first collection

Riprap in 1959, and Barney Rosset, founder-editor of Grove Press and of the virtual house journal of the Beats, *Evergreen Review.*

Beat, too, has always had its own identifying geographies. Ginsberg, Kerouac (once beyond his Lowell, Massachusetts, origins), and Corso find their first measure in the New York of Columbia University, the Village, St. Mark's, and The Chelsea Hotel. San Francisco follows the West Coast literary world in which Ferlinghetti and his City Lights press and bookshop serve as working center. Other California locales range from Big Sur as both Henry Miller and Kerouac turf to Bubb's Creek where Snyder and Ginsberg traveled and which becomes a vital place-reference in their verse.

California, in fact, supplies a web of writerly connections. One prime constellation includes the poets Michael McClure, Gary Snyder, Lew Welch, Philip Whalen, Robert Duncan, Jack Spicer, and, always, the vintage painter-versemaker Kenneth Patchen.[3] At a slight remove there need, also, to be included the California of Richard Brautigan (he took his own life in Bolinas, California) and the Oregon of Ken Kesey who, in fiction like *A Confederate General from Big Sur* (1964) and *One Flew Over the Cuckoo's Nest* (1977), give a larkier, satiric-experimental flavor to Beat life. As late 1950s and early 1960s Beatdom gave way to a subsequent 1960s and 1970s Hippiedom, jazz to rock/punk (Kerouac's beloved Charlie Parker, John Coltrane, and Dizzie Gillespie to groups from "The Grateful Dead" to "The Soft Machine"), and dope to acid, was it not Neal Cassady, no less, who drove the bus with its LSD colorations for Kesey's "Merry Pranksters" up and down, and often beyond, the West Coast?

Beat geography, moreover, goes well beyond the two Coasts; notably the Colorado of Neal Cassady's Denver or the Boulder that became the site of The Naropa Institute under the guidance of Chogyam Trungpa Rinpoche, Ginsberg, and Anne Waldman. It embraces the Paris of the "Beat Hotel" as run by Mme. Rachou, and where Ginsberg, Orlovsky, Corso, Burroughs, and Brion Gysin lived in the mid-1950s. Tangiers takes on a matching force, varyingly drug garden, Gay outpost, and literary colony headed by Paul and Jane Bowles, and whose lugubrious other key presence was Burroughs himself with Gysin as restaurant owner. Kyoto, where Gary Snyder and Joanne Kyger were married, offered a temple culture and Zen practices that drew Ginsberg among others. Mexico City doubles in

Beat iconography as the site of Burroughs's shooting of his wife, Joan
Vollmer, and of where, in 1955, Kerouac wrote *Mexico City Blues*.
Latterly, Vienna's *Schule für Dictung*, founded in 1991 and whose
poetics and poetry teaching draw their inspiration from Naropa, has
become Austria's matching Beat academy.

III

Beatdom, literary and otherwise, needs equally to be identified
for its international circuits and outreach. No doubt, in part because
of the shared language, Beat found more than a literary echo in
Britain—however deceptive the analogies often made with Angry
(actually deeply conservative) Young Man figures like the playwright
John Osborne or the novelist Alan Sillitoe. Anyone present at the
momentous Albert Hall Beat reading in London in 1965, the auditori-
um heavy in pot haze and with readings by Ginsberg and Corso, an
almost spectral voice recording of Burroughs reading *The Naked
Lunch*, sound poetry from Austria, a Finnish voice in the poet and
translator Anselm Hollo, and a selection of British poets from
Christopher Logue to Adrian Mitchell, would have been in little
doubt. Confirmation, too, lay in the ensuing anthology *Wholly
Communion* (1965).

Jeff Nuttall, poet, chronicler, teacher, maker of performance
scripts, has long been more than willing to acknowledge the Beat
component in his challenges to British class division and etiquette in
so influential a work as *Bomb Culture* (1968). The Beat use of spoken measure runs through "the Liverpool poets," the wry, lyrical
Brian Patten, the more oral-populist Roger McGough (the energy
behind the group *The Scaffold*), or the lyric, intelligently whimsical
Adrian Henri. This overlap of Mersey voice and anglo-Beatdom also
has its mark in the very naming of the Beatles that John Lennon
explicitly linked to his reading of *Howl*.

Adrian Mitchell, in an accusation poem akin to the antimilitary
verse of Ferlinghetti or Corso like "Tell Us Your Lies," took on the
obfuscations of British establishment power and especially its military and nuclear accoutrements. The London poetry circuit could
look to an anarchist, language-play seam in Michael Horovitz and
Peter Brown (Scotland supplied Iain Sinclair). Even an otherwise
wholly un-Beat poet like George MacBeth, who ran BBC Radio's

"Third Programme" poetry from 1955–76 and who took aim at the Beats in his tepid satire "Owl," together with the London-centered circuit of Edward Lucie-Smith, Peter Redgrave, and Alan Brownjohn who became known as "The Group," however hard they tried, found it difficult to ignore Beat ease and expansiveness.[4] A major debt, by contrast, has to be paid to Eric Mottram, critic, poet, and London University teacher, whose longtime championing of the Beats and editorship of *Poetry Review* in the 1970s was seminal.[5]

The further reach is to be heard in the Scottish-born Alexander Trocchi's anthology work and fiction (Weaver, et al. 1963), the latter as expressed in a drug chronicle ("the mind under heroin") like *Cain's Book* (Trocchi 1960) or a powerful obsessive love portrait ("It is the word 'I' which is arbitrary and which contains within itself its own inadequacy and its own contradiction") like *Young Adam* (Trocchi 1961). In Jan Cremer's *I Jan Cremer* (1965) The Netherlands supplied its own Beat literary bad boy ("I'm the kid on the corner, the boy who's always hanging around"), the self-appointed drugs, sex, and jazz itinerant roué of the modern city be it in Europe or the States. Simon Vinkenoog, poet, author of the novel *Hoogseizoen/High Season* (1962), centers more on Amsterdam as Beat-European city. His translation of "*Howl*" into Dutch adds its own confirmation.

A far different voice, yet still with its Beat affiliation, belongs to Andrei Voznesensky, harbinger of a Russia reborn from Sovietism and whose massively popular reading tour of the United States in 1966 (and friendship with Ginsberg) signaled a historic challenge to received Cold War convention. His "A Beatnik's Monologue: The Revolt of the Machines" (1967), particularly, calls up *Howl* both in its dystopian vision and its measure: "Howling, caterwauling, hordes of fuming machines repeat their cry: 'Meat! Human meat!'"

Contrastingly again, from Australia, a name like that of Richard Neville features (along with a then often psychedelically clad celebrity and TV intellectual presence like Germaine Greer). As Beat-hippie founder of *Oz* magazine he would become a frequent court figure on grounds of supposed obscenity. His Sydney to "swinging London" odyssey is fondly recalled in his conglomerately titled *Hippie, hippie shake: the dreams, the trips, the trials, the love-ins, the screw ups ... the sixties* (1995).

Even as distant as Japan a Beat note would sound, not least in the form of an "alternative" fiction of dropout, sex, and drugs. Ryu Murakami's *Kagirinaku Tomeini Chikai Blue/Almost Transparent Blue* (1976), within a GI-Japanese friendship, unravels a whole youth underground. Haruki Murakami's *Kaze No Uta O Kike/Listen to the Singing of the Wind* (1979) and *Norway No Mori/Norwegian Wood* (1987; the title taken from a Beatles' song) explores the drift born of postwar urban Japanese affluence. Kaoru Shoji's *Akazukinchan Ni Ki O Tsukete/Be Careful, Little Red Riding Hood* (1981) encloses its love saga in a Beat patina.

IV

> "When you speak of civil rights, civil liberties, etc. you think of black vs. white. When there's talk of investigation of these rights, of federal grants for education, of cheap housing, in other words, discrimination, you speak of Negroes. At the Chinese banquet when all the big whigs [sic] got up to talk, they mentioned first Negroes, and, second Chinese. . . . And that's the way it goes. All America is divided into three parts, white, black and yellow. . . . How about me?"

> Letter to Willie L. Brown, Jr. resigning from Brown's campaign for Speaker of the California House of Representatives, 1970 (Acosta 1996, 114)

The Brown Buffalo. La cucaracha. On his own writerly reckoning "The Samoan." Hunter Thompson's 300 pound "Samoan." Dr. Gonzo in *Fear and Loathing in Las Vegas* (1972). Under any or all of these sobriquets, Oscar Zeta Acosta (1935-74) supplies a stirring, if often marginalized, name in the making of 1960s American counterculture.

To associate him with the Beat Movement, even so, might at first surprise, a hitherto unacknowledged co-spirit in literature as life from out of the ranks of *Chicanismo*. It also pays a due calculated to further rescuing Acosta from a "mainstream" oversight as unfair as it has too often been negligent. Indeed Acosta's Beat *vita* grows more plausible, not to say more vivid, with each remembered detail.

There is Acosta the anarcho-libertarian *Chicano* raised in California's Riverbank/Modesto and who makes his name as a Legal Aid lawyer in Oakland and Los Angeles after qualifying in San Francisco in 1966. There is the Air Force enlistee who, on being sent to Panama, becomes a Pentecostal convert and missionary there (1949-52) before opting for apostasy and a return to California. There is the jailee in Ciudad Juárez, Mexico, in 1968, forced to argue in local court for his own interests in uncertain street Spanish (or *caló*) after a spat with a hotelkeeper. Finally there is the Oscar of the barricades, the battling lawyer of the schools and St. Basil's protest in 1968. This is the "buffalo" who becomes *La Raza Unida* independent candidate for Sheriff of Los Angeles in 1970, who regularly affirms his first allegiance by signing himself "Oscar Zeta Acosta, Chicano lawyer," and who finally leaves for Mexico in despair, madness even, at the internal divisions of *Chicano* politics.

To these, always, have to be added the rumbustious tequila drinker and druggie ten years in therapy, the hugely overweight ulcer sufferer who spat blood, the twice-over divorcee, and the eventual *desaparecido* in 1974 aged 39 who was last seen in Mazatlán, Mexico, and whose end has long been shrouded in mystery. Was he drug or gunrunning, a kind of *Chicano* Ambrose Bierce who created his own exit from history, or a victim of kidnap or other foul play? Above all, from a literary perspective, there has to be Acosta the legendary "first person singular" writer of *The Autobiography of a Brown Buffalo* (1989a) and *The Revolt of The Cockroach People* (1989b).

Even in summary Acosta can hardly be said not to invite attention as an American one-off, an original. But a Beat writer, too? The response allowing for all reservations and if at first sight seemingly a no, somehow, and also, has to be a yes.

Undeniably he became an energy, however maverick, in the rise of Brown Power, the *Chicano/latino* movement akin to the Black Power of Malcolm X, the Panthers, SNCC, and other radical activism. Is not the 1968 Delano grape strike its equivalent of Selma or of Wounded Knee? This best known of the agricultural-worker strikes (*las huelgas*), led by César Chávez and his United Farm Workers, belongs, too, to other activism admired by Acosta, whether José Angel Gutíerrez's La Raza Unida in Texas or "Corky" Gonzalez's Crusade for Justice in Denver.

Yet, and at the same time, Acosta's life gives off its own nothing if not Beat, or at the very least Beatlike, flavor. It would be hard to pretend that there was ever the one Beat identikit or, if there were, that Acosta supplied in his life and art a perfect fit. But a Beat "personality" is always very much there to be met with. It embraces his own will to a would-be Zen or Ghandian transcendental spirituality—whatever the calls of his own gargantuan and "too too solid flesh." His own "on the road" escapades equally count, not only in California but also in Texas and Colorado. There is an undoubted Beatdom in his wish to find a lived, dynamic "spontaneity" both in writing and the everyday round, even in his court and legal work.

Other Beat or Beat-related accoutrements lie in the frequent resort, besides the drinking, to pot and amphetamines and eventually to LSD and other chemical stimulus. His womanizing, and hetero-machismo, might not be entirely from the *fellahin* ethos, but it comes close, including biases which often lie close to misogyny. His politics, be they for *Chicano/a* tenant rights or anti-Vietnam, and which saw him as frequently carrying a revolver and accompanied by a body-guard as handling a court or related legal brief, invite their own comparison with any number of Beat arrests and happenings. Ginsberg and "The Fugs" resolving to levitate the Pentagon, or Kesey's prankster activism, come to mind. In these, as in other respects, Acosta both extends, and at the same time quite problematizes, what it is to belong to both Chicano and Beat lineage, hybridity full of challenge to the usual categories.

The literary implications similarly suggest interzone, shared imaginative terrain. On the one hand Acosta is associated with the literary "Chicano Renaissance" of names like José Antonio Villarreal in *Pocho* (1959) with its intergenerational and Mexican-American family history, or Tomás Rivera in his bilingual migrant worker story-cycle "... *y no se lo tragó la tierra/ ... and the earth did not part*" (1971), or Rudolfo Anaya in *Bless Me, Ultima* (1972) with its lyric memories of a postwar New Mexico childhood of *brujería* (magic) and *curanderismo* (healing). None of this, however, disguises his Bad Boy status in *Chicano* literary ranks—the no-holds scatology and "bad" language, or his swipes at ethnic piety, the gaps in Anglo and Hispanic Catholicism and the sentimentalization of Mexico. He was ever his own man.[6]

On the other hand there can also be little mistaking the footfalls of Kerouac and Cassady, and, more obliquely, of Ginsberg and Ferlinghetti. Hunter Thompson's fond recall of Acosta in vintage argot likens him to one of the great founding Beat luminaries. "Oscar was a wild boy," he writes, "crazier than Neal Cassady" (1989, 5-7). Yet, once again, he is not to be locked into simply the one Beat style or phase. For all that Kerouac's echoing road ethos invites its recognition, as does each turn and swerve of a countercultural life, so his own "gonzo" style is not to be denied—Acosta, again as ever, as his own kind of performance figure.

Acosta's writing itself likewise pulls two ways. *Brown Buffalo* (1989a) and *Cockroach People* (1989b) evidently can look to a context in other first person *Chicano/a* writing. That, of necessity, calls up so historic a *corrido* or oral-written anthem of *Chicanismo* as Rodolfo "Corky" Gonzalez's *I Am Joaquín/Yo Soy Joaquín* (1972) with its panoramic unfolding of "Aztlán"; or Richard Rodriguez's *Hunger of Memory* (1981) and *Days of Obligation: An Argument with My Mexican Father* (1992), each, controversially, given over to his assimilationist rite of passage from Chicano to American; or Ray Gonzalez's El Paso border history under the quasi-Proustian title *Memory Fever* (1993.)

At the same time both Acosta volumes also yield their own Beat styling and temper. The confessional spontaneity, the pace, again calls up Kerouac, whether *On the Road* or the novels that make up the Duluoz cycle. Nor would it be hard to discern a shared spirit with other ranking "confessional" Beat texts: John Clellon Holmes's *Go* (1952) as early Beat portraiture, Carl Solomon's *Mishaps, Perhaps* (1966) as a self-portrait of breakdown within a larger generational pathology, or Neal Cassady's *The First Third* (1971) as an itinerary and high-adrenaline American life made over into narrative. LeRoi Jones/Amiri Baraka's *The Autobiography of LeRoi Jones/Amiri Baraka* (1984) also serves, another life study in which a onetime Beat affiliation plays into, and once more complicates, a politics of ethnic nationalism (and, subsequently, his own brand of Marxism).

As to Acosta's other writings, the three-part San Joaquín story, "Perla is a Pig" (1971), published in the journal *Con Safos*, offers a portrait of *Chicano* community internally prejudiced against one of its own as an "eccentric." The very outsiderness of the protagonist Huero, a maybe oblique figure for Acosta's own singularity within the culture of his birth, leads to the wasted sacrifice of his pig and renders him still rejected and ultimately exiled. That the story, for all its vernacular immediacy, avails itself also of underpinnings from Biblical parable and Aztec-Chicano myth suggests a yet further intertextual subtlety. Acosta's uncollected verse in "Poems For Spring Days" (1996, 55-61) does likewise, again full of *Chicanismo* yet also

Snyder-like in contemplative quality, given over to a "bardic," lyric line measure yet also buttressed with allusion to seeming Beat, or in its wake white Hippie figures from Bob Dylan to The Beatles.

On the other hand, incontrovertibly, there is Acosta's own sumptuously bad-mouthed disavowal in *The Autobiography of a Brown Buffalo* of any working affinity with the Beats as a movement:

> I speak as a historian, a recorder of events with a sour stomach. I have no love for memories of the past. Ginsberg and those coffee houses with hungry-looking guitar players never did mean shit to me. They never took their drinking seriously. And the fact of the matter is that they got what was coming to them. It's their tough luck if they ran out and got on the road with Kerouac, then came back a few years later with their hair longer and fucking marijuana up their asses, shouting Love and Peace and Pot. And still broke as ever. (Acosta 1989a, 18)

Perverse it may be, but the case could, and likely should, be made that this offers a kind of "Beat" anti-Beat declaration. Given every acknowledgement of Acosta's *Chicanismo* is there not here a style, a flourish, to recall Kerouac's "bop," or William Burroughs's laconicism, or the dark comic wordplay of any of Bob Kaufman's *Abomunist* (1959) manifestos?[7] Acosta, in other words, and in life as much as on the page, again gives serious grounds to be thought literary kin or cousinship to the Beats.

V

The "I" persona assumed by Acosta in *The Autobiography of a Brown Buffalo* bows in with a suitably Beat gesture of self-exposure: "I stand naked before the mirror." He sees a body of "brown belly," "extra flesh," "two large hunks of brown tit" (1989a, 11). Evacuation becomes a bathroom opera of heave, color, the moilings of fast-food leftovers. Hallucinatory colloquies open with "Old Bogey," Cagney, and Edward G. Robinson. In their wake he turns to "my Jewish shrink," Dr. Serbin, the therapist as accuser, and whose voice echoes like some mock Freudian throughout. Glut rules, a buildup of "booze and Mexican food," Chinese pork and chicken, ulcers, pills for dyspepsia, and his shower room tumescence and betraying fantasy coitus with Alice, the leggy, blond, Minnesota partner of his friend Ted Casey on overseas war duty in Okinawa.

This is an opening ventriloquy busy and comic in its own right, at once self-serious yet self-mocking. There is even an "on the road" intertextual shy as Acosta plunges "headlong" in his green Plymouth into San Francisco morning traffic. The Beat allusions, furthermore, quickly cluster. "I'm splitting" (1989a, 33) he writes in Beat idiom to his office mate. Procol Harum sings "A Whiter Shade of Pale." He buys drink from a liquor store opposite City Lights Bookshop, "a hangout for sniveling intellectuals" (1989a, 36) and throws in a reference to Herb Caen long celebrated for his coining, however facetious, of the term "beatnik." Memories of marijuana and his first LSD come to mind. He roars drunk into Dr. Serbin's in the guise of *faux* barbarian, "another wild Indian gone amok" (1989a, 42). Acosta so monitors "Acosta." The one text patrols the other.

At "Trader JJ's," watering hole talkshop, he gives vent to a bar room and wholly un-pc macho patois of "Chinks and fags" (1989a, 43). The Beatles's "Help" spills its harmonies and plaintiveness on to Polk Street for him. Ted Casey tempts him with mescaline. "Powdered mayonnaise" (1989a, 67) appears at the Mafia restaurant. Women, his ex-lover June MacAdoo, Ted's girl Alice and her friend Mary, all weave into his sexual fantasies even as he frets and, with reason, doubts his own male prowess. The diorama is motleyed, a comic cuts weave of illusion and fact. Ginsberg's "hungry fatigue," as he calls it in "A Supermarket in California (1958)," and Kerouac's "whole road experience," in a phrase from *On the Road*, have been made over, hybridized, fondly mocked, into a new "brownskin" West Coast odyssey.

So it is, too, on July 1, 1967, that Acosta announces himself as "The Samoan," island brown hulk, ethnic transvestite, a figure of guise, mask, harlequinry. "I've been mistaken for American Indian, Spanish, Filipino, Hawaiian, Samoan, and Arabian" he witnesses, adding ruefully, "No one has ever asked me if I'm a spic or greaser" (1989a, 68). Is this not "Oscar" as living American multitext, *Latino* lawyer yet also *Latino* outlaw, *Chicano* yet also Beat outrider? Is not, too, the figure of John Tibeau, "Easy Rider" biker poet on a Harley Davidson, his *alter ego*, a latter-day and Beat-styled West Coast fantasy troubadour, a fusion of Lord Byron and the Bob Dylan he listens to with admiration?

Chicano and Beat Acosta compete and yet collude throughout. On the one hand he looks back to his Riverbank boyhood with its gang allegiance and fights against the Okies ("I grew up a fat, dark Mexican—a Brown Buffalo—and my enemies called me a nigger"

[1989a, 86]), his fantasy wargames, peachpicking, clarinet playing and early first loves. On the other hand he heads into a Pacific Northwest with the hitchhiker Karin Wilmington, a journey busy in allusions to Tim Leary, Jerry Garcia, and The Grateful Dead, and more *faux* Indian pose in Hemingway country at Ketchum, Idaho. Both come together as he then circles back into his Panama years, his onetime bid to serve as "a Mexican Billy Graham" (1989a, 132).

As he weaves his way through more drugs, figures like Scott ("a full time dope smuggler and a salesman for Scientology" [1989a, 158]), Beatdom, unflatteringly or not, again supplies "Oscar" as would-be author with a benchmark reference—"The beatniks in the colleges were telling brown buffaloes like me to forget about formal education" (1989a, 152). For all that he can self-mockingly tell the waitress Bobbi that "My family is the Last of the Aztecs" (1989a, 140), the call is equally to a Beat spontaneity, the free flow of life and pen.

Hippiedom, overdoses, bad trips, a succession of women, memories of writer alcoholics like Al Mathews, car crashes and blackouts in Alpine, and odd jobs in Vail, Colorado, all play against the memory of his detention in Juarez jail amid "the ugliest pirates I ever saw" (1989a, 192), and need to prove, as if the playing out of a formula migrant script, his "American" identity at the border ("You don't *look* like an American, you know?" [1989a, 195]).

Almost inevitably, given a journey text as Kerouac-mythic as actual, the pathway back into Los Angeles becomes the hallowed, iconic Route 66. He speaks of a time soon to come when he will become "Zeta," as taken from the last letter of the Spanish alphabet (and, as *The Revolt of The Cockroach People* confirms, also from the name of the hero in the movie *Las Cucarachas*), "Oscar" as *auteur* equally in life as art. For the moment, however, he gives as his working certificate of identity the following:

> What I see now, on this rainy day in January, 1968, what is clear to me after this sojourn is that I am neither a Mexican nor an American. I am neither a Catholic nor a Protestant. I am a Chicano by ancestry and a Brown Buffalo by choice. (Acosta 1989a, 199)

Back, finally, in East LA, the *barrio* known vernacularly in street *caló* as "East Los" and "the home of the biggest herd of brown buffaloes in the world" (1989a, 199), he opts for a moment of rest, of temporary and recuperative pause. To hand is "Oscar" as both

Chicanismo's own literary *vato loco* and yet Beat warrior, its own would-be Sheriff of Los Angeles and yet Beat roadrunner, all to be continued over into the "another story" (1989a, 199) pending in *The Revolt of The Cockroach People*.

VI

I stand and observe them all. I who have been running around with my head hanging for so long. I who have been lost in my own excesses, drowned in my own confusion. A faded beatnik, a flower vato, an aspiring writer, a thirty-three-year old kid full of buffalo chips is supposed to defend these bastards. (Acosta 1989b, 53)

So, in antic pose (his name card reads "Buffalo Z. Brown, Chicano Lawyer, Belmont Hotel, LA" [1989b, 48]), the "Oscar" of *Cockroach People* positions himself in relation to the *Chicano* militants involved in the local school strikes of 1968. This authorial "I" again gives off a beguiling equivocation of self and persona, activist and spectator.

On the one hand, as novel cum autobiography, the text yields an "actual" Acosta of LA courtroom and barricade, counsel in the St. Basil 21 and East Los Angeles 13 Trials, would-be exposer of the Robert Fernandez and "Roland Zanzibar" murders, conferee with César Chávez and Corky Gonzalez, and candidate for Sheriff of Los Angeles County.

On the other, it yields an Acosta always the writer *semblable* who sees his own silhouette in the Aztec warrior founder god Huitzilopochtli (11), speaks of himself as "Vato Número Uno" (13) and "singer of songs" (207), uses the court to give a parable history of *Chicanismo* with due allusion to Quetzacoatl, Moctezuma, Córtes and la Malinche through to 1848 and the "Anglo" appropriation of the southwest and its latterday aftermath, casts himself as first person and yet, alterity itself, third person participant in the Chicano Militant bombing of a Safeway store and Bank of America branch, and envisions himself as the *carnal* (brother/dude) edging into madness at the spies and fifth columnists, the delusions and betrayals, within *Chicano* activism.

Throughout, and in an address to a "court" as much of appealed-to history as the law, he again emphasizes a *Chicano*/Beat nexus: "A hippie is like a cockroach. So are the beatniks. So are the Chicanos. We are all around Judge. And Judges do not pick us to serve on

Grand Juries"(1989b, 228). Any number of shared Beat/Beatnik and "Gonzo" markers give added support throughout *Cockroach People*. The LA cathedral built by the Vietnam War supporting and autocratic Cardinal McIntyre becomes his "personal monstrosity" (1989b, 11), McIntyre's outward architectural show, as Oscar construes it, of an inward spiritual blight. The *Chicano* poor who protest against this high tier-Catholicism, in the text's hallucinatory telling, transpose into a "gang of cockroaches" (1989b, 11), replete with Gloria Chavez, goldclub swinging heroine.

As "a religious war" (1989b, 14) erupts, Oscar envisions himself as both his own familiar and stranger: "'Come on', our lawyer exhorts. I, strange fate, am this lawyer" (1989b, 14). The whole then veers into seriocomic Beat opera, a politics of the real and yet the surreal, as signaled in each rallying placard: "YANKEES OUT OF AZTLAN" (1989b, 32) or, during the fracas over the schools, "MENUDO EVERYDAY" (1989b, 41), or, in the author's own rise to fame, "VIVA EL ZETA!" (1989b, 164).

Questing, as he says, for "my Chicano soul" (1989b, 47), Zeta also looks back, and with a mix of reproach and nostalgia, to "my beatnik days" (1989b, 65). Both hold for him. To one side stands his trial work with the St. Basil 21 and East LA 13, his flurry of contempt imprisonments (Prisoner "Zeta-Brown, 4889") and eventual political campaign. To the other he gives himself to heady flights of Beat phantasmagoria. "We are the Viet Cong of America," he proclaims (1989a, 198). Sexual euphoria, aided by an ingestion of Quaalude-400s, takes the form of his would-be Sheik of Araby practices with his three girl followers and the love tryst with the black juror Jean Fisher. If not actually, then again in his mind's eye, he finally has the entire California judicial bench subpoenaed on grounds of historic racism.

Two sequences give added particularity to this use of text as also metatext. First Acosta offers the arrest, self-hanging and, above all, autopsy of Robert Fernandez. The corpse ("just another expendable Cockroach" [1989b, 101]), anatomically sliced and jarred under the guidance of Dr. Thomas A. Naguchi, LA County Coroner, yet, with just the right exoticism, also "Coroner to the stars," becomes Acosta's own textual autopsy of the abused larger body of all *Chicanismo*. The same holds for the police shooting of "Roland Zanzibar," based on the death of the journalist Reuben Salazar of Station KMEX.

Acosta anything but hides his view that an iconographic and more inclusive process has been involved, a ritual silencing of unwanted *Chicanismo*. "Someone still has to answer for Robert Fernandez and Roland Zanzibar" he writes, both to memorialize yet also to prompt future action (1989b, 258).

This doubling, or reflexivity, holds throughout. He depicts both the *vatos*, *cholos*, and *pintos* of barrio or street, and the cops and white authorities who make up *los gabachos*, as belonging to their own 1960s yet also to far older white-brown historic clashes and timelines. Acosta enters the text on shared terms, lawyer yet meta-lawyer, as he engages in each reeling, absurdist exchange with Judge Alacran during the "Chicano Militants" and Gonzalez trials. In his role as "Zeta" he offers himself as located in both a Los Angeles court-room and the courtroom of history.

In fact all the text's main actual figures are pitched to take on their own kind of mythicism, none more so than César Chávez and Corky Gonzalez—legatees, as Acosta sees them, of an "Aztec" warrior-dom of Zapata and Pancho Villa. Mayor Sam Yorty plays Janus, smiling sympathizer yet *agent provocateur* who in bad faith counsels *Chicano* insurrection. A crazed Charlie Manson, "acid fascist" (1989b, 98), hovers as presiding spirit of a Los Angeles Acosta terms "the most detestable city on earth" (1989b, 23). Gene McCarthy features as a radical from the mainstream, one politician in two guises. Robert Kennedy enters and exits as both Democratic Party and *campesino* supporting martyr, killed by Sirhan Sirhan as "mysterious Arab" (1989b, 98). A celebrity, and appropriately on-stage, performance of support for his campaign for sheriff is given by "hidden" *Chicanos* like Anthony Quinn and Vicki Carr. Acosta's technique is always to emphasize this duality of time and place, one timeline held inside another.

And, fittingly, Hunter Thompson makes his appearance as "Stonewall," yet another life figure consciously given textual or virtu-al identity. He serves as journalist confessor to the author's own "Zeta." For Acosta, too, has his own "other" self to add to the parade, his own mediation of reality and word, of the turnings of *Chicanismo*, yet also, and whatever the modulations, of American Beat legacy.

VII

Beat *Chicano. Chicano* Beat. Whether as Oscar Zeta Acosta, or as "Oscar Zeta Acosta," the author of *The Autobiography of a Brown Buffalo* and *The Revolt of The Cockroach People* hovers teasingly between and as both. If the Beat pantheon is yet further to be expanded can he not claim overdue rights of application, not to say of acceptance and membership? And if granted a Beat credential how does that challenge, or reenforce, received notions of Beatdom?

A last roster of considerations comes into play. It needs, first, to be asked how "Beat," in truth, the Beats themselves remained—Kerouac in his later ill-spirited phase, Ginsberg in his populist acclaim, Burroughs as elder statesman satirist, Ferlinghetti as "visual" poet, or Snyder out of sorts at forever being identified with the movement.

Acosta himself is essentially a late-1960s writer whose books draw on an America in which Beat, the Beatnik, fuse into other counterculturism—with Bob Dylan as a symptomatic swing figure. Hippie, rock, flower power, the emerging fashionability of Afro dress and related styles, and anti-Vietnam protest, all play into his own "gonzo" politics. He also makes his literary bow just at the moment when "ethnicity" becomes a newly charged working term, one of identity culture in which *Chicanismo*, Brown Power, runs parallel with Black, Native, and Asian calls to self-awareness and activism.

If, in all respects, Acosta emerges as both problematic Beat and problematic Chicano writer, and certainly no respecter of piety in either tradition, that does not close down the invitation or the challenge. Rather it asks that we accord his overlap, his very hybridity, welcome recognition: a *Chicanismo* nothing if not imbued with Beat spirit, a Beatdom nothing if not under "buffalo" and "cockroach" guise.

Notes

1 I have given an account of these poets in Lee (1995, 158–77).
2 See, especially, Rexroth (1957, 28–41).
3 An anthology symptomatic of the time would be Melzer (1971).
4 For an informed and useful account of this British response to The Beats, see Challis (1985, 191–200).
5 See, in this respect Mottram (1972, 1977, 1989, 1992). Mottram was also a greatly influential teacher for my own UK generation of Americanists and, before his death in 1995, I was able to edit a *Festschrift* dedicated to him (Lee 1993).

6 Scholarship on the *Chicano* renaissance has been extensive, but see especially: Sommers and Ybarra-Frausto (1979), Bruce-Novoa (1982), Tatum (1982), Martínez and Lomelí (1986), Shirley and Shirley (1988), Lomelí and Shirley (1989), Saldívar (1990), Calderón and Saldívar (1991), and Lee (1995, 320–39).

7 All three of these manifestos, *Abomunist Manifesto* (1959), *Second April* (1959) and *Does The Secret Mind Whisper?* (1960), the originals now collector's items, are republished in Kaufman (1959).

Works Cited

Acosta, Oscar Zeta. 1971. "Perla is a Pig." *Con Safos* 2.7: 34–46.

———. 1989a. *The Autobiography of a Brown Buffalo*. 1972. Reprint. New York: Vintage.

———. 1989b. *The Revolt of The Cockroach People*. 1973. Reprint. New York: Vintage.

———. 1996. *Oscar "Zeta" Acosta: The Uncollected Works*. Ed. Ilan Stavans. Houston: Arte Público Press.

Allen, Donald, ed. 1960. *The New American Poetry 1945–1960*. New York: Grove Press.

Anaya, Rudolfo. 1972. *Bless Me, Ultima*. Berkeley: Quinto Sol Publications.

Baraka, Amiri (LeRoi Jones). 1964. *Dutchman*. In *Dutchman and The Slave*. New York: Morrow and Co.

———. 1984. *The Autobiography of LeRoi Jones/Amiri Baraka*. New York: Alfred A. Knopf.

Brautigan, Richard. 1964. *A Confederate General from Big Sur*. New York: Grove Press.

Bremser, Bonnie. 1969. *Troia: Mexican Memoirs*. New York: Croton Press.

———. 1971. *For Love of Ray*. London: London Magazine Editions.

Brossard, Chandler. 1952. *Who Walk in Darkness*. New York: New Directions.

Bruce-Novoa, Juan. 1982. *Chicano Authors: A Response to Chaos*. Austin: University of Texas Press.

Burroughs, William. 1962. *The Naked Lunch*. 1959. Reprint. New York: Grove Press.

Calderón, Héctor, and José David Saldívar, eds. 1991. *Criticism in the Borderlands: Studies in Chicano Literature, Culture, and Ideology*. Durham: Duke University Press.

Cassady, Carolyn. 1976. *Heart Beat, My Life with Jack and Neal*. Berkeley: Creative Arts.

———. 1990. *Off the Road, My Years with Cassady, Kerouac and Ginsberg*. New York: Morrow.

Cassady, Neal. 1971. *The First Third*. San Francisco: City Lights Books.

Challis, Chris. 1985. "The Rhythms of My Own Voice: A Brit on the Beats." In *Beat INDEED!*, ed. Rudi Horemans. Antwerp: Restant/Exa Publishers.

Charters, Ann, ed. 1992. *The Portable Beat Reader*. New York: Viking.

Corso, Gregory. 1958. *Gasoline, The Vestal Lady on Brattle and Other Poems*. San Francisco: City Lights Books.

——. 1989. *Minefield, New and Selected Poems*. New York: Thunder's Mouth.

Cremer, Jan. 1965. *I Jan Cremer*. New York: Shorecrest.

di Prima, Diane. 1969. *Memoirs of a Beatnik*. New York: Olympia Press.

——. 1973. *Loba, Part I*. Santa Barbara: Carpa Press.

——. 1978. *Loba: Parts I-VII*. Berkeley: Wingbone Press.

Ferlinghetti, Lawrence. 1958a. *A Coney Island of the Mind*. New York: New Directions.

——. 1958b. "Constantly Risking Absurdity." In *Endless Life*. New York: New Directions.

Ginsberg, Allen. 1956. *Howl and Other Poems*. San Francisco: City Lights Books.

——. 1959. "Notes for *Howl and Other Poems*." Fantasy Records 7006.

——. 1996. Foreword to *The Beat Book: Poems and Fictions of the Beat Generation*, ed. Anne Waldman. Boston: Shambhala.

Gonzalez, Ray. 1993. *Memory Fever*. Seattle, WA: Broken mon Press.

Gonzalez, Rodolfo. 1972. *I Am Joaquín*. New York: 1967. Reprint. Bantam Books.

Holmes, John Clellon. 1952. *Go*. New York: Ace.

——. 1988a. "The Philosophy of the Beat Generation." In *Passionate Opinions: The Cultural Essays*. Fayetteville: University of Arkansas Press.

——. 1988b. "This is the Beat Generation." In *Passionate Opinions: The Cultural Essays*. Fayetteville: University of Arkansas Press.

Huncke, Herbert. 1990. *Guilty of Everything: The Autobiography of Herbert Huncke*. New York: Paragon House.

Jones, Hettie. 1990. *How I Became Hettie Jones*. New York: E. P. Dutton.

Johnson, Joyce. 1983. *Minor Characters*. New York: Simon and Schuster.

Jones, Ted. 1969. *Black Pow-Wow: Jazz Poems*. New York: Hill and Wang.

——. 1970. *Afrodisia*. New York: Hill and Wang.

Kaufman, Bob. 1959. *Abomunist Manifesto*. San Francisco: City Lights Books.

——. 1965. *Solitudes Crowded with Loneliness*. 1959. Reprint. New York: New Directions.

——. 1967. *Golden Sardine*. San Francisco: City Lights Books.

——. 1981. *The Ancient Rains: Poems 1956-1978*. New York: New Directions.

Kaufman, Eileen. 1987. "Laughter Sounds Orange at Night." In *The Beat Vision: A Primary Sourcebook*, ed. Arthur Knight and Kit Knight. New York: Paragon House Publishers.

Kerouac, Jack. 1957. *On the Road*. New York: Viking.

——. 1958a. "Essentials of Spontaneous Prose." *Evergreen Review* 2.5 (Summer).

——. 1958b. *The Subterraneans*. New York: Grove Press.

——. 1959. *Mexico City Blues*. New York: Grove Press.

——. 1988. *Trainsong*. New York: Henry Holt.

Kesey, Ken. 1977. *One Flew Over the Cuckoo's Nest*. New York: Viking/Penguin.

Kingston, Maxine Hong. 1989. *Trickmaster Monkey: His Fake Book*. New York: Knopf.

Kyger, Joanne. 1965. *The Tapestry and the Web*. San Francisco: Four Seasons Foundation.

——. 1983. *Going On, Selected Poems 1958-80*. New York: Dutton.

Lee, Robert A. 1995. "*Chicanismo* as Memory: The Fictions of Rudolfo Anaya, Nash Candelaria, Sandra Cisneros, and Ron Arias." In *Memory and Cultural Politics: New Approaches to American Ethnic Literatures*, ed. Amritjit Singh, Joseph T. Skerrett, Jr., and Robert E. Hogan. Boston: Northeastern University Press.

———. ed. 1993. *A Permanent Etcetera: Cross-Cultural Perspectives on Post-War America*. London: Pluto Press.

———. ed. 1995. "Black Beats: The Signifying Poetry of LeRoi Jones/Amiri Baraka, Bob Kaufman and Ted Joans." In *The Beat Generation Writers*. East Haven, CT: Pluto Press.

Lomelí, Francisco A., and Carl R. Shirley, eds. 1989. *Chicano Writers First Series*. Vol. 82, *Dictionary of Literary Biography*. Detroit: Bruccoli Clark Layman.

Mailer, Norman. 1957. *The White Negro*. San Francisco: City Lights Books.

Martínez, Julio A., and Francisco Lomelí, eds. 1986. *Chicano Literature: A Reference Guide*. Westport, CT: Greenwood Press.

Melzer, David, ed. 1971. *The San Francisco Poets*. New York: Ballantine.

Miller, Henry. 1934. *Tropic of Cancer*. Paris: Obilisk Press.

———. 1939. *Tropic of Capricorn*. Paris: Obilisk Press.

———. 1945. *The Air-Conditioned Nightmare*. New York: Avon.

Mottram, Eric. 1972. *Allen Ginsberg in the Sixties*. Seattle: Unicorn Books.

———. 1977. *William Burroughs: The Algebra of Need*. 1971. Reprint. London: Marion Boyars.

———. 1989. *Blood on the Nash Ambassador: Investigations in American Culture*. London: Hutchinson Radius.

———. 1992. *The Algebra of Need: William Burroughs and the Gods of Death*. London: Marion Boyars.

Murakami, Haruki. 1979. *Kaze No Uta O Kike* (Listen to the Singing of the Wind). Tokyo: Kodansha.

———. 1987. *Norway No Mori* (Norwegian Wood). Tokyo: Kodansha.

Murakami, Ryu. 1976. *Kagirinaku Tomeini Chikai Blue* (Almost Transparent Blue). Tokyo: Kodansha.

Neville, Richard. 1995. *Hippie, hippie shake: the dreams, the trips, the trials, the love-ins, the screw ups . . . the sixties*. London: Bloomsbury.

Nuttall, Jeff. 1968. *Bomb Culture*. London: McGibbon and Kee.

Parkinson, Thomas, ed. 1961. *A Casebook on The Beat*. New York: Thomas Y. Crowell.

Rexroth, Kenneth. 1957. "Disengagement: The Art of the Beat Generation." In *New American Writing*. No. 11. New York: The New York American Library.

Rivera, Tomás. 1971. "*. . . y no se lo tragó la tierra*" (and the earth did not part). Berkeley: Quinto Sol Publications.

Rodriguez, Richard. 1981. *Hunger of Memory*. Boston: Codine.

———. 1992. *Days of Obligation: An Argument with My Mexican Father*. New York: Viking Penguin.

Saldívar, Ramón, ed. 1990. *Chicano Narrative: The Dialectics of Difference*. Madison: University of Wisconsin Press.

Shirley, Carl R, and Paula W. Shirley, eds. 1988. *Understanding Chicano Literature*. Columbia, SC: University of Carolina Press.

Shoji, Kaoru. 1981. *Akazukinchan Ni Ki O Tsukete* (Be Careful, Little Red Riding Hood). Tokyo: Chuokoronsha.

Solomon, Carl. 1966. *Mishaps, Perhaps*. San Francisco: City Lights Books.

Sommers, Joseph, and Tómas Ybarra-Frausto, eds. 1979. *Modern Chicano Writers: A Collection of Critical Essays*. Englewood Cliffs, NJ: Prentice-Hall.

Spellman, A. B. 1965. *The Beautiful Days*. New York: Poets Press.

———. 1966. *Four Lives in the Bepop Business*. New York: Schocken. [Retitled in 1970 as *Black Music: Four Lives*.]

Stavans, Ila, ed. 1996. *Oscar "Zeta" Acosta: The Uncollected Works*. Houston: Arte Público Press.

Tatum, Charles M. 1982. *Chicano Literature*. Boston: Twayne.

Thompson, Hunter. 1972. *Fear and Loathing in Las Vegas*. New York: Random House.

———. 1989. Introduction to *The Autobiography of A Brown Buffalo*. New York: Random House.

Trocchi, Alexander. 1960. *Cain's Book*. New York: Grove Press.

———. 1961. *Young Adam*. London: Heinemann.

Villarreal, José Antonio. 1959. *Pocho*. New York: Doubleday.

Vizenor, Gerald. 1987. *Griever: An American Monkey King in China*. Normal, Ill: Illinois State University/Fiction Collective.

Voznesensky, Andrei. 1967. *Antiworlds*. London: Oxford University Press.

Waldman, Anne. 1983. *Fast Speaking Woman and Other Chants*. San Francisco: City Lights Books.

———. ed. 1996. *The Beat Book: Poems and Fictions of the Beat Generation*. Boston: Shambhala.

Weaver, Richard, Terry Southern, and Alexander Trocchi, eds. 1963. *Writers in Revolt*. New York: Frederick Fells.

Wholly Communion. 1965. London: Lorrimer Films/Publications.

Williams, William Carlos. 1946. *Paterson*. New York: New Directions.

CHAPTER THIRTEEN

The Ambivalence of Kotzeinle's Beat and Bardo Ties
Robert E. Kohn

A neglected, then rediscovered, but still underappreciated American novel is *The Fan Man* by William Kotzwinkle.[1] Its protagonist is Horse Badorties, an aging stoned-out, wild-eyed, unbathed Lower East Side New York hippie, who wears unmatched tennis shoes and carries an incredibly stuffed satchel and a gigantic umbrella. In the few days spanned by the novel, the frenetic Badorties recruits and rehearses his Love Chorus of fifteen-year-old "chicks" for their first public performance, cons NBC for live television coverage of the dubious event but is then so stoned that he misses the performance. The concert goes on successfully without him, while he recovers inner peace and renewal in the park of his childhood memories. This is a strange book, and not surprisingly, it was poorly received by reviewers when it first appeared in 1974. Richard Todd complained that Horse

> says "man" quite a bit. Extrapolating from a few pages, I'd guess the word "man" appears maybe three thousand times? Some days Badorties only says the word "dorky," that being "dorky day" for Horse Badorties. What to make of this? . . . For my part, I think this book is so cute it could hug itself. (Todd 1974, 129)

Valentine Cunningham, likewise confounded by the repetitive "mans" and "dorkys," derided this "bizarre offering" but allowed that "*The Fan Man*'s energetically disposed reflections on urbanity will at least earn it a footnote in someone's thesis on city fiction" (1974, 871). The critics were not aware that "man" and "dorky" have special significance in the context of Kotzwinkle's novel, nor that these "energetically disposed reflections on urbanity" would ultimately make *The Fan Man* a cult book, whose devotees would undertake pilgrimages to Horse Badorties's Lower East Side, walking the inner circle of Tompkins Square Park and climbing the steps to the balcony of St. Mark's Church in the Bowery (St. Nancy's in the novel) to see where Horse might have directed his Love Chorus.

In the one favorable review, an admiring William Kennedy pictures Horse Badorties:

> Wearing one Japanese, one Chinese shoe, uncoding "The Tibetan Book of the Dead" and . . . walk[ing] into American literature a full-blown achievement, a heroic godheaded head, a splendid creep, a sublime prince of the holy trash pile. Send congratulations to William Kotzwinkle, also a hero, man. (Kennedy 1974, 33)

Kennedy's review provides the crucial link between *The Fan Man* and Tibetan Buddhism.

The novel was largely ignored by the literary establishment until fourteen years later, when Herbert Gold, in a collection of essays by "important writers . . . [on] neglected fiction," connected *The Fan Man* to "the Beat period . . . summer-of-love, hippie. . . . Aquarian sensibility . . . LSD, marijuana, . . . and the freedom to be nobody" (1988, 107–08). Although Gold's essay ignores the essential link to Tibetan Buddhism, it does add the other pivotal element, that of the Beat Generation, to understanding *The Fan Man*. The present paper brings together the insights of Kennedy and Gold, and explores the Buddhist and Beat Generation subtexts of the novel and the relationship between them. During the late 60s and early 70s, when Kotzwinkle was composing the novel, there was a productive but controversial interaction of poets and writers of the Beat Generation with Tibetan Buddhist gurus who had fled the Chinese occupation of their country in 1959 and found their way to New York and San Francisco. *The Fan Man* addresses that controversial interaction with a message that has proved prophetic. Early in the novel, we learn that it contains a message: "This is Horse Badorties, man, tape recording a message for the great time capsule to be buried in concrete and dug up tomorrow" (Kotzwinkle 1994, 33). Indeed, it was only two years after *The Fan Man* was first published that the notorious Halloween scandal occurred at the Buddhist Institute in Colorado, followed by further calamitous consequences of the interaction between the Beat Generation and Tibetan Buddhists.

In the first part of this paper, following Kennedy, the Tibetan Buddhist subtext of *The Fan Man* is examined. Many of these connections are traced to seminal works in Tibetan Buddhism by the Oxford-educated American scholar, W. Y. Evans-Wentz (1958, 1960, 1968), who for many years was the only translator of sacred Tibetan texts. The three of his interpretative translations, including *The Tibetan Book of the Dead*, that were published in paperback between 1958 and 1968 appear to have been carefully read by Kotzwinkle.[2] In the second part of the paper, following Gold, a number of themes in the novel are traced back to the literature of the Beat Generation. It is often the case that images and events in *The Fan Man* have simultaneous counterparts in both Tibetan Buddhism and Beat Generation literature. The third part of the paper briefly recounts the controversial interaction between Tibetan Buddhist gurus in America and the poets and authors of the Beat Generation who interacted with them. Although that interaction was richly productive for both sides, there were excesses that appear to have been very disturbing to Kotzwinkle and that motivated his novel. It is suggested that the author's own infatuation with the beatnik culture of Greenwich Village and the Beat Generation writers—not generally known until Lewis's (1996) important biography of this reclusive author was recently published—together with his profound commitment to Buddhism made Kotzwinkle deeply ambivalent about an interaction that could ultimately discredit Buddhism in America. This ambivalence could explain Kotzwinkle's masterful creation of Horse Badorties. Although Kotzwinkle reminds us repeatedly that this hippie character is an undeserving reprobate, he nevertheless manages to create a personality, larger than life, that has inspired an enduring cult following. Kotzwinkle's own ambivalence is successfully transmuted into the artful ambiguity of *The Fan Man*.

The Tibetan Buddhist Subtext of *The Fan Man*

The Buddhist "godheads" to which Kennedy alerts us are three-fold. They are: the semilegendary Padmasambhava, an eighth-century scholar who brought the teachings of Buddhism from India to Tibet and is credited with writing *The Tibetan Book of the Dead*; the deity, Hayagriva, who is Padmasambhava's wrathful manifestation; and the bodhisattva, Avalokiteshvara, who is Padmasambhava's peaceful manifestation (Evans-Wentz 1968, 28, 133, 160). The incessant "dorkys" and ubiquitous "mans" that baffled critics relate to Padmasambhava and Avalokiteshvara. Padmasambhava was venerably called "The Irresistible *Dorje* King"; *Dorje* is Tibetan for "thunderbolt of the gods" and has the spiritual clout of a mantra (115, 159). Except for the "j" instead of a "k," it sounds like the "dorky" that Badorties intones more than a thousand times in one chapter. The Tibetan mantra that is specifically used "for making direct appeal to the bodhisattva, Avalokiteshvara," the well-known *Om Mani Padme Hum*, resonates in the "I am alone in my pad, man" that begins the novel (Kotzwinkle 1994, 9). The second word of the mantra, *mani*, which means "jewel," significantly contains the appellation that appears so many times in *The Fan Man* (Evans-Wentz 1968, 173n). The repeated recitation of this (man)tra is expressed by the hum (which concludes the mantra) of Buddhist prayer wheels, which become the ubiquitous "fans" in the novel.

The Godhead, Hayagriva

The connection of Horse Badorties to the deity, Hayagriva, is made known in the second paragraph, when he needs "a tie, and here is a perfectly good rubber Japanese toy snake, man, which I can easily form into an acceptable knot" and later, when looking into

> the subway window. And since it is dark in the tunnel and lighted in the subway car, I can see my Horse Badorties head reflected with hair sticking out in ninety different directions. Weird looking Horse Badorties. Horse Badorties making demon little ratty face, crawling eyeballs into corners, wrinkling nose up rodentlike, pulling gums back, sticking teeth out, making slow chewing movements. Freaking myself out, man, and several other people in the car. (Kotzwinkle 1994, 10, 29)

The wrathful deity, Hayagriva, is typically depicted in Tantric art with live snakes around his neck, symbolizing his role as "Subjugator of Nagas" (Rhie and Thurman 1991, 54; Lipton and Ragnubs 1996,

113). Although the Nagas are giant eels rather than snakes in *The Fan Man*, there is the same "poisonous lake" in both contexts (Evans-Wentz 1968, 140). Like Badorties, the wrathful Hayagriva has upswept hair and is more fully bearded than other deities. It clinches the identity that Hayagriva is Tibetan for "the Horse-necked one" and that "his primary characteristic is the presence of three horse heads in his red, upswept hair" (Rhie and Thurman 1991, 112-13). The wrinkled-up nose, popping eyes, pulled back gums, and fangs that Badorties projects in the subway window are typical of wrathful deities in Tantric art (see Figure 1). As in *The Fan Man*, they are primarily mental visualizations rather than real beings with supernatural powers. They are often depicted with five sets of arms, which explains Horse's "fifty fingers, all over the strings," standing unevenly on two dissimilar prostrate figures, which explains the "two different shoes, man, one yellow plastic Japanese, the other red canvas Chinese, and my walking, man, will be hopelessly unbalanced" (Kotzwinkle 1994, 17, 124). Horse even speaks of his "third eye," as befits a Tantric deity. Finally, Horse's incredibly packed satchel proxies for the many implements that a Tantric deity carries at once in his multiple arms.

After "making his demon little ratty face . . . what else, man, is needed? Only one other thing, man, and that is a tremendously deep and resonant Horse Badorties Tibetan lama bass note which he is now going to make:'Braaaaaaaaaaaaauuuuuuuuuuuuu mmmmmmmmm-mmnnnnnnnnn'" (Kotzwinkle 1994, 29). This resonating blast from Horse's sphincter, which he repeats in the Museum of Natural History, epitomizes the significant contradictions that pervade *The Fan Man*. It is a gross vulgarity directed at the Indian creator god, Brahma, whose "severed head (in Tantric art is) our own head (and) represents the Buddha's triumph over the temptation to become a god" (Rhie and Thurman 1991, 18). At the same time, the sound evokes the haunting blast of the twenty-foot Tibetan horns and the magnificently drawn-out "om" of the Tibetan monks in polyphonic chorus. In Tibetan Buddhism, moreover, "the nine doors of the body," which include the sphincter, have meditational significance (Evans-Wentz 1958, 200, 200n).

The Godhead Author of Ancient Texts, Padmasambhava

Padmasambhava, whose wrathful emanation is Hayagriva, is the second Buddhist godhead of Horse Badorties (Evans-Wentz 1968, 132–33). His appellation, "*Dorje*," explains the huge umbrella that Horse duplicitously obtains from a hot dog vendor's wagon: "Walking along, man, carrying an incredible umbrella, man, big as a fucking flag pole. . . . I'm so happy, man, to have this umbrella with my insignia on it of crossed hot dogs on a bun" (Kotzwinkle 1994, 32). The umbrella represents the large staff or *khatvanga* that deities, including Padmasambhava, hold in their arm (Lipton and Ragnubs 1996, 224).[3] At the top of the *khatvanga* is the pronged handle commonly called by its Sanskrit name, *vajra*, which is "*dorje*" in Tibetan and hence Horse's "insignia" as well as his "dorky." Likewise the "crossed hot dogs" painted on the big umbrella remind Horse of the double *dorje*, which is one of the important logos of Tibetan Buddhism. There may also be a connection here between "hot dog" and "*k'hot dorje.*"

According to legend, the *Guru Rimpoche* or "Precious Teacher," Padmasambhava, rose from a lotus only eight years after the death in 483 bc of the Great Buddha, and being "immune to illness, old age, and death," survived into the eighth century, when he wrote what became *The Tibetan Book of the Dead* (Evans-Wentz 1968, 25, 27, 157, 179, 192). He is said to have buried his sacred manuscripts in numerous caves and temples, where they remained safely hidden until their miraculous discovery in the fifteenth century, many of them by Karma Lingpa, who is held to be an emanation of Padmasambhava himself (1960, 74). Horse Badorties is connected to Padmasambhava through the latter's spiritual link to Hayagriva and also through Padmasambhava's presumed authorship of *The Tibetan Book of the Dead*, known to Tibetan Buddhists as *The Great Liberation Through Hearing in the Bardo* (Freemantle and Trungpa, 1975). In the very first chapter, Horse announces his entry into the *Bardo* of Dreams; in the twelfth chapter, into the *Bardo* of Rebirth; and in the thirteenth chapter, into the *Bardo* of Death. *Bardo*, which means "in between," in this case between death and rebirth, is repeated hundreds of times in the novel when Badorties narcissistically invokes his own name, which by moving a single letter becomes "*Bardo* ties."

The Tibetan Book of the Dead portrays earthly existence as beginningless rounds of deaths and rebirths called *Samsara*, in which an individual's mind or mental energy passes from one sentient being to another. Such cycles of death and rebirth are suggested by the circular motions of the novel: "I've gone down three flights of steps, man, and I am turning around and going back up them again" (Kotzwinkle 1994, 18), or "I am going an extra stop, man, with my beard caught in the door, so I can approach Chinatown from ten or fifteen blocks below" (30). Similarly, the many fans in the novel connote the cycles of rebirth, just as the Wheel of Life does in Tibetan Buddhism (Evans-Wentz 1958, 357n): "Digging into satchel and withdrawing fan. Turning on the little blades, man, and the warm air is blown against my face and I am alive again, man, in the humming breezes" (Kotzwinkle 1994, 28). The cycles of death and rebirth are poignantly characterized by Horse's getting out of bed and going back again repeatedly in the first chapter, and near the end of the book by his departure from one pad to another: "I leave it behind me, man, stuffed to the ceilings, just as I have left other pads behind me in New Orleans, Acapulco, San Francisco, Miami Beach, Pittsburgh, and Poughkeepsie—sacred temples, man, jammed to the framework with possessions. . . . You have had the Great Death, man" (164-65).

Through meditation exercises, the Tibetan Buddhist seeks to develop a mental energy that will survive his or her own death, and unconsciously cycle itself into an auspicious human womb at a time of conception (Freemantle and Trungpa 1975, 89; Thurman 1994, 18, 28, 57, 68, 113). For Horse Badorties, his tape recorder is that enduring mind or mental energy:

> I'm turning on the tape recorder, man, to record the sound of the door closing as I go out of my pad. . . . It is the sound of liberation, man, from my compulsion to delay over and over again my departure . . . Later on, when I have forgotten who I am, I can always turn on the tape recorder and find out that I am Horse Badorties. (Kotzwinkle 1994, 17, 23)

In the *Bardo* of Dreams, the separated mind may experience the Hungry Ghost Realm: "I cannot speak a moment longer, man, without something to eat. I am weak from hunger, man" (Kotzwinkle 1994, 12), or the Realm of Hell: "while other passengers are sweltering in the summer heat, Horse Badorties swelters twice as much because he is wearing an overcoat (29)," or the Realm of Animals, where a cockroach is reading a book about the Dalai Lama and a crab is trying to climb a tree, or finally the Realm of Gods, which, because Buddhism is non-theistic, is the realm of pride, ego-intoxication and self-absorption that befits the extreme narcissism of Horse Badorties. But there are also hopeful periods in which Horse is in the Human Realm of the *Bardo*, developing "awareness of the immediacy of death" and the sadness of *Samsara* (Thurman 1994, 19–33). "Lonely life, man, on the planet Earth. I'd recognize it anywhere, gravity holding me down.... The only way to get off the earth, man, is die, and I am definitely dying, man. The all-important question is: Will I be able to take fan satchel and umbrella with me when I go?" (Kotzwinkle 1994, 89).

The Godhead Semideity, Padmasambhava

The connection of *The Fan Man* to Padmasambhava goes beyond the latter's legendary authorship of *The Tibetan Book of the Dead*. According to Evans-Wentz, Padmasambhava would "drink to the point of intoxication, and taught his disciples to do likewise.... [He had an] utter disregard of social, moral, and dogmatic religious conventionalities or established codes of conduct.... Conventional concepts of sex morality [were] completely ignored by him" (1968, 32, 35, 36, 120n).[4] With his stoned-out addiction to marijuana, his inveterate deceitfulness, and his depraved quest for fifteen-year-old "chicks who will be there, man, and perhaps, man, I will stuff my meat in their buns (Kotzwinkle 1994, 38-39)," Horse Badorties is following in the footsteps of the Padmasambhava that Evans-Wentz depicts. But the issue of sexuality in *The Fan Man* is complex. According to Tibetan Buddhist literature, the voluptuous maidens in Tantric art are intended to channel sexuality into spirituality. "Overtly sexual portrayals of union between male and female deities, commonly found in Tibetan art, are not meant to be regarded sensually, but rather are symbolic of the union of wisdom (female) and compassion (male), the two qualities necessary to achieve enlightenment" (Lipton and Ragnubs 1996, 32).[5] Often, the male deity in these unions is standing, which explains Horse's "We'll have to do it standing up, baby" (Kotzwinkle 1994, 50). Although his underage partners are inexplicably attracted to him, Horse is apparently not yet ready to achieve enlightenment through the union of wisdom and compassion, for he consistently eludes intercourse.

But there is ambiguity in his sexuality. Based on the legends recounted by Evans-Wentz, Padmasambhava frequently transformed himself into birds, even a pair of hawks. Accordingly Horse Badorties, remembering from past lives as a bird how to "make flapping motions with [his] arms" (Kotzwinkle 1994, 103), tells his blonde chick "I'm far-out, man, looking out over the rooftops, like Hawkman himself, and I am flying, man" (138). Because it is time for the Love Chorus rehearsal, Horse once again puts off sex, suspiciously telling the blonde chick "Leave this window open, baby, to air the place out. So long, so long, man" (139). Could the speaker actually be Padmasambhava, wanting to relive the sexual exploits that Evans-Wentz attributes to him? Perhaps it is really that same Padmasambhava, who cannot resist the "sweet blonde chick . . . beautiful blue eyes . . . nice skin . . . gorgeous boobs" (136) and who has simultaneously become *both* Hawkman and Horse so that the latter can go to his rehearsal while the former rapes the girl. Tellingly, Horse is not surprised when the girl informs him of her assault.

The one admirable quality that Horse and Padmasambhava share is their musical ability. Horse is "master of every opening and closing rhythm pattern known to the mind of man" (Kotzwinkle 1994, 123) and identifies with the original "master musician," Padmasambhava, when he remembers that "Long time ago, man, I used to float around in the sky with a sitar, a celestial musician, man, who has fallen from the heights" (89). Many events of Padmasambhava's life, according to Evans-Wentz took place in caves that ancient Buddhist monks carved in mountainsides. The openings that Horse chops out from one apartment to another evoke a similar chopping of rock in the Aurangabad Caves of southeastern India fifteen hundred years ago (Berkson, 1986, 2). Perhaps Horse is remembering his past lives in such caves, when he tells his chick,

> That is correct, baby, a hole in the wall, which I took the precaution of chopping out yesterday. If the landlord should by any chance discover that I am living in this number two pad, it won't matter, because we will now slip through this secret passage—go ahead, baby, through those broken slats and falling plaster—through this hole in the wall to my Horse Badorties number three pad. (Kotzwinkle 1994, 133)

Just as archaeologists call the rooms at Aurangabad "Cave 1, Cave 2, etc.," so does Horse identify his pads by numbers. He calls them "pads" because the Sanskrit word for lotus is *padma* and the word for risen is *sambhava*; so like the Precious Teacher, Horse Badorties rises from his *padma(n)*.

It is evident to Horse and to us that he is living an "abominable life," perhaps because of bad karma from some previous life, and that his life remains abominable until the last chapter, when for once he goes,

> straight out the door, without breakfast, without looking around, without fucking off, without looking over my piles of stuff. I am in the actual sunlight of the street already, man, closing my store, and walking along. Man, I must be straightening out my life, if I am able to leave my store-pad so easily. I must be shaping up, man. . . . (Kotzwinkle 1994, 179–80)

Having formulated his plans to revisit Van Cortlandt Park, Horse congratulates himself: "What a wonderful and well-reasoned program this is, Horse Badorties. You should be a college professor." (177)[6]

The Bodhisattva Godhead, Avalokiteshvara

The peaceful deity, Avalokiteshvara, is the highly reverenced manifestation of Padmasambhava, and hence his connection to Horse (Rhie and Thurman 1991, 54; Evans-Wentz 1968, 145, 160, 160n). It is believed that Avalokiteshvara "takes successive human births as the Dalai Lama" (Lopez 1996, 27; Evans-Wentz 1968, 160n), which explains "Horse Badorties, man, having a taste of good old samadi, feeling like the Dalai Lama" (Kotzwinkle 1994, 138). Avalokiteshvara is the most important of all bodhisattvas, holy people that have renounced the opportunity to enter *Nirvana* and that continue to be reborn again and again in order to help other people achieve the Great Liberation and become Buddhas (Evans-Wentz 1968, 173n). The emphasis on bodhisattvas is "the most famous feature of the *Mahayana*," which means great vehicle or great path. The reincarnated faithful, conscious of their past lives and seeking enlightenment, are called *yogins*. Evans-Wentz claims that *yogins* and bodhisattvas recognize one another instantly (1960, 171n). In *The Fan Man*, this code for recognition appears to be "man"; even women are sometimes addressed as "man" by Horse, for as Evans-Wentz explains, *(man)i* is part of the mantra for appealing to Avalokiteshvara, whose Tibetan name can either mean "the keen-seeing lord" or "the lord who is seen within" (1968, xxvi; 1958 233n). Thurman believes that "Companions may seem to be ordinary beings, but they are actually Buddhas and Bodhisattvas, there to help you realize your own enlightenment" (1994, 70). That is the subtext when Horse learns that his neighbor, Luke, is going to Japan: "There goes Luke, man, down the steps for the last time, to a Buddhist monastery. He's on the Path, man, and so am I" (Kotzwinkle 1994, 61).

When Horse finally emerges from a subway train that has typically taken him past his destination, he goes: "Up the subway steps, man, walk up, see where I am. I am on Brooklyn Heights, man, there is the sea below. A wild wind is blowing and the sun is dropping toward the ocean. The water is gold and the tugboat goes through the gold. I am with you again on the Heights, man" (Kotzwinkle 1994, 117). With that startling line, readers sense that they too may be in the Human Realm with their own golden bodhisattva. In the very next paragraph, Horse speaks of "my head on backwards" (119). Later, at the church, "I give them my face in three-quarter profile," and then "I am peering at them from on high, sideways" (170). These facial allusions evoke familiar portrayals of the eleven-headed Avalokiteshvara.[7] The many heads, especially when each is reinforced by a third eye, enhance Avalokiteshvara's ability to recognize aspiring *yogins*: "Apply to third eye, stimulate visions" (122).

The master musicianship of Padmasambhava and the *mahayana* aspirations of Avalokiteshvara are joined when "Maestro Badorties keeps the Love Chorus together, man, in supreme polyphonic harmony. This music, man, is from the angel of radiant joy in the central realm of the densely-packed, and when it is done right, it elevates my hot dog soul to the region of ecstasy" (Kotzwinkle 1994, 45). The music of the Love Chorus dates back to the fifteenth century, when polyphonic singing began in Tibetan monasteries. Even today, Mullin and Weber claim that

> performing or hearing multiphonic singing is considered to be a transformative experience, that the vibration that the music creates clears and balances the subtle body and brings the blessings of the "dakas" and "dakinis" from etheric dimensions into the human world. Negative energies are dispersed and innate radiance and clarity are reinforced. (Mullin and Weber 1996, 70, 118–23)

The *dakas* and *dakinis* are the male and female angels "of radiant joy," which appear in the "central realm" of the lineage "trees" in Tibetan tangka scroll paintings, which are indeed "densely-packed" with row after row of buddhas, lamas, mediational deities, *dakas* and *dakinis*.[8] The fifteen-year-old chicks that Horse recruits for the Love Chorus appear to be earthly manifestations of these *dakini* angels, continuing their ancient pedagogical relationship—mentioned in a footnote by Evans-Wentz—with their Precious Mentor, Padmasambhava (1968, 177n).

For "the final purification process in music" (Kotzwinkle 1994, 170), the Love Chorus must take the imaginary "Uncle Skulky out and air him, man, let him run around and skulk a bit, after which he goes back down into his horrible secret chamber" (170). This suggests the popular "Black Hat Dance," described by Mullin and Weber, in which Tibetan monks wearing skull masks do a skulking, weaving dance that symbolizes their release of "old negativities" and their transcendence over ego-centeredness (1996, 72). In *The Fan Man*, these are equivalent to "Uncle Skulky, man . . . the impossibly mad relative we all have sleeping in our souls" (Kotzwinkle 1994, 170).

Nirvana versus Samsara

From the third chapter on, Horse longs for a particular tree in Van Cortlandt Park, and when he finally gets there in the last chapter of the book, he,

> remembers, man, he remembers sweet and innocent childhood here in the park. When I was a little kid, man, I used to see strange things in my head, man. Used to see guys in turbans, chanting. And Chinese cats, man, playing flute. And a mountain, man, in Tibet, where they were blowing twenty-foot horns, man. I came into this world, man, remembering where I'd been. (Kotzwinkle 1994, 185)

While Horse is remembering his past lifetimes, just as The Buddha did under the Bo Tree when he attained *Nirvana* at Bodh Gaya, the Love Chorus in Tompkins Square Park is struggling to carry on without him. The spaced-out Horse Badorties has inexplicably gotten it in his head that the concert is scheduled for the following day. This final chapter of *The Fan Man* resounds like the grand finale of an opera in which singers, situated in separate times or places but on the same stage and supposedly unseen and unheard by each other, join their voices in rich duets, trios and quartets. While Badorties meditates under his tree: "Different lifetimes gathering around, and I go in and out, man of ever-widening bands of sensitive awareness" (183), the saxophone player calls for him in vain: "Hello, Horse, man—please, man, where are you? I can't hold them off any longer, man. The NBC director is getting nervous, man, over—'You can't reach him, Frank?'—No, Father, he's out of walkie-talkie range" (184). Frank has no choice but to lead the concert: "Where are you, Horse, you motherfucker, I never directed no chorus before, man, and my hand is shakin" (186).

But there is an alternative interpretation of this *Nirvana-Samsara* duet. Perhaps, Horse has *purposely* forgotten the date. The emphasis shifts to the saxophone player, who for the first time is identified by his proper name. We remember that "the trombone and saxophone are gut musicians, man, go anywhere, play anything, not afraid to leap around with their axes, man" (Kotzwinkle 1994, 125). Because Tantric deities typically carry a battle ax in one of their many hands, it is now apparent that the saxophone player is a Tantric *yogin* in the *Bardo* preparing for his own enlightenment, and that Avalokiteshvara is there to assist (Freemantle and Trungpa 1975, 60; Rhie and Thurman 1991, 18). The triumph of the final chapter belongs to Frank, the saxophone player. He directs the Love Chorus masterfully. Whereas Horse would surely have had an ugly confrontation with the obstinate Puerto Rican drummers, Frank successfully engages them to join in:

> We are singin it perfect, man, the chicks, Father, me, and the PR drummers, man, it's real, man, it is workin out, now, to the end, man, keep them all harmonic, don't nobody fall off the notes, man. The chicks, man, their hair is blowin out, risin gently from the breezes of the fans, man. Horse's fans, man, keep you cool and in the music. That's all, that's it, now, now, now, hold that note soprano bass tenor alto hold it, let it shimmer and shine up there in the evenin air, in the trees in the quiet. (Kotzwinkle 1994, 188)

In this alternative interpretation, it is Frank that is achieving *Nirvana*, while Horse remains behind in *Samsara* to continue helping other *yogins* achieve enlightenment.

Evans-Wentz hails the awakening from cycles of Samsara and the attainment of Nirvana that comes with "the Supreme Realization that both Nirvana and the Samsara are eternally indistinguishably one.... [This merging] constitutes the Great Liberation" of *The Tibetan Book of the Dead* (1968, 70-71). The finale of *The Fan Man* epitomizes the grand conjunction of *Nirvana*, which is the bliss of Horse "dreaming deep into my ancient feelings, man ... [going] in and out, man, of ever-widening bands of sensitive awareness" (Kotzwinkle 1994, 183) while the saxophone player is still agonizing in *Samsara*: "Man, my guts are jumpin, man, this conductin gives you an ulcer, man" (188). Alternatively Frank is soaring in *Nirvana*: "we are together, man, the chords are sweet the way Horse likes them, and strong, risin up through the trees, man, out over the park and I am flappin my wings, man, takin off into the sky, lookin for Horse, man, where are you, man?" (187), while Horse, consumed by fantasies of urban violence and Ho Chi Minh, continues to flounder in *Samsara*.

The merging of *Nirvana* and *Samsara*, to attain the Great Liberation of *The Tibetan Book of the Dead*, is not the only merging of opposites in *The Fan Man*. From the first chapter on, Horse speaks in contradictions: "Very good, that was terrible, the worst singing I ever heard except for one of two moments which were magnificent beyond relief" (Kotzwinkle 1994, 45) or "music should be the only thing I ever do. Which is why I am going to become a used-car salesman instead, man" (124). The novel builds on contradiction, laying the foundation for the author's "message for the great time capsule," that the excesses of the Beat Generation, the glorification of drugs and sexual anarchy, are contrary to traditional Buddhist purity and practice. These contradictions ultimately reflect the underlying ambivalence of Kotzwinkle himself.

The calm ending of the novel is reminiscent of the downpour that struck while The Great Buddha, ill and near death, was meditating under his chosen tree. The thunder, lightening and torrential rain caused his younger disciples to take cover under trees, while The Buddha remained unmoved (Kalupahana and Indrani1982, 220-21). Feeling raindrops, Horse finally opens his gigantic umbrella:

> It is up, man. It is up and over my head. Listen, man, to the raindrops beating down on it. The soccer players are running for cover, man, in the bushes, but I'm covered already, man. I am slowly heading across the huge green lawn toward the subway, man, satchel in one hand, umbrella in the other, stepping through puddles. Everything is cool, man, beneath the great umbrella. Horse Badorties is ready for the monsoon. (Kotzwinkle 1994, 191)

Likewise, it was after Padmasambhava became the Enlightened One, that Evans-Wentz recounts how "there was a fall of rain for seven days, all diseases disappeared, and . . . lucky signs appeared" (1968, 159).

The Beat Generation Subtext of *The Fan Man*

Much of the imagery of *The Fan Man* can also be traced to the literature of the Beat Generation and the personalities of the authors who defined it. Attracted to Buddhism, these authors allied themselves with Tibetan teachers who were developing a faithful following in the United States. The interchange of cultures was intellectually and spiritually productive, but in some quarters, the merging of Buddhist meditation and ego nullification with the Beat Generation's glorification of psychedelic drugs and free love was ominously excessive. This gave rise to a spirited controversy, in the context of which, Horse Badorties's ambiguous role in *The Fan Man* can be understood.

The Fan Man's Link to Beat Literature

In his "Footnote to Howl," Allen Ginsberg declares that "The bum is as holy as the seraphim! the madman is holy as you my soul are holy" (1956, 21). Likewise, Jack Kerouac's most famous novel finds the frenetic Dean Moriarty in,

> tattered shoes . . . not shaved, his hair . . . wild and bushy, his eyes bloodshot . . . goofing all the time . . . the HOLY GOOF . . . BEAT-the root, the soul of Beatific . . . Angel Dean . . . holy con-man . . . preparations had to be made to widen the gutters of Denver and foreshorten certain laws to fit his suffering bulk and bursting ecstasies. [The] moth-eaten overcoat he brought specially for the freezing temperatures of the East. (Kerouac 1991, 188, 194, 195, 211, 213, 259, 309)

but wears in warmer San Francisco, further identifies Dean, who is Neal Cassady in real life, as a model for Horse Badorties, who likewise wears an old overcoat in summer. Horse Badorties is also modeled after Ray Smith, narrator of *The Dharma Bums*, who wears the familiar "earmuff cap," looks like a "Bodhisattva in its frightful aspect," and remembers where he had "worn out a little path going to meditate under a favorite baby pine." Despite the orgies that went on around him, Ray "never had girls of [his] own," not even when "a beautiful brunette consented to go up the hill." Like Horse, he was either interrupted at the critical moment or else had an "overwhelming urge to close his eyes in company" and meditate (Kerouac, 1958, 26, 106, 147, 152, 153).

Allen Ginsberg and Jack Kerouac were themselves models for Horse Badorties. Ginsberg surely looked the part with his full beard and long hair, while his East Village apartment, like Horse's, was furnished with "discarded furniture found on the street" (Schumacher 1992, 405–06). Indeed, Horse's avoidance of sexual intercourse with his "chicks" has an entirely different interpretation in the context of Ginsberg's homosexuality. That they are called "chicks" in *The Fan Man* evokes Kerouac's own term for the dozens of girls he psychotically slept with in the few years after *On the Road* was published, while Horse's offensive slurs of Puerto Ricans seems to have been inspired by the intense prejudices that Kerouac inherited from his parents (Nicosia 1983, 105, 415, 555, 560, 582, 642).

Many of the arcane images in *The Fan Man* can be traced to Kerouac's novels. The cockroaches that navigate in paper boats and read sacred texts in Horse's apartments are reminiscent of long passages in Kerouac in which the humanity of cockroaches, "their sense of discretion, their feelings, their emotions, their thoughts" are praised (1950, 403). The outlandish scene in *The Fan Man* in which a chick gets off the subway "in a hurry, leaving behind her on the seat, a TURD, man" (Kotzwinkle 1994, 39) connects to the astonishing parable in Kerouac of the disciple who upon asking his Zen Master "What is the Buddha?," "experienced sudden enlightenment" at the master's reply that "The Buddha is a dried piece of turd" (1958, 136). The "crazy colored guy" playing bongo drums in *The Dharma Bums*, that everybody declared "must be a Bodhisattva," may be the model for Frank, the saxophonist in *The Fan Man*, while Kotzwinkle's license to use so many words with "fuck" in their roots is authorized early in *The Dharma Bums*, "fuck being a dirty word that comes out clean" (Kerouac 1958, 14, 154). Horse's lawlessness in passing bad checks and stealing, his drunken stupors, his frenetic pursuit of multiple sexual liaisons, his penchant for entering his pads by climbing through windows, and even his memory of dying and being reborn numberless times, all have precedence in the antics of the two main characters in *On the Road* (1991, 44, 60, 62, 173, 220–21).

The Beat Generation and Tibetan Buddhism

The seemingly irrelevant incident in *The Fan Man* in which Horse's neighbor, Luke, announces that he is going to Japan to enter a Buddhist monastery is a reference to Japhy Snyder in *The Dharma Bums*, who sails for Japan to stay in a monastery. In reality, Japhy

Snyder is the poet Gary Snyder, who, like Ginsberg and Kerouac, began his studies of Buddhism in the 50s (Fields 1992, 210-11, 213). Their friend, Timothy Leary, who for a while elevated psychedelics to the level of academic research at Harvard, used *The Tibetan Book of the Dead* as a guidebook in his writing (Leary, Metzner, and Alpert 1964). Leary is not mentioned in *The Fan Man*, but his presence there is implied by Kotzwinkle's references to *I Ching*, the ancient Chinese writings in which rectangular diagrams containing whole and half lines are used to divine fate. Leary featured a different one of these cryptic diagrams along with an esoteric saying from the *I Ching* on the first page of each of the chapters, called "trips," in his book, which he "dedicated to the ancient sacred sequence of turning-on, tuning-in, and dropping-out" (1968). The esoteric sayings from the *I Ching* are parodied in *The Fan Man* with the astrological imitation, "A mixed or muddled order and chaos threatens" (Kotzwinkle 1994, 25).

According to Fields, it was through Chögyam Trungpa, the eleventh incarnation of Trungpa Rimpoche and the leading Tibetan-born interpreter writing in English, that Allen Ginsberg became part of the Tibetan Buddhist establishment in America (1992, 367). Chögyam Trungpa is another of the many models for Horse Badorties. When Trungpa first came to the United States in May of 1970, his

> appearance was disquieting and puzzling to many. . . . He ignored health food and ate whatever he wanted, from Japanese haute-cuisine—in New York he managed to find an all-night sushi bar off Forty-second Street—to good old English roast beef. He also drank and smoked without apology, and sampled all the good things that Western civilization had come up with, from the halls of Oxford to the then-fashionable psychedelics—which he laughingly characterized as a kind of double illusion or sugar samsara. (Fields 1992, 309)

Trungpa's late-night culinary expeditions are replayed in *The Fan Man*, as is the sensitive issue of eating meat. The "rotten" in Ginsberg's famous poem, "who cooked rotten animals lung heart feet tail . . . dreaming of the pure vegetable kingdom" (1956, 13) resonates when Horse, in the bake shop, longs for "the hot-stuffed buns, stuffed with ground-up cooked-up delicious dead cow, turn rotten in my guts fuck my mind up with death anxiety putrification. I can't do it, man. I am passing up the stuffed meatbun. . ." (Kotzwinkle 1994, 38).[9]

Chögyam Trungpa was a distinguished teacher, who, though he learned English late in life, wrote important works in that language including a translation with Francesca Fremantle of *The Tibetan Book of the Dead* (1975). The Naropa Institute, that he started in Colorado as the Rocky Mountain Dharma Center, eventually became the first Buddhist-inspired college to achieve accreditation in the United States. It may be significant that earlier in his life, Trungpa undertook a retreat to the very cave in Bhutan "where Padmasambhava had meditated more than a thousand years before," for in many ways he was a modern version of the first Guru Rimpoche, Padmasambhava (Fields 1992, 301). Trungpa "became controversial for teaching a 'crazy wisdom' that allegedly justified his own public drunkenness, sexual promiscuity, and violence" (Kamenetz 1994, 8).[10] It may have encouraged Trungpa's excesses that the anti-establishment poet, Allen Ginsberg, had a student/teacher relationship with him and taught a course in "spiritual poetics" at his Institute. The image of "The Lion of Dharma"—a name given to Ginsberg by Trungpa—chanting lengthy mantras at his well-attended public lectures epitomizes the amalgamation of the Beat Generation and Tibetan Buddhism (Fields 1992, 316-17).

The Impact of the Beat Generation on Tibetan Buddhism in America

The Hope and the Reality

In the 1950s, there was great hope that the Buddhism of the Beat Generation, the "Zen Free Love Lunacy" and the "Zen intellectual artistic Buddhism" of Allen Ginsburg, Gary Snyder and Jack Kerouac,[11] would complement and enrich the traditional Buddhism of the Tibetan monks (Fields 1992, 222). Optimism persisted well into the 60s that psychedelic drugs could productively shortcut and enrich the meditative experience. Gary Snyder, who is Japhy Ryder in *The Dharma Bums* and Luke in *The Fan Man*, lauded the "remarkable results [that students of the sacred texts achieve] when they take LSD. . . . They often feel they must radically reorganize their lives to harmonize with such insights" (1969, 109). However, these expectations became increasingly controversial and were challenged in a series of papers in the October 1971 issue of *The Eastern Buddhist*.

Kotzwinkle appears to have taken a strong stand alongside the traditionalists, using *The Fan Man* as his vehicle. He clearly ridicules the "rapturous blissful state" (138), the "incredible subtleties . . . of rare and extraordinary design" (42) that allegedly appear after only a few puffs of "sacred smoke." The "chicks" of the Love Chorus, who are promised "instant musicianship," supposedly attain it when they are finally "making reptilian Horse Badorties faces" (146). To the contrary, "reptilian" connotes Timothy Leary's account of a psychedelic trip turned nauseous, in which Peter Orlovsky's gestures look "REPTILIAN" (1968, 118),[12] and may even allude to the wretched addicts "known as Reptiles" in that nadir of Beat literature, *Naked Lunch*, by Burroughs (1959, 51).

Kotzwinkle's disdain for "Beat Buddhism" is epitomized by the repulsive character of Horse Badorties. We are continually reminded of his unsavory faults, his blatant inconsiderateness, inveterate deceitfulness, ethnic prejudice, vulgar behavior, willful destruction of private property, entrapment of teenage girls, foisting of drugs on minors, passing bad checks, using foul language, stealing, staying stoned, never bathing except by accident, and what is significantly contrary to Buddhist precept, his unremitting egotism. It is true that Horse will eventually be enlightened. The end of the novel suggests that he will, and indeed it is a basic tenet of Buddhism that the worst among us, even murderers, will eventually, if not in the present lifetime then in some future lifetime, attain *nirvana*. In the meantime, Horse Badorties is visiting a lot of bad *karma* on the planet.

Kotzwinkle's "message for the great time capsule," his warning that psychedelic drugs and "free love lunacy" would be harmful to Buddhism, turned out to be prophetic. Two years after *The Fan Man* was published, a scandal occurred at Chögyam Trungpa's Colorado Institute. A prominent poet and his female companion, attending a three-month study seminar there, had not expected that participants would be abruptly required by the drunken Trungpa to remove all their clothing at a Halloween party and thereby symbolize their necessary "sacrifice of ego" and "exposure of . . . neuroses." As Sanders (1979), Clark (1980) and Schumacher (1992, 612-15) tell the story, the two escaped to their room, only to be besieged and after a bloody assault, led back to the hall and forcibly disrobed by Trungpa's guards. In the course of this ugly incident, Trungpa hinted his disappointment that a woman "of Oriental heritage . . . would be seeing a white man," at which the poet's companion responded by calling him a Nazi. Rick Fields does not mention this sordid incident in his history of American Buddhism, but it appears to be the first sign "that the meeting of East and West heralded by the heady sixties and early seventies (would turn) into nothing less than a head-on collision" (1992, 362). The collision that Fields documents, that began, remarkably, with one of the models for Horse Badorties, was the abuse of power, particularly in sexual and financial areas, by both Asian and American teachers of Buddhism. It became public knowledge by the early 80s that respected teachers had been having affairs with their students (Fields 1992, 362-67). A high-placed regent appointed by Chögyam Trungpa, had AIDS, kept it a secret, and believing that his faith would cleanse him, infected one of his students. The unraveling of institutional Buddhism was painful but led to bold reexamination and reform. In retrospect, it is unfortunate that the Tibetan Buddhist community ignored *The Fan Man* (there is no mention of William Kotzwinkle in Rick Field's history), for had its message been heard and understood, there might have been less of the "obedience, devotion, and blind acceptance" of teachers by their students that the Dalai Lama openly blamed for this sad setback of Tibetan Buddhism in America (Fields 1992, 379).

Kotzwinkle's Ambivalence

The Fan Man is William Kotzwinkle's masterpiece. The repugnant actions of its omnipresent protagonist convey the author's "message for the great time capsule," that the beatnik dissoluteness of *On the Road*, *The Dharma Bums*, *Naked Lunch*, and *High Priest* has no place in traditional Buddhism. The astonishing fact for American literature is that the disreputable Horse Badorties would become what Wakefield calls "a consummate hippie" (1996, 31), that he would inspire a cult following for the book, causing it to be republished six times (including translations into German and Spanish) and to become what Lewis calls "an almost sacred text" (1991, 790). That Horse Badorties's "abominable life" would inspire a sacred text is a significant achievement in American literature, an achievement engendered by Kotzwinkle's own ambivalence regarding the hippie writers.

Kotzwinkle's love for traditional Tibetan Buddhism is evident, not only in *The Fan Man's* sacred imagery and scholarly foundation, but also in his reverent remembrance in *Doctor Rat* that,

> The musicians of Tibet once fashioned great horns, some as long as fifty feet, which they blew down the Himalaya mountain passes. These were their offerings to the Absolute. They were, as you know, wiped out by war, and few men now living can produce that music. Men have forgotten what the whales, with their great brains, do not forget. . . . That the purpose of our lives is to celebrate the grandeur of the cosmos. (Kotzwinkle 1976, 102)

The Buddhist belief in the human sentience of whales, rats, and other animals, that motivates *Doctor Rat*, is carried still further in Kotzwinkle's *The Bear Went Over the Mountain* (1996), while his faith in Buddhist *karma* surely underlies the "Fragments of Papyrus from the Temple of the Older Gods" (1998).

Only recently, and fortuitously for the present essay, has more insight on Kotzwinkle's ambivalence come to light. Leon Lewis has gotten past the famous reclusiveness of the novelist and published a substantial biographical study, revealing that Kotzwinkle's early writings were "shaped by the beat writers he read in college," that he had "hitchhiked to New York City in 1957 and embraced the beatnik culture of Greenwich Village," and that when he listened to Jack Kerouac reading poetry, it struck him "like a rocket!" (1996, 99, 101). One wonders whether the impressionable young Kotzwinkle was, in fact, attracted to Tibetan Buddhism by the examples of Kerouac, Ginsberg, and other Beat writers.

How ambivalent Kotzwinkle must have felt when he became aware in the 60s that the writers he cherished were undermining the religion he worshipped. This ambivalence reveals itself, on the one hand, in the sordid excesses of Horse Badorties, and, on the other, in the sweet rapport that the scruffy narrator establishes with his readers, in the sadness he confesses, and in the energetic humor of his exploits.[13] Nowhere is that ambivalence more extreme than in the sphincter of *The Fan Man*, which at best is the drawn-out "Horse Badorties Dalai Lama bass note" (Kotzwinkle 1994, 107) that resonates with meditational significance, but, at worst, the disgusting "asshole [that] started talking on its own" in Burrough's *Naked Lunch* (1959, 132-33). Understanding Kotzwinkle's ambivalence is the key to understanding *The Fan Man's* ambiguity.

Concluding Remarks

Although it is an incredibly short paperback, barely 140 pages long when one deducts for its fully and partially blank pages, *The Fan Man* carries with it so many levels of meaning and interpretation that it is the equivalent of a much longer, denser tome. There is a subtext of Tibetan Buddhism and another, often overlapping, subtext of the Beat Generation. There may also be a political subtext, for Kotzwinkle cannot help but reflect some of the deep resentment that the Tibetan Buddhist community feels toward the Chinese Communists for an invasion that took away their homeland, caused the deaths of more than a million Tibetans and destroyed 90 percent of their cultural artifacts. Perhaps, the "Commander Schmuck Imperial Red Chinese Army hat" with "the thick pile-stuffed earflaps" (Kotzwinkle 1994, 23) represents the deafened ears of the conqueror; the "precious valuable worthless objects" (33) that Horse buys in Chinatown are an indictment of the Chinese materialistic economy that replaced the Tibetan religious culture; and the hundred-year-old Chinese eggs that "have been allowed to age for an entire year" (39) are a metaphor for the invaders' deceitful promises.

There may also be an autobiographical subtext to the novel. That so much of Horse's business is transacted from a telephone booth reflects Kotzwinkle's own proclivity to keep "in touch with editors and agents from a public pay phone" ("Paperback Talk" 1982, 31). Greenwich Village was an exciting place to live, and as a resident, Kotzwinkle appears to have been influenced by Richard Foreman, whose *avant-garde* Ontological-Hysteric Theatre productions began in 1968 in the Village. The first play, *Angelface*, in which a celestial being appears on the stage, thrusting his body forward and flapping his wings, plus Foreman's theatrical philosophy that "calls for an emptying of the mind in the experience of art, so that the mind is more alert, more awake," is strongly reminiscent of Horse's direction of the Love Chorus (Davy 1981, 1, 199). So also is Foreman's call for "a courageous tuning of the old self to new awareness" (Carlson 1984, 463). It also appears that Kotzwinkle was strongly influenced by Thomas Pynchon's *The Crying of Lot 49*, which may have been the conceptual model for *The Fan Man*. Both are novels of quest built around *The Tibetan Book of the Dead*. Significantly, the interim between death and rebirth in the *Bardo* and the span of Pynchon's novel are both exactly 49 days (Newman, 1986, 82; Petillon, 1991, 137; Chambers, 1992, 116).[14] Pynchon's heroine is O(edipa) M(aas), and, according to Petillon, Dr. Hilarius is Timothy Leary (1991, 127). The "used-car salesman" that Horse plans to become (Kotzwinkle 1994, 124) is an allusion to Oedipa's husband, Mucho Maas, who, like Horse, uses psychedelic drugs and pursues teen-aged girls, while Horse's Hayagriva face (see Figure 1) appears earlier in Pynchon (1966, 18). The "Not so loud, hey . . . They're watching. With binoculars." in Pynchon (1966, 57) is the kind of contradiction that Kotzwinkle (1974, 45, 124) plays with, while the "humming out there," that is a major focus of Petillon's interpretation of *The Crying of Lot 49*, becomes the pervasive humming of fans in *The Fan Man* (1991, 130-34). Both novels conclude with similarly intense ambiguity.

The richness of *The Fan Man*, its many levels of interpretation, and its exquisitely cadenced sentences, some of which are reproduced in this paper, remain to be more fully appreciated, especially by scholars. It is surprising to learn from the current publisher that *The Fan Man* does not appear to be "part of any major university's curriculum or suggested reading list"[15] and from Lewis that a consensus of critics "has kept serious studies of Kotzwinkle's writings out of academic journals" (1996, 106). However, the omission of such post-beat masterpieces from university curricula and scholarly discourse is now being confronted (Skerl 2000), and studies such as the present essay may be ". . . only the beginning of what is to come" (2).

A quarter of a century has passed since *The Fan Man* was first published. It remains a time capsule of an interesting period in American literature when poets and authors of the Beat Generation embraced an esoteric, eastern religion. "Only now" writes Tonkinson, "with the . . . revival of popular interest in the Beats are we beginning to appreciate the pivotal role these writers played in the transmission of Buddhism to America" (1995, viii). The foreboding message of Kotzwinkle's time capsule has played itself out, and Tibetan Buddhism is now stronger for the infusion of American talent that the Beat Generation brought to it. Among the early hippies was Robert A. F. Thurman, who became fluent in Tibetan, translated sacred texts including his modernized version of *The Tibetan Book of the Dead*, helped found the American Institute of Buddhist Studies in New York, and is a highly respected, nationally known professor at Columbia University (Fields 1992, 292-94). There are now more than 250 Tibetan Buddhist Learning Centers in the United States, and more Americans than ever have become familiar with the history, art, and music of this culture (Kamenetz 1994, 278).[16] Symbolic of this renaissance is the glossy coffee-table magazine, *Tricycle: The Buddhist Review*, now in its tenth year of publication, which reveals how far we have come from the message of doom in Kotzwinkle's time capsule. While Chögyam Trungpa Rimpoche, who died in 1987, is remembered in its pages as "the most superior Dharma teacher to work in the West (Tworkov 1997, 41), his "crazy wisdom" that celebrated alcohol, drugs and sexual contact between teacher and students, is emphatically proscribed (Alexander 1998; Bays 1998).

The Fan Man is a significant part of Tibetan Buddhist history in America and should be recognized as such. It is also a unique contribution to American culture, because its author anticipated the destructive influence of beatnik excesses upon the ancient religion. Because of Kotzwinkle's strong emotional ties both to the Beat Generation writers and to traditional Tibetan Buddhism, he experienced an anguished ambivalence of which American literature is the beneficiary. That ambivalence enabled Kotzwinkle to create a hero/anti-hero unique in literature and has made *The Fan Man* one of the most unusual novels of the mid-twentieth century.

Notes

1 I am indebted to my Buddhist cousin, Martin Marvet, for answering all of my questions about his adopted religion and for his insightful rearrangement of "Badorties," which appears in the title of this paper. I thank the anonymous readers for *College Literature* for their guidance and acknowledge the help of my book group, especially Judy and Larry Baker, Ann Bader, Bryna Blustein, Charles Werner, and Claire Hyman, who read early drafts. I am grateful to my wife, Martha B. Kohn, for her pivotal editing of the first draft and for a profound interpretation of cadence in *The Fan Man*. Finally, I thank Paul E. Chambers for the connection to Thomas Pynchon.

2 My hypothesis that Kotzwinkle read these paperbacks is supported by his declaration in *Contemporary Authors* that he was himself a Buddhist (1974, 293–94).

3 For a picture of Padmasambhava holding a *khatvanga*, see Evans-Wentz (1968) frontispiece.

4 Padmasambhava is highly revered to this day by Tibetan Buddhists, who reason that when he introduced Buddhism to the materialistic populous of ninth-century Tibet, it was advantageous for him to act unconventionally.

5 See also the frontispiece and its explanation in Rhie and Thurman, 1991.

6 This appears to be a whimsical allusion by Kotzwinkle to a footnote in which Evans-Wentz (1968, 183n) acknowledges an earlier (1960, 74) error that he had made: "Certain scholars in the Occident have stated that Padmasambhava was a professor in the Buddhist University at Nalanda at the time the Tibetan King invited him to Tibet. . . . Now it appears from the original textual account that it was the Great Pandita Bodhisattva, and not Padmasambhava, who was the professor in Nalanda" (74).

7 For a beautiful example of the three-quarter profile of Avalokiteshvara, see the photograph in Rhie and Thurman (1991, 322).

8 For more discussion of "the Central Realm of the Densely-Packed," see Evans-Wentz (1960, 107).

9 Many American Buddhists are vegetarian on religious grounds. The conflict over meat evokes an uncharacteristic footnote in Evans-Wentz, regarding a twenty-three-hundred-year-old Buddhist edict prohibiting "the slaying of any animal, either in sacrifice or food." Present-day Tibetans, he writes "excuse their meat-eating on the grounds of climatic and economic necessity [but this] seems to be chiefly an unconscious attempt to cover up a racial predisposition, inherited from nomadic and pastoral ancestors, for a flesh diet" (1960, 170n).

10 For his posthumously published lectures, see Trungpa (1991).

11 These epithets for Beat Buddhism are expressed by Alvah Goldbook (Allen Ginsberg) and Japhy Ryder (Gary Snyder) in Kerouac (1958, 26, 91).

12 Allen Ginsberg and his companion, Peter Orlovsky, were both on this "trip" with Leary. The capitalization of REPTILIAN is Leary's.

13 Wakefield writes that this "hilarious saga" made him "laugh so hard that (he) fell off a chair" (1996, 31).

14 The conventional view is that Oedipa is in the transitional stage (Grant, 1994, 37), but the Tibetan Buddhist perspective that comes from studying *The Fan Man*, together with numerous hints from Pynchon, suggests that it may be the recently deceased lover of Oedipa who is in the *Bardo*, while she is the intended conduit for his rebirth.

15 Private communications (email) with Linda Rosenberg, Random House, February 20, 1997.

16 In a later book, Kamenetz tells how some of the early participants in the interaction of Beat writers and Tibetan monks became rabbis and incorporated Buddhist prayer practices in a robust new movement called Jewish Renewal (1997).

Works Cited

Alexander, William. 1998. "Twelve Steps and Dharma Drunks." *Tricycle: The Buddhist Review*. 8 (Fall): 60–71.

Bays, Jan Chozen. 1998. "What the Buddha Taught About Sexual Harassment." *Tricycle: The Buddhist Review*. 8 (Fall): 55–59.

Berkson, Carmel. 1986. *The Caves at Aurangabad*. New York: Mapin.

Burroughs, William S. 1959. *Naked Lunch*. New York: Grove Press.

Carlson, Marvin. 1984. *Theories of the Theatre*. Ithaca: Cornell University Press.

Chambers, Judith. 1992. *Thomas Pynchon*. New York: Twayne.

Clark, Tom. 1980. *The Great Naropa Poetry Wars*. Santa Barbara: Cadmus.

Contemporary Authors. 1974. Vols. 45–48. Detroit: Gale Publishing.

Cunningham, Valentine. 1974. "Provincial." *New Statesman* 88 (December 13): 871.

Davy, Kate. 1981. *Richard Foreman and the Ontological-Hysteric Theatre*. Ann Arbor: UMI.

Evans-Wentz, W.Y. 1958. *Tibetan Yoga and Secret Doctrines*. London: Oxford.

———. 1960. *The Tibetan Book of the Dead*. New York: Galaxy.

———. 1968. *The Tibetan Book of the Great Liberation*. London: Oxford.

Fields, Rick. 1992. *How the Swans Came to the Lake: A Narrative History of Buddhism in America*. Boston: Shambhala.

Freemantle, Francesca, and Chögyam Trungpa, 1975. *The Tibetan Book of the Dead: The Great Liberation Through Hearing in the Bardo*. Berkeley: Shambhala.

Ginsberg, Allen. 1956. *Howl and Other Poems*. San Francisco: City Lights Books.

Gold, Herbert. 1988. "Herbert Gold on William Kotzwinkle's *The Fan Man*." In *Rediscoveries II: Important Writers Select Their Favorite Works of Neglected Fiction*, ed. David Madden and Peggy Bach. New York : Carroll and Graf.

Grant, J. Kerry. 1994. *A Companion to "The Crying of Lot 49."* Athens: University of Georgia Press.

Kalupahana, David J., and Indrani. 1982. *The Way of Siddhartha*. Berkeley: Shambhala.

Kamenetz, Roger. 1994. *The Jew in the Lotus*. San Francisco: Harper.

———. 1997. *Stalking Elijah*. San Francisco: Harper.

Kennedy, William. 1974. "Horse Badorties." *The New Republic*. 2 (March): 32–33.

Kerouac, Jack. 1950. *The Town and the City*. New York: Grosset and Dunlap.

———. 1958. *The Dharma Bums*. New York: Signet.

Kotzwinkle, William. 1976. *Doctor Rat*. New York: Alfred A. Knopf.

———. 1991.*On the Road*. New York: Viking Press, 1957. Reprint. New York: Penguin.

———. 1994. *The Fan Man*. New York: Harmony Books. 1974. Reprint. Vintage Contemporaries.

———. 1996. *The Bear Went Over the Mountain*. New York: Henry Holt.

———. 1998. "Fragments of Papyrus from the Temple of the Older Gods." *Omni Publications International*. 10 (April): 85–89.

Leary, Timothy. 1968. *High Priest*. New York: World Publishing.

Leary, Timothy, Ralph Metzner, and Richard Alpert. 1964. *The Psychedelic Experience: A Manual Based on "The Tibetan Book of the Dead."* New Hyde Park: University Books.

Lewis, Leon. 1991. "William Kotzwinkle." *Beacham's Popular Fiction Update*. Washington, D.C.: Beacham.

———. 1996. William Kotzwinkle. *Dictionary of Literary Biography*. Vol. 173. Detroit: Gale Research.

Lipton, and Ragnubs. 1996. *Treasures of Tibetan Art*. New York: Oxford.

Lopez, Donald S., Jr. 1996. *Tibetan Buddhism*. In *Treasures of Tibetan Art*, ed. Barbara Lipton and Nina Dorjee. New York: Oxford University Press.

Mullin, Glen H., and Andy Weber. 1996. *The Mystical Arts of Tibet*. Atlanta: Longstreet.

Newman, Robert D. 1986. *Understanding Thomas Pynchon*. Columbia: University of South Carolina Press.

Nicosia, Gerald. 1983. *Memory Babe: A Critical Biography of Jack Kerouac*. New York: Grove Press.

"Paperback Talk." 1982 .*The New York Times* 11 July, 31.

Petillon, Pierre-Yves. 1991. "A Re-cognition of Her Errand into the Wilderness." In *New Essays on "The Crying of Lot 49,"* ed. Patrick O'Donnell. Cambridge: Cambridge University Press.

Pynchon, Thomas. 1966. *The Crying of Lot 49*. Philadelphia: Lippincott.

Rhie, Marilyn M., and Robert A. F. Thurman. 1991. *Wisdom and Compassion: The Sacred Art of Tibet*. New York: Harry N. Abrams.

Sanders, Ed. 1979. *The Party: A Chronological Perspective on a Confrontation at a Buddhist Seminary*. Woodstock: Poetry, Crime and Culture Press.

Schumacher, Michael. 1992. *Dharma Lion: A Critical Biography of Allen Ginsberg*. New York: St. Martin's Press.

Skerl, Jennie. 2000. "Introduction: The Unspeakable Visions of the Individual in Academe." *College Literature* 27.1 (Winter): 1-7.

Snyder, Gary. 1969. *Earth House Hold*. New York: New Directions.

Thurman, Robert A. F. 1994. *The Tibetan Book of the Dead*. New York: Bantam.

Todd, Richard. 1974. "Om." *Atlantic*, May, 129-30.

Tonkinson, Carole. 1995. "Preface." In *Big Sky Mind: Buddhism and the Beat Generation*, ed. Carole Tonkinson. New York: Riverhead.

Trungpa, Chögyam. 1991. *Crazy Wisdom*. Boston: Shambhala.

Tworkov, Helen. 1997. "A New Place, A New Time." *Tricycle: The Buddhist Review* 7 (Winter): 38-43.

Wakefield, Dan. 1996. "To See What He Could See." *The Nation* 4 November, 31-32.

CHAPTER FOURTEEN

"Blissful, Torn, Intoxicated":
Brinkmann, Fauser, Wondratschek, and the Beats
Anthony Waine and Jonathan Wooley

> Germany was swallowed up by a thousand different American things,
> bombs, drugs, music, cinema. Our longings were not built into the
> German Volkswagen. They drifted over from Hawaii, from Los Angeles,
> and later from New York. The economic recovery was at first like an
> American imitation. And for a while German parents had American boys
> and girls as their children. They all chewed gum, wore jeans, liked Elvis or
> jazz—or philosophized on asphalt-covered earth, from which roads and
> petrol stations and skyscrapers were popping up. (Wondratschek 1987,
> 273)[1]

This thumb-nail sketch of the first couple decades of life in the
newly founded Federal Republic of Germany is extracted from a
lecture given by Wolf Wondratschek in a number of North American
cities in 1977. At that time Wondratschek was in the process of establishing himself as West Germany's most popular poet, indeed as *the*
Pop Poet of his generation, at least in terms of sales and renown.[2] In
the course of this essay we shall be arguing that Wolf Wondratschek
(born in 1943), and two other writers, Rolf Dieter Brinkmann (born
in 1940) and Jörg Fauser (born in 1944), belonged to a generation
whose dates of birth exposed them fully to the multifarious manifestations of American politics, economics, and culture in postwar

Western Europe. One of these manifestations was the writing, morality, and lifestyle of the Beats which Wondratschek was surely alluding
to in the phrase "philosophized on asphalt-covered earth," for
German thinking had hitherto been an activity carried out in solip-
sistic seclusion, far removed from public spaces and urban settings.

Wondratschek's slightly tongue-in-cheek evocation of the degree
of Americanization of West German society and culture, especially
youth culture, has to be understood historically if one is not to
assume that throughout this century his country was slavishly
dependent on foreign fads and fashions and little more than a colony
for imported American values. Between 1933 and 1945 Germany's
leaders had put into practice an ideology which effectively cut their
people off from cultural trends which were internationalist, cosmopolitan, or even modern. Furthermore, during the thirteen years preceding the Third Reich, when the first (Weimar) Republic had been
open-minded towards non-German ideas, art, and entertainment,
their impact was limited to the big cities and to social classes which
could afford to indulge in the newly emerging leisure pursuits. Nor
did the intelligentsia uniformly welcome the westernization of
Weimar Germany, some preferring to look eastward (to the Soviet
Union), others, like Bertolt Brecht, regarding it as being synonymous
with full-blown capitalism, but many still seeing it as a bastardization
of true Germanic values, spiritual as well as political. And there was
still one further deeply entrenched attitude prevalent in learned and
scholarly circles which became entangled with the reaction to the
import of American ways of life after the First World War. This attitude reaches as far back as the early nineteenth century and is
described succinctly by Lothar Jordan:

> Lenau's declamation of 1832: "Brothers, these Americans are petty mind-
> ed people who turn the heavens' stomachs. Dead to all things intellectual,
> as dead as a doornail" illustrates one of these stereotypes which are hand-
> ed right down into the twentieth century and according to which German
> intellectuals and writers judge Americans. They are disappointed because
> of having too high expectations: the hatred of an inhuman and money-
> grabbing America which can only turn out cowboys and gunboat diplo-
> mats but no culture goes hand in hand with the predominant picture of a
> better life in a better country (politically, economically and in terms of
> natural environments). (Jordan 1994, 38)

Jordan's claim that his country's intellectual and artistic elites have consistently denied that Americans possess "Kultur" raises of course the question as to what Germans (and, to be truthful, European elites in general) understand by this term. The question is relevant, we believe, for the ensuing discussion of why the Beat Generation has been significant not only for our three representative German writers but as part of a broader movement in their country which has resulted in the gradual demolition of the very stereotype which Jordan has identified as having bedeviled American-German discourse. Here, too, it is helpful to refer to Wondratschek's 1977 lecture which turns the tradition of this discourse on its head, for early on in it he is already bemoaning the fact that "in a way literature in my country is repulsed by simple things, in fact by triviality, vulgarity and frankness in general; it's as if it detests ordinary life" (1987, 269). Wondratschek's simple assertion goes to the very heart of the matter. He is rejecting the conception of culture as only being about the creation and the appreciation of works of unique and lasting art and about the concomitant need to segregate the individual artist and his/her creativity from the everyday processes of humdrum reality. Instead he is making a revolutionary call, at least by German standards, for culture to encompass the entire gamut of human experience, customs, and values—scholarly rational and popular-visceral, verbal-creative and physical-sensual. For such an insight Wondratschek readily acknowledges his indebtedness to the American tradition:

> There was something hovering above the books which I loved. A great weight, an enormous readiness for adventure, nausea, oddness, illness. They weren't authors, they were real people. The genre of the artistic work wasn't being obeyed, but a moral code. Jack Kerouac. Ken Kesey. Ginsberg. Burroughs. Later Dylan. Figureheads. Father figures who acted like adolescents, like madmen, like prophets, wicked, addicted, free. (Wondratschek 1987, 271)

Here were figures from the American counterculture with whom it was easier for the war-baby generation of Brinkmann, Fauser, and Wondratschek to identify than with writers from their own German (or European) tradition. Indeed in expressing their affinity with modern American heroes, they were shunning quite consciously and provocatively their own fathers' generation of poets, novelists, essayists and, even more, were rejecting the social and political values of

their country's leaders. All three writers had been involved in the
Student Movement which in Germany had begun to ferment around
1966 and had reached its zenith two years later. This movement had
vented its wrath against international ills and injustices, most notably
the US involvement in the Vietnam War, and against domestic
oppressiveness and repressiveness as inherent in the authoritarian
structures of the German family, educational system, public institutions, and that which had come to constitute the West German establishment. The figure of the father, symbolic or real, became an object
of the younger generation's ire, frustration, and disenchantment.[3]
This is not so surprising when one remembers that it was the
fathers' generation which had been personally involved in the rise of
German fascism and its subsequent atrocities. This may well explain
why Wondratschek explicitly referred to the American writers listed
as being "father figures." But his reference to them using such overtly
psychobiological terminology does beg the question as to why
American role models rather than home-grown ones? Here it may be
instructive to mention West Germany's most important postwar literary institution, the Gruppe 47.

Group 47 took its name from the year, 1947, in which the first
meeting of an informal coterie of writers and publishers took place,
several of whom had spent time in American prisoner of war
camps.[4] They wished to encourage new German writing in a style
that was purged of National Socialist trappings and which would
deliver democratic, realistic works for a readership perceived as
being in need of such literature after twelve years of incessant propaganda. One man, Hans Werner Richter, soon established himself as
the organizer and leader (and father figure?) of the Group which
never had an official constitution, nor an offical membership list, nor
a fixed meeting place. Richter alone decided who should be invited
to read their (unpublished) work at the meeting, sending a postcard
to the selected person. Critics would also be invited. The readings
followed a ritual designed to inculcate in the writer an acceptance
of criticism and democratic debate which had been so conspicuous-
ly lacking in the Nazi Germany in which they had grown up. The
writer would sit in a chair (which soon became known as the "electric chair" for good reason), read for about half an hour until arbitrarily stopped by Richter who would then invite spontaneous reactions

from the assembled writers and critics whilst the writer in question remained completely silent. A good "performance" frequently resulted in a contract being offered by a publishing house whose representatives were also there to spot new talent. A particularly benevolent guest at Group meetings was the young, charismatic editor of West Germany's anti-establishment news magazine *Der Spiegel*, Rudolf Augstein. His magazine, founded in the British zone of occupation in 1946 and modeled partly on American weeklies such as *Time* and *Newsweek*, gave considerable free publicity to the Group and to individual members. By the early 60s the Group had become more successful than it had ever imagined (or perhaps even intended), and many observers viewed it as being more or less representative of West German literature *per se*. Eventually some of its "members" became embarrassed by its quasi-monopoly status and distanced themselves from it. In 1967 it held its last meeting.

There are some parallels to the genesis and philosophy of the Beat movement. It too was a loose grouping of like-minded spirits who strove to break free from their traditional national heritage or at least from dominant strands within it. It too was filled with a distrust of ideology, and its representatives used their power as intellectuals to challenge orthodoxy and conformism. The burgeoning materialism of their society was anathema to them. In an essay published in 1958 in *Akzente*, one of the Federal Republic's most influential literary magazines, Gregory Corso informed German readers: "He [the new American writer—AEW] despises conformity, the standard of the middle classes and money" (Corso 1958, 103). The Beats, too, sought to forge a new language, a new tone, and new rhythms to express a changing sense of identity, both as social beings and as writers. Finally, they, too, understood that some degree of organized activity and of self-publicity was necessary if the still relatively unknown writers were to break out of being a clique of friends and colleagues and have their voice, individually and collectively, heard in the wider public domain. But there was one decisive difference. The Beats embodied a more anarchic view of the world and consequently never evolved the structures and rites around which Gruppe 47 cohered for the best part of twenty years. The Beat movement seemed happy to mutate and dissipate, geographically, artistically, and collectively, with no attempt to impose a corporate philosophy, or to promote a unique identity, and thereby cultivate exclusivity.

Corso's essay, published under the title "Dichter und Gesellschaft in Amerika" (Writer and Society in America), is nevertheless evidence of the desire by German intellectuals and publishers to present their readers with the work and ideas of contemporary writers around the globe—after twelve years of Nazi isolationism a laudatory undertaking. Nor was it accidental that Corso had been approached to produce this personal and up-to-date portrait for *Akzente*. One of *Akzente*'s joint editors was the ubiquitous and immensely prolific Professor of English and American Literature, Walter Höllerer. Höllerer, it should be added, also happened to be one of Gruppe 47's resident critics and therefore a crucial conduit for postwar German-American literary relations. That Höllerer had clearly approached Corso for the article as a personal friend and colleague, can be gleened from Höllerer's own lengthy, knowledgeable, and enthusiastic essay published just one year after Corso's essay entitled "Junge amerikanische Dichtung" (New American Writing). Höllerer, uniquely to our knowledge, explained the word "beat" for the benefit of German readers, gave very acceptable translations of it, quoted at length from poems by Ginsberg, Corso, and Koch, and finished by giving a brief portrait of every principal and subsidiary new American writer. Corso and Höllerer went on to edit an anthology for the Hanser Verlag entitled *Junge amerikanische Lyrik* covering no fewer than 39, mainly young, writers. Another member of Gruppe 47, Hans Magnus Enzensberger, has played a role equally crucial as Höllerer's in the reception of the new American poetry. In 1962 his translation of and introduction to the poems of William Carlos Williams brought to the attention of German readers for the first time the work of an older American poet who, ironically, had been better known before Enzensberger's translation as the enthusiastic promotor of Ginsberg's poems for German readers. He called Williams the "doyen and patriarch of a poetry which has prised itself away from dependence on Europe and spread across a whole continent from New York to San Francisco" (1962, 29).

Whilst Höllerer and Enzensberger had in fact visited Ginsberg in Paris in 1957 (Jordan 1994, 165), Enzensberger's poetry, considered by many critics to represent some of the very best West German poetry produced in the 50s and 60s, shares few common characteristics with the Beats' output. On the other hand the very title of Wondratschek's collection of poems from the 70s betrays his "torn" American-German identity. It is called *Chuck's Zimmer*. Not only does it contain some poems actually written in English, it also presents poems inspired by his travels in America, including the following one to which he gave an English title (1981, 204), referring as it does to a famous site in the States of California and Nevada;

DEATH VALLEY
The dead straight road went on and on.
I hummed the same tune over and over.
I felt the muck of a hundred cigarettes
on my tongue. I drove an old Chevy.
The wind whistled through old gaps in my teeth.
To the left and right desert,
the end of mankind
a Genesis without God,
stones, little hares and the sign
LAS VEGAS 78 MILES.
I was looking forward
to losing.

One is instantly struck by the unpoetic, unaesthetic texture of this prosaic hymn to the American West. It is a hymn sung most fervently by Kerouac, certainly in the age of highways and automobiles. It is also a landscape and an experience immortalized in dozens of road movies and documentary films. It has been relived by countless tourists. It is infinitely reproducible. The author knows this prehistory, plays with it, and gently parodies it ("an old Chevy"). It is nevertheless still defiantly personal, the "I" being reiterated four times in a twelve-line poem. German writers steeped in Beat art like Wondratschek have been encouraged by its unfettered and unembarrassed subjectivity and autobiographical authenticity. The personal subject matters, is part of the reality being evoked, and wants to draw the reader into that real individual's world. And what a subject he is! Deglamourized, deintellectualized, and pretty kaput, like the old Chevy he is driving. The final word "losing" laconically reinforces the subject's sense of self and of his existence in general. The starkness and infinity of Death Valley fail to inspire him to lyrically extol nature and its pantheistic qualities, rather, just when his imagination is turning towards metaphysical ruminations ("a Genesis without

God") the muse is rudely cut short by the intrusion of metropolitan realities ("LAS VEGAS 78 MILES") writ large to emphasize their concreteness. The asphalt cowboy alias the lyric narrator is thankfully nearing the end of his pilgrimage to a mecca with decidely materialistic overtones, and one which promises worldly, though elusive pleasures ("I was looking forward to losing"). Las Vegas, the embodiment of global popular culture, is the very antithesis of that world of higher, more refined, and sublime pleasures and emotions one traditionally associates with "true" poetry. Such a myth was well and truly shattered by Williams and the Beats, and Wondratschek is following merrily and self-ironizingly in their tire marks.

The Beats not only taught Wondratschek to look at their country in a particular way and also to record his feelings in an idiom which brought it closer to German vernacular than many of his German predecessors but also encouraged him to look at his countrymen in a detached, critical yet realistic way. For whilst it is certainly true that the Beats achieved a style of writing which broke free from European patterns and conventions, they did not deploy this style to then pen anthems to America but rather to excoriate certain elements of it whilst celebrating other aspects. In other words from "Howl" onward their poetry, fiction, and essays have never shied away from embracing political topoi both on a small and a large scale. Let us move then from Death Valley back to Germany. "Deutschlandlied" is the official name of the German national anthem. Wondratschek has also entitled one of his poems "Deutschlandlied" (1981, 154-56), but its spirit is aggressively non-jingoistic and iconoclastic.

> SONG OF GERMANY
> "We just are the best in the world in certain things"—
> I heard that over cocktails,
> one person had read all of Nietzsche
> Another is a Nazi only in private
> Lovers of music, something German
> like a love of pets and hatred of people
> this industry in thinking, in killing—
> every hungry dog that creeps across an empty street
> would make life so much nicer
> than your brand new Mercedes.
> . . . .
> But the world successes of the West bore me.

A hundred little crooks appeal to me more
than this ensemble of butter and theory,
the wife
the spouse
the subconscious half ajar
self painted water colours
a negro's prick from hell
the whole stirring atomic age.
A rundown café at the end of the world
has more to offer,
nothing works,
the objects have exchange value
something as primitive as light and air
reason comes home from the heads
into the bodies.
. . . .
You can finger my balls,
you German tourists
you men of arrogance
I saw whole stretches of country become ugly
I saw you browbeating a foreign smile
and ruling the world
The German mind—welded together
from blood and soil
"we just are the best in the world in certain things"—
no thanks.
(edited by the author-translators)

Of course Germany has its own impressive tradition of political verse which evokes and comments on its nation's past and present. It stretches from Hölderlin through Heine and Brecht to Enzensberger. Wondratschek will have been familiar with all these major figures, at least two of whom, Heine and Brecht, had to go into exile on account of their anti-nationalist stance. What characterizes this poem is what has been emanating from the USA since the mid-50s. There is a passion driving it which is frequently concealed by his earlier fellow-writers beneath layers of irony and erudition. Wondratschek certainly wants us to think about his critique but wants us to feel and empathize with his anger and his estrangement. He discards modernist "alienation effects" taking us straight into the lion's den in the very opening line. Moreover, he vents his disillusionment with the directness we take for granted now in a post-Beat culture: "But the world successes of the West bore me"; "A rundown café at the end of the world / has more to offer"; "A hundred little crooks appeal more to me." Indeed, is not this last line an allusion to the Beats' strong sympathies for crooks like Huncke and others who flouted the laws of the land? And if there are such allusions to the Beats' moral code, are there not also citations of certain stylistic hallmarks? When the narrator exclaims "I saw whole stretches of country become ugly / I saw you browbeating a foreign smile" we are reminded of the opening of "Howl": "I saw the best minds of my generation etc.," especially since Wondratschek too is intoning a negative vision. The reference to "a negro's prick" and the sarcastic exhortation "You can finger my balls" echo Ginsberg and others' sexual explicitness far more than any pre-1968 indigenous writing which had certainly treated and evoked the erotic but in a "tasteful" and almost self-censoring way. Plain vulgarities, subcultural vernaculars, everyday images, pedestrian street scenes imbue his "Song of Germany" with a very contemporary and demotic realism.

Considerable space has been given so far to the critical thoughts of Wolf Wondratschek, as well as to two contrasting poems, and further attention will be paid to the Beat leanings of Jörg Fauser. This has been a conscious decision by the authors to broaden the base of what might be termed the "alternative canon" of contemporary German literature. Hitherto one name has been pinned to the mast of that "alternative canon" and with very good reason. The author in question is of course Rolf Dieter Brinkmann, and certainly in the second half of the 60s Brinkmann's desire to move not only his native literature but also his native culture into another gear and down another highway (Highway 68?!) was pursued with crusading zeal and gutsy determination. Britain and the United States were major catalysts for his evolving aesthetics (Waine, 1992), and his forewords to three anthologies written in the space of 18 months in 1968 and 1969 are significantly new milestones in the ongoing West German reception of the Beats which has already been briefly documented. However, the reception that took place in the late 60s was not only quantitatively different but also qualitatively so. The earlier Höllerer-led appreciation was part of a postwar "Nachholbedarf" (need to catch up). This is symbolized in the anthology edited by Enzensberger in 1960 entitled *Museum der Modernen Poesie* (*Museum of Modern Poetry*). Whilst Höllerer and Enzensberger quickly established transatlantic friendships with the new American writers, the cultural climate of the Federal Republic, even in the early 60s, was still rather conservative and conformist, with bohemianism expressed through adherence to existentialist credos and private forms of social dissent. Furthermore, the generation preceding the arrival of Wondratschek, Fauser, and Brinkmann was, spiritually, deeply affected by the knowledge of their nation's sinful past. Consequently they confronted their responsibility both to help atone for these sins and to prevent fascism from ever again being cultivated in the German soil.[5] Wondratschek's "Song of Germany" demonstrates how even the following generation of postwar writers, though so much more Dionysian and transatlantic in their outlook, is still haunted by this legacy.

Germany's recent political history was not the only troubling inheritance German writers faced. There was also the entrenched notion of the poet's lifestyle and social function. The preconceived image was that of a rather remote figure, inhabiting a world of "Geist" (spirituality wedded to intellect), romantically possessing gifts not found in the nether world of quotidian reality and commercial imperatives, and aspiring upward to an ethereal sphere of "Kunst" (real art) and "Sein" (true being). The Beats gave Brinkmann new signposts. "The new American literature" he declaimed "like the whole new cultural scene in the USA begins in the present with contemporary material and does not have any set, internalized patterns to lose . . ." (1982, 224). Brinkmann set out to deconstruct such "set, internalized patterns," especially those surrounding the aforementioned notion of the writer. In his introduction to the poetry of Frank O'Hara, a poet who, incidentally, had been popularized in Germany as part of the Beat Generation, Brinkmann informs his German readers:

> The professional title of "poet" possesses hardly any further attractiveness for the new American writers since the arrival of the Beat authors as the social conditioning expressed by that word has been more or less consciously seen through by the individual authors. The literary products seem to arise alongside other matters, seem to have come about coincidentally—the fact that one has done them is important, writing is conceived as doing. (Brinkmann 1982, 218–19)

Four further legacies were bequeathed directly or indirectly by the Beats to this young German cultural urban guerrilla. They were, first-

ly, the belief that images or pictures were as influential as words for
the contemporary author; secondly, the need to place the sensual
(be it tactile, erotic, optical, artificial or natural) above the academic
(or "academicized" as he liked to pejoratively term it) and rational;
thirdly, to savour popular culture and utilize its materials, styles, and
rhythms in a poetry which expresses the core psychological-bio-
chemical mind as opposed to its cultivated parts; and, finally, not
unrelated to the first three, the legitimate use of mind-altering and
expanding drugs to seek a new awareness of temporal and spacial
being and movement.

In the essay "Der Film in Worten," from which some of the above
quotations are taken and whose title was directly inspired by
Kerouac, Brinkmann takes his countryman Enzensberger to task for
having taken some words uttered by Kerouac out of context and for
accusing the latter of being close to fascist thought.[6] His defence of
Kerouac revolves around the dichotomy of intellect versus sensuality:

> Enzensberger's rejection of Kerouac's statement can be regarded as symp-
> tomatic of the well-known lack of sensuality in the thinking of Western
> intellectuals who today quite rightly see themselves as being excluded
> from a movement which demands an increased sensuality which has
> digested thinking and reflexivity in a quite natural way. Indeed I cannot
> understand why a thought should not have the attractiveness of the tits of
> a nineteen year old which one enjoys fondling. (Brinkmann 1982, 227)

This last sentence, printed in 1969, was considered shocking especially coming from a person purporting to be a serious writer. But
Brinkmann was bringing into German literary discourse a new tone,
and in his championing of sensuality, a new texture and mood in
keeping with the era of postmodernity dawning in Western Europe.[7]
This era was to be partially characterized according to another of
Brinkmann's North American mentors, Leslie Fiedler, by the bridging
of the gap between high and popular culture, and Brinkmann certainly sensed amongst the Beats a non-discriminatory attitude
towards this realm, indeed a readiness to participate in and derive
pleasure from it. Finally, when in the knowingly named anthology
ACID Brinkmann writes, "At the same time William Burroughs 'the
one at the mixing machine, boys, that's me' showed the direction
'Breakthrough in the Grey Room,' by which he meant the brain, a
grey room constricted by regulations and paralysed as a taboo"
(1982, 229), we infer that part of this breakthrough is to be affected

by drugs which allow one to overcome the regulations and to unlock the taboos (Kramer 1995, 156).

Though in the course of the next five years, 1970-75, Brinkmann was to revise certain ideas and modify some of his attitudes, his prose and his poetry still showed him adapting for his own work the materials he had so assiduously researched and collected during the previous decade. His last published volume of poetry, *Westwärts 1&2* (1975), contains examples of verse which marry the two traditons, German and American, in a manner unsurpassed subsequently by German poets. He did for German cities like Cologne what Frank O'Hara had done for New York, and which Gregory Corso summed up in a beautiful line of a poem which he had written as a retrospective on the Beat Generation and their subsequent personal developments. He spoke of "a subterranean poesy of the streets" (Honan 1987, 34). Here is Brinkmann's own attempt to do the same:

HEARING ONE OF THOSE CLASSIC
black tangos in Cologne at the end of
August, where the summer's already
turned to dust, shortly after shops
shut, coming out of the open door of a
pub which is owned by a Greek, is almost
a miracle: for a moment a
surprise, to pause for a moment,
respite for a moment in this street
which nobody loves and which makes you
breathless while walking through it. I
wrote everything down before
this moment evaporated
in the cursed hazy
paralysis of Cologne.

Brinkmann's muse for this poem (1975, 25) is unashamedly metropolitan. He, the poet, is responding viscerally as well as verbally to a few moments of unadultered street culture. And although this piece of music is exotically foreign (originating as sensual South American dance music with African rhythms), it is nevertheless well known (a "classic"). The street is a well-trodden one too and one presumes in the very heart of the city. The music is not live but recorded, one of those pieces played often and in many public places. It is indeed coming from a pub, probably one which the poet frequented himself as he knows its owner, a Greek. Brinkmann therefore takes great care to stress that he has not experienced some unique vision of artistic beauty but something banal, familiar, almost mechanically reproducible. Yet it is so profoundly and sensuously moving that it stops him in his tracks and compels him to capture in quite plain diction, striking an almost colloquial tone, simultaneously the uniqueness and the ephemerality of the metropolitan experience. The uniqueness and the ephemerality are captured in the word "moment," used four times no less. The almost obsessive concern with the miraculous moment and his decision, recorded in the poem itself, to commit it instantly to paper, produce in the reader a strong sensation of spontaneity. This spontaneity is conveyed syntactically to the reader as both s/he and the narrator participate from the opening image of the title down to the first and only full stop in the suddeness, strength, and elementariness of the process of hearing and responding. Counterpointed with this moment of magic, and yet strangely interwoven with it, is the city of Cologne, as we are told twice, at the beginning and the end. It would seem to be a barren landscape, having "turned to dust," with streets "which nobody loves" and "which make you breathless" and which, for good measure, is inanimated by a "cursed hazy paralysis." The poet's malaise about the city is frankly articulated. Yet, paradoxically, he is able to turn this malaise into a statement about the real possibility of transcending the condition and experiencing perhaps even a beatific state: "is almost a miracle."

In a foreword, written in 1969, for the anthology of American poetry, *Silverscreen*, Rolf Dieter Brinkmann spells out his own poetic philosophy at that time, which would result in little masterpieces such as "Hearing One of Those Classic." He celebrates a refreshing, new sensibility to be found in these American poems, "that first and foremost they are just there" (1982, 248). They are unaffected expressions of existence which do not pretend to transcend the parameters of the text; they immortalize instances of wonder at the immediate or present (they meet the reader "there"), moments of epiphany. Moreover, the poet notes approvingly that his American counterparts are not writing in order to further the concept of "literature," they feel no compulsion to tackle any of the grand narratives, their efforts are instead channeled into realizing themselves. His compendium, *Standfotos* (1980), furnishes early examples of this evolving (post)modern aesthetic.

The valedictory poem of this compendium, "Wolken" (Clouds; 1980, 361) illustrates Brinkmann's retreat from "the imperious gesture of knowing-it-all, of instruction" (1982, 249) which had become a standard trait of the poetic figure. From the title one may surmise that Brinkmann is dealing with nature, even a metaphysical, discursive theme. However, the opening lines place him firmly on the ground refuting any omniscience or indeed any wish for such omniscience, "A few clouds more or less up there / I don't mind. . . . I can't grasp the whole picture." At the same time he is empowered, in that his subjective agency is the driving force of the poem, his aesthetic judgement determines what is assimilated, "A few words. . . . A few which I like." Through this he registers a delight at his own creativity so that at times one is left to wonder whether he is making an observation or writing a running critique of the poem itself. On picking up a tissue in his room he notes, "That is a beautiful contrast to the blue / between the clouds." The poem is furthermore infused with spontaneity in this way since Brinkmann shares with the reader the trivial, everyday dilemma of whether to finish reading yesterday's paper, and makes him/her participate not just in the unfolding of this snatch of experience but in the production of the poem. Insights are to be gained in the personal rather than universal sense, "When I've got <<high>> enough, these things become clearer," writes Brinkmann. The "high" here is marked off as it denotes not the lofty overview one might associate with poets and clouds alike but quite the opposite, a heightened, drug-enhanced sentient perception of minutiae in Brinkmann's immediate, domestic environment: the tissue on his floor, for example. This holds no secondary, metaphorical meaning; it is merely a tangible item which holds a meaning for Brinkmann as it contains something of his life, "A Tempo tissue, in which *you* are." As if to reiterate this he then uses it to blow his nose. By the end of the poem all barriers between his surrounding reality and the poem have been erased, as he looks to the clouds and notes, "They are the same which are in the word clouds, on this piece of paper, in my room, inside of me, blue."

For some critics the poet was highly influential in awakening German literature and culture to the excitement of surface detail. As

Hermann Peter Piwitt puts it, "He taught us to see" (Geduldig and Sagurna 1994, 169). He had the ability to reproduce a familiar scene with the astonishment of one registering it for the first time. The simple picture he reproduces in the poem of the same name ("Einfaches Bild") is the seductiveness and sensuality of a passing girl in black stockings as registered by the spectator, the male gaze. It is not multiple imagery but minimalism which captures this captivating scene. The girl's appearance is not elaborated beyond her ladderless stockings and so strikes one more as the product of synchronic observation than subsequent deliberation. The circular structure mirrors Brinkmann's gaze as it pans 180 degrees, while this fixation is consolidated by the attachment of the adjective "schön" (beautiful) to both her approach and departure; her sexiness is located in her movement. Ironically, this symmetrical, highly visual poem has no core; its central lines seem to lose sight of the girl, "Her shadow / on the street / her shadow / on / the wall" betraying the fleetingness of such a sight. Still, the girl remains tantalizing until the last; her stockings have no ladders, Brinkmann unclear as to whether this perfection continues or trails out under the skirt.

Finally, we shall consider the reception of American culture in general and the Beat generation in particular as evidenced in the writings of Jörg Fauser. In a short, selective biographical essay on Jack Kerouac, Fauser recalls the first time he read *On the Road* as a late teenager in the early 60s. The book's impact was, not surprisingly, physical rather than intellectual, "like a dig in the ribs, a casual clicking with the tongue; pure jazz: Go, man, go!" (1985, 61). It prodded and lured Fauser like a cool, vitalizing, immediately familiar stranger from the stewing, ruminating humanism, terminal "Vernunft" (common sense) and phlegmatic conservatism which had grown out of the war's rubble. His generation, the "children of the war rubble," had known nothing else but this steady adherence to an equally steady "reconstruction," the ubiquitous insipidity and a country dominated (indeed governed) by grey-haired old men; tedium festering in "eternal Sunday afternoons with the mowing of lawns" (1985, 61). Initially then, Fauser received "Beat" as in the interpretation, "beatific" which he, in turn, translates as "Glückselig, zerrissen, berauscht" (blissful, torn, intoxicated). By breaking down this first adjective one is left with the instructive noun "Glück." Alternatively translated as "happiness" or "luck," there is (because of the relatively transparent nature of the German language) always cross-field resonance: that is to say, the two meanings are never entirely separable. Certainly in Fauser's understanding of "happiness," luck, chance, risk, and contingency play an important role. "Glück" is not a state (unlike a cognate such as "Zufriedenheit," literally "being at peace") but ingrained in the process of ruddering one's fate in serendipity and discovery, instead of bowing down to grand narratives such as history and progress. In other words, "Glück" expresses no sense of an *earned* happiness or spiritual fulfillment; it is happiness where one can get it. Notably, "Glück" forms a central theme in Fauser's serious thriller *Der Schneemann* (1983) and finds its way into his 1979 collection of poetry, *Trotzki, Goethe und das Glück*. In both it emits a sense of hedonism which had previously been denied by a remorseful cultural dominant. Meanwhile, to be "zerrissen" is to rupture the idea of "re-construction," to embrace the irrational, to skirt even on the edge of "madness." This is closely linked to the third adjective listed by Fauser, "berauscht." To be Beat was to be intoxicated not only by the exhiliration or "Rausch" (rush) of perpetual motion but also by the intake of "Rauschmittel" (drugs) which pushed the writer to the extremes of experience.

And Fauser definitely did push his frame to these extremes. His thinly veiled persona, Harry Gelb, in the autobiographical novel-cum-documentary *Rohstoff* (1984) even manages to flabbergast the scarcely calvinist William S. Burroughs by his reckless indulgence. On learning that Gelb has taken raw, untreated opium intravenously, Burroughs tells him, "You must have been completely mad." As revealed by the same passage, it was Burroughs who introduced Fauser to Apomorphine and recommended that he spend some time in the notorious Junkies' Colony in Istanbul in order to beat his addiction. If Fauser's awareness of the possibilities of literature owes a great deal to Kerouac, he has Burroughs to thank for averting an even more premature death.

While this life of excess, as promoted by the Beats, is poles apart from conventional, settled ways of life, it shares according to Clive Bush (Lee 1996, 131-32) the same "psychological goal," namely exhaustion. Nonetheless, unlike the former who press themselves into a ready-made rut of "homogeneous repetition," that is, convince themselves of the scarcity of possibilities, of the exhaustion of alternatives and desire that nothing will happen, the Beats set out to exhaust as much of the apparently infinite available experience as they can. A peculiar and paradoxical mixture of appetite and exhaustion threads its way through Fauser's poetry. On the one hand, he is beset at times by a pathological fear of missing out, as crystallized by a text such as "Alt genug" (Old enough; Fauser 1979, 58) where he tells his female bedfellow, "I would very much like to take you in my arms / but world is world / and roars by." Perpetual motion through experience is the only antidote to an inherent feeling of insuffiency and inadequacy. If one skims over the titles included in *Trotzki, Goethe und das Glück* (1979), this hungry motion appears to be echoed in a cosmopolitan welter of place-names and addresses such as "Tanger Sutra" (Tangiers Sutra), "Nevada," "Back in the USSR," "Bar Brazil" and "Paris, im Vorübergehen" (Paris, in Passing). Yet these belie a frequent and pronounced sense of stagnation and *déjà vu* in his work, a waning belief in unique experience *per se*. Even in the exotic, far eastern setting of "Eine Art Abschied" (A Kind of Departure), Fauser understands himself to be just *another* conduit-like sensor for this particular experience, "Later the taste of cold sheets / and smell of a flat / which tomorrow is left." His location in time and space is blurred and blunted in contrast to the pinprick present of Brinkmann's work which strips away all other times and places to leave senses of epiphany. If Brinkmann imagines himself to be a pioneer, Fauser writes as a shadow engaged in second-hand consumption and never leaves the reader in any doubt that theirs is third-hand.

One explanation for this difference could be attributed to their respective relationships to drugs and the function these drugs serve in their poetry. While Brinkmann *experimented* with mind-altering chemicals, Fauser was, it should be remembered, a heroin addict. As such the former had a much tighter control on the effects of his drugs since they only extended and intensified his *perception,* while Fauser's encroached upon his body, nervous system, and emotional faculties. One's impression is that Brinkmann's poetry is written from within the state of mental stimulation, of the "high" induced by LSD and so on, whereas Fauser pens his work while in some state of withdrawal or come-down. As a result Fauser registers little of the romance and wonder in the present as does Brinkmann and displays none of the emotional intensity found in Kerouac's *On the Road,* for example. While a number of his poems read like a physical stream of consciousness, Fauser tends to rationalize emotion, perhaps in order to regain the control surrendered while intoxicated on heroin. Certainly in a poem such as "Vor der Tagesschau" (Before the Daily News; Fauser 1979, 9) the onus seems to be on the poet holding himself together both psychologically and emotionally; the repetition, cluttering of concrete nouns, and vertical imagery betraying an almost paranoid need to delineate order.

Bound up with Fauser's preference for the primitive and physiological is a rejection of the political posturing, sloganizing, and foisting of empty ideals in the 60s. He trusted rather his thirst, libido, addictions; these become the only things worth believing in and following. Again, this precipitates a kind of exhaustion which brings to mind Walter Höllerer's interpretations of "Beat" back in 1959 where the writer is "worn-out by a supply of propagandistic arguments and contradictory educational slogans" (1959, 30). That the mottos being bandied around Germany in the 60s tended to deny and exclude the everyday wants and concerns of the individual was inevitably redressed by a trend emerging in the early 70s, labeled "New Subjectivity." This encompassed a brand of poetry which, in terms of form and language, bordered on rhythmatic prose and, in terms of subject matter, tended as little toward the esoteric as pop music, homing in on quotidien activities of the poet, trips to the cinema or pub, highly subjective accounts of travel, friendships, and relationships. As noted by Manfred Durzak the birth of this reassertion of a particular side of self can be traced to the dissolution of the Student Movement (1981, 81).

If the poem, "Trotzki, Goethe und das Glück" is to be believed, Fauser's disengagement and skepticism predate this dissolution. Contrary to the promise of the title, Fauser does not deliver any lofty, academic treatise but recounts one episode or subtext from his love life spent in a commune full of Trotzkyists. "No sooner had I come off the needle, / I lumbered into the next trap: the revolution," he starts the poem, implying, one might think, that he immersed himself in political activity with the same voracity he had expended on his heroin addiction. In truth, this "revolution" denotes instead the turning of the poet's head by a beautiful young Parisian, who merely happens to be a Trotzkyist, "The revolution was called Louise / had incredibly slim hips, / flashing eyes, fluttering black / hair, came from Paris and was a Trotzkyist." Although outwardly converted to her politics, his participation in the Trotzkyist demonstrations is begrudging and tactical, "I palavered / when palaver was called-for / waved flags when flags were called-for." Ironically, his one act of rebellion is to flout the doctrine "of the Great Chairman" (i.e., Trotzki) himself by indulging in a decadent breakfast, which interestingly appears to go unchecked by his "comrades." It is only when he verbally challenges the point of their activities and dares to suggest that contentment may lie in more personal interaction that Louise snaps indignantly, "And Trotzki? / And the comrades in prison? / Your bourgeois happiness, pah! Beer / and poems while the revolution is being organized." It would seem that to bad-mouth Trotzkyism is more heinous a crime than to act in a manner which clearly contravenes its basic principles. Fauser's cynicism toward this political hot-air is ultimately vindicated as years later he bumps into a girl who still has contact with Louise. On hearing she has returned to Paris, Fauser asks whether she is working in the "Zentralkomitee." This notion is promptly dispelled by the girl who tells him that she has married a Goethe researcher; hardly the epitome of anti-bourgeois values. Elsewhere in Fauser's novels as well as his poetry, his interest lies in and his kinship lies with the utterly disaffiliated of society; the outsiders, the losers, the ignorant, and the indifferent.

Fauser's poem, "Dichter in New York" (Poet[s] in New York; Fauser 1985, 21) incorporates different facets or nuances of Beat. It is a diary-like account of one evening the poet spends before, during, and after a reading by Charles Bukowski at St. Mark's Church, the Bowery, in the summer of 1976. The title leads one initially to wonder whether Fauser is referring to an individual subject ("Der Dichter," either himself or Bukowski) or to a more generalized plural, to the spirit or essence of poets in New York. In the course of the text, it becomes clear that Fauser is at once spinning his own unapologetically autobiographical story while confessing his interchangeability with the implied packs of writers in transit around the city. This is a poem about lifestyle, or rather, about how poetry and lifestyle have become entwined in this deacademized milieu. Throughout the poem runs a duality of exhaustion and fluidity. As one joins the narrative, Fauser impresses upon the reader the dense, stifling heat and humidity clogging the city's air, "As if you were running in an Iron Lung through long corridors / and then the power runs out." This is a heaviness carried through the sensual environment with "dark beer," "sweat," "smoke," a woman's "greasy envelope," and steam from the sewers that stands like "flags of smoke" and which is also consolidated by recurrent impressions of satiety. When Fauser first meets his friends, they are already "pretty much sloshed," or literally, "filled-up"; his friend Jack has developed a prominent beer-belly, the venue of the reading is already at bursting-point when they arrive.

Nevertheless the poem is driven by a dynamism which refuses to surrender to this sense of fatigue; the literal "electricity" may have packed up, but the characters can draw on a stored current of energy. Indeed, just as the cream which Jack has regularly to rub into his hemorrhoids could be read as another cause for exasperation, it acts, amusingly, as a kind of metaphor for the lubricated style and movement of characters within the account. Fauser may not engage in Kerouac's "spontaneous, get-with-it, unrepressed word-slinging," the poem being more a product of meticulously naturalistic and narrated detail, but he taps into the "motor activity" of this Beat's work through a preference for dialogue and an anecdotal/conversational tone overall. And while the poem's rhythm may not exude the "bop prosody" found in Kerouac but seems rather to be entrenched in a tired groove dragging the poet on, the text is peppered with instances of slick wit. For example, one lady's attempts to chat up Jack are hampered by his obligatory visits to the toilet every fifteen minutes to treat his hemorrhoids, so that "she couldn't really get hold of him," neither figuratively nor literally is the implication.

In fact, not only do characters slip in and out of the narrative, where their paths do intersect, they are shown to operate at crossed purposes. The lady from Philadelphia tells one of the men, "You look like Bob Dylan at 80," intending it as a compliment but inducing merely disgruntlement. Fauser likewise registers this lack of meaningful exchange at the reading itself; "he could have peed on them or fallen down dead, they would have giggled and applauded" so that behind their boisterous reaction lies a kind of apathy; they have come to react in this way regardless of the content of Bukowski's set. Their applause is shown to be all the more insincere when set against Fauser and his friends' beat state. Futhermore, the poem contains no hermeneutic code; Bukowski's reading may be the pivotal event but is not built up to as a climax but slots into the rhythm of the rest of the text. Bukowski has no inflated sense of importance, being neither intoxicated by his own words nor fooled by the audience's response, and leaves discreetly. Fauser, although he has great respect for Bukowski, does not dwell on the content of the American's performance but seems more interested in the audience and atmosphere of the spectacle. Indeed, despite its insistent dynamic, the poem remains uneventful. The result is a searching transience. As Jack comments "On this road a load of people have died," he is not occupied by any feelings of tragedy but takes the fact as a promise of incident, "He stared out. Perhaps someone was dying right now." Fauser ends the text by drawing an analogy between poetry and sleep, "afterwards everyone complains they didn't get enough," amalgamating the notions of creation, exhaustion, and hunger/thirst.

Jörg Fauser's poem about "Poets in New York," which includes himself as German participant and observer, and written in 1976, is an appropriate conclusion to our analysis of this episode of German-American discourse. Americans have long since ceased to be "petty minded people who turn the heavens' stomachs. Dead to all things intellectual, as dead as a doornail" to requote Lenau's indictment of 1832. Fauser, Brinkmann, and Wondratschek have imbibed America, both third-hand via its myriad postwar German copies and imitations, second-hand via its literatures, and first-hand via actual "study visits" to its shores and to its cultural meccas, be they Las Vegas or St. Mark's Church, The Bowery. In general terms too Germans' concept of culture has broadened irreversibly since the end of the war, and this broadening, this opening out and indeed this democratizing of "Kultur" has made them less bigoted, less elitist, and less eurocentric than when Lenau uttered his opinion, symbolically in the year of Goethe's death and therefore at the high point of German Classicism. A modern, if not postmodern pluralism has been visible since the late 60s in West Germany, and the consensus, real or imagined, as represented by Gruppe 47, has long since splintered. The Beats stand for one component of "otherness" which has helped to subvert the German cultural status quo, a status quo built upon the principles relentlessly deconstructed by Brinkmann, Fauser, and Wondratschek: theory, logicality, academic objectivity, party political *engagement*, personal and collective responsibility, moral leadership, ironic detachment. The otherness of the Beats was defined pithily by Wondratschek as their being "wicked, addicted, free," whilst Fauser saw them as being "blissful, torn, intoxicated." In short the Beats helped a new generation of West German writers, born between 1940 and 1950, and who discovered and devoured the Beats between 1960 and 1970, to set out more confidently on the road of self-discovery, self-liberation, and self-awareness.

Ironically, and tragically, Rolf Dieter Brinkmann was to die, aged 35, in April 1975 on the road in the heart of London, run over by a car as he and a friend were crossing over to one of Brinkmann's favorite London pubs, The Shakespeare. Jörg Fauser too died on the road, the night he was celebrating his 43rd birthday in June 1987 with friends in Munich, after mysteriously wandering on to an autobahn outside the city where he was knocked down by a lorry and killed instantly.

Notes

1 This and all subsequent translations are those of the joint authors.
2 The four collections of 70s poetry which make up *Chuck's Zimmer* have sold over 125,000 copies. How quintessentially American the Christian name is, whilst even the apostrophe is an anglicization.
3 Many modern German writers have written novels, stories, essays, and plays about the father, and have helped to spawn an entire subgenre of so-called "father-literature."
4 Gruppe 47 has attracted considerable scholarly attention and consequently there are numerous articles and books devoted to the topic. For documentary information see Lettau (1967). For a literary and sociological analysis see Arnold (1980).
5 In 1962, 15 years after the first meeting of Group 47, Hans Werner Richter stated that the founding fathers:
once and for all wanted to prevent a repetition of what had happened and to lay the foundations for a new, democratic Germany, for a better future and for a new literature, which is conscious of its responsibility towards social and political developments as well. They believed that the world of German writing and publishing could not exonerate itself from what had happened. (Richter 1962, 8)

6 Brinkmann was not the only German to object to Enzensberger's defamatory
   remarks contained in his essay "Aporien der Avantgarde" (1962, 50–80). See, for
   example, Hartung (1971).
7 The case for viewing Brinkmann as a postmodernist is well made by
   Gemünden (1995).

Works Cited

Arnold, Heinz Ludwig, ed. 1980. *Die Gruppe 47: Ein kritischer Grundriß*.
   Sonderband Text + Kritik. Munich: edition text + kritik.

Brinkmann, Rolf Dieter, ed. 1969. *Silverscreen. Nene Amerikanische Lyrik*.
   Cologne: Kiepenheuer & Witsch Verlag.

———. 1975. *Westwärts 1&2*. Reinbek bei Hamburg: Rowohlt.

———. 1980. *Standfotos 1962-1970*. Reinbek bei Hamburg: Rowohlt.

———. 1982. "Der Film in Worten." Reinbek bei Hamburg: Rowohlt.

Corso, Gregory. 1958. "Dichter und Gesellschaft in Amerika." *Akzente*: 101–12.

Durzac, Manfred. 1981. "Neue Subjektivität. Zur Literatur der siebziger Jahre in der
   Bundesrepublik Deutschland." In *Deutsche Gegenwartsliteratur:
   Ausgangspositionen und aktuelle Entwicklungen*, ed. M. Durzac. Stuttgart:
   Philipp Reclam jun.

Enzensberger, Hans Magnus. 1960. *Museum der Modernen Poesie*. Frankfort a
   Main: Suhrkamp.

———. 1962. *Einzelheiten II: Poesie und Politik*. Frankfurt a Main: Suhrkamp.

Fauser, Jörg. 1979. *Trotzki, Goethe und das Glück*. Munich: Rogner & Bernhard.

———. 1983. *Der Schneemann*. Reinbek bei Hamburg: Rowohlt.

———. 1984. *Rohstoff*. Frankfurt a. Main. Berlin. Vienna: Verlag Ullstein.

———. 1985. *Strand der Städte*. Basel: Nachtmaschine.

Geduldig, Gunter, and Marco Sagurna, ed. 1994. *Too much: das lange Leben des
   Rolf Dieter Brinkmanns*. Aachen: Alano-Verlag.

Gemünden, Gerd. 1995. "The Depth of the Surface, or, What Rolf Dieter Brinkmann
   Learned from Andy Warhol." *German Quarterly* 68 (Summer): 235–50.

Hartung, Harald. 1971. "Pop als 'postmoderne' Literatur: Die deutsche Szene:
   Brinkmann und andere." *Neue Rundschau* 82: 723–42.

Höllerer, Walter. 1959. "Junge amerikanische Literatur." *Akzente*: 29–43.

Honan, Park, ed. 1987. *The Beats. An Anthology of "Beat" Writing*. London.
   Melbourne: J.M.Dent & Sons.

Jordan, Lothar. 1994. *Europäische und nordamerikanische Gegenwartslyrik im
   deutschen Sprachraum 1920-1970; Studien zu ihrer Vermittlung und
   Wirkung*. Tübingen: Max Niemeyer Verlag.

Kramer, Andreas. 1995. "Schnittpunkte in der Stille: Rolf Dieter Brinkmann und
   William S. Burroughs." In *William S. Burroughs*, ed. M. Bayer and A. Kramer.
   Eggingen: Edition Klaus Isele.

Lee, A. Robert, ed. 1996. *The Beat Generation Writers*. East Haven, CT: Pluto
   Press.

Lettau, Reinhard, ed. 1967. *Die Gruppe 47: Bericht. Kritik. Polemik*. Neuwied und
   Berlin: Luchterhand Verlag.

Richter, Hans Werner, ed. 1962. *Almanach der Gruppe 47: 1947-1962*. Reinbek bei Hamburg: Rowohlt.

Waine, Anthony. 1992. "Fatal Attractions: Rolf Dieter Brinkmann and British Life and Culture." *The Modern Language Review* 87 (April): 376–92.

Wondratschek, Wolf. 1981. *Chuck's Zimmer*. Munich: Wilhelm Heyne Verlag.

———. 1987. *Menschen. Orte. Fäuste*. Zurich: Diogenes.

CONTRIBUTORS

Baldwin, Douglas G.
An "ABD" from Yale University's English Department, he has published in *The Faulkner Journal* and *Studies in Short Fiction*; he is currently an Assessment Specialist at Educational Testing Service.

Bennett, Robert
A graduate student in English at the University of California. he has published essays on various twentieth-century American and postcolonial writers. He is currently completing a dissertation on interart representations of post-WWII New York City.

Diggory, Terence
Courtney and Steven Ross Professor of Interdisciplinary Studies at Skidmore College. He is the author of *Yeats and American Poetry: The Tradition of the Self* (1983) and *William Carlos Williams and the Ethics of Painting* (1991).

Douglas, Ann
Parr Professor of Comparative Literature at Columbia University and the author of *The Feminization of American Culture* (1977) and *Terrible Honesty: Mongrel Manhattan in the 1920s* (1995).

Grace, Nancy McCapbell
Associate Professor of English at The College of Wooster in Ohio. She is the author of *The Feminized Male Character in 20th-Century Literature* (1995) and the co-editor of *Beat Women and Beat Writing* (forthcoming).

Johnson, Ronna C.
Lecturer in English and American Studies at Tufts University. She has published on Kerouac and Beat writing and is currently completing a book-length study on Kerouac.

Kern, Robert
Associate Professor at Boston College. He has published articles on modern and post-modern American poetry and is the author of *Orientalism, Modernism, and the American Poem* (1996).

Kohn, Robert E.
Professor Emeritus of Economics at Southern Illinois University and the author of *Pollution and the Firm* (1998).

Lee, A. Robert
Professor of English at Nihon University, Tokyo. He is the editor of *The Beat Genertion Writers* (1996), and author of *Designs of Blackness: Mappings in the Literature and Culture of Afro-America* (1998), and *Postindian Conversations* (1999; with Gerald Vizenor).

Murphy, Timothy S.
Assistant Professor of English at the University of Oklahoma. He is the author of *Wising Up the Marks: The Amodern William Burroughs* and English translation coordinator for the Deleuze Web, an internet archive of seminars given by the late French philosopher.

Myrsiades, Kostas
Professor of Compartive Literature and editor of *College Literature* at West Chester University in Pennsylvania. He is the author, editor, translator of seventeen books on Greek literature and cuture and the teaching of literature.

Paton, Fiona
Assistant Professor of English at the State University of New York at New Paltz where she teaches Kerouac and the Beats at the graduate and undergraduate levels.

van der Bent, Jaap
Professor of English at the Univesity of Nymegen, The Netherlands.

Waine, Anthony
Professor in the Department of European Languages and Cultures at Lancaster University, England and author of two books on Martin Wallser.

Wilson, Steve
A member of the English faculty at Southwest Texas State University where he teaches graduate and undergraduate courses on the Beat Generation.

Wooley, Jonathan
A PhD. candidate in the Department of Germanic Studies at the University of Sheffield, England.

INDEX